The Catherine Code

Printed by IngramSpark

ISBN: 978-0-6456106-3-5

ACKNOWLEDGMENTS

This book could not have been written without ancestry charts from fabpedigree. com run by American amateur genealogist Jamie Allen (whose eccentric website is much more 'authoritative' than his disclaimer suggests) and the excellent skills of my friend Fred Baker. Special thanks to Claudia Joseph and Elizabeth Roberts for permission to use photographs, and thanks also to the many people who provided images to Wikipedia and websites such as Pinterest. Sincere apologies if I have left out any names.

The Catherine Code

Contents

The Catherine Code

'Veneration felt for [St Catherine of Alexandria] by William the Conqueror — and, in particular, his son Henry I — led to the introduction of the cult into England.'
— *2003 thesis by Christine Louise Walsh, Queen Mary University of London.*

'The mitochondrial DNA used to identify the body of Richard III with two currently living descendants of his sister was inherited from his great-grandmother Katherine Swynford.'
— *Facebook post by The Katherine Swynford Society, February 2013.*

'His mother was daughter unto John, Duke of Somerset, son unto John, Earl of Somerset, son unto Dame Katherine Swynford and of her double advoutrow (adultery) gotten.'
— *Richard III's proclamation against the future Henry VII.*

'By its very nature the evidence for Edmund Tudor's parentage is less than conclusive, but such facts as can be assembled permit the agreeable possibility that Edmund 'Tudor' and Margaret Beaufort were first cousins and that the royal house of 'Tudor' sprang in fact from Beauforts on both sides.'
— *Historian G L Harriss.*

'There is much debate as to whether Catherine of Valois and Owen Tudor married. No documentation of marriage exists and, even if they did marry, their marriage would not have been been legal due to the act regarding the remarriage of a queen dowager.'
— *Susan Flantzer, unofficialroyalty.com 2013.*

'Catherine of Aragon held a stronger claim [than Henry VII] to the English throne through her great-great-grandmother Catherine of Lancaster who was a legitimate daughter of John of Gaunt.'
— *Marnie Camping-Harris, Edinburgh University's* Retrospect *Journal (2023).*

'I have discovered strong evidence that Katherine Carey was Henry VIII's daughter, notably in a poem written by Sir Philip Sidney for Katherine's granddaughter.'
— *Alison Weir, author of* Mary Boleyn: The Mistress of Kings *(2011).*

'St Catherine of Siena had a vision in which she married Jesus Christ and his foreskin served as the wedding ring.'
— *Wikimedia Commons.*

'During the middle ages, there were at least fourteen claimants to the title of the Holy Prepuce in churches around Europe. In 1421, Henry V sent for one of them, the Holy Prepuce of Coulombs in France, because it was believed that its sweet scent would help his wife Catherine of Valois have an easy childbirth.'
— The Guardian, *February 2007.*

'Macalpine and Hunter have detected four descendants of the royal houses of Hanover and Hohenzollern with biochemical evidence of variegate porphyria. They traced clinical evidence back from Edward, Duke of Kent, and Frederick the Great, converging on Margaret Tudor, sister of Henry VIII. The suggestion is made here that the condition might be traced back further to [Catherine of Valois' father] Charles VI of France.'
— *Lindsay C Hurst, 'Porphyria Revisited' (2012).*

'Lady Kinloss was a Scottish peeress who sat in the House of Lords from 1963... She was also the Tudor claimant to the throne of England, being the senior surviving descendant of Lady Jane Grey's sister Lady Catherine.'
— Sydney Morning Herald, *November 2012.*

'Catherine of Braganza's enthusiasm for tea made (it) a hallmark and fetish for the status-chasing elites... slavery has always been an integral part of the sugar and tea economy (and) revenues filled the British royal navy coffers enabling them to conquer distant lands at a terrible human cost, especially in Africa and the West Indies.'
— The Dark and Devious History of Tea *(2019), by Darius Okolla.*

'[Art historian Graeme Cameron] looked deeply into the layers of the Mona Lisa with special technology and found that the sublayer of the painting depicted a 60+ year old female bearing the features of da Vinci's mother Caterina... A younger Caterina is also believed to be the inspiration of the female sitting to the right of Jesus in the Last Supper.'
— *Article on businesswire.com August 2015.*

'A time may yet come, perchance, when a descendant of one of these simple artisans may arise, not unworthy of the Conyers' ancient renown; and it will be a gratifying discovery to some future genealogist when he succeeds in tracing in the quarterings of such a descendant the unsullied bearing of Conyers of Durham.'
— *Sir Bernard Burke's 1861 prophecy about the daughters of Kate's impoverished ancestor Sir Thomas Conyers.*

'Kate Middleton appears to be mostly "English". One of her great-great-great-great-great-great-great-grandfathers was a child of Huguenot refugees, and one of her great-great-grandfathers was a child of Scottish parents, thus her ethnic ancestry (as far as is currently known) can be shown as: 93.555% English, 6.25% Scottish and 0.195% French.'
— *William Addams Reitwienser,* The Ancestry of Catherine Middleton *(2011).*

'The grainy home video captured a thirteen-year-old Kate speaking to a sooth-sayer wearing a scarf and gold hoop earring. "Will he fall in love with me?" inquires Kate when she is told she will meet a rich landowner named William. "Indeed he will," responds the fortune-teller. "And marry me?" asks Kate. "And marry you," he confirms, after reading her palm. "It is all I ever dreamed of," she confides to the audience, adding to much laughter, "Oh how my heart flutters."
— Kate: The Future Queen *(2013), by Katie Nicholl.*

'Here is the perfected rounded sphere which reveals the eternal pattern of the universe.'
— *Inscribed around Westminster Abbey's famous Cosmati Pavement on which Kate was married on St Catherine of Siena's feast day (29th April) in 2011.*

THESE famous buildings feature in both *The Da Vinci Code* and *The Catherine Code*. Dan Brown's novel starts in the Louvre Museum (top left) and involves two of da Vinci's masterpieces (the Mona Lisa and Madonna of the Rocks) which may have been inspired by Caterina Sforza, from whom Kate's children descend through illegitimate offspring of Charles II and James II. The albino monk murders a nun in the Church of Saint-Sulpice (top right) which venerates St Catherine of Alexandria in a stained glass window. Kate's ancestor William Marshall the Protector was buried in London's Temple Church (bottom right) and she was married in Westminster Abbey (centre) on St Catherine of Siena's feast day. Rosslyn Chapel (bottom left) was built by Prince William's ancestor William St Clair whose patron saint was St Catherine of Alexandria.

The most amazing part," Katherine said, "is that as soon as we humans begin to harness our true power, we will have enormous control over our world. We will be able to design reality rather than merely react to it.

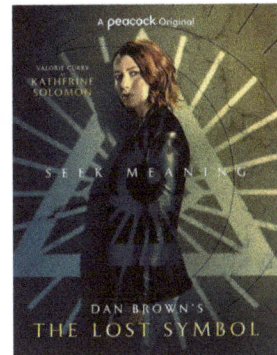

'Noetic scientist' Katherine Solomon was Robert Langdon's partner in The Lost Symbol *(2009), a sequel to* The Da Vinci Code *that was made into a short-lived American TV series.*

THE TWO most important Caterinas in *The Catherine Code* are the unmarried slave or peasant girl who gave birth to Leonardo da Vinci in 1452, and an illegitimate daughter of the Duke of Milan. According to German-born art historian Maike Vogt-Luerssen (in an article on kleio.org) Caterina Sforza inspired the Madonna in da Vinci's Annunciation (top) but that is unlikely because the famed Countess of Forli was aged only nine when the painting was started around 1472.

My theory is that most of Leonardo's Madonnas, and possibly the Mona Lisa, were based on his mother Caterina (who resembled Caterina Sforza). Madonna of the Rocks (above left), which provides a vital clue in *The Da Vinci Code*, was replicated for the Milan church in which Caterina was buried. And The Virgin and Child with St Anne (above right) is significant because it was unfinished when da Vinci died in 1519. Note that St Anne, the Madonna's mother, resembles da Vinci's male lover Salai.

IT SEEMS that da Vinci's mother Caterina and/or Caterina Sforza inspired many contemporaneous depictions of St Catherine of Alexandria, including Pietro Perugino's palm-holding version with the Madonna (above) and another (right) presumably copied from a painting by Bernardino Luini who was greatly influenced by da Vinci. The Luini painting, attributed to Giampietrino, was first recorded at Kensington Palace in 1710 and described as 'after Leonardo'. Another portrait in the Royal Collection, featuring the saint and two child angels, is 'after a painting traditionally supposed to be by Leonardo'. One possibility is that da Vinci's depiction of his mother as her namesake saint, like Leda and the Swan, has not survived.

Catherine of Aragon (above), mother of Mary I, was depicted as Mary Magdalene who is pictured with St Catherine of Alexandria (top) and St Catherine of Siena (left). Some believe Mary's alabaster jar was the Holy Grail.

CONTRARY to *The Da Vinci Code*, Jesus and Mary Magdalene (above left) have countless millions of descendants or none at all. Mary is pictured (top) kneeling next to St Catherine of Alexandria as she mystically marries baby Jesus. St Catherine of Siena did the same (above right), allegedly receiving the messiah's foreskin as a wedding ring. One of St Catherine of Siena's letters dated around 1374 supports the claim that Mary Magdalene preached in Marseille in southern France where, coincidentally, Kate's great-aunt Mary Glassborow and twin sister Valerie were born in 1924. Kate usually celebrates Christmas in St Mary Magdalene Church at Sandringham where Princess Mary, daughter of Queen Mary and granddaughter of Mary of Cambridge, was baptised in 1897.

CHARLES II's wife Catherine of Braganza (above) and his long-term mistress Barbara Palmer (right) were both depicted as St Catherine of Alexandria. Kate's children descend from Barbara's bastard son Henry Fitzroy whose grandmother Henrietta Maria, like her illegitimate ancestor Caterina Sforza, was also depicted as St Catherine. Catherine the Great (inset), who had at least one illegitimate son, wore the Order of St Catherine which was founded for her grandmother-in-law Catherine I. Another recipient of the order was Kate's great-grandmother-in-law Princess Alice of Battenberg who, like Catherine of Braganza's husband and Catherine the Great, had an all-female bloodline from Catherine of Foix (See chart on Page 103).

Foreword

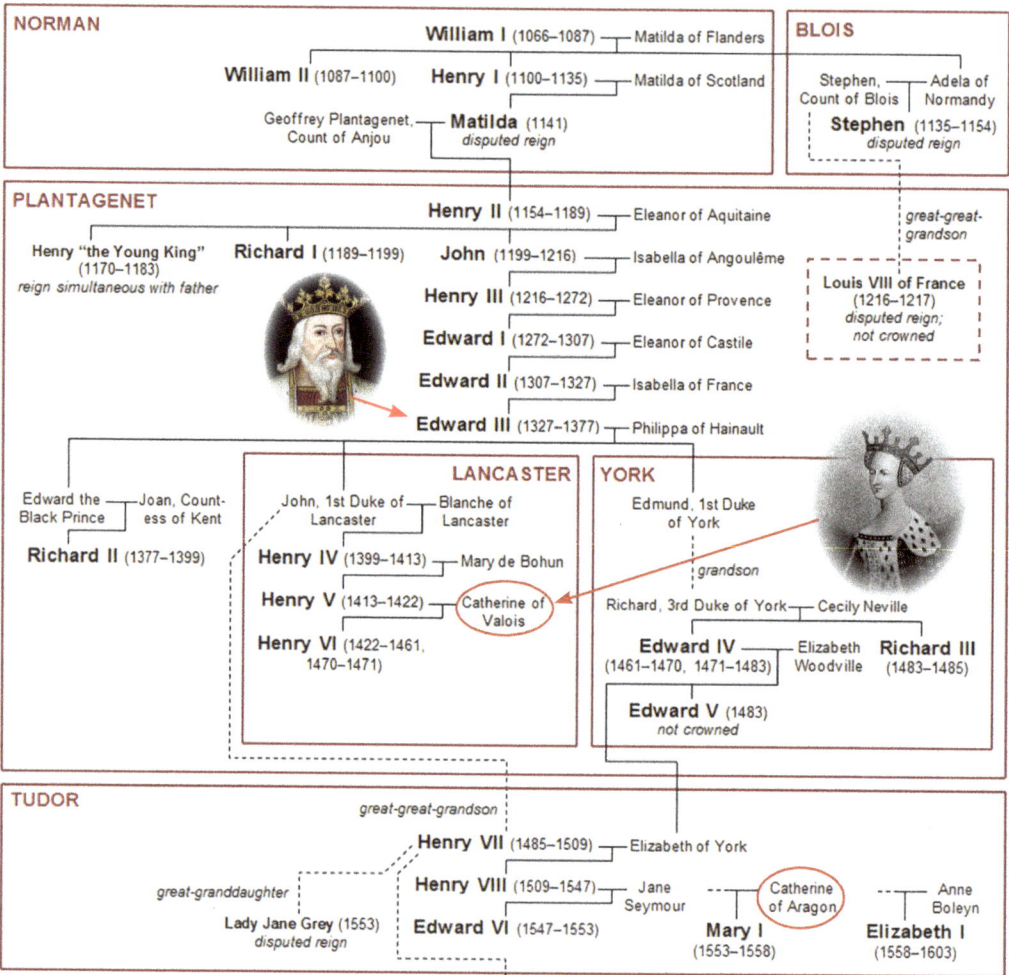

NORMAN

William I (1066–1087) — Matilda of Flanders

William II (1087–1100)　Henry I (1100–1135) — Matilda of Scotland

Geoffrey Plantagenet, — Matilda (1141)
Count of Anjou　　　　*disputed reign*

BLOIS

Stephen, — Adela of
Count of Blois │ Normandy

Stephen (1135–1154)
disputed reign

PLANTAGENET

Henry II (1154–1189) — Eleanor of Aquitaine

great-great-grandson

Henry "the Young King" (1170–1183)　Richard I (1189–1199)　John (1199–1216) — Isabella of Angoulême
reign simultaneous with father

Louis VIII of France
(1216–1217)
*disputed reign;
not crowned*

Henry III (1216–1272) — Eleanor of Provence

Edward I (1272–1307) — Eleanor of Castile

Edward II (1307–1327) — Isabella of France

Edward III (1327–1377) — Philippa of Hainault

LANCASTER

Edward the — Joan, Count-
Black Prince │ ess of Kent

Richard II (1377–1399)

John, 1st Duke of — Blanche of
Lancaster　　　　Lancaster

Henry IV (1399–1413) — Mary de Bohun

Henry V (1413–1422) — Catherine of Valois

Henry VI (1422–1461, 1470–1471)

YORK

Edmund, 1st Duke
of York

grandson

Richard, 3rd Duke of York — Cecily Neville

Edward IV — Elizabeth　Richard III
(1461–1470, 1471–1483) │ Woodville　(1483–1485)

Edward V (1483)
not crowned

TUDOR

great-great-grandson

Henry VII (1485–1509) — Elizabeth of York

great-granddaughter

Lady Jane Grey (1553)
disputed reign

Henry VIII (1509–1547) — Jane Seymour ---- Catherine of Aragon ---- Anne Boleyn

Edward VI (1547–1553)　Mary I (1553–1558)　Elizabeth I (1558–1603)

ILLEGITIMACY, inbreeding and bad behaviour have shaped the British royal family since William the Conqueror, commonly known as William the Bastard, seized the throne from King Harold in 1066.

It is therefore fitting that the future William V has no legitimate royal bloodline from his Norman namesake through Henry VII who seized the throne from Richard III. As shown above, Henry VII was a great-great-grandson of John of Gaunt, the first Duke of Lancaster and second husband of Katherine Swynford who has a major role in *The Catherine Code*.

Henry VII's bloodline was through Katherine Swynford's oldest illegitimate son John 'Fairborn' Beaufort and his granddaughter Margaret Beaufort. She married Henry VII's father Edmund Tudor, the oldest illegitimate son of Catherine of Valois and her second husband Owen Tudor. (Before marrying Owen, Catherine had an affair with Margaret's uncle Edmund Beaufort so it is possible that he sired Edmund Tudor.)

Henry VIII's bloodline through Richard of York is also dubious because, while his son (Edward IV) may not have been illegitimate, his father (Richard of Connisburgh)

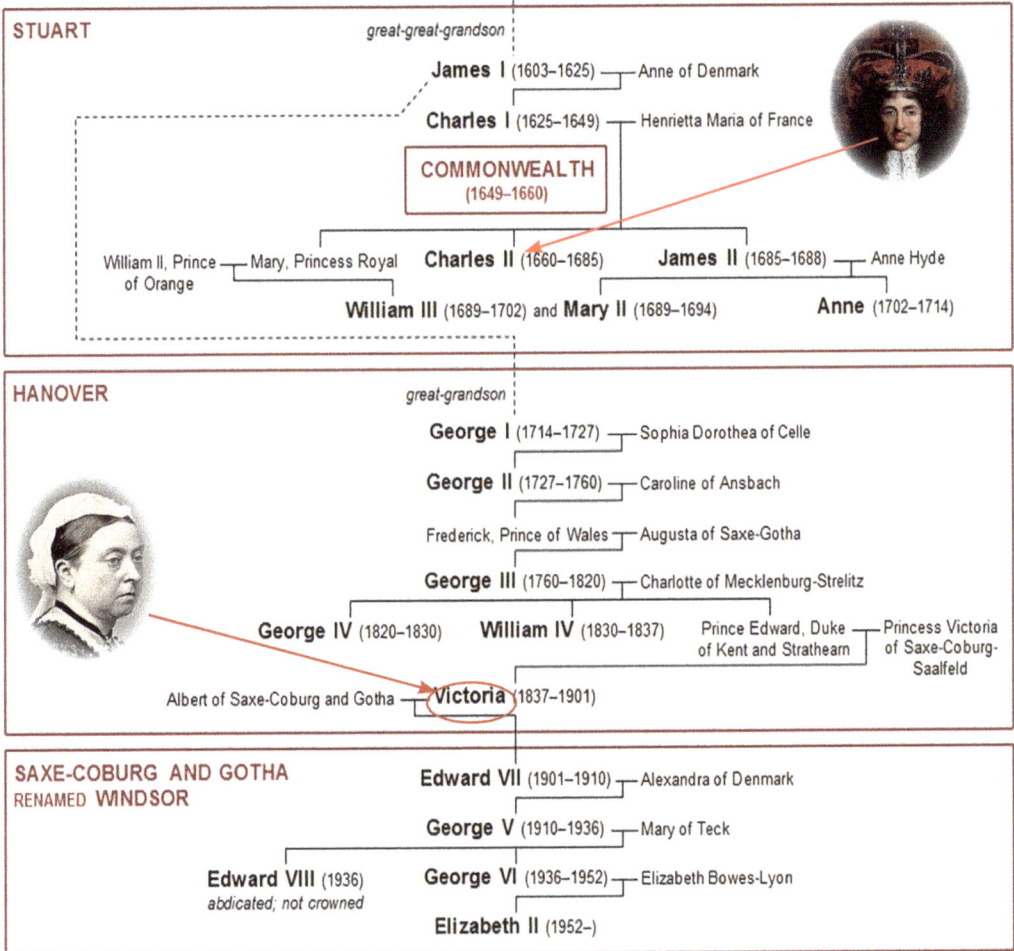

STUART

great-great-grandson

James I (1603–1625) ——— Anne of Denmark

Charles I (1625–1649) ——— Henrietta Maria of France

COMMONWEALTH (1649–1660)

William II, Prince of Orange ——— Mary, Princess Royal   **Charles II** (1660–1685)   **James II** (1685–1688) ——— Anne Hyde

William III (1689–1702) and **Mary II** (1689–1694)   **Anne** (1702–1714)

HANOVER

great-grandson

George I (1714–1727) ——— Sophia Dorothea of Celle

George II (1727–1760) ——— Caroline of Ansbach

Frederick, Prince of Wales ——— Augusta of Saxe-Gotha

George III (1760–1820) ——— Charlotte of Mecklenburg-Strelitz

George IV (1820–1830)   **William IV** (1830–1837)   Prince Edward, Duke of Kent and Strathearn ——— Princess Victoria of Saxe-Coburg-Saalfeld

Albert of Saxe-Coburg and Gotha ——— Victoria (1837–1901)

SAXE-COBURG AND GOTHA
RENAMED WINDSOR

Edward VII (1901–1910) ——— Alexandra of Denmark

George V (1910–1936) ——— Mary of Teck

Edward VIII (1936) *abdicated; not crowned*   **George VI** (1936–1952) ——— Elizabeth Bowes-Lyon

Elizabeth II (1952–)

---

was almost certainly the bastard son of John Holland (See chart on Page 9).

Prince William descends from Henry VIII's alleged illegitimate daughter Catherine Carey whose stepmother Catherine of Aragon had a strong claim to the throne through John of Gaunt's legitimate daughter Catherine of Lancaster, also known as Catherine of Castille. Prince William also descends from sisters of Henry VIII's last two wives, Catherine Howard and Catherine Parr, and from two illegitimate stepsons of Catherine of Braganza, the childless wife of Charles II.

Charles III does not descend from his namesake but Princess Diana did. Consequently, Prince William will be the first sovereign descended from the Merry Monarch.

William the Bastard needed papal permission to marry Matilda of Flanders, his third cousin once removed, because they did not have the seven degrees of separation required by the Catholic Church. If that rule had been strictly maintained until modern times, most royal marriages would have been illegal.

Note: All the monarchs shown above descended from William the Bastard and so did most of the 200 Catherines mentioned in this book. One of Kate's bloodlines is through an illegitimate daughter of Edward IV and a bastard son of Henry I.

Catherine Elizabeth MIDDLETON

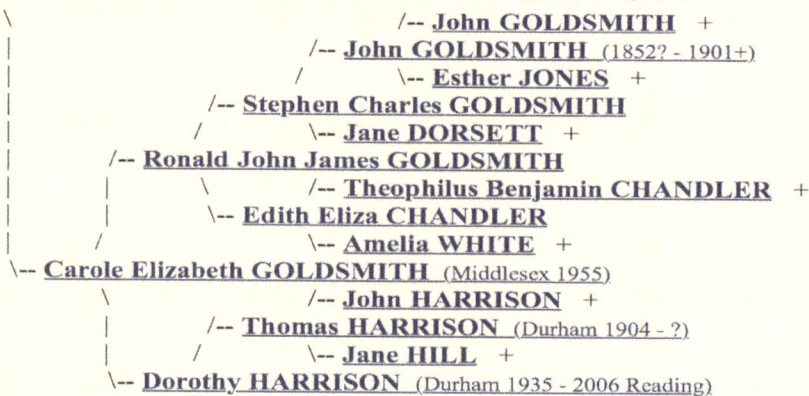

Born: Reading 1982

Husband/Partner: **William Arthur Philip Louis WINDSOR**

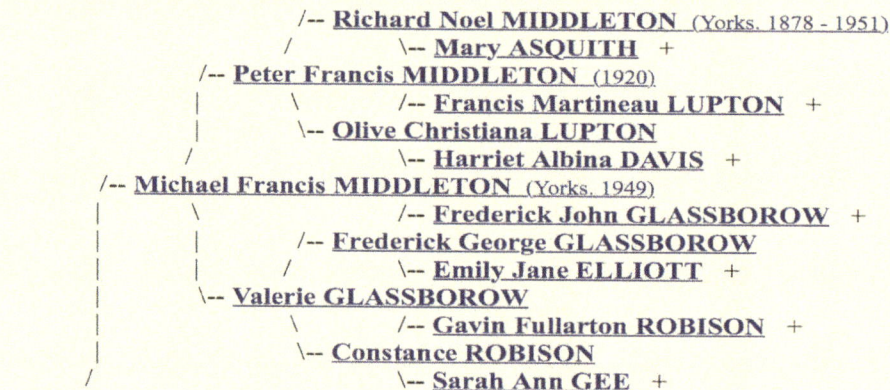

```
                          /-- Richard Noel MIDDLETON (Yorks. 1878 - 1951)
                       /         \-- Mary ASQUITH  +
                   /-- Peter Francis MIDDLETON (1920)
                   |         \         /-- Francis Martineau LUPTON  +
                   |          \-- Olive Christiana LUPTON
                   /                  \-- Harriet Albina DAVIS  +
               /-- Michael Francis MIDDLETON (Yorks. 1949)
               |   \                  /-- Frederick John GLASSBOROW  +
               |    |          /-- Frederick George GLASSBOROW
               |    |         /         \-- Emily Jane ELLIOTT  +
               |    \-- Valerie GLASSBOROW
               |          \              /-- Gavin Fullarton ROBISON  +
               |           \-- Constance ROBISON
           /                        \-- Sarah Ann GEE  +
```

-Catherine Elizabeth MIDDLETON

```
               \                  /-- John GOLDSMITH  +
               |           /-- John GOLDSMITH (1852? - 1901+)
               |          /         \-- Esther JONES  +
               |      /-- Stephen Charles GOLDSMITH
               |     /         \-- Jane DORSETT  +
               |  /-- Ronald John James GOLDSMITH
               |  |    \              /-- Theophilus Benjamin CHANDLER  +
               |  |     \-- Edith Eliza CHANDLER
               |  /                  \-- Amelia WHITE  +
               \-- Carole Elizabeth GOLDSMITH (Middlesex 1955)
                   \              /-- John HARRISON  +
                   |      /-- Thomas HARRISON (Durham 1904 - ?)
                   |     /         \-- Jane HILL  +
                   \-- Dorothy HARRISON (Durham 1935 - 2006 Reading)
```

GIVEN the title of this book, Kate's grandmother Valerie Glassborow and her twin sister Mary deserve a special mention because they were code-breakers during World War II. Valerie married Spitfire pilot Captain Peter Middleton, who flew with Prince Philip on his tour of South America in 1962, and Mary married Peter's older brother Anthony.

Valerie's and Mary's father Frederick George Glassborow was interned in the Netherlands while serving with the Royal Navy during World War I, and Frederick's grandfather was an inmate in Holloway Prison (See Page 155).

Introduction

WHILE it may not inspire a Dan Brown novel, the 'Catherine code' is a remarkable series of genealogical, genetic and other connections involving the future Queen Catherine and her many namesakes, including five previous Queen Catherines plus Kate's ancestor Katherine Swynford whose illegitimate offspring could have a hundred million living descendants.

In other words, nearly everyone reading this book descends from at least one royal bastard and is distantly related to the current Princess of Wales (although proving it is another matter).

As shown opposite, Kate was definitely a commoner when she married Prince William on 29th April 2011 which, coincidentally, was the feast day of St Catherine of Siena, not to be confused with St Catherine of Alexandria whose cult was introduced to Britain in 1066 by William the Conqueror, known to his contemporaries as William the Bastard.

Kate has a bloodline from an illegitimate daughter of Edward IV through the most recent aristocrat in her family tree, Sir Thomas Conyers, who died in poverty in 1810. His granddaughter Jane Hardy was the grandmother of Jane Liddle who married coalminer John Harrison, and their son, also named John Harrison, married Jane Hill. Many of Kate's other maternal ancestors were labourers, including Joseph Middleton who was born in Norfolk around 1781.

Most of Kate's paternal ancestors were middle class, including solicitor Richard Noel Middleton whose mother Mary Asquith, like Queen Victoria, married her first cousin. And the marriage of William Middleton and his deceased wife's sister is notable because it was illegal for the same reason that Henry VIII cited against Catherine of Aragon.

As shown on famouskin.com Kate and Prince William are twelfth cousins once removed through their most recent ancestor Jane Lambton. Another important common ancestor was Agnes Gascoigne whose family lived at Gawthorpe Hall in Yorkshire, not far from the Stockeld Middletons.

Kate's children have a bloodline from Catherine Mydelton (née Vavasour) who was living in Wakefield 300 years before William Middleton was born there

in 1807. The Middleton between Wakefield and Leeds is one of more than 30 Middletons that could be Kate's ancestral home

There are several other Catherine Middletons in Prince William's family tree, including the mother of the first Earl of Middleton, a Scottish soldier of fortune who married a great-grandniece of Henry VIII's allegedly illegitimate daughter Catherine Carey.

P RINCE WILLIAM epitomises the 'Catherine code' because, as well as having thousands of individual bloodlines from Katherine of Flanders through illegitimate offspring of Katherine Swynford, he has a rare form of Indian mitochondrial DNA inherited from Katherine Scott Forbes.

Anyone with predominantly English heritage probably descends from a majority of the people living in England a thousand years ago but, unlike Kate and most other commoners, the royals have records of births, deaths and marriages to prove it. According to fabpedigree.com Prince William descends from Katherine of Flanders through nearly all of his great-great-great-grandparents.

The future William V has a bloodline from Catherine the Great's possibly illegitimate son through Prince Philip who, coincidentally, had the same mtDNA as the Russian tsarina inherited through a separate all-female bloodline from Catherine of Foix.

Another matrilineal descendant of Catherine of Foix was Charles II, an ancestor of Prince William but not Charles III. Consequently, William will be the first British sovereign descended from the his father's namesake — albeit through two of his illegitimate sons — and Kate, fittingly, will be the first Queen Catherine since Catherine of Braganza.

William Arthur Philip Louis WINDSOR

Born: London 1982

Wife/Partner: Catherine Elizabeth MIDDLETON

```
                  /-- Andrew (Prince) of GREECE & DENMARK
          /          \-- Olga Constantinovna ROMANOV of RUSSIA  +
       /-- Philip MOUNTBATTEN (Prince) of GREECE & DENMARK
       |      \           /-- Louis (H.S.H.) of BATTENBERG (MOUNTBATTEN)
       |       \-- Alice (Princess) von BATTENBERG
       /                  \-- Victoria Alberta of HESSE AND BY RHINE  +
    /-- Charles Philip Arthur George WINDSOR (Prince of WALES)
    |      \            /-- George V WINDSOR (King) of ENGLAND  +
    |       \-- George VI Albert WINDSOR (King) of ENGLAND
    |       |    /          \-- Mary (Princess) of TECK  +
    |       \-- Elizabeth II Alexandra Mary WINDSOR (Queen) of ENGLAND
    |           \          /-- Claude George BOWES-LYON  +
    |            \-- Elizabeth Angela Marguerite (Lady) BOWES-LYON
    /                      \-- Nina Cecilia CAVENDISH-BENTINCK  +
```

‑William Arthur Philip Louis WINDSOR

```
    \                   /-- Frederick (4th Earl) SPENCER  +
    |                /-- Charles Robert (6th Earl) SPENCER
    |               /     \-- Adelaide Horatia Elizabeth SEYMOUR  +
    |            /-- Albert Edward John (7th Earl) SPENCER
    |            |     \-- Margaret (Hon.) BARING  +
    |         /-- Edward John (8th Earl) SPENCER
    |         |   \           /-- James Albert Edward HAMILTON  +
    |         |    \-- Cynthia Elinor Beatrix (Lady) HAMILTON
    |         /                \-- Rosalind Cecilia Caroline (Lady) BINGHAM  +
    \-- Diana Frances (Lady) SPENCER
              \              /-- James Boothby Burke ROCHE  +
              |           /-- Edmund Maurice Burke ROCHE
              |           /    \-- Frances Eleanor (Ellen) WORK  +
              \-- Frances Ruth Burke (Hon.) ROCHE
                          \    /-- William Smith (Colonel) GILL  +
                           \-- Ruth Sylvia (Lady) GILL
```

Prince William has a bloodline from Catherine of Valois' illegitimate son Edmund Tudor through Henry VIII's illegitimate daughter Catherine Carey. William also descends from sisters of three of Henry VIII's wives — Catherine of Aragon, Catherine Howard and Catherine Parr — and from two claimants to the throne, Katherine Pole and Lady Catherine Grey, either of whom could theoretically have been crowned Catherine I.

Coincidentally, Katherine Pole and Catherine Grey, whose son was declared illegitimate by Elizabeth I, had the same mitochondrial DNA as Henry VIII and so did his great-aunt Catherine Woodville and her ill-fated nephews, commonly known as the Princes in the Tower.

Significant common ancestors of Kate and Prince William include Katherine Grandison, who may have inspired the Order of the Garter; Katherine Percy, a granddaughter of the legendary 'Hotspur'; Katherine Clifford's granddaughter Catherine Mortimer, who had a bloodline from Lady Godiva; and Katherine Swynford's grandson Edmund Beaufort who had an affair with Catherine of Valois before she married Owen Tudor.

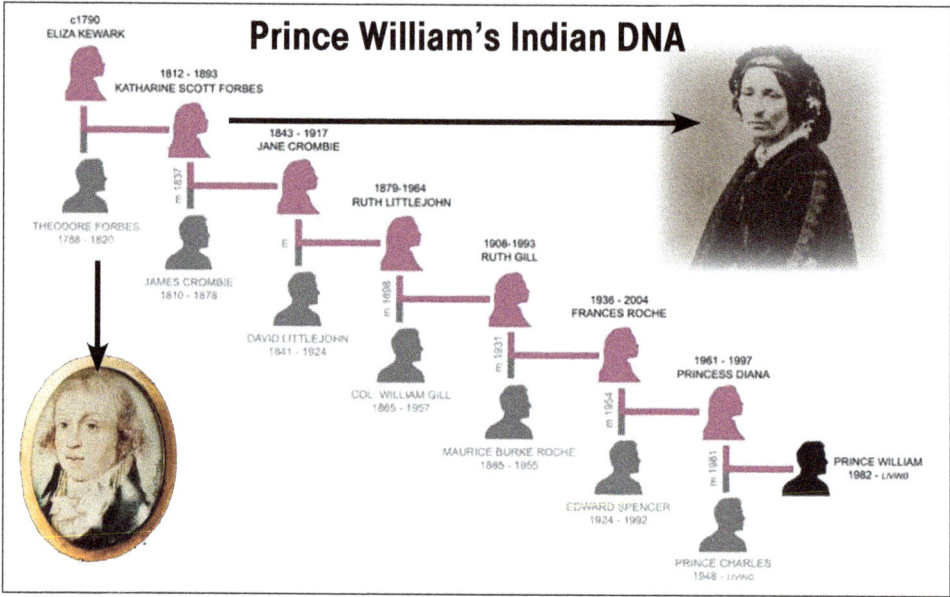

Prince William's Indian DNA

c1790
ELIZA KEWARK

1812 - 1893
KATHARINE SCOTT FORBES

1843 - 1917
JANE CROMBIE

1879-1964
RUTH LITTLEJOHN

THEODORE FORBES
1788 - 1820

m 1837

JAMES CROMBIE
1810 - 1878

1908-1993
RUTH GILL

m 1898

DAVID LITTLEJOHN
1841 - 1924

1936 - 2004
FRANCES ROCHE

m 1931

COL. WILLIAM GILL
1865 - 1957

1961 - 1997
PRINCESS DIANA

m 1954

MAURICE BURKE ROCHE
1885 - 1955

m 1981

PRINCE WILLIAM
1982 - LIVING

EDWARD SPENCER
1924 - 1992

PRINCE CHARLES
1948 - LIVING

While this may prove nothing, apart from the fact that Catherine has long been a popular name, the interconnectedness of Kate's namesakes is suggestive of in-breeding which can greatly increase the risk of genetic disorders.

Incredibly, one Mormon researcher identified two thousand individual blood-lines from Edward III to Charles III, about half of which must have been through Katherine Swynford's illegitimate children.

SHORTLY before Kate added her mtDNA (haplogroup unknown) to the royal gene pool, British newspapers announced that Prince William has a rare form of haplogroup R inherited through an all-female bloodline from Katherine Scott Forbes whose father Theodore worked for the East India Company in Bombay.

According to Ian Jack in *The Guardian* (June 2013), the claim was based on DNA tests taken by third cousins of Prince William's maternal grandmother Frances Shand Kydd. 'This, in the words of BritainsDNA, confirms beyond doubt that the housekeeper-mistress Eliza Kewark was of Indian heritage,' Jack wrote. '(But) such a degree of certainty invites questions… could the rare DNA in his distant relations have a different source?' That seems highly unlikely because, as far as we know, Prince William has never challenged the claim.

About six years before Prince George was born,

Tsar Nicholas II inherited haplogroup T from Katharina von Pfannberg and his son Alexey, who had haemophilia, inherited haplogroup H from Catherine of Foix through Queen Victoria.

The PEDIGREE of

Katherine PLANTAGENET

Husband/Partner: **William HERBERT**

```
                              /-- Edward III (WINDSOR; King) of ENGLAND +
                    /-- Edmund of LANGLEY (PLANTAGENET) (1341 - 1402)
                    |    \ / OR: poss. John (K.G.) HOLLAND +
                  /     \-- Philipa d' AVESNES of HAINAULT +
          /-- Richard PLANTAGENET of CONISBURGH
          |       \       /-- Pedro `the Cruel' (King) of CASTILE +
          |        \-- Isabel PEREZ (Princess) of CASTILE
          /              \-- Maria Juana de PADILLA (PEDILLA) +
      /-- Richard PLANTAGENET-YORK
      |   |                   /-- Edmund `the Good' de MORTIMER +
      |   |          /-- Roger de MORTIMER
      |   |         /       \-- Philippa of CLARENCE (PLANTAGENET) +
      |   \-- Anne de MORTIMER (1390 - 1411)
      |           \       /-- Thomas (II; de) HOLLAND +
      |            \-- Alianore (Lady) HOLLAND
      /                  \-- Alice (Lady of Arundel) FitzALAN +
  /-- Richard III (PLANTAGENET; King) of ENGLAND
  |      \                 /-- Ralph (2nd Baron of RABY; de) NEVILL +
  |      |        /-- John (III; de) NEVILL (1327+ - 1388)
  |      |        /     \-- Alice (de) AUDLEY +
  |      /-- Ralph I NEVILL (de NEVILLE) (1363? - 1425)
  |      |   |     \       /-- Henry (IV; III; 2nd Lord; de) PERCY +
  |      |   |    \-- Matilda (Maud Mary) de PERCY (1342? - 1379)
  |      |   /              \-- Idonea (Idoine de) CLIFFORD +
  |      \-- Cecily (Lady) NEVILLE (1415 - 1495)
  |          \                 /-- Edward III (WINDSOR; King) of ENGLAND +
  |          |        /-- John (BEAUFORT) of GAUNT
  |          |        /     \-- Philipa d' AVESNES of HAINAULT +
  |          \-- Joan (Lady; de) BEAUFORT (1379? - 1440)
  |                  \       /-- Paon (Sir; of GUIENNE) de ROET +
  |                   \-- Katherine ROELT
```

- Katherine PLANTAGENET
    \-- poss. Katherine HAUTE (mistress)

scientists identified Alexey Romanov's remains through a sample from Prince Philip who had the same mtDNA as Alexey inherited from Catherine of Foix. Another sample, taken from a matrilineal descendant of Nicholas II's sister, confirmed that the Tsar inherited haplogroup T from Katharina von Pfannberg (See The Last of the Romanovs, Page 120).

There was another breakthrough in 2012 when DNA samples from two living matrilineal descendants of Katherine Swynford (Roelt) helped scientists to identify Richard III's remains. Not much is known about his illegitimate daughter Katherine Plantagenet whose mother may have been Katherine Haute.

Katherine Swynford's husband John of Gaunt should have had the same Y-DNA as Richard III, a patrilineal descendant of Gaunt's brother Edmund of Langley. However, because there was no match with living patrilineal descendants, there must have been a 'false paternity event'.

John of Gaunt was possibly a bastard son of Edward III, but it is much more likely that Richard of Conisburgh was sired by John Holland (shown above).

Matrilineal Ancestors of British Monarchs — 1

	Matrilineal Ancestors	Mitochondrial Haplogroup		Matrilineal Ancestors	Mitochondrial Haplogroup
Henry VI	Catherine of Valois (Mother)		Mary I	Catherine of Aragon (Mother)	
Edward IV	Katherine Swynford	J	Charles I	Katharina von Pfannberg	T
Edward V	Catherine Woodville (Maternal aunt)	U	Charles II	Catherine of Foix	H
Richard III	Katherine Swynford	J	James II	Catherine of Foix	H
Henry VIII	Catherine Woodville (Maternal great-aunt)	U	William III	Catherine of Foix	H

CENTRAL to the 'Catherine code' are the British monarchs with known mitochondrial haplogroups inherited from four of Kate's namesakes: Katherine Swynford; Katharina von Pfannberg, Katherina Polyxene and Catherine of Foix. Henry VIII and Edward V did not descend from Catherine Woodville but they all had the same haplogroup as Jacquetta of Luxembourg and her sister Catherine.

The rare Indian haplogroup of the future William V was determined in 2013 by DNA tests on some of his maternal relatives, and Prince George's haplogroup may eventually be revealed in the same way.

Without access to royal tombs, the haplogroups of many long-dead monarchs will never be known. However, there could be more chance discoveries of remains like those of Richard III and the Romanovs.

In the meantime, the popularity of DNA testing is creating a huge database. A search

	Matrilineal Ancestors	Mitochondrial Haplogroup		Matrilineal Ancestors	Mitochondrial Haplogroup
George I	Katharina von Pfannberg	T	George V	Katharina von Pfannberg	T
George III	Katharina von Pfannberg	T	Edward VIII	Katherina Polyxene	H
George IV	Katharine von Waldeck-Eiseberg		George VI	Katherina Polyxene	H
Queen Victoria	Catherine of Foix	H	* William V	Katherine Scott Forbes	R
Edward VII	Catherine of Foix	H	* George VII	Catherine Middleton (Mother)	

* Future Monarchs

has already begun for living matrilineal descendants of Edward II's sisters to find out if he died in northern Italy and not in Berkeley Castle, reputedly by having a red-hot poker inserted in his anus. (Google The Auramala Project for details.)

The haplogroup of Catherine of Valois' first husband Henry V could be determined by testing someone with an all-female bloodline from Irish princess Aoife who, coincidentally, had the same mtDNA as Catherine's lover Edmund Beaufort.

Several monarchs could have been added to the charts above, including Catherine Grey's sister Lady Jane, queen for just nine days in 1553, who had the same haplogroup U as Catherine Woodville; James I, who had an all-female bloodline from Princess Katherine's sister through Catherine de Vendome and Catherine d'Artois; and William IV who had the same mtDNA as his brother George IV.

George VI and his brother Edward VIII were matrilineal descendants of Katherina

Charles 'the Mad'

'Mad' King George III

Polyxene and so is Denmark's Queen Margrethe who, according to a list on fam-ilytreedna.com has haplogroup H. Margrethe descends from Queen Victoria and is in the British line of succession.

T HE NOTION that Kate's children could be at risk from a genetic disorder in-troduced by Catherine of Valois 600 years ago is not completely far-fetched.

According to a theory first espoused in the 1960s by Ida Macalpine and Richard Hunter, George III inherited porphyria from Mary Queen of Scots. About twenty years later, in an article (available online) titled 'Porphyria Revisited', Lindsay C Hurst traced the disorder back to Catherine of Valois' father Charles 'the Mad'.

As shown opposite, Catherine's son Henry VI had symptoms of porphyria but his half-brother Edmund Tudor, Henry VII and Henry VIII did not. The health problems of Mary Queen of Scots, including violent stomach pains, are well document-ed; and James I famously had wine-coloured urine, a well-known sign of porphyria.

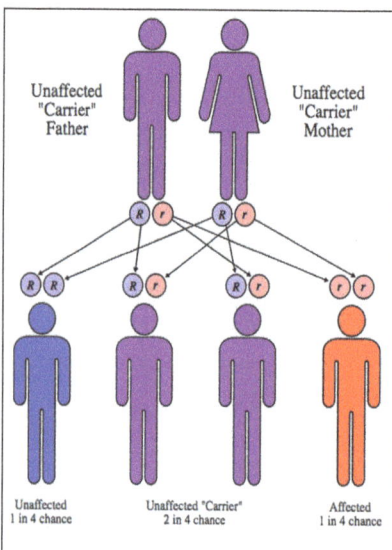

Unaffected "Carrier" Father

Unaffected "Carrier" Mother

R r   R r

R R   R r   R r   r r

Unaffected
1 in 4 chance

Unaffected "Carrier"
2 in 4 chance

Affected
1 in 4 chance

Professor Timothy Peters has disputed the porphyria theory. Using computer-based di-agnostics he concluded that James I had two syndromes: Lesch-Nyhan and Asperger's. It has also been claimed that George III was bipolar and that he may have been poisoned by arsenic. However, because the porphyria theory was prominent in *The Madness of King George* (1994), it is still widely accepted.

Porphyria is a group of liver diseases which normally have three inheritance options: affected, unaffected and transmitter.

HOUSES OF VALOIS, LANCASTER, TUDOR AND STUART

☐ TRANSMITTERS
⚏ POSSIBLE TRANSMITTERS

▲ INSANE
● CLINICAL EVIDENCE OF PORPHYRIA.
△ DISCOLOURED URINE

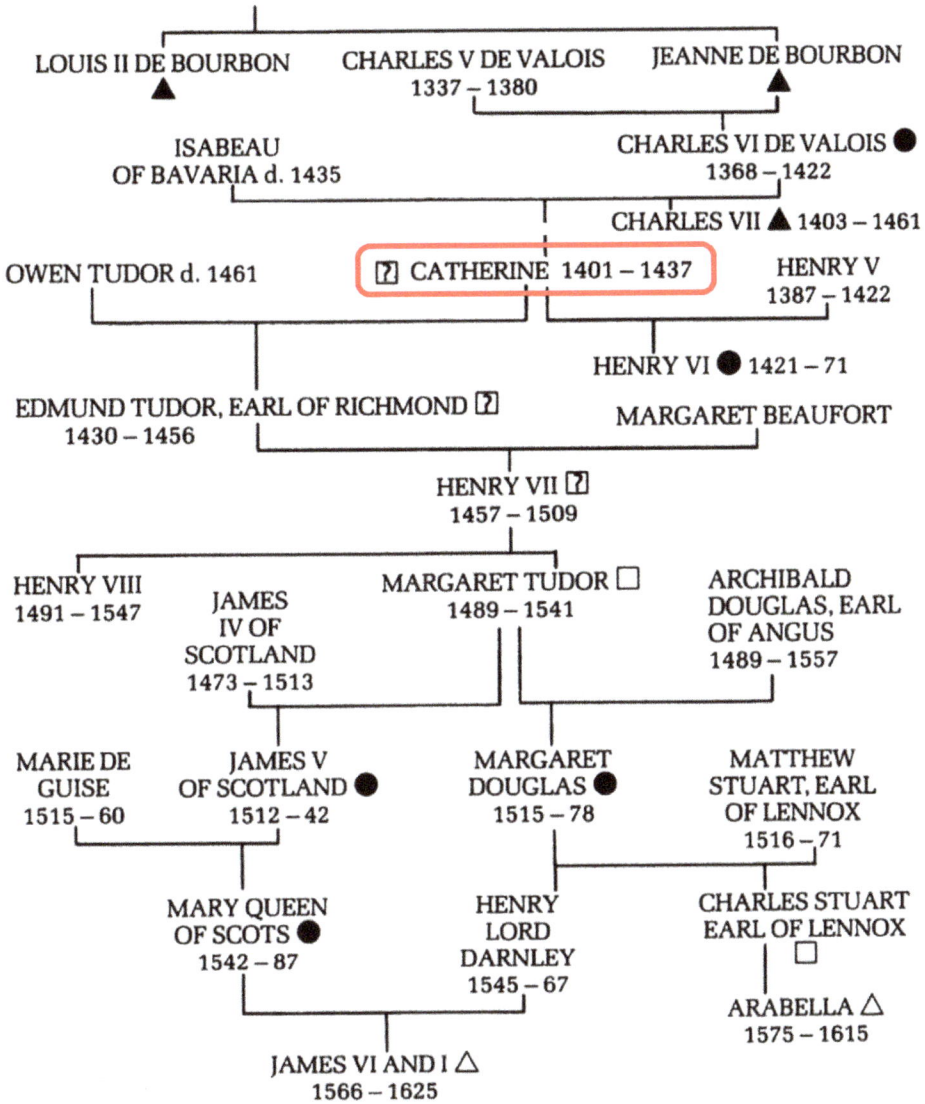

LOUIS II DE BOURBON ▲

CHARLES V DE VALOIS
1337 – 1380

JEANNE DE BOURBON ▲

ISABEAU OF BAVARIA d. 1435

CHARLES VI DE VALOIS ●
1368 – 1422

CHARLES VII ▲ 1403 – 1461

OWEN TUDOR d. 1461

⚏ CATHERINE 1401 – 1437

HENRY V
1387 – 1422

HENRY VI ● 1421 – 71

EDMUND TUDOR, EARL OF RICHMOND ⚏
1430 – 1456

MARGARET BEAUFORT

HENRY VII ⚏
1457 – 1509

HENRY VIII
1491 – 1547

JAMES IV OF SCOTLAND
1473 – 1513

MARGARET TUDOR ☐
1489 – 1541

ARCHIBALD DOUGLAS, EARL OF ANGUS
1489 – 1557

MARIE DE GUISE
1515 – 60

JAMES V OF SCOTLAND ●
1512 – 42

MARGARET DOUGLAS ●
1515 – 78

MATTHEW STUART, EARL OF LENNOX
1516 – 71

MARY QUEEN OF SCOTS ●
1542 – 87

HENRY LORD DARNLEY
1545 – 67

CHARLES STUART EARL OF LENNOX ☐

ARABELLA △
1575 – 1615

JAMES VI AND I △
1566 – 1625

Regardless of whether Charles 'the Mad' and George III had porphyria, their physical and mental problems were probably exacerbated by inbreeding, starting with Charles' parents who were half-first cousins once removed.

Mary Queen of Scots married her half-first cousin Henry Darnley (who had the same mtDNA as Henry VIII); George I married his first cousin Sophia Dorothea; and Queen Victoria married her first cousin Prince Albert.

Queen Victoria may have transmitted porphyria to Princess Feodora of Prussia

Joan of North Wales   *Joan 'The Fair Maid of Kent'*

who died in 1945, and to Prince William of Gloucester who died in a plane crash in 1972, just ten years before Kate was born.

THE current Princess of Wales descends from one of the first Welsh princesses through the first English Princess of Wales, both of whom were named Joan.

Joan of North Wales, an illegitimate daughter of England's King John, married Llewelyn the Great around 1205. And Joan, nicknamed 'The Fair Maid of Kent', was Princess of Wales while married to Edward III's oldest son, nicknamed the Black Prince, who was Katherine Swynford's brother-in-law.

The remains of the Welsh Joan are in a church in Anglesey, not far from where Kate and Prince William lived before they married in 2011. Joan, who had a notorious affair with 'Black William' de Braose, is a central character in Sharon Kay Penman's novel *Here Be Dragons* (1985).

As shown opposite, the English Joan was the great-grandmother of Edmund Beaufort who had an affair with Henry V's widow Catherine of Valois. Kate descends from Beaufort, who had the same mtDNA as Henry V, through Katherine Spencer and Catherine Clifford

The second English Princess of Wales was Anne Neville, the teenage wife of Catherine of Valois' grandson Edward of Westminster, followed by Catherine of Aragon who was Princess of Wales while briefly married to Prince Arthur.

After Camilla married Prince Charles in 2005, she chose not to be known as Princess of Wales out of respect for Princess Diana who, strictly speaking, should never have been known as such because her official title was Diana, Princess of Wales.

Edmund (Knight of the Garter) BEAUFORT

1st Duke of Somerset

Born: Midx. abt. 1406   Died: 22 May 1455   k. at Battle of St. Alban's

HRH Charles's 16-Great Grandfather. Lady Diana's 14-Great Grandfather.

poss. Wives/Partners: Eleanor (Lady; de) BEAUCHAMP ; Margaret (Eleanor's sister)

Children: Margaret (de) BEAUFORT ; Eleanor (Countess of WILTSHIRE) BEAUFORT ;
      Henry (Sir) BEAUFORT

```
                        /-- Edward III (WINDSOR; King) of ENGLAND
               /             \-- Isabella `the She-Wolf' of FRANCE  +
            /-- John (BEAUFORT) of GAUNT
            |       \        /-- William (Guillaume) III d' AVESNES  +
            |       |   \-- Philipa d' AVESNES (Countess) of HAINAULT
            |       /             \-- Jeanne de VALOIS  +
         /-- John `Fairborn' (K.G.; de) BEAUFORT
         |      \               /-- poss. Paon (Comte) de ROET  +
         |      |        /-- Paon (Sir; of GUIENNE) de ROET
         |      \-- Katherine ROELT
```

-Edmund (K.G.) BEAUFORT

```
         |            /-- Thomas (de) HOLAND  (1314? - 1360)
         |        /          \-- Maud (la) ZOUCHE  +
         |     /-- Thomas (II; de) HOLLAND  (1350? - 1397)
         |     |      \          /-- Edmund of KENT (PLANTAGENET)  +
         |     |      \-- Joan `Fair Maid' PLANTAGENET  (1328 - 1385)
         |     /             \-- Margaret (Baroness) WAKE  +
         \-- Margaret (of Kent) HOLAND  (1384? - 1439)
                 \          /-- Edmund FitzALAN  +
                 |    /-- Richard I `Copped Hat' FitzALAN
                 |    /      \-- Alice de WARENNE  +
                 \-- Alice (Lady of Arundel) FitzALAN
                          \        /-- Henry of MONMOUTH (PLANTAGENET)  +
                          \-- Eleanor (Alianor) (of LANCASTER) PLANTAGENET
                              \ / or: poss. Isabel DESPENCER, q.v.
                                \-- Maud (de) CHAWORTH  +
```

Catherine, Princess of Wales is still Duchess of Cambridge but has several new titles, including Duchess of Cornwall and Duchess of Rothesay (used only in Scotland). And Kate will almost certainly join Queen Margrethe of Denmark as a Colonel-in-Chief of the Princess of Wales' Royal Regiment.

Because of strong Welsh opposition to the Prince of Wales title going to heirs of the British throne, it will not be surprising if Prince William and Kate end this tradition following the death of Charles III.

Note: Although she became Princess William of Wales in 2011, Kate had to curtsy to 'blood princesses' Beatrice and Eugenie. From now on, they will have to curtsy to the future Queen Catherine who is second in the order of female precedence.

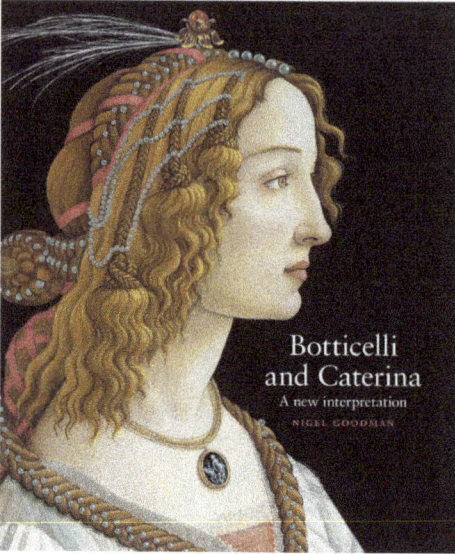

Botticelli
and Caterina
A new interpretation
NIGEL GOODMAN

CATERINA SFORZA IST MONA LISA

THROUGH illegitimate offspring of Charles II and James II, Kate's children descend from Caterina Sforza, an illegitimate daughter of the Duke of Milan who may have been one of Botticelli's models for Venus, otherwise known as Aphrodite, and also the real Mona Lisa.

As shown above, the Mona Lisa claim was made by German art historian Magdalena Soest whose 2011 book features a portrait of Caterina Sforza by Lorenzo di Credi. Another possible sitter was Caterina's first cousin (and sister-in-law) Isabella of Aragon, a second cousin once removed of Catherine of Aragon.

Regardless of the sitter's identity, the world's most famous painting is probably an idealised portrait of Leonardo da Vinci's mother Caterina. As Viacheslav Chirikba wrote in *The Mystery of Caterina* (2018): 'The evidence of the exceptional emotional significance that this female image carried for the artist is the fact that Leonardo did not part with the painting for the rest of his life. This would be incomprehensible were it simply a portrait of a minor customer's wife.'

Nigel Goodman made his claims about Botticelli in a book published in 2022.

After studying images of Caterina Sforza in the Sistine Chapel frescoes, Goodman concluded that she was the model for the goddess of love in Venus and Mars (and for an attendant in The Birth of Venus); for the goddess of health in Pallas and the Centaur; and for all three of the graces in Primavera.

(Caterina Sforza's Visconti ancestors claimed descent from Venus/Aphrodite and so

Caterina Sforza may have been the model for Madonna of the Rocks (the anagram SO DARK THE CON OF MAN) which features in The Da Vinci Code.

— 16 —

Catherine of Aragon challenged Henry VIII and Anne Boleyn by commissioning this cipher mixing HENRICUS REX with her own name, which she spelled with a K. The pet monkey in the portrait was another bold statement: The king could roam but he was tied to his first wife.

did Kate's allegedly illegitimate ancestor Edward IV who cited a dubious bloodline through Brutus of Troy, Aphrodite's great-great-grandson, to boost his claim to the throne.)

The Birth of Venus, Pallas and the Centaur, and Primavera are in the Uffizi Gallery which Kate frequented while studying in Florence before starting her art history course at St Andrews University..

Note: Leonardo's mother Caterina died in 1494 and Caterina Sforza died in May 1509, exactly two weeks before Catherine of Aragon married Henry VIII.

L IKE *The Da Vinci Code, The Catherine Code* has a lot to do with religion, and especially with the mythical St Catherine of Alexandria.

Edward the Confessor somehow obtained healing oil originating from St Catherine's tomb at Mt Sinai and deposited it in Westminster Abbey which he started rebuilding around 1042. William the Conqueror, who introduced the saint's cult to Britain, was crowned in the abbey on Christmas Day 1066.

Work started on the abbey's St Catherine Chapel in the mid-1100s and a century later an elaborate shrine was erected for Henry III's short-lived youngest daughter Princess Katherine. England once had about fifty churches dedicated to St Catherine, including London's St Katherine Cree founded in 1280.

Catherine of Valois, Catherine of Aragon and Catherine Parr venerated their namesake saint. And, like her mother-in-law Henrietta Maria, and arch rival Barbara Palmer, Catherine of Braganza was depicted as St Catherine by a renowned artist.

Prince George and his siblings descend from William Sinclair, builder of Scotland's mysterious Rosslyn Chapel which features in Dan Brown's novel. St Catherine of Alexandria was the family's patron saint and that explains why there is a Catherine wheel on Sinclair's tomb.

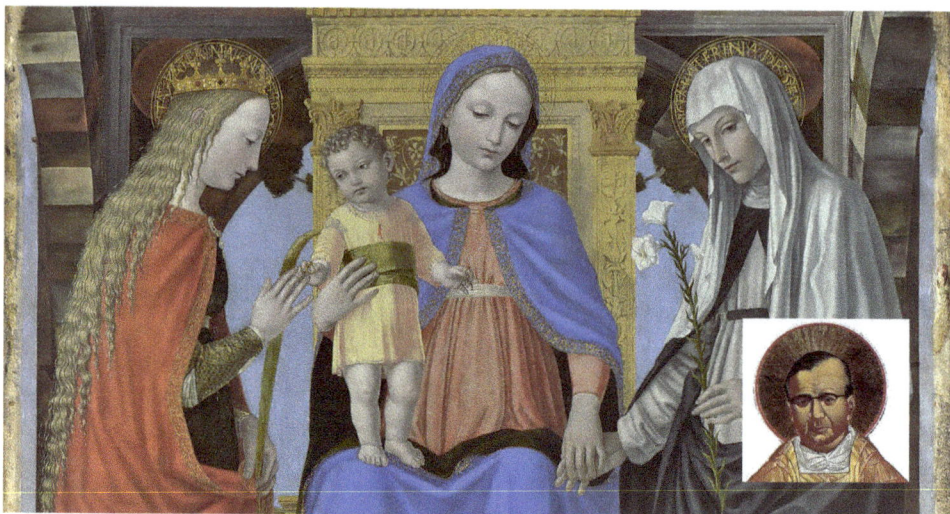

Not far from Rosslyn Chapel is St Catherine's well which, according to legend, started flowing after drops of healing oil from the saint's tomb were accidentally spilled at Liberton. The well was visited each year by nuns from the convent of St Catherine of Siena in Edinburgh.

Princess Katherine and Catherine of Braganza were born on St Catherine of Alexandria's feast day (25th November) and so, presumably, was Katherine Swynford who had three Catherine wheels on her coat of arms.

On 25th November 2007, as an unmarried 25-year-old woman, Kate became a 'Catherinette' (See Wikipedia for details of the French tradition). She and Prince William got engaged almost exactly three years later and they married on the feast day of St Catherine of Siena (29th April) in 2011. The Bishop of London Dr Richard Chartres quoted from the saint during his speech: 'Be who God meant you to be and you will set the world on fire.'

Note: In 1964, controversial Opus Dei founder Josemaria Escriva (inset), whose birthday (9th January) is shared by Kate, named St Catherine of Siena as an 'intercessor' of the secretive Catholic organisation which features in *The Da Vinci Code*.

The Catherine Code

Part I

Katarina of Yugoslavia

Tatiana Sfiris

FOUR DAUGHTERS OF EVE

MITOCHONDRIAL DNA inherited through namesakes of Kate who lived in the Middle Ages has enabled modern-day scientists to make some truly amazing discoveries.

As Bryan Sykes explained in *The Seven Daughters of Eve* (2001), every woman alive today has an all-female bloodline from Mitochondrial Eve who lived in Africa about 150,000 years ago (See map opposite). He named the 'daughters' according to their haplogroups, including H (Helena) and T (Tara) which are common throughout Europe.

Like her great-uncle Prince Philip, whose mtDNA helped scientists to identify Alexey Romanov's remains, Katarina of Yugoslavia inherited haplogroup H from Catherine of Foix who died around 1494 (See chart on Page 103). Katarina, not to be confused with Katherine, the Crown Princess of Yugoslavia, is patron of the Society of Genealogists.

Charles II, James II, William III, Queen Victoria and Edward VII had all-female bloodlines from Catherine of Foix and so did Russia's Catherine the Great and France's Louis XIV. Louis, nicknamed the 'Sun King', inspired *The Man in the Iron Mask* (See Page 100). Other matrilineal descendants include two living European monarchs: Spain's Felipe VI and Sweden's Carl XVI Gustaf.

Identification of Nicholas II's remains was confirmed by a sample from Tatiana Sfiris' mother Xenia, a matrilineal descendant of Katharina von Pfannberg (haplogroup T) who died around 1375. Charles I, George I, George III and George V had the same mtDNA and were even more closely related because the three Georges, and many other monarchs, descended from Katharina von Pfannberg through most of their great-great-grandparents.

Thanks to the late John Ashdown-Hill, we know that Australian-born Wendy

— 20 —

Wendy Duldig

Elizabeth Roberts

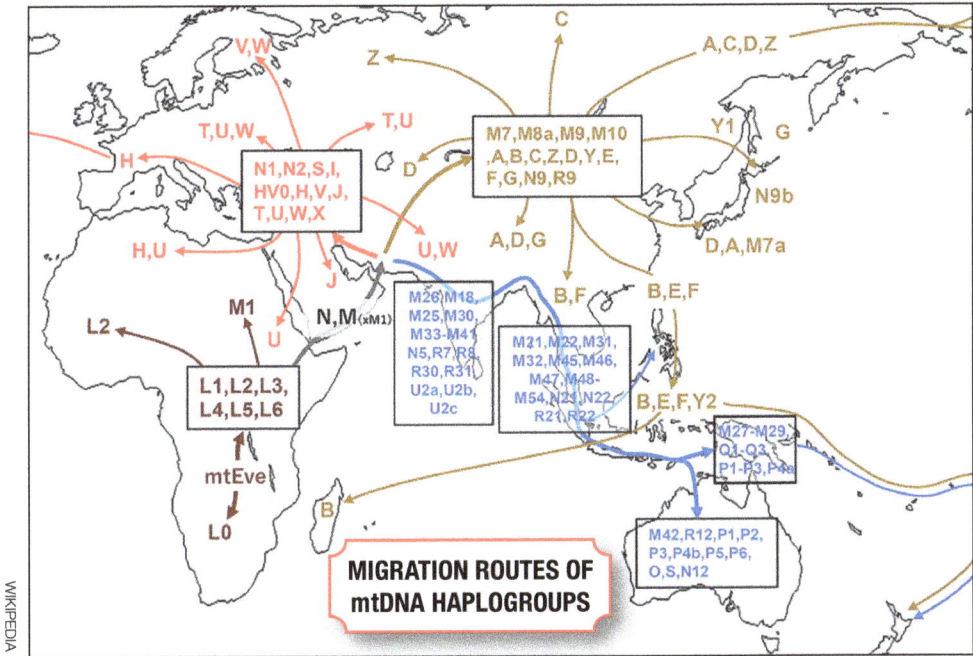

MIGRATION ROUTES OF mtDNA HAPLOGROUPS

Duldig has an all-female bloodline from Jasmine (haplogroup J) through Katherine Swynford and Richard III's sister (See Page 105). Kate descends from an illegitimate daughter of Richard III's brother who may not have had the same male DNA (See Edward IV's Illegitimacies, Page 62).

While trying to solve the Princes in the Tower mystery, John Ashdown-Hill tracked down opera singer Elizabeth Roberts who descends from Ursula (haplogroup U) through Jacquetta of Luxembourg (whose sister Catherine died in 1492). Henry VIII inherited Jacquetta's mtDNA and possibly her Kell-positive blood, which could explain Catherine of Aragon's pregnancy problems.

THE KATHERINA POLYXENE CODE

REMARKABLY, all of the monarchs pictured opposite inherited the same mitochondrial DNA, presumably haplogroup H, through all-female bloodlines from Katherina Polyxene of Solms-Rodelheim (inset above) who died in 1765, proving conclusively that until recently European royals were a separate ethnic group (See More German Than British, Page 50).

Wilhelm I of Germany was an uncle of Catherine the Great's great-grandson Alexander II who had four illegitimate children with his mistress Catherine Dolgorukova. Kate's children descend from Alexander II's brother-in-law Prince Alexander of Hesse and by Rhine who was either illegitimate or dangerously inbred (See Badges of Bastardy, Page 98). Wilhelm I, Alexander II, George VI (and his brother Edward VIII) all descended from Katherine Swynford and Catherine of Valois through George I.

Sweden's Oscar II and his son Gustaf V had all-female bloodlines from Katherina Polyxene and so did Gustaf's grandson Gustavus Adolf Bernadotte, father of the current monarch Carl XVI Gustaf who has an all-female bloodline from Catherine of Foix (See Catherines of Sweden, Page 86).

Oscar II's great-great-granddaughter Margrethe II of Denmark, who descends from Katherina Polyexene through all of her great-great-grandparents (including Queen Victoria), has multiple cousinships with Harald V of Norway whose parents were first cousins.

Harald V's first cousin Albert II of the Belgians, who sired an illegitimate daughter now known as Her Royal Highness Princess Delphine, abdicated in

Wilhelm I of Germany

Alexander II of Russia

George VI of Britain

Oscar II of Sweden

Margrethe II of Denmark

Harald V of Norway

Albert II of the Belgians

Willem-Alexander

Grand Duke Henri

2013 and so did Queen Beatrix of the Netherlands, mother of Willem-Alexander whose daughter Catharina-Amalia is heir apparent.

Not surprisingly, Grand Duke Henri of Luxembourg, a first cousin of Belgium's current monarch King Philippe, descends from Katharina von Pfannberg through all of his great-great-grandparents.

Many Scandinavian and Benelux monarchs have been members of an Order of the Dragon founded by Willem I of Brunant in 1602, two centuries after another Order of the Dragon was co-founded by Barbara of Cilly, from whom all of the monarchs pictured above descend through Katherina Polyxene.

Note: Katherina Polyxene had a bloodline from William the Conqueror through Katharina von Sachsen-Lauenburg and Katherine of Anhalt-Bernburg.

FIVE QUEEN CATHERINES

WHILE Kate is not descended from any of her royal namesakes, her children have bloodlines from Catherine of Valois (pictured above with her first husband Henry V); from Henry VIII, husband of Catherine of Aragon, Catherine Howard and Catherine Parr; and from Catherine of Braganza's husband Charles II.

Catherine of Valois was widowed just nine months after giving birth to the future Henry VI at Windsor Castle, which supposedly cursed both him and his father (See Page 112). Five years later, after being forced to end her affair with Katherine Swynford's grandson Edmund Beaufort, Catherine started an illegal relationship with Owen Tudor (which meant that their sons Edmund and Jasper Tudor were illegitimate).

Henry VIII married Catherine of Aragon in 1509. Two decades later, with no male heir, Henry claimed he was cursed because of Catherine's previous marriage to his brother. Henry divorced Catherine — making their daughter Mary I illegitimate — and then married Anne Boleyn, breaching canon law because he had previously slept with her sister Mary.

Anne Boleyn's daughter Elizabeth I was declared illegitimate after Anne was executed for alleged adultery. Anne's first cousin Catherine Howard suffered the same fate, and Catherine

Catherine of Aragon was depicted as the Madonna (left) and also as Mary Magdalene whose alleged bloodline was the basis for The Da Vinci Code.

Catherine Howard

Catherine Parr

Parr narrowly avoided execution after arguing with Henry VIII about religion.

After outliving Henry VIII, Catherine Parr married her true love Thomas Seymour but died soon after child birth. The child died in infancy and Seymour was executed for treason in 1549.

As well as several failed pregnancies, the convent-educated Catherine of Braganza had to endure Charles II's many mistresses and bastard children, including two ancestors of Kate's children.

Note: Before Richard II married Catherine of Valois' six-year-old sister Isabella in late 1396, Katherine Swynford (as Duchess of Lancaster) was briefly England's first lady with arms featuring three Catherine wheels.

THE TEMPLAR CURSE

ALL OF Kate's royal namesakes, through their husbands, were possible victims of a famous curse laid on Philip IV of France by Jacques de Molay (right), last grandmaster of the Knights Templar, shortly before he was burned to death in 1314. The curse supposedly lasted for thirteen generations.

Henry V was a fifth generation descendant of Philip IV through Katherine Swynford's husband John of Gaunt; Henry VIII was an eighth generation descendant; and Charles II, husband of Catherine of Braganza, was in the 13th generation.

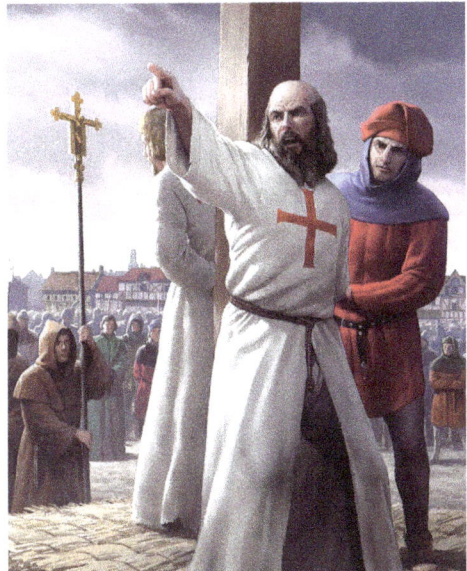

Jacques de Molay issues his famous curse

CATHERINES OF WESTMINSTER

THE FUTURE Queen Catherine outshone her five royal namesakes by getting married on the Cosmati Pavement in Westminster Abbey. And, barring unforeseen circumstances, Kate will be the first British-born Queen Catherine to be crowned on the famous mosaic which supposedly predicts the end of the world (See Page 254).

French princess Catherine of Valois married Henry V at Troyes in 1420; Spanish princess Catherine of Aragon married Henry VIII at Greenwich in 1509; Catherine Howard married Henry VIII at Oatlands Palace in 1540; Catherine Parr married Henry VIII at Hampton Court in 1543; and Portuguese princess Catherine of Braganza married Charles II in Portsmouth in 1662.

Catherine of Valois was crowned on the Cosmati Pavement in 1421 and Catherine of Aragon was crowned on the same spot in 1509. There were no coronation ceremonies for Catherine Howard and Catherine Parr, and Catherine of Braganza could not be crowned because she was Catholic.

The pavement was laid down in the sanctuary (highlighted opposite) on the orders of Henry III, father of Britain's first Princess Katherine who had the same mitochondrial DNA as Catherine of Valois' father Charles 'the Mad' (See Page 110).

After Princess Katherine died in 1257, her grief-stricken father erected an elaborate shrine behind the sanctuary but it disappeared during construction of Henry VII's chapel.

Princess Katherine, who may have been deaf mute, was born in 1253 on the feast day of St Catherine of Alexandria (25th November) and died aged three.

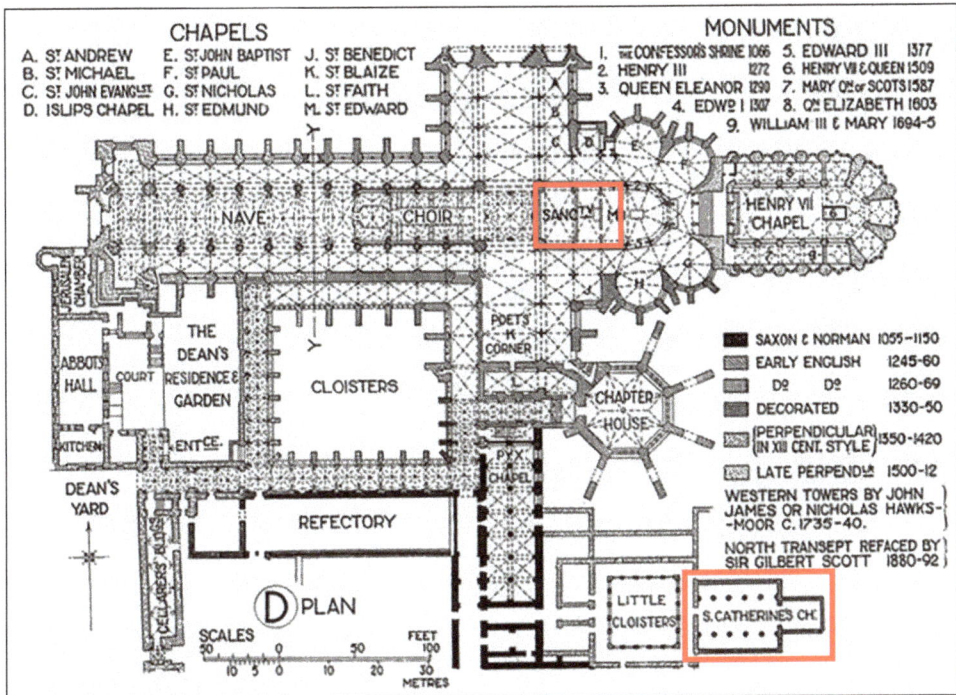

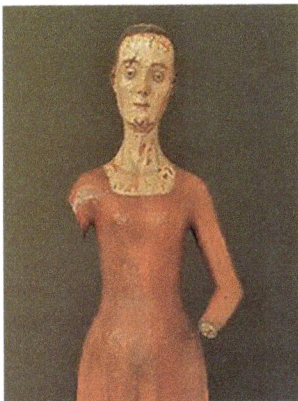

St Catherine's Garden (above) is all that remains of St Catherine's Chapel built in the 1100s by King Stephen's bastard son Gervase of Blois.

In 1669, on his 36th birthday, Samuel Pepys famously kissed the embalmed corpse of Catherine of Valois (effigy above) whose sons Edmund and Jasper Tudor were illegitimate. Henry VIII's alleged illegitimate daughter Katherine Knollys (Catherine Carey) was buried nearby and so was James II's and Catherine Sedley's illegitimate daughter Catherine Darnley who was a friend of the poet Alexander Pope.

Also buried in the abbey, near her half-uncle Isaac Newton (whose tomb and Alexander Pope feature in *The Da Vinci Code),* was Catherine Barton and her daughter Catherine Conduitt. The older Catherine reputedly told the story about a falling apple which provides a vital clue in Dan Brown's novel.

SWORDS OF ST CATHERINE

BOTH St Catherine of Alexandria (above left) and her Siena namesake mystically married Jesus but only the latter received a foreskin wedding ring.

Kate's mythical Alexandrian namesake was beheaded with a sword after breaking her torture wheel, hence the swords in many of her portraits. And according to another legend, a St Catherine sword belonged to Joan of Arc (above right) who had a sister named Catherine.

After seeing St Catherine in a vision, Joan supposedly located her sword in Sainte-Catherine-de-Fierbois and wielded it while supporting Catherine of Valois' brother Charles VII against the English. (In their 2007 book *L'Affaire Jeanne d'Arc*, Roger Senzig and Marcel Gay sensationally claimed that Joan was Catherine of Valois' illegitimate half-sister.)

Before being burned at the stake, Joan was interrogated by Katherine Swynford's bastard son Cardinal Henry Beaufort whose illegitimate daughter Joan is an ancestor of Kate's children through Katherine Stradling (See chart on Page 239).

Kate's children may descend from another illegitimate Joan, the daughter of a nun allegedly seduced by William de la Pole (nicknamed Jackanapes) who fought Joan of Arc at the Siege of Orleans. Prince George and his siblings also descend from Jackanapes' sister Isabel through Henry Fitzroy, a bastard son of Charles II and Barbara Palmer who, like Catherine of Braganza and Catherine's mother-in-law Henrietta Maria, was depicted as St Catherine (See Page 70).

St Catherine of Alexandria is depicted in a stained glass window of Paris' Church of Saint-Sulpice visited by the murderous albino monk in The Da Vinci Code.

…AND A FORESKIN WEDDING RING?

WHEN Kate Middleton married Prince William in Westminster Abbey on 29th April 2011 many people were vaguely aware that it was the feast day of St Catherine of Siena whose mystical marriage to Jesus inspired many paintings, including the one above by Giovanni di Paulo di Grazia.

But few, if any royal watchers knew that St Catherine's mythical wedding ring was Jesus' foreskin which, after being preserved for 1400 years, was allegedly given to Catherine of Valois by Henry V.

During the Middle Ages, Christians venerated at least twenty different holy prepuces, including one held at Coulombs Abbey near Chartres which may have been borrowed by the hero of Agincourt in 1420. Some say that Henry V placed the relic in his wedding bed to boost Catherine's fertility; others say it ensured a painless delivery. Either way, Henry VI was born the following year but that wasn't good news for his father (See Catherine of Valois' Curses, Page 112).

Note: Since Queen Victoria's youngest son Prince Leopold was not diagnosed with haemophilia until shortly after his second birthday, presumably he and his male relatives were not circumcised. However, it is well documented that Charles III was snipped by mohel Jacob Snowman in 1948. And, based on Prince Harry's book *Spare* released in early 2023, it seems that he and brother William were circumcised soon after they were born.

KNIGHTS OF ST CATHERINE

KATE has a tenuous connection to St Catherine of Alexandria through her distant ancestor Richard 'the Fearless' of Normandy (shown opposite) who, according to legend, was flown by 'ghost-knights' to the saint's monastery at Mt Sinai in Egypt (above).

The monastery contains the alleged body of St Catherine which was found by monks around 800 AD. One of the saint's fingers ended up at Rouen in northern France and that resulted in an abbey being built on nearby St Catherine's Hill. The abbey also had some holy oil from St Catherine's tomb, some of which was presumably obtained by St Edward the Confessor and given to Westminster Abbey.

William the Bastard, who championed the cult of St Catherine in Britain, died in Rouen in 1087; Kate's ancestor Edward IV was born there in 1442; and Catherine of Valois' former lover Edmund Beaufort surrendered to her brother Charles VII in Rouen in 1449.

According to a website run by the St Pachomius Library, American adventurer Wendell Phillips (inset above), an alleged prototype of the fictional Indiana Jones, was made a Knight of St Catherine after visiting Mt Sinai in 1951, about 2000 years after Richard 'the Fearless', son of Sprota the concubine, was flown there by a band of supernatural knights who expiated their sins by fighting demons.

Not much is known about the original Knights of St Catherine who reputedly guarded the monastery and its caravan-lines, but they may have inspired the Knights Templar, founded in Palestine around 1120, and also the Order of the Garter founded by Edward III in 1348.

A website run by a branch of the Lusignan family invites worthy candidates to join their Order of St Catherine with Mt Sinai which was purportedly founded in 1063. And the Canadian-based Order of the Knights of St Catherine of Sinai claims to possess one of the saint's fingers, presumably not taken from her 'incorrupt' left hand which remains at the monastery.

The PEDIGREE of

William the CONQUEROR (Duke) of NORMANDY

Born: 1027 Died: 9 Sep 1087

Wives/Partners: Maud PEVEREL ; Matilda (Maud) FLEMING ; (NN), a concubine
Children: William `the Elder' PEVEREL de NOTTINGHAM [alt ped] ; Robert II CURTHOSE;
Henry I BEAUCLERC (King) of ENGLAND ; Adela Alice (Princess) of ENGLAND ; William II `Rufus'

```
                /-- Richard I `the Fearless' (Count) of NORMANDY
             /     \-- Sprota de BRETAGNE (concubine)  +
          /-- Richard II `the Good' of NORMANDY  (963? - 1027)
          |     \         /-- Herbastus (Herfastus) (Sire) de CREPON  +
          |     |      |       | or: (NN), a Dane
          |     |      /       | or: Forquelar of CIRQUES
          |     \-- Gunnora (Gonnor) de CREPON  (936? - 1031?)
          |          \| OR: prob. not Emma de FRANCE  +
          |          || OR: prob. not Gunnora (HARALDSDOTTIR) DENMARK  -
          |          \-- poss.  Cynthia of OBATRIDES  +
          |               | or: poss. Cyrid of SWEDEN
       /-- Robert II (Duke) of NORMANDY  (1000? - 1035 Turkey)
       |     \              /-- prob.  Juhel (Judhael) BERENGER  +
       |     |           /     | OR: poss. Judicael BERENGER [alt ped]  +
       |     |        /-- Conan I `the Crooked' (Count/Duke) of BRITTANY
       |     |        |     \-- Gerberge (poss. of NANTES)  +
       |     |        /          | OR: poss. Gerberga of SAXONY  +
       |     \-- Judith (Princess) of BRITTANY
       |              \         /-- Geoffrey I `Grisgonelle' (Count) d' ANJOU  +
       |              \-- Ermangarde d' ANJOU  (952? - 992)
       /                   \-- Adelaide (Adelais) of VERMANDOIS  +
```

- William the CONQUEROR (Duke) of NORMANDY

```
       \                   /-- Rollo (BRICO) THURSTAN  +
       |              /-- Askytel
       |         /-- Reynald de FALAISE
       |      /-- Fulbert `the Tanner' de FALAIS  (974? - ?)
       |   /          | OR: prob. not Fulbert de FALAIS [alt ped]  +
       \-- Herleve (Salburpyr) de FALAISE  (1003? - 1050?)
```

'SAINT' KATHERINE OF LEDBURY

KATE'S children have a bloodline from Richard 'the Fearless' through the saintly Katherine of Ledbury, also known as Catherine Giffard, who was immortalised in a sonnet by William Wordsworth.

After her husband Baron Nicholas de Audley died around 1299, Katherine became an 'anchoress', or hermit, in Herefordshire and is best remembered for a story about church bells ringing unaided. (Some say the bells sounded during an earthquake.)

Katherine, who was never officially canonized, has often been confused with St Catherine of Alexandria whose cult spread throughout Britain after being introduced by William the Conqueror.

Note: According to fabpedigree.com and geni.com Katherine was a great-granddaughter of King John's illegitimate daughter Joan of North Wales.

ROYAL BASTARD BLOODLINES

LIKE KATE, many millions of people around the world are eligible to join the Descendants of the Illegitimate Sons and Daughters of the Kings of Britain, an American genealogical group founded in Virginia in 1950 and commonly known as the Royal Bastards.

On fabpedigree.com most of Katherine Swynford's grandchildren have bloodlines from William the Conqueror through three prominent royal bastards: Henry I's son Robert of Gloucester, Henry II's son William Longespee, and King John's daughter Joan of North Wales.

Katherine Swynford's son-in-law and daughter-in-law also descended from Henry II's illegitimate half-brother Hameline d'Anjou whose daughter Suzanne may have been one of King John's mistresses.

Both Kate and Prince William descend from an illegitimate daughter of Edward IV, and from three illegitimate daughters of William I of Scotland. Prince William has many other bastard bloodlines, including one from Catherine of Valois' niece Antigone of Gloucester through two Catherine Copleys.

Catherine of Valois, Catherine of Aragon, Catherine Howard, Catherine Parr and Catherine of Braganza descended from William the Bastard, and so did Kate's noble namesakes Katherine Spencer, Katherine Percy and Katherine Clifford.

Prince Philip had an all-female bloodline from Catherine of Foix, whose grandparents all descended from William the Bastard, and Philip's father-in-law George VI had an all-female bloodline from Katherina Polyxene who possibly descended from William the Bastard through all of her grandparents.

The bend sinister on the Royal Bastards' badge commonly but not always signified illegitimacy (See Beaufort Bastard Bloodlines, Page 239).

— 32 —

THE PEDIGREE OF

Katherine CARY

Born: abt. 1524 Died: 1569

HRH Charles's 12-Great Grandmother. Lady Diana's 11-Great Grandmother.

Husband/Partner:　　Francis (K.G.; of Rotherfield) KNOLLYS
Children:　　Anne KNOLLYS ; Richard KNOLLYS ; Katherine KNOLLYS ; Lettice KNOLLYS ;

```
                              /-- Owen (Sir) TUDOR  +
                      /-- Edmund TUDOR  (1430? - 1456)
              /           \-- Catherine de VALOIS  +
      /-- Henry VII TUDOR (King) of ENGLAND
      |       \           /-- John (K.G.) BEAUFORT  +
      |        \-- Margaret BEAUFORT
      /           \-- Margaret (of BLETSOE) BEAUCHAMP  +
  /-- Henry VIII TUDOR  (London 1491 - 1547 London)
  |       \ | OR: prob. not William (Esq.) CAREY  +
  |       |                     /-- Richard PLANTAGENET-YORK  +
  |       |               /           | or: poss. BLAYBOURNE the Archer (cuckolder)
  |       |        /-- Edward IV 'of Rouen' PLANTAGENET-YORK
  |       /           \-- Cecily (Lady) NEVILLE  +
  |      \-- Elizabeth (of YORK) PLANTAGENET
  |             \           /-- Richard (K.G.) WYDEVILLE  +
  |              \-- Elizabeth (Lady) WOODVILLE
  /                   \-- Jacquette de LUXEMBOURG  +
```

- Katherine CARY

```
  \                         /-- Geoffrey (Sir) BOLEYN  +
  |                  /-- William (K.B.; of Blickling) BOLEYN
  |                /           \-- Anne HOO  +
  |       /-- Thomas (K.G.) BOLEYN  (1477 - 1539)
  |       |       \           /-- Thomas (le BOTILLER) BUTLER  +
  |       |        \-- Margaret (Lady) BUTLER  (1455 - 1537?)
  |       /                   \-- Anne HANKEFORD  +
  \-- Mary BOLEYN  (Norfolk 1504? - 1543 Staffords.)
         \                    /-- John (K.G.; 1st Baron) HOWARD  +
         |            /-- Thomas HOWARD (Earl of SURREY)
         |            /       \-- Catherine MOLINES (MOLEYNS)  +
         \-- Elizabeth (Lady) HOWARD
```

FROM HENRY VIII TO KATE?

THE CLAIM that Kate is descended from Henry VIII's illegitimate daughter Catherine Carey (Katherine Cary), first made in *The Spectator* in 2011, was based on the misidentification of her ancestor William Davenport whose father was involved in the trans-Atlantic slave trade (See Page 164). However, as shown above, Kate's children have bloodlines from Mary Boleyn's daughter through both Charles III and Princess Diana.

DNA tests on the remains of Catherine Carey (right) and Elizabeth I in Westminster Abbey would presumably determine if they were half-sisters. It has long been rumoured that Catherine's brother Henry Carey was also sired by Henry VIII. If so, Catherine and Henry were descended from Katherine Swynford through both John and Joan Beaufort.

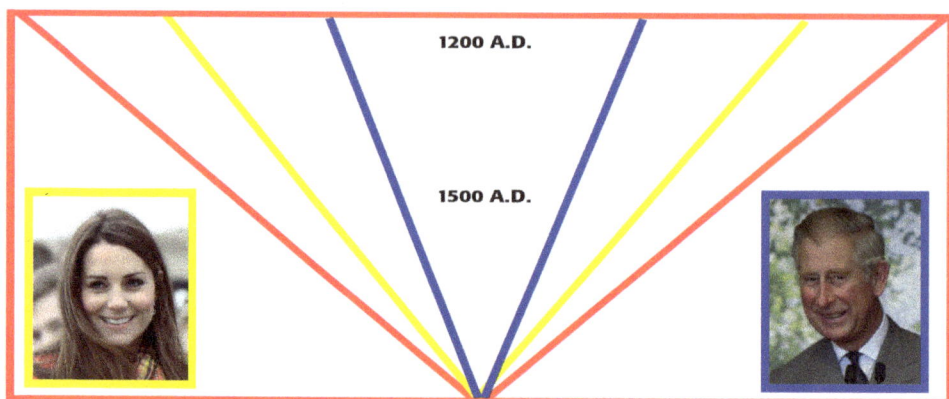

KATE'S COLLAPSING PEDIGREE

SINCE we all have two parents, four grandparents, eight great-grandparents, and so on, our family trees should be V-shaped. In reality, pedigree collapses caused by accumulated inbreeding lead to an ever-increasing number of duplicate ancestors.

Both Kate and Prince William are descended from first cousins who married in the 1800s. Queen Victoria's mother and Prince Albert's father were siblings and so were John William Middleton's mother and mother-in-law, Mary and Ellen Ward (See chart on Page 146). However, the royals have a long history of consanguineous marriages and, as shown above, Charles III's V-shaped pedigree (in blue) is a lot narrower than Kate's.

According to Mormon royal expert Robert Gunderson, Charles has more than 2000 individual bloodlines from Edward III. Gunderson also claimed that Charles' 14th great-grandparents numbered only 23,000 when, theoretically, there should have been 65,536 (2^{16}).

The pedigree collapse of Kate's children starts with their royal great-grandparents who were more closely related than most people realise. As well as being second cousins once removed through Christian IX of Denmark, Elizabeth II and Prince Philip were third cousins through Queen Victoria; fourth cousins through Friedrich III of Hesse-Cassel; fourth cousins once removed through George III; and double fifth cousins through Mary Hanover.

George V was descended from Katharina von Pfannberg through all of his great-great grandparents, and Prince William is descended from Katherine of Flanders through nearly all of his great-great-great-grandparents.

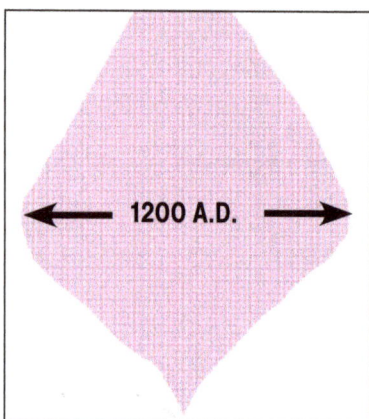

Present-day family trees are roughly diamond-shaped with a maximum number of ancestors around 1200 AD and a Mitochondrial Eve who lived somewhere in Africa in the very distant past.

Pedro (III) 'the Cruel' (King) of CASTILE

Born: 1334   Died: 1369   executed

HM George I's 10-Great Grandfather.

Wives/Partners: Maria Juana de PADILLA (PEDILLA) ; Juana de CASTRO, mistress
Children: Constance Pedra (Princess) of CASTILE ; Isabel PEREZ (Princess) of CASTILE

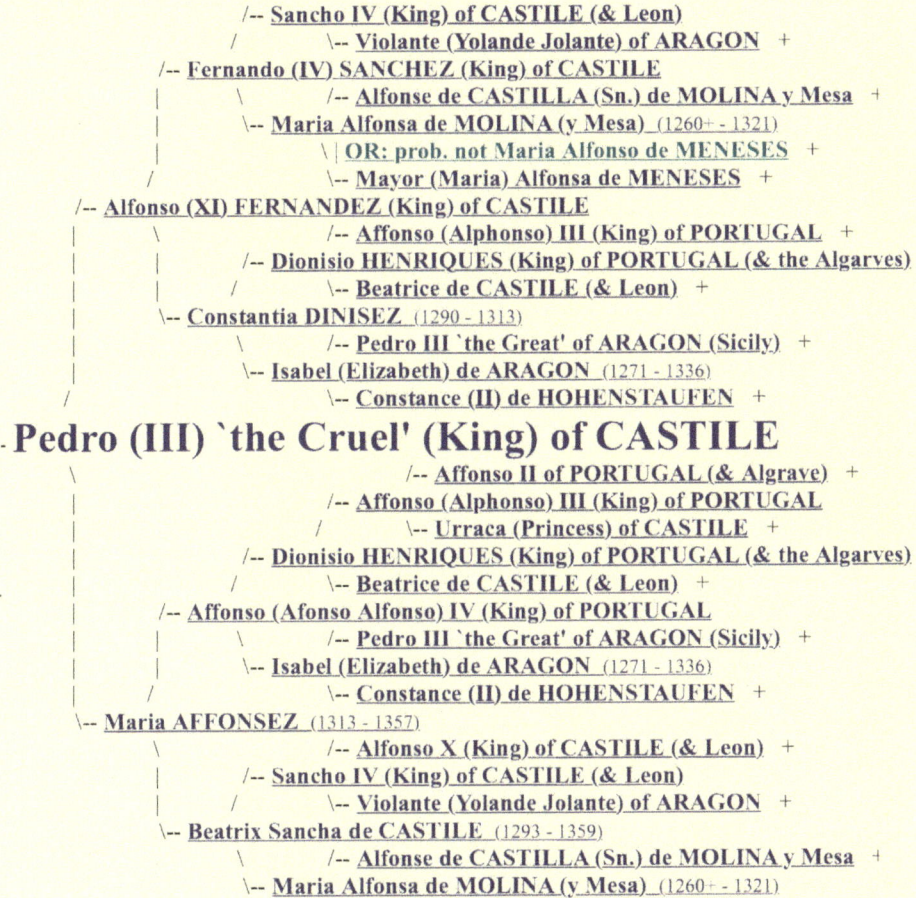

```
                       /-- Sancho IV (King) of CASTILE (& Leon)
                      /        \-- Violante (Yolande Jolante) of ARAGON  +
              /-- Fernando (IV) SANCHEZ (King) of CASTILE
              |       \        /-- Alfonse de CASTILLA (Sn.) de MOLINA y Mesa  +
              |        \-- Maria Alfonsa de MOLINA (y Mesa)  (1260+ - 1321)
              |              \| OR: prob. not Maria Alfonso de MENESES  +
              /                 \-- Mayor (Maria) Alfonsa de MENESES  +
        /-- Alfonso (XI) FERNANDEZ (King) of CASTILE
        |       \             /-- Affonso (Alphonso) III (King) of PORTUGAL  +
        |       |       /-- Dionisio HENRIQUES (King) of PORTUGAL (& the Algarves)
        |       |       /       \-- Beatrice de CASTILE (& Leon)  +
        |        \-- Constantia DINISEZ  (1290 - 1313)
        |               \           /-- Pedro III `the Great' of ARAGON (Sicily)  +
        |                \-- Isabel (Elizabeth) de ARAGON  (1271 - 1336)
        /                      \-- Constance (II) de HOHENSTAUFEN  +
```

Pedro (III) `the Cruel' (King) of CASTILE

```
        \                  /-- Affonso II of PORTUGAL (& Algrave)  +
        |             /-- Affonso (Alphonso) III (King) of PORTUGAL
        |             /       \-- Urraca (Princess) of CASTILE  +
        |       /-- Dionisio HENRIQUES (King) of PORTUGAL (& the Algarves)
        |       /       \-- Beatrice de CASTILE (& Leon)  +
        /-- Affonso (Afonso Alfonso) IV (King) of PORTUGAL
        |       |       \           /-- Pedro III `the Great' of ARAGON (Sicily)  +
        |       |        \-- Isabel (Elizabeth) de ARAGON  (1271 - 1336)
        |       /              \-- Constance (II) de HOHENSTAUFEN  +
        \-- Maria AFFONSEZ  (1313 - 1357)
                \                /-- Alfonso X (King) of CASTILE (& Leon)  +
                |       /-- Sancho IV (King) of CASTILE (& Leon)
                |       /       \-- Violante (Yolande Jolante) of ARAGON  +
                 \-- Beatrix Sancha de CASTILE  (1293 - 1359)
                        \           /-- Alfonse de CASTILLA (Sn.) de MOLINA y Mesa  +
                         \-- Maria Alfonsa de MOLINA (y Mesa)  (1260+ - 1321)
```

ONLY FOUR GREAT-GRANDPARENTS

KATE'S most inbred ancestor on fabpedigree.com is Peter the Cruel (right) whose parents, as shown above, were double first cousins with the same grandparents. It was the genetic equivalent of a half-sibling marriage.

Both Kate and Prince William descend from Peter the Cruel through his possibly illegitimate daughter Isabel Perez; through Isabel's alleged illegitimate son Richard of Conisburgh; and through an illegitimate daughter of the allegedly illegitimate Edward IV (See Page 62).

A HUNDRED MILLION DESCENDANTS?

MANY millions of people have bloodlines from Katherine Swynford through two of her illegitimate children, John 'Fairborn' Beaufort and his sister Joan. And everyone descended from John or Joan is also descended from Edward III, pictured above counting the French dead after the Battle of Crecy in 1346.

According to historian and genealogist Leo van de Pas, Edward III had 321 great-great-great-grandchildren, including Catherine Woodville's husband Henry Stafford who, as shown opposite, had bloodlines from both John and Joan Beaufort. Kate is descended from John Beaufort through Katherine Spencer, and from Joan Beaufort through Katherine Percy (See charts on Pages 199 and 211).

British genealogist Andrew Millard has estimated that about 240 of Edward III's great-great-great-grandchildren were living in England around 1460 and, based on fabpedigree.com and other websites, at least half of them had Beaufort bloodlines. The Black Death killed some royals but they still maintained a growth rate of more than three times per generation.

If 120 Beaufort descendants born around 1460 multiplied at the same rate for another four generations, by the 1580s there would have been more than 9000 of them in a population of 3.8 million; and if they multiplied at the average rate of 2.28 times per generation, the total would have been around 3000. (Both estimates are hugely deficient because of overlapping generations.)

Based on the lower estimate, the likelihood that an English person living in

FABPEDIGREE.COM

The PEDIGREE of

Henry (Knight of the Garter) STAFFORD

Born: 1455 Died: 2 Nov 1483 Salisbury

Lady Diana's 13-Great Grandfather. HRH Charles's 14-Great Grandfather.

Wife/Partner: Catherine WYDEVILLE (WYDVILLE)
Children: Elizabeth (Lady) STAFFORD ; Henry (K.G.) STAFFORD ;
         Anne (Lady of Buckingham) STAFFORD ; Edward (K.G.) STAFFORD

```
                              /-- Ralph de STAFFORD  +
                      /-- Hugh (2nd Earl; de) STAFFORD
                      /        \-- Margaret (Baroness) de AUDLEY  +
              /-- Edmund (5th Earl; K.G.) de STAFFORD
              /        \-- Philipa (Philippa; de) BEAUCHAMP  +
      /-- Humphrey (K.G.) STAFFORD  (15/8/1402 - 10/7/1460)
      |        \        /-- Thomas of WOODSTOCK (PLANTAGENET)  +
      |        \-- Anne of GLOUCESTER (PLANTAGENET)  (1383 - 1438)
      /              \-- Eleanor (Alianor) (Lady) de BOHUN  +
  /-- Humphrey II STAFFORD  (1424? - 22/5/1455 (or '57+))
  |        \              /-- John (III; de) NEVILL  +
  |        |        /-- Ralph I NEVILL (de NEVILLE)  (1363? - 1425)
  |        |        /        \-- Matilda (Maud Mary) de PERCY  +
  |        \-- Anne (de) NEVILLE  (1411? - 1480)
  |              \        /-- John (BEAUFORT) of GAUNT  +
  |              \-- Joan (Lady; de) BEAUFORT  (1379? - 1440)
  |                    \ | or: poss. Margaret de STAFFORD, q.v.
  |                    \-- Katherine ROELT  +
```

-Henry (K.G.) STAFFORD

```
  \                      /-- Edward III (WINDSOR; King) of ENGLAND  +
  |                /-- John (BEAUFORT) of GAUNT
  |                /        \-- Philipa d' AVESNES of HAINAULT  +
  |        /-- John `Fairborn' (K.G.; de) BEAUFORT
  |        /        \-- Katherine ROELT  +
  |    /-- Edmund (K.G.) BEAUFORT  (Midx. 1406? - 22/5/1455)
  |    |        \        /-- Thomas (II; de) HOLLAND  +
  |    |        \-- Margaret (of Kent) HOLAND  (1384? - 1439)
  |    /              \-- Alice (Lady of Arundel) FitzALAN  +
  \-- Margaret (de) BEAUFORT  (? - 1474?)
          \              /-- Thomas de BEAUCHAMP  +
          |        /-- Richard (de) BEAUCHAMP  (1382 - 1439 Normandy)
          |        /        \-- Margaret (de) FERRERS  +
          \-- Eleanor (Lady; de) BEAUCHAMP  (1408 - 1468 London)
```

1587 was descended from Katherine Swynford is 3000 divided by 3,800,000 = 0.0007. However, based on research by American demographer Kenneth Wachter, the odds that Kate Middleton is NOT descended from Katherine Swynford are even smaller because an English person born around 1977 descends from about 15,000 people living in 1587 ($0.9993^{15,000} = 0.00002$ or .002 per cent).

Put more simply, it is more than 99.99 per cent certain than anyone with predominantly English heritage is descended from a Beaufort bastard, although proving it is another matter.

In an online article dated 2008, Andrew Millard concluded that Edward III has around 100 million living descendants, including most of England's population plus many millions in the USA, Canada, and Australia. Half a generation later, the total for Katherine Swynford must be almost the same.

Note: The 'incestual roots' of Henry Stafford, the Duke of Buckingham, are outlined on the fabpedigree website.

FROM KATALIN OF THE CUMANS...

LONG before Meghan Markle married Prince Harry, Elizabeth II's own gene-alogists cheerfully acknowledged her multiracial ancestors. And, as shown below, Iain Moncreiffe and Don Pottinger emphasised Her Majesty's African her-itage by placing a dancing native on the cover of their book *Blood Royal* (1956).

Historians are still debating whether George III's wife Queen Charlotte inher-ited her 'mulatto' features from Madragana, the Moorish mistress of Affonso III of Portugal who lived several centuries earlier. The alternate history TV series *Bridgerton* is based on this notion (See Page 248).

One of Queen Charlotte's closer ancestors was the dark-skinned Dorothea of Denmark who, coincidentally, had the same mitochondrial DNA as George I, George III and George V.

Both Queen Charlotte and Dorothea of Denmark descended from Katalin (Catherine) of Hungary (inset above), daughter of Elizabeth of the Cumans from whom Kate and Meghan Markle are descended through Elizabeth Percy and Philippa of Hainault, mother of Katherine Swynford's husband John of Gaunt. (Gaunt had an all-female bloodline from Elizabeth of the Cumans so he must have had the same mitochondrial DNA as Katalin of Hungary.)

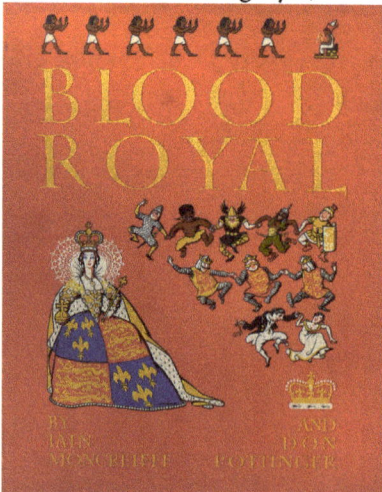

Before she married Edward III, Queen Philippa was famously described as 'brown of skin all over' but there is no evidence that she had Moorish ancestors. The most likely explanation is that she had a Mediterranean complexion.

The PEDIGREE of
Katalin (Princess) of HUNGARY

Born: ? Died: 1317

HRH Charles's 20-Great Grandmother.

Husband/Partner: **Stefan IV DRAGUTIN (King) of SERBIA**
Child: **Jelisaveta NEMANJIC (Regent) of SERBIA**

```
                        /-- Andreas (Masodik Endre) II (King) of HUNGARY
               /              \-- Agnes (Anne) de CHATILLON-SUR-LOING  +
       /-- Bela IV ARPAD (King) of HUNGARY  (1206 - 1270)
       |       \           /-- Berthold VI (IV; III) of ANTIOCH  +
       |        \-- Gertrude von MERAN (de MERANIE)  (1185? - 1213)
       /              \-- Agnes von GROITZSCH-ROCHLITZ  +
   /-- Istvan V (King) of HUNGARY  (1239 - 1272)
   |   \            /-- Manuel (Manolis) Panhypersebastos LASCARIS  +
   |    |       /-- Theodore I Comnenus LASCARIS  (1173? - 1222)
   |    |      /    \-- Ioanna (PHOKAINA) KARATZAINA  +
   |    \-- Maria LASKARINA (LASCARINA; of LASKARIS-NIKAIA)
   |          \| OR: prob. not Maria LASKARINA  +
   |           |       /-- Alexius (Alexios) III ANGELOS (ANGE)  +
   |           \-- Anna (ANGELINA) KOMNENE  (1176? - 1212?)
   |               \| OR: prob. not Philippa RUBENID  +
   /                \-- Euphrosyne Kamateros (KAMATERINA) DOUKANIA  +
```

- Katalin (Princess) of HUNGARY

```
   \                    /-- Begluk(?), son of Aepa II  +
   |                 /-- Kotian (Khan) of KUMANS
   |              /-- Suthoi (KHAN) of the KUMANS
   |          /-- Kuthen (Zayhan) of CUMANIA  (1214? - 1240?)
   \-- Erzsebet (Princess) of CUMANIA  (1240? - 1290+)
         \            /-- Isiaslav II (Grand Prince) of KIEV  +
         |        /    | or: Rostislav I Mikhail (q.v. : Isiaslav's brother)
         |     /-- Mstislav II (Grand Prince) of KIEV (von KIEW)
         |    |       \| OR: Mstislav MSTISLAVICH von NOWGOROD  +
         |    |    \-- prob. not  Agnes von SCHWABEN  +
         |    /           | OR: (NN), unknown 1st wife
         \-- Erzsebet(?) (Princess) of GALICIA
```

...TO THE QUEEN OF SHEBA

THE mysterious Cumans, who once ruled much of Central Asia with the Kipchaks, were fair-skinned with blonde hair and blue eyes, but they almost certainly had Chinese and Indian ancestors.

Through Katalin of Bulgaria, Katalin of Hungary may have been descended from Attila the Hun; Katalin of Hungary was also supposedly descended from the legendary Queen of Sheba (right), wife of King Solomon.

Based on genetic research, the real Queen of Sheba may have lived in Ethiopia about 3000 years ago.

ENGLAND
AND FRANCE
1066

THE KATHERINE WHO NEVER WAS?

SEVERAL genealogical websites, including geneanet.com and myheritage.com agree with fabpedigree.com that Katherine of Flanders married Alphonso de Vere around a thousand years ago and had a son Alberic or Aubrey, nicknamed 'the Monk'. But according to geni.com and thepeerage.com there is no such connection, and the blunt assessment of wikitree.com about Katherine of Flanders is: 'Research suggests that this person may never have existed.'

Either way, an astonishing number of people are descended from Alberic de Vere's mother, including Prince William who has bloodlines through nearly all of his great-great-great-grandparents.

Katherine of Flanders reportedly died at Hedingham in Essex three decades before William the Bastard won the Battle of Hastings. He introduced the cult of St Catherine so, if Alberic de Vere's mother was named Katherine, she may have been the first of her namesakes living in England. At Gosfield, not far from Hedingham and Sudbury Middleton, there is a church dedicated to St Catherine which got financial support from the de Veres.

Alphonso de Vere, the alleged husband of Katherine of Flanders, claimed descent from the legendary Melusine (See The Starbucks Mermaid, Page 42).

(See The Starbucks Mermaid, Page 42).

If Katherine of Flanders was the granddaughter of Arnulf II (left) then she was a first cousin once removed of Matilda Fleming, wife of William the Bastard.

WIKIPEDIA

— 40 —

Katherine of FLANDERS

HM George I's 18-Great Grandmother.
poss. Husbands/Partners: Alphonso (Alphonsus) de VERE ; Alphonso (Alphonsus) de VERE [alt ped]
Child: Alberic (I) 'the Monk' de VERE

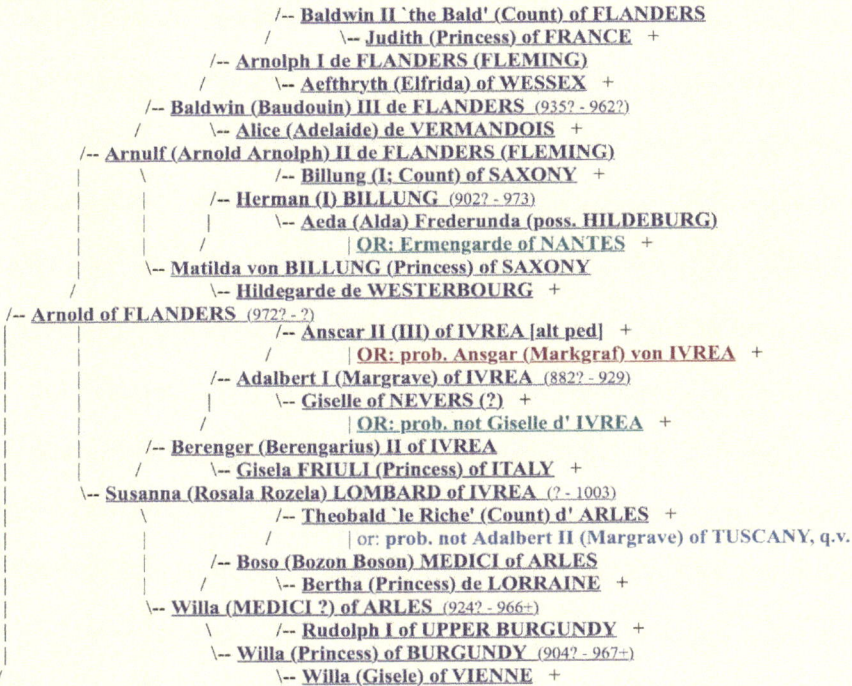

```
                              /-- Baldwin II 'the Bald' (Count) of FLANDERS
                             /      \-- Judith (Princess) of FRANCE  +
                      /-- Arnolph I de FLANDERS (FLEMING)
                     /      \-- Aefthryth (Elfrida) of WESSEX  +
               /-- Baldwin (Baudouin) III de FLANDERS  (935? - 962?)
              /      \-- Alice (Adelaide) de VERMANDOIS  +
       /-- Arnulf (Arnold Arnolph) II de FLANDERS (FLEMING)
      |     \                 /-- Billung (I; Count) of SAXONY  +
      |      |         /-- Herman (I) BILLUNG  (902? - 973)
      |      |        |       \-- Aeda (Alda) Frederunda (poss. HILDEBURG)
      |      |       /         | OR: Ermengarde of NANTES  +
      |      \-- Matilda von BILLUNG (Princess) of SAXONY
      /              \-- Hildegarde de WESTERBOURG  +
  /-- Arnold of FLANDERS  (972? - ?)
  |     |                 /-- Anscar II (III) of IVREA [alt ped]  +
  |     |                /       | OR: prob. Ansgar (Markgraf) von IVREA  +
  |     |       /-- Adalbert I (Margrave) of IVREA  (882? - 929)
  |     |      |          \-- Giselle of NEVERS (?)  +
  |     |      |           | OR: prob. not Giselle d' IVREA  +
  |     |     /-- Berenger (Berengarius) II of IVREA
  |     |    /      \-- Gisela FRIULI (Princess) of ITALY  +
  |     \-- Susanna (Rosala Rozela) LOMBARD of IVREA  (? - 1003)
  |            \                 /-- Theobald 'le Riche' (Count) d' ARLES  +
  |             |               /       | or: prob. not Adalbert II (Margrave) of TUSCANY, q.v.
  |             |       /-- Boso (Bozon Boson) MEDICI of ARLES
  |             |      /      \-- Bertha (Princess) de LORRAINE  +
  |             \-- Willa (MEDICI ?) of ARLES  (924? - 966+)
  |                    \                 /-- Rudolph I of UPPER BURGUNDY  +
  |                     \-- Willa (Princess) of BURGUNDY  (904? - 967+)
  /                            \-- Willa (Gisele) of VIENNE  +
```

Katherine of FLANDERS

Kate has a personal connection to Flanders because three of her great-great-uncles died in that region during World War I.

In 2014 the *Daily Mail* linked these tragedies to the so-called 'Middleton millions'. It was a tale of heartbreak 'symbolised by a simple headstone that stands among the poignant rows of graves at the Rue-Petillon Military Cemetery... the last resting place of Maurice Lupton, a 28-year-old captain in the 7th battalion of the West Yorkshire Regiment, who died on 19th June 1915.'

A year later, Maurice's brother Lionel (who joined up with Princess Diana's grandfather Albert Spencer) was killed during the Battle of the Somme, and in 1917 Francis Lupton was killed by a bomb near Miraumont.

In 2017 Kate attended services in Belgium marking the centenary of the Battle of Passchendaele, during which there were half a million casualties.

ALAMY

THE STARBUCKS MERMAID

LIKE most people who have drunk Starbucks coffee, Kate probably knows next to nothing about the alluring creature on the company's logo.

The mermaid has clear connections to the legendary fish-tailed Melusine (pictured above), from whom Kate and millions of other coffee lovers are allegedly descended through Katherine of Flanders' husband Alphonso de Vere.

According to fabpedigree.com there are two Katherine de Veres in Prince William's family tree who were both supposedly descended from the mythical Melusine through all of their grandparents. Both Katherines were also descended from Robert de Vere, the third Earl of Oxford, who may have been the original Robin Hood (See Page 176).

The Katherine de Vere featured opposite may have been the illegitimate daughter of John de Vere KG and an unknown mother. Either way, Katherine and her granddaughter Katherine Broughton — an aunt of Catherine Howard who married Henry VIII — had bloodlines from Raymond de Vere who allegedly married Melusine de Lusina, also known as the Elven Dragon Princess of the Picts.

The Plantagenets claimed descent from Melusine who was, according to an oft-repeated joke by Richard the Lionheart, 'the Devil's daughter'. Like nearly everyone

The Starbucks mermaid has always had two tails and is actually a siren.

The PEDIGREE of

Katherine de VERE

Died: aft. 1504

Lady Diana's 14-Great Grandmother.

Husband/Partner: **Robert (Sir) BROUGHTON**
Child: **John (of Toddington) BROUGHTON**

```
                      /-- Richard de VERE  (1385? - 1417)
                     /          \-- Alice (Lady of) FitzWALTER  +
          /-- John de VERE
          |          \          /-- Richard (II; Sir) SERGEAUX (CERGEAUX)  +
          |           \-- Alice SERGEAUX (CERGEAUX)  (1384? - 18/5/1452)
         /                      \-- Philippa FitzALAN de ARUNDEL  +
     /-- John (K.G.) de VERE  (1442 - 1513)
     |    \                      /-- John (III; Sir) HOWARD  +
     |     |          /-- John (Knight) HOWARD  (? - 1409)
     |     |         /          \-- Margaret (de) PLAIZ  +
     |     \-- Elizabeth HOWARD  (1410? - 1475)
     |                \          /-- Richard (Sir) WALTON  (? - 1431)
     /                 \-- Joan WALTON  (? - 1424)
```

- Katherine de VERE

```
     \                      /-- Ralph (2nd Baron of RABY; de) NEVILL  +
     |          /-- John (III; de) NEVILL  (1327+ - 1388)
     |         /          \-- Alice (de) AUDLEY  +
     |     /-- Ralph I NEVILL (de NEVILLE)  (1363? - 1425)
     |     |   /          \-- Matilda (Maud Mary) de PERCY  +
     |    /-- Richard (NEVILLE) de NEVILL  (1400? - 1460)
     |    |    \          /-- John (BEAUFORT) of GAUNT  +
     |    |     \-- Joan (Lady; de) BEAUFORT  (1379? - 1440)
     |    /                \-- Katherine ROELT  +
     \-- Margaret de NEVILLE  (? - 1506+)
```

with English heritage, Kate has dubious bloodlines from this Melusine through Katherine Swynford's in-laws, Ralph Neville and Margaret Holland, and the illegitimate offspring of Henry I.

There were several other Melusines, including one who married one of Kate's Lusignan ancestors and built a huge chateau near Poitiers in France in just 15 days, and another who allegedly bewitched an ancestor of Henry VIII's great-grandmother Jacquette de Luxembourg and built a castle on the Bock Promontory.

Through Elizabeth Woodville and Elizabeth of York, Jacquette de Luxembourg may have been the source of Henry VIII's Kell-positive blood which allegedly caused Catherine of Aragon's pregnancy problems (See Page 158).

The *Game of Thrones* character Melisandre was obviously based on Melusine, who in some legends could magically transform into a flying dragon.

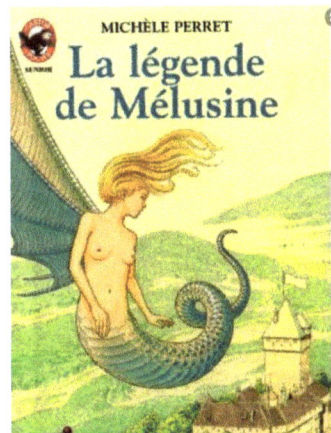

MICHÈLE PERRET

La légende de Mélusine

THE LADY GODIVA SOCIETY

A S WELL AS meeting the strict requirements of the Royal Bastards society, Kate is eligible to join another American society which commemorates Lady Godiva who supposedly rode naked through the streets of Coventry around 1050 watched only by Peeping Tom.

The society recognises dozens of gateway ancestors who arrived in America in the 1600s, including Katherine Hamby from Ipswich in Suffolk, a direct ancestor of President Franklin Roosevelt. Many of the accepted Godiva bloodlines are through 'Black William' de Braose (See Catherine Mortimer chart on Page 205) who had more than a dozen grandchildren born in the 1200s.

Kate and Prince William have numerous descents from Lady Godiva's son Aelfgar through Katherine Swynford's son-in-law Ralph Neville, the first Earl of Westmorland, and Katherine's daughter-in-law Margaret Holland, both of whom were descendants of 'Black William' de Braose. There are many other bloodlines through Thomas Conyers and also through Thomas Fairfax.

Thomas Fairfax's paternal grandmother Catherine Neville was born at Thornton Bridge in Yorkshire in 1428. According to fabpedigree.

Many millions of people are eligible to join the Society of Descendants of Lady Godiva based in Jacksonville, Florida.

— 44 —

The PEDIGREE of
Catherine NEVILLE
Poss. HRH Charles's 21-Great Aunt. Lady Diana's 15-Great Grandmother.

Husbands/Partners:	William (Esq.; of Walton) FAIRFAX ; (2nd) Richard Percy
Possible Children:	Mary FAIRFAX [alt ped] ; Thomas (K.B; of Walton & Gilling) FAIRFAX

```
                                /-- Randolph (Ranulph; Ralph) de NEVILLE  +
                        /-- Ralph (2nd Baron of RABY; de) NEVILL
                        /        \-- Euphemia (FitzROBERT; de) CLAVERING  +
                /-- Ralph (of Cundall) de NEVILLE  (1332? - 1380?)
                /        \-- Alice (de) AUDLEY  +
        /-- Alexander de NEVILLE  (? - by 1420)
        |       \        /-- Alexander LEDES
        |        \-- Elizabeth de LEDES
        /                \-- Margaret d' EIVILLE  +
   /-- Alexander (Sir) de NEVILLE  (? - 1457?)
  /        \-- Margery
```

Catherine NEVILLE

```
        \                       /-- John (de) EURE  +
        |                 /-- John (Sir; de) EURE  (1341? - 1393)
        |                 /        \-- Margaret
        |           /-- Ralph (Sir; of Witton Castle; de) EURE
        |           /        \-- Isabel de CLIFFORD  +
        |     /-- William (Sir; of Witton) EURE  (? - 1465?)
        |     |       |       /-- William (2nd Baron) de ATON  +
        |     |       \-- Catherine de ATON (AYTON)
        |     /                \-- Isabel PERCY  +
        \-- Catherine EURE  (? - 1459)
                \                /-- Henry (3rd Baron) FitzHUGH  +
                |         /-- Henry (4th/3rd Baron) FitzHUGH
                |         /        \-- Joan le SCROPE  +
                \-- Maud (Matilda) FitzHUGH  (Yorks. ? - 1467)
```

com she had possible bloodlines from Lady Godiva through Euphemia Clavering, Sir John Eure and Joan le Scrope (shown above).

Through her mother Catherine Eure and great-grandmother Catherine de Aton, Catherine Neville had multiple bloodlines from the de Veres, Lusignans and Plantagenets who all claimed descents from the legendary Melusine.

Burlesque dancer Katrina Darling — who is Kate's second cousin once removed through John and Jane Harrison — received plenty of attention after the 2011 royal wedding, including a *Playboy* front cover. Like Kate, Katrina has bloodlines from Lady Godiva through an illegitimate daughter of Edward IV who bolstered his claim to the throne by claiming descent from Adam and Eve, and also from a great-great-grandson of Aphrodite (See Page 66).

Katrina's most popular routine was a risqué version of God Save the Queen.

THE PEDIGREE OF

Katherine (Lady) HASTINGS

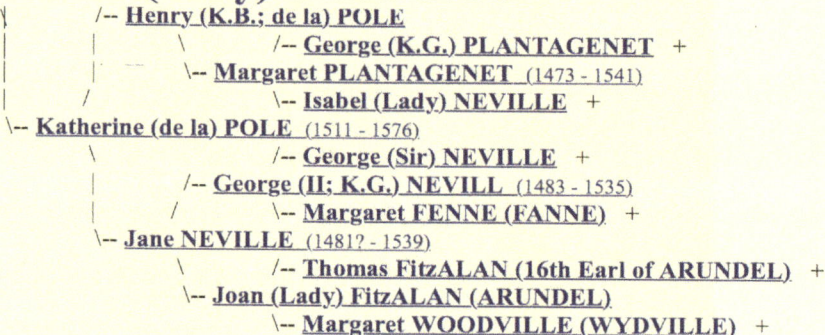

Born: abt. 1542   Died: abt. 1579
HRH Charles's 13-Great Aunt. Lady Diana's 11-Great Aunt.

Husband/Partner: Henry (FIENNES; K.B.) CLINTON
Children: Thomas (3rd Earl of Lincoln) CLINTON ; Edward CLINTON

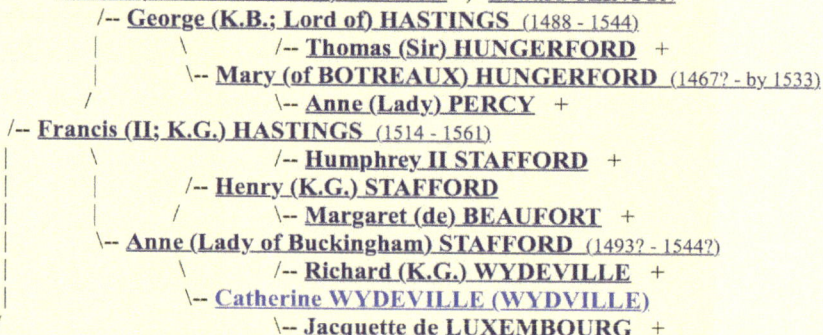

```
          /-- George (K.B.; Lord of) HASTINGS  (1488 - 1544)
          |      \              /-- Thomas (Sir) HUNGERFORD  +
          |       \-- Mary (of BOTREAUX) HUNGERFORD  (1467? - by 1533)
          /                     \-- Anne (Lady) PERCY  +
   /-- Francis (II; K.G.) HASTINGS  (1514 - 1561)
   |      \                      /-- Humphrey II STAFFORD  +
   |       |              /-- Henry (K.G.) STAFFORD
   |       |             /        \-- Margaret (de) BEAUFORT  +
   |       \-- Anne (Lady of Buckingham) STAFFORD  (1493? - 1544?)
   |                      \        /-- Richard (K.G.) WYDEVILLE  +
   |                       \-- Catherine WYDEVILLE (WYDVILLE)
   /                              \-- Jacquette de LUXEMBOURG  +
```

- Katherine (Lady) HASTINGS

```
   \       /-- Henry (K.B.; de la) POLE
   |       |      \              /-- George (K.G.) PLANTAGENET  +
   |       |       \-- Margaret PLANTAGENET  (1473 - 1541)
   |       /                     \-- Isabel (Lady) NEVILLE  +
   \-- Katherine (de la) POLE  (1511 - 1576)
          \                      /-- George (Sir) NEVILLE  +
          |              /-- George (II; K.G.) NEVILL  (1483 - 1535)
          |             /        \-- Margaret FENNE (FANNE)  +
          \-- Jane NEVILLE  (1481? - 1539)
                         \        /-- Thomas FitzALAN (16th Earl of ARUNDEL)  +
                          \-- Joan (Lady) FitzALAN (ARUNDEL)
                                   \-- Margaret WOODVILLE (WYDVILLE)  +
```

HYPOTHETICAL QUEEN CATHERINES

KATE'S children descend from two hypothetical Queen Catherines who both had bloodlines from Katherine of Flanders through nearly all of their great-grandparents. And through all-female bloodlines from Jacquetta of Luxembourg, Catherine Grey and Katherine Pole (and her husband) had the same mitochondrial DNA as Henry VIII who executed Katherine's father Henry Pole and his mother Margaret.

An alternative line of succession, based on Edward IV's illegitimacies, is from his brother George Plantagenet KG through Katherine Pole's son George Hastings. According to this theory, Britain's 'real monarch' is the eldest son of Australian farmer Michael Abney-Hastings (left), the 14th Earl of Loudon.

[As shown above, Kate's children do not descend from Katherine Hastings but they do descend from Catherine Hastings (died 1636) whose brother could, theoretically, have been Henry X.]

Catherine (Lady of Suffolk) GREY

Born: 1540   Died: 1568 Suffolk
HRH Charles's 11-Great Grandmother.   Lady Diana's 11-Great Grandmother.

Husband/Partner: **Edward SEYMOUR (1st Earl of HERTFORD)**
Child: **Edward (Lord BEAUCHAMP) SEYMOUR**

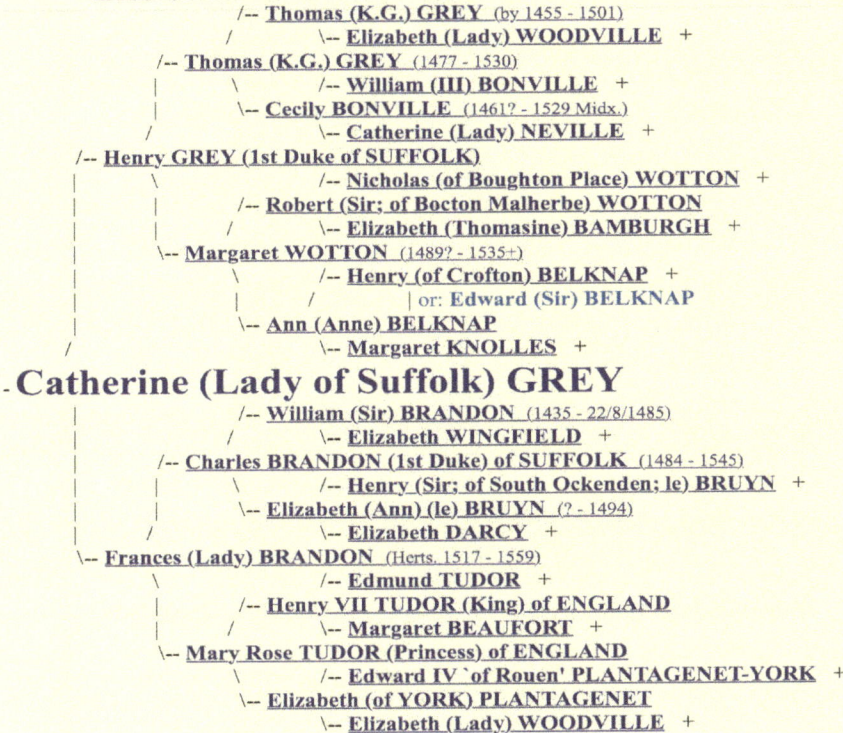

```
                              /-- Thomas (K.G.) GREY  (by 1455 - 1501)
                             /      \-- Elizabeth (Lady) WOODVILLE  +
                    /-- Thomas (K.G.) GREY  (1477 - 1530)
                   |      \      /-- William (III) BONVILLE  +
                   |       \-- Cecily BONVILLE  (1461? - 1529 Midx.)
                  /                \-- Catherine (Lady) NEVILLE  +
         /-- Henry GREY (1st Duke of SUFFOLK)
        |          \        /-- Nicholas (of Boughton Place) WOTTON  +
        |           |      /-- Robert (Sir; of Bocton Malherbe) WOTTON
        |           |     /      \-- Elizabeth (Thomasine) BAMBURGH  +
        |           \-- Margaret WOTTON  (1489? - 1535+)
        |                   \        /-- Henry (of Crofton) BELKNAP  +
        |                    |      /      | or: Edward (Sir) BELKNAP
        |                    \-- Ann (Anne) BELKNAP
        |                           \-- Margaret KNOLLES  +
```

-Catherine (Lady of Suffolk) GREY

```
        |                  /-- William (Sir) BRANDON  (1435 - 22/8/1485)
        |                 /      \-- Elizabeth WINGFIELD  +
        |        /-- Charles BRANDON (1st Duke) of SUFFOLK  (1484 - 1545)
        |       |          \        /-- Henry (Sir; of South Ockenden; le) BRUYN  +
        |       |           \-- Elizabeth (Ann) (le) BRUYN  (? - 1494)
        |       |                   \-- Elizabeth DARCY  +
        \-- Frances (Lady) BRANDON  (Herts. 1517 - 1559)
                 \        /-- Edmund TUDOR  +
                  |      /-- Henry VII TUDOR (King) of ENGLAND
                  |     /      \-- Margaret BEAUFORT  +
                  \-- Mary Rose TUDOR (Princess) of ENGLAND
                           \        /-- Edward IV `of Rouen' PLANTAGENET-YORK  +
                            \-- Elizabeth (of YORK) PLANTAGENET
                                  \-- Elizabeth (Lady) WOODVILLE  +
```

Another alternative line is from Henry VIII's sister Mary Tudor through Catherine Grey whose sister Jane succeeded Edward VI but was executed nine days later. Catherine of Aragon's daughter 'Bloody Mary' ruled for the next five years followed by her half-sister Elizabeth I who, like Mary, was declared illegitimate by Henry VIII.

Elizabeth I was furious after Catherine Grey secretly married Edward Seymour and had two sons while imprisoned in the Tower of London. Catherine's sons were declared illegitimate and she died of a broken heart in 1568.

Based on Catherine Grey's claim, Britain's 'real monarch' is the eldest daughter of Mary Freeman-Grenville, the 12th Lady Kinloss. Mary and Michael Abney-Hastings both died in 2012.

Catherine Grey (right) and Katherine Pole got posthumous revenge when their joint descendant Elizabeth II was crowned in 1953 and that revenge will be even sweeter if one of Kate's descendants is crowned Catherine I.

Katherine of Flanders	
Katherine Forbes	**Catherine de Ufford**
Katherine Gordon*	**Katherine Neville***
Katherine Duff*	**Katherine Herbert***
Catherine Duff*	**Katherine Purcell***
Katherine Morison*	**Catherine Copley I***
Katherine Scott Forbes*	**Catherine Copley II***
Prince William	**Kate Middleton**

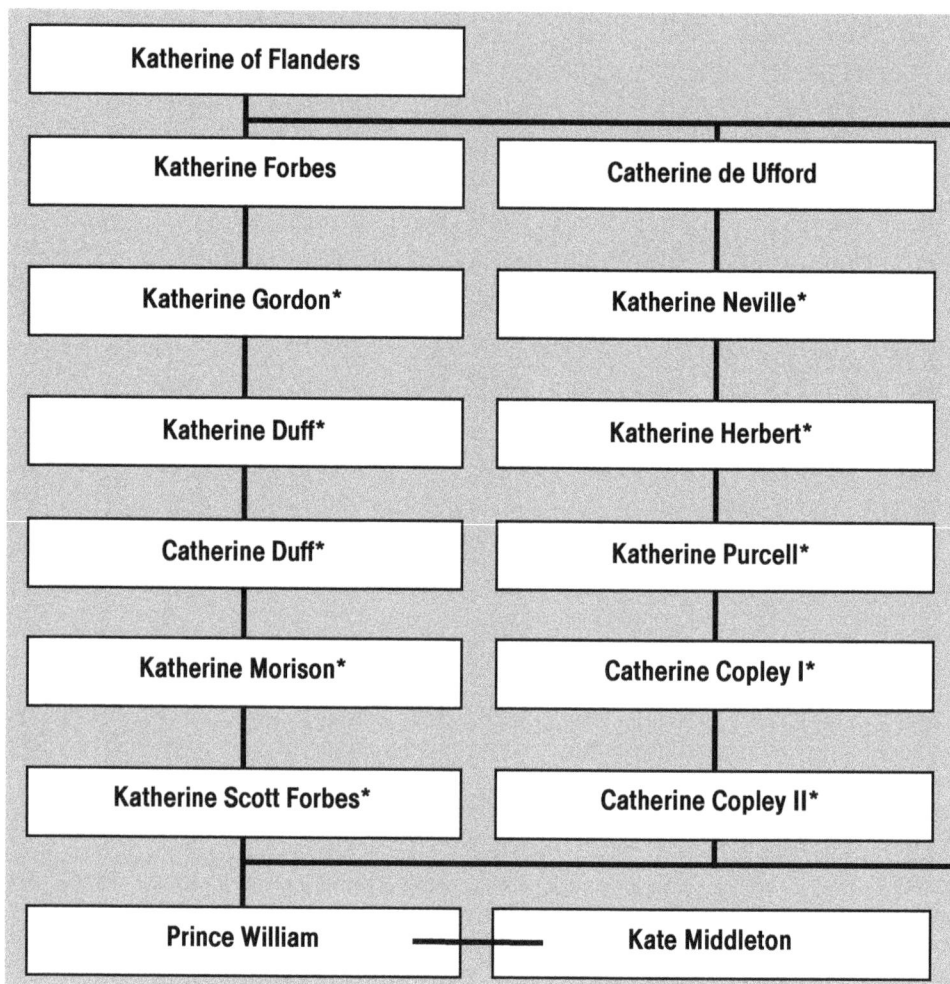

AN ABUNDANCE OF CATHERINES

SOMEONE with superb computer skills and a lot of spare time may eventually confirm that Kate's children have more than a million individual bloodlines from William the Conqueror plus a surprising number from most of his contemporaries, including Katherine of Flanders who died around 1030. And many of those bloodlines are through Katherine's namesakes.

Thanks to Mormon expert Robert Gunderson, we know that Charles III has at least 2000 individual bloodlines from Edward III, about half of which are through Katherine Swynford's grandchildren. And, given her noble pedigree, Princess Diana must have had a similar number of descents from the Beaufort bastards.

On fabpedigree.com bloodlines can be quickly traced to Katherine of Flanders through nearly all of Prince William's 32 great-great-great-grandparents, including Edward VII and Queen Alexandra.

While Prince William's pedigree collapses by about two-thirds after twenty generations, Kate has reliable bloodlines from Katherine of Flanders and Katherine

Catherine Mortimer	
Catherine Stafford	Katherine Clifford
Katherine Pole*	Catherine Southwell
Catherine Hastings*	Katherine Mapes
Catherine d'Arcy*	Katherine Guybon
Catherine Shorter*	Catherine Doughty

Also descended from Katherine Swynford

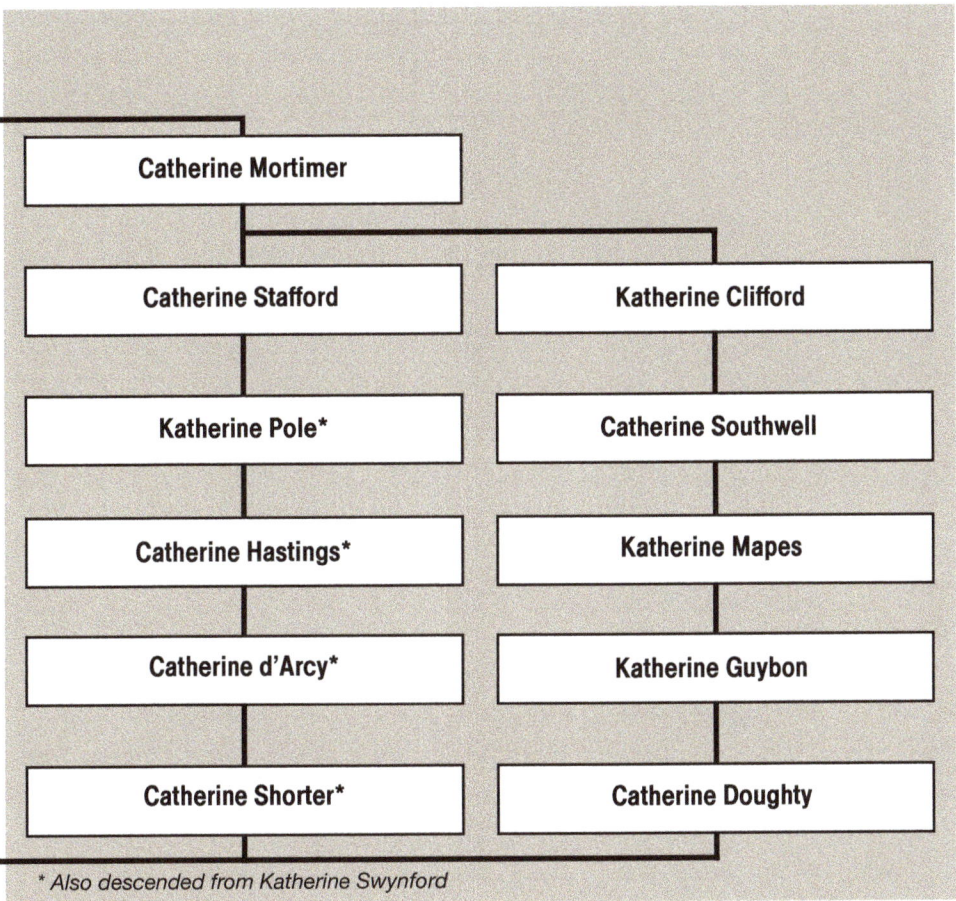

Swynford through only two of her great-great-grandparents, Francis Martineau Lupton and John Harrison, so we will never know the extent of her pedigree collapse. However, because Kate descends from an illegitimate daughter of Edward IV, she and Prince William have numerous ancestors in common.

Not surprisingly, there are hundreds of Catherines and Katherines in Prince William's family tree. William inherited a rare form of mtDNA from Katherine Scott Forbes; Katherine Pole had the same mtDNA as Lady Catherine Grey and Catherine Woodville; and Katherine Purcell is noteworthy because she was a matrilineal descendant of Irish princess Aoife (See chart on Page 196).

Note: While the focus on Catherines is obviously arbitrary this approach reveals connections that would otherwise be hidden.

The main character in John Green's 2006 'young adult' novel dates nineteen girls named Katherine.

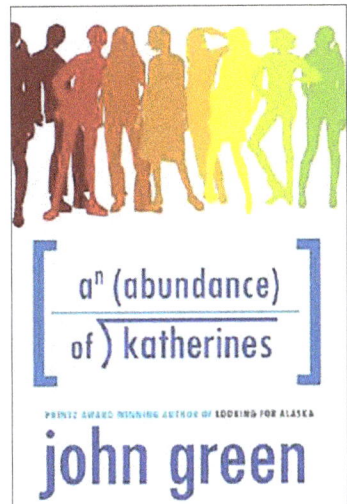

[aⁿ (abundance) / of) katherines]

PRINTZ AWARD WINNING AUTHOR OF *LOOKING FOR ALASKA*

john green

MORE GERMAN THAN BRITISH?

WHILE Kate's Britishness is indisputable, the heritage of her children is, according to American genealogist William Addams Reitwiesner, much harder to define.

In 2006 he wrote: 'Long study of the genealogies of the European Royals can lead one to the realisation that (they) can be considered a separate ethnic group. The only way they differ from other ethnic groups is that they are not geographically discrete, but in other respects they meet all the qualifications of an ethnic group...especially their mating habits.'

Reitwiesner, who died in 2010, acknowledged that the vast majority of 'royals' were actually German, which is apparent in the chart opposite. Like all monarchs back to George III, George VI was born in Britain, and he was an inspirational leader during World War II, but that did not change his ethnicity.

According to Reitwiesner, George VI was about 77 per cent 'royal', 12 per cent Hungarian, and less than 6 per cent German. Conversely, the Queen Mother was about 90 per cent British, five per cent French, and three per cent Irish. Surprisingly, their most recent common ancestors were Henry VIII's parents.

Because Prince Philip was more 'royal' than Elizabeth II (77 per cent to 39 per cent), Charles III is 58 per cent 'royal' and only 22 per cent British.

Anti-German sentiment during World War I forced George V to change the name of the royal house from Saxe-Coburg and Gotha to Windsor.

— 50 —

George VI Albert WINDSOR (King) of ENGLAND

Born: York Cottage, Norfolk 14 Dec 1895   **Died:** 6 Feb 1952 Sandringham
HRH Charles's Grandfather.

Wife/Partner: Elizabeth Angela Marguerite (Lady) BOWES-LYON
Children: Elizabeth II Alexandra Mary WINDSOR (Queen) of ENGLAND ; Margaret Rose

```
                          /-- Ernst I (Duke) of SAXE-SAALFELD-COBURG
                 /            \-- Augusta Caroline Sophia of REUSS-EBE.  +
         /-- Albert Augustus Charles (Prince) of SAXE-COBURG-GOTHA
         /            \-- Luise (Dorothea) (Duchess) of SAXE-GOTHA  +
     /-- Edward VII of SAXE-COBURG-GOTHA (King) of ENGLAND
     |       \            /-- Edward Augustus of GREAT BRITAIN & I.  +
     |        \-- Victoria of HANOVER (Queen) of ENGLAND
     /            \-- Victoria (Duchess) of SAXE-SAALFELD-COBURG  +
 /-- George V WINDSOR (King) of ENGLAND
 |       \                  /-- Wilhelm SCHLESWIG-HOLSTEIN-SONDERBURG-GLU.  +
 |        |          /-- Christian IX OLDENBURG (King) of DENMARK
 |        |         /    \-- Luise Caroline von HESSE-CASSEL  +
 |        \-- Alexandra Caroline Marie (Princess) of DENMARK
 |             \          /-- Wilhelm (X; Landgrave) of HESSE-CASSEL  +
 |              \-- Louise Wilhelmina Fredericka Caroline A. J. of HESSE-CASSEL
 /                  \-- Luise Charlotte (Princess) of DENMARK  +
```

George VI Albert WINDSOR (King) of ENGLAND

```
 \                       /-- Friedrich II (Duke) of WUERTTEMBERG  +
 |                /-- Ludwig Friedrich Alexander (Duke) of WUERTTEMBERG
 |               /    \-- Friederike Sophia Dorothea of BRANDE.  +
 |        /-- Alexander Paul Ludwig Constantine (Duke) of WUERTTEMBERG
 |       /    \-- Henriette (Princess) of NASSAU-WEILBURG  +
 |   /-- Franz (Francis) (1st Duke) of TECK
 |   |   \         /-- Laszlo (Count) RHEDEY de KIS-RHEDE  +
 |   |    \-- Claudine Susanne RHEDEY (RHEDY) de KIS-RHEDE
 |   /         \-- Agnes (Baroness) INCZEDY de NAGY-VARAD  +
 \-- Mary (Princess) of TECK
     \                  /-- George III (King) of ENGLAND  +
     |          /-- Adolphus Frederick (Prince) of GREAT BRITAIN & Ireland
     |         /    \-- Sophia Charlotte von MECKLENBURG-STRELITZ  +
     \-- Mary Adelaide (Princess) of CAMBRIDGE
          \          /-- Friedrich (III; Landgrave) of HESSE-CASSEL  +
           \-- Augusta Wilhelmina Louisa (Landgravine) of HESSE-CASSEL
               \-- Caroline (Princess) of NASSAU-USINGEN  +
```

But because Princess Diana was mostly English and Scottish, Prince William is roughly 50 per cent British and 30 per cent 'royal', plus small percentages of German, Irish, French, Anglo-Irish and Hungarian. (Most people will agree that Reitwiesner's 'royal' classification is no longer relevant.)

Through George V, Kate's children have a bloodline from William the Conqueror through Katharina von Arnsberg, Katharina of Solms-Burgsolms, Katharina von Isenburg-Grenzau, Katherine von Solms-Lich, Katherine von Waldeck-Eiseberg, Katharina of Everstein, and Katharina Elisabeth von Schonburg-Lichtenstein (died 1656).

George V descended from Katharina von Pfannberg through all but two of his 32 great-great-great-grandparents. And because one of those bloodlines was all-female, George V had the same mitochondrial DNA as George I and George III (See chart on Page 95).

QUINTESSENTIALLY BRITISH

STRICTLY SPEAKING, the former Catherine Middleton will be Britain's most ethnically British queen consort.

Exhaustive research by royal expert William Addams Reitwiesner showed that Kate is 99.8 per cent British, including 93.55 per cent English heritage plus 6.25 per cent Scottish heritage through the paternal grandparents of Constance Robison (shown opposite). Kate is 0.2 per cent French through her Huguenot ancestor Gaston Martineau who arrived in England in the 1600s.

Queen Camilla is slightly less British than Kate because one of her great-great-grandmothers was French-Canadian. And it is remotely possible that Camilla descends from Edward VII because one of his mistresses was Camilla's great-grandmother Alice Edmonstone. If so, Camilla is Charles III's second cousin once removed, the same relationship that Elizabeth II had to Prince Philip.

The royal family's ethnicity may have been very different if George VI had been born first in line to the throne because there was a long tradition of British monarchs marrying their European cousins. After Edward VIII's abdication, the Queen Mother — who was more than 90 per cent British and about five per cent French — succeeded her mother-in-law Mary of Teck who was 68 per cent 'royal' and 25 per cent Hungarian.

Kate's Englishness is evident in her father's arms granted in 2011. The three acorns represent Kate and her siblings and the trees in Berkshire where they were born. Oak is also a long established symbol of England and strength.

The PEDIGREE of
George Alexander Louis of CAMBRIDGE

Born: London 22 Jul 2013

```
                               /-- George I (King) of the HELLENES  +
                         /-- Andrew (Prince) of GREECE & DENMARK
                        /       \-- Olga Constantinovna ROMANOV of RUSSIA  +
                 /-- Philip MOUNTBATTEN (Prince) of GREECE & DENMARK
                /       \-- Alice (Princess) von BATTENBERG  +
           /-- Charles Philip Arthur George WINDSOR (Prince of WALES)
           |    \           /-- George VI Albert WINDSOR (King) of ENGLAND  +
           |    |      /-- Elizabeth II Alexandra Mary WINDSOR (Queen) of ENGLAND
           |    /          \-- Elizabeth Angela Marguerite BOWES-LYON  +
     /-- William Arthur Philip Louis WINDSOR  (London 1982)
     |    \                   /-- Albert Edward John (7th Earl) SPENCER  +
     |    |           /-- Edward John (8th Earl) SPENCER
     |    |          /    \-- Cynthia Elinor Beatrix (Lady) HAMILTON  +
     |    \-- Diana Frances (Lady) SPENCER
     |                  \       /-- Edmund Maurice Burke ROCHE  +
     |                   \-- Frances Ruth Burke (Hon.) ROCHE
     /                          \-- Ruth Sylvia (Lady) GILL  +
```

George Alexander Louis of CAMBRIDGE

```
     \                     /-- John William MIDDLETON  +
     |              /-- Richard Noel MIDDLETON  (Yorks. 1878 - 1951)
     |             /    \-- Mary ASQUITH  +
     |      /-- Peter Francis (Capt.) MIDDLETON  (1920 - 2010)
     |     /          \-- Olive Christiana LUPTON  +
     |    /-- Michael Francis MIDDLETON  (Leeds, Yorks. 1949)
     |    |    \           /-- Frederick George GLASSBOROW  +
     |    |      \-- Valerie GLASSBOROW
     |    /             \-- Constance ROBISON  +
     \-- Catherine Elizabeth MIDDLETON  (Reading 1982)
          \                 /-- Stephen Charles GOLDSMITH  +
          |           /-- Ronald John James GOLDSMITH
          |          /    \-- Edith Eliza CHANDLER  +
          \-- Carole Elizabeth GOLDSMITH  (Middlesex 1955)
```

According to Reitwiesner, Princess Diana was 51 per cent English, 28.5 per cent Scottish, 3.5 per cent Anglo-Irish and 0.5 per cent Welsh. (Full details at wargs. com in a 2006 article titled 'The Ethnic ancestry of Prince William'.)

Thanks to the Queen Mother, Diana and Kate, Prince George will probably be the most ethnically British monarch since Elizabeth I, but such comparisons are no longer meaningful.

On fabpedigree.com there are numerous bloodlines from Kate's distant aristocratic ancestors, including the Percys, Nevilles and Cliffords who married Beauforts and other descendants of Katherine Swynford. But, frustratingly, there are few bloodlines from Kate's more recent ancestors with common surnames including Smith, Jones, Ablett, Dawson, Finch, Hughes, Jenkins, Marshall, Matthews, Powell, Ward, Webster and White.

COAL MINER'S GRANDDAUGHTER

WHILE Kate's parents have been described as 'upper Middleton class', many of her maternal ancestors were upper or lower working class and she will, undoubtedly, be Britain's 'commonest' queen.

When Kate's grandmother Dorothy Harrison was born in 1935 her father Thomas was working in Hetton-le-Hole in Durham as a carpenter, unlike his father and grandfather, both named John, who were coal miners. Dorothy's husband Ronald Goldsmith also broke the mould by becoming an engineer, unlike his grandfather and great-grandfather, both named John, who were labourers. Ronald's maternal grandfather James Dorsett was a street sweeper (See The Princess and the Pauper, Page 130).

Thomas Harrison could easily have suffered the same fate as his brother Anthony who died in the Eppleton pit in 1895. After being told that two of his fellow miners were missing, Anthony rushed to the rescue but was overcome by poisonous gas.

Carole Goldsmith grew up in London and met Captain Michael Middleton while working as a stewardess. In 1987 they started a successful party supply company, and have been described as 'self-made millionaires', however Michael did have a sizeable Lupton inheritance.

Kate's maternal Middleton ancestors from Norfolk, presumably unrelated to her paternal ancestors, were at the bottom of the working class. As shown on her marriage

Dorothy Harrison

THE PEDIGREE OF

Dorothy HARRISON

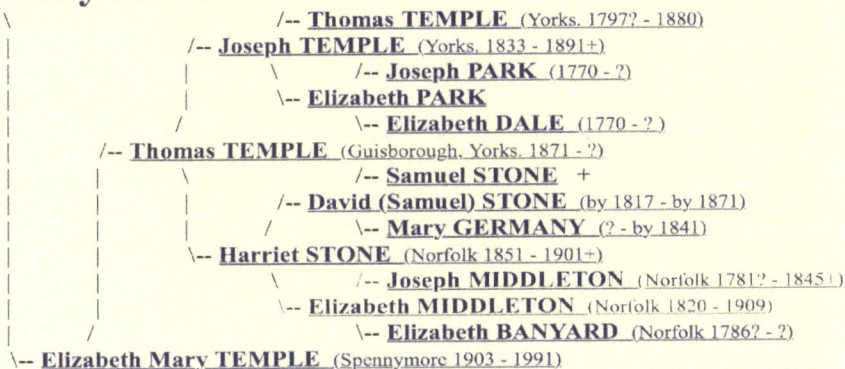

Born: Durham 1935   Died: 2006 Reading

Husband/Partner: **Ronald John James GOLDSMITH**
Child: **Carole Elizabeth GOLDSMITH**

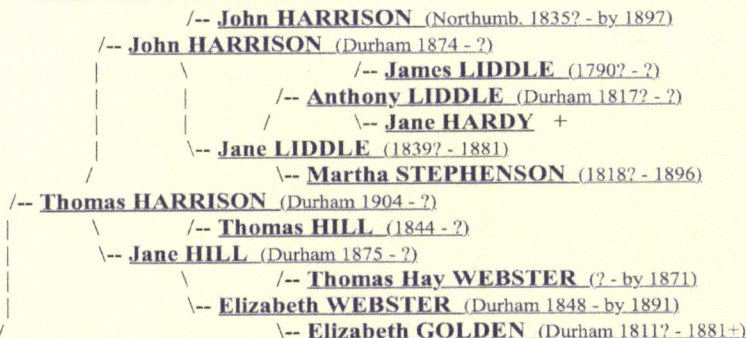

```
                            /-- John HARRISON (Northumb. 1835? - by 1897)
            /-- John HARRISON (Durham 1874 - ?)
            |         \              /-- James LIDDLE (1790? - ?)
            |         |      /-- Anthony LIDDLE (Durham 1817? - ?)
            |         |      /       \-- Jane HARDY +
            |         \-- Jane LIDDLE (1839? - 1881)
            /                \-- Martha STEPHENSON (1818? - 1896)
       /-- Thomas HARRISON (Durham 1904 - ?)
       |         \      /-- Thomas HILL (1844 - ?)
       |         \-- Jane HILL (Durham 1875 - ?)
       |                \        /-- Thomas Hay WEBSTER (? - by 1871)
       |                \-- Elizabeth WEBSTER (Durham 1848 - by 1891)
       /                      \-- Elizabeth GOLDEN (Durham 1811? - 1881+)
```

- Dorothy HARRISON

```
       \                /-- Thomas TEMPLE (Yorks. 1797? - 1880)
       |         /-- Joseph TEMPLE (Yorks. 1833 - 1891+)
       |         |      \        /-- Joseph PARK (1770 - ?)
       |         |      \-- Elizabeth PARK
       |         /              \-- Elizabeth DALE (1770 - ?)
       /-- Thomas TEMPLE (Guisborough, Yorks. 1871 - ?)
       |         \              /-- Samuel STONE +
       |         |      /-- David (Samuel) STONE (by 1817 - by 1871)
       |         |      /       \-- Mary GERMANY (? - by 1841)
       |         \-- Harriet STONE (Norfolk 1851 - 1901+)
       |                \        /-- Joseph MIDDLETON (Norfolk 1781? - 1845+)
       |                \-- Elizabeth MIDDLETON (Norfolk 1820 - 1909)
       |         /              \-- Elizabeth BANYARD (Norfolk 1786? - ?)
       \-- Elizabeth Mary TEMPLE (Spennymore 1903 - 1991)
```

CERTIFIED COPY OF AN ENTRY OF MARRIAGE   GIVEN AT THE GENERAL REGISTER OFFICE

Application Number   W129229

No.	When Married.	Name and Surname.	Age.	Condition.	Rank or Profession.	Residence at the Time of Marriage.	Father's Name and Surname.	Rank or Profession of Father.
73	April 28	David Stone	full age	Bachelor	Labourer	Hetherset	Samuel Stone	Labourer
		Elizabeth Middleton	full age	Spinster	---	Hetherset	Joseph Middleton	Labourer

A certified copy dated 31st October 2006

certificate, Elizabeth Middleton's husband David Stone was a labourer and so were both of their fathers, Joseph Middleton and Samuel Stone. After working as a nurse, Elizabeth spent her last years in Guisborough, Yorkshire where her son-in-law Joseph Temple was an ironstone miner.

The most recent aristocrat in Kate's family tree is Thomas Conyers, from whom she is descended through Jane Liddle and Jane Hardy (shown above).

KATE OF THE CONYERS

LIKE THE eponymous heroine in Thomas Hardy's classic novel *Tess of the d'Urbervilles,* Kate descends from a noble family that fell on hard times.

As shown opposite, Sir Thomas Conyers of Horden had a bloodline from Sir William Blakiston, owner of Gibside (above), who was one of England's richest men. However, Conyers inherited no money with his title and died in 1810 after spending his last years in a workhouse in Chester-le-Strreet, not far from Lumley and Lambton castles (See map on Page 60).

Fifty years later, British genealogist Sir Bernard Burke wrote these prophetic words about Thomas' three daughters: 'A time may yet come, perchance, when a descendant of one of these simple artisans may arise, not unworthy of the Conyers' ancient renown; and it will be a gratifying discovery to some future genealogist, when he succeeds in tracing in the quarterings of such a descendant the unsullied bearing of Conyers of Durham.'

Kate descends from Emma Turberville (born Yorkshire c1154) through Henry Constable of Burton, and Kate's children descend from Catherine Turberville (born Wales c1314) through Katherine Stradling (See chart on Page 239).

Through several Lumleys, possibly including Isabel (shown opposite), Thomas Conyers had bloodlines from an illegitimate daughter of Edward IV. Conyers may also have descended from some legendary dragon slayers (See Page 60) and from several Robin Hood contenders (See Page 176).

According to famouskin.com Kate and Prince

THE PEDIGREE OF

Thomas (9th Baronet; of Horden) CONYERS

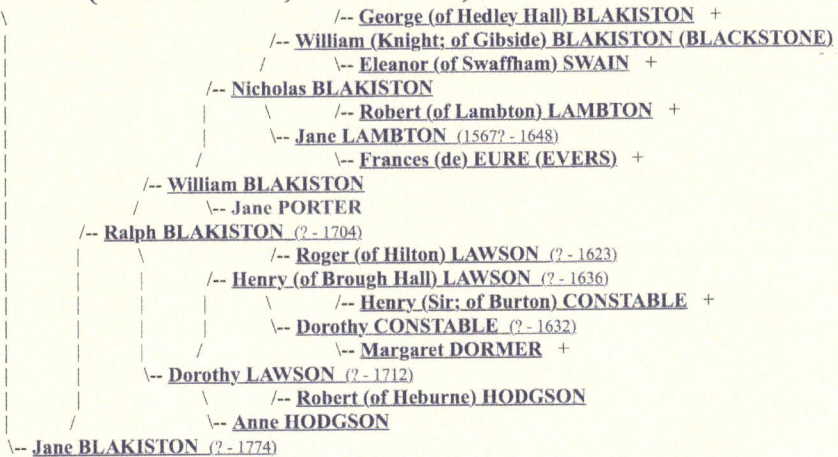

Born: 1731   Died: 1810

Wife/Partner: Isabel LAMBTON
Child: Jane CONYERS

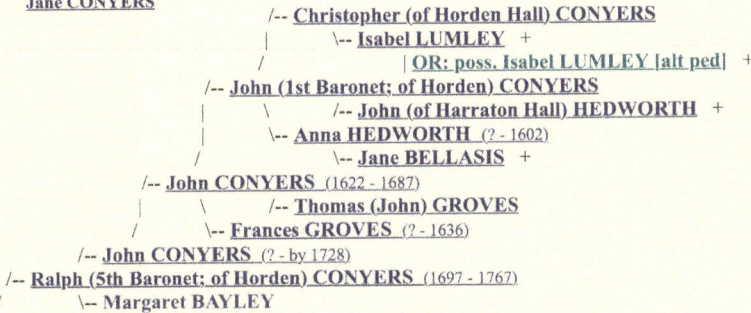

```
                              /-- Christopher (of Horden Hall) CONYERS
                              |   \-- Isabel LUMLEY  +
                          /   |       | OR: poss. Isabel LUMLEY [alt ped]  +
                      /-- John (1st Baronet; of Horden) CONYERS
                      |   \       /-- John (of Harraton Hall) HEDWORTH  +
                      |   \-- Anna HEDWORTH  (? - 1602)
                      /                \-- Jane BELLASIS  +
                  /-- John CONYERS  (1622 - 1687)
                  |   \         /-- Thomas (John) GROVES
                  /   \-- Frances GROVES  (? - 1636)
              /-- John CONYERS  (? - by 1728)
          /-- Ralph (5th Baronet; of Horden) CONYERS  (1697 - 1767)
          /   \-- Margaret BAYLEY
```

- Thomas (9th Baronet; of Horden) CONYERS

```
          \                   /-- George (of Hedley Hall) BLAKISTON  +
          |               /-- William (Knight; of Gibside) BLAKISTON (BLACKSTONE)
          |               /   \-- Eleanor (of Swaffham) SWAIN  +
          |           /-- Nicholas BLAKISTON
          |           |       /-- Robert (of Lambton) LAMBTON  +
          |           |   \-- Jane LAMBTON  (1567? - 1648)
          |           /       \-- Frances (de) EURE (EVERS)  +
          |       /-- William BLAKISTON
          |       /   \-- Jane PORTER
          |   /-- Ralph BLAKISTON  (? - 1704)
          |   |   \         /-- Roger (of Hilton) LAWSON  (? - 1623)
          |   |   |     /-- Henry (of Brough Hall) LAWSON  (? - 1636)
          |   |   |     |       /-- Henry (Sir; of Burton) CONSTABLE  +
          |   |   |     |   \-- Dorothy CONSTABLE  (? - 1632)
          |   |   |     /       \-- Margaret DORMER  +
          |   |   \-- Dorothy LAWSON  (? - 1712)
          |   |             \-- Robert (of Heburne) HODGSON
          |   /               \-- Anne HODGSON
          \-- Jane BLAKISTON  (? - 1774)
```

William are 12th cousins once removed through Jane Lambton (their most recent common ancestor), from whom Kate descends through Jane Blakiston, Jane Conyers, Jane Hardy and Jane Liddle.

On a visit to New York in 2014, Kate and Prince William inspected a physical reminder of their joint ancestry, the Blakiston-Bowes cabinet (right) created around 1700 to celebrate the marriage of Sir William Blakiston's great-granddaughter Elizabeth to a Bowes ancestor of the Queen Mother.

Note: The Conyers arms (inset opposite) feature three cinquefoils, Venus-related flower symbols which inspired a ribald discussion in *The Da Vinci Code* about clitorises and church doorways.

METROPLITAN MUSEUM OF ART

THE GHOST OF LILY LUMLEY

WHEN Kate was entertaining her school friends with impressions of Joanna Lumley's character in *Absolutely Fabulous,* the future queen had no idea that she and the former model are both related to an illegitimate daughter of Edward IV.

Lumley Castle (above) in Chester-le-Street is supposedly haunted by the ghost of Ralph Lumley's first wife Lily who may have been the step-mother of Sir John Lumley (shown opposite). According to legend, two priests murdered Lily because of her religious beliefs and threw her body down a well. Ralph Lumley's only known wife was Eleanor Neville, sister of the Ralph Neville who married Katherine Swynford's daughter Joan Beaufort.

Many visitors to the castle, now a luxury hotel, have been frightened by Lily's ghost, including members of the Australian and West Indian cricket teams.

Another alleged murder involved Sir John Lumley's grandson George, the third Baron Lumley. George and Giles Thornton, the illegitimate brother of George's wife Elizabeth, fought a duel over a disputed inheritance. Some sources claim that George's son Thomas was the duellist; either way, it seems that Thornton was killed in a ditch at Windsor Castle.

Kate's ancestor Ralph Lumley, pictured with Richard II, was executed in 1400 after rebelling against Henry IV whose half-brother Thomas Swynford allegedly murdered Richard II in Pontefract Castle.

THE PEDIGREE OF

Isabel LUMLEY

Born: Derby abt. 1558

HRH Charles's 13-Great Aunt. Lady Diana's 15-Great Aunt.

Husband/Partner: **Richard CONYERS**
Possible Child: **Christopher (of Horden Hall) CONYERS**

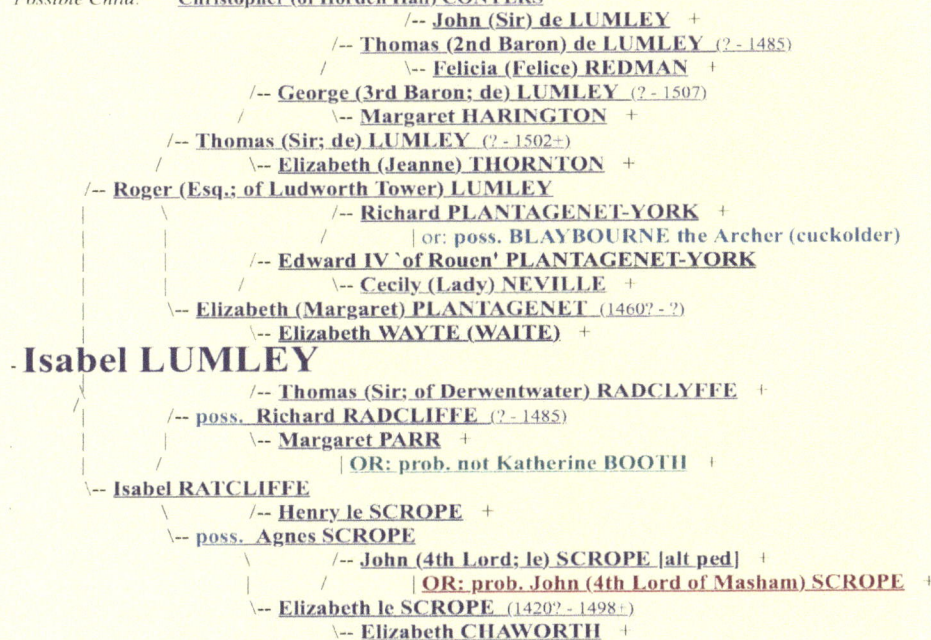

```
                                    /-- John (Sir) de LUMLEY  +
                        /-- Thomas (2nd Baron) de LUMLEY  (? - 1485)
                        /           \-- Felicia (Felice) REDMAN  +
                /-- George (3rd Baron; de) LUMLEY  (? - 1507)
                /           \-- Margaret HARINGTON  +
        /-- Thomas (Sir; de) LUMLEY  (? - 1502+)
        /           \-- Elizabeth (Jeanne) THORNTON  +
    /-- Roger (Esq.; of Ludworth Tower) LUMLEY
    |       \               /-- Richard PLANTAGENET-YORK  +
    |       |               | or: poss. BLAYBOURNE the Archer (cuckolder)
    |       |       /-- Edward IV `of Rouen' PLANTAGENET-YORK
    |       |       /       \-- Cecily (Lady) NEVILLE  +
    |       \-- Elizabeth (Margaret) PLANTAGENET  (1460? - ?)
    |               \-- Elizabeth WAYTE (WAITE)  +
```

Isabel LUMLEY

```
                        /-- Thomas (Sir; of Derwentwater) RADCLYFFE  +
    |       /-- poss. Richard RADCLIFFE  (? - 1485)
    |       |       \-- Margaret PARR  +
    |       /               | OR: prob. not Katherine BOOTH  +
    \-- Isabel RATCLIFFE
        \               /-- Henry le SCROPE  +
        \-- poss. Agnes SCROPE
            \               /-- John (4th Lord; le) SCROPE [alt ped]  +
            |       /       | OR: prob. John (4th Lord of Masham) SCROPE
            \-- Elizabeth le SCROPE  (1420? - 1498+)
                    \-- Elizabeth CHAWORTH  +
```

Kate's children have up to three Lumley bloodlines from Edward IV's illegitimate daughter Margaret Plantagenet (often wrongly named Elizabeth) whose mother may have been Elizabeth Wayte or Elizabeth Lucy. Prince George and his siblings also descend from Ralph Lumley's daughter Catherine Lumley through Catherine Chidioc and Katherine Popham (died 1588).

Margaret Plantagenet, Thomas Conyers, and many of their Lumley and Lambton relatives, were buried in St Mary and St Cuthbert's church in Chester-le-Street, not far from the workhouse in which Thomas spent his last years.

FABULOUS IMPRESSIONS

IN *Kate: The Future Queen* (2013), one of her teachers at St Andrews prep school in Berkshire recalled: 'She used to do an impression of Joanna Lumley and would always joke to her friends when she thought the teacher wasn't listening. 'That's absolutely fabulous, darling!'

The actress spent a night in her ancestral home while filming her 2021 TV series *Joanna Lumley's Britain.*

LEGENDARY DRAGON SLAYERS

THROUGH his parents' most recent common ancestor Jane Lambton, Prince George can claim descents from three legendary dragon slayers.

First and foremost, the future George VII is supposedly descended from St George, the patron saint of England and the Order of the Garter (See Page 64). Coincidentally, the parish of Middleton St George is not far north of Sockburn (See map opposite).

The other two alleged dragon killers were Sir John Conyers, slayer of the Sockburn Worm, and Sir John Lambton of Lambton Castle which, as shown above, is not far from Lumley Castle.

According to legend, a worm found by young Lambton in the River Wear grew into a rampaging monster. Integral to the story is a curse on the Lambton family which supposedly lasted for nine generations.

One of Prince George's favourite films is *How to Train Your Dragon* so he may be shocked to learn about his dragon-slaying ancestors. However, he will probably be thrilled to learn about the dragon connections of his ancestor Henry VII which inspired *Game of Thrones* (See Page 186).

Lewis Carroll started writing his famous nonsense poem about the Jabberwock (left) when he was a boy living at Croft-on-Tees in County Durham and was probably familiar with both the Sockburn and Lambton worms. And Kate is very familiar with Carroll because her university thesis was about his photography.

The PEDIGREE of

Jane LAMBTON

Born: abt. 1567   Died: 1648

HRH Charles's 10-Great Grandmother.   Lady Diana's 12-Great Grandmother.

Husband/Partner: **William (Knight; of Gibside) BLAKISTON (BLACKSTONE)**
Children: **Ralph (1st Baronet; of Gibside) BLAKISTON ; Nicholas BLAKISTON**

```
                          /-- Thomas (William?) LAMBTON
                          /        \-- poss. Elizabeth (? - 1479+)
                  /-- John (of Lambton) LAMBTON (? - 1549)
                  |        \           /-- Thomas ROKEBY
                  |         \-- poss. (Miss) ROKEBY
                  /               \-- Elizabeth AYSCOUGH
          /-- Robert (of Lambton) LAMBTON (? - 1583)
          |       \                  /-- Thomas (Sir; de) LUMLEY  +
          |        |        /-- Roger (Esq.; of Ludworth Tower) LUMLEY
          |        |        /        \-- Elizabeth (Margaret) PLANTAGENET  +
          |        \-- Anne (of Ludworth) LUMLEY (1510? - 1564)
          |            \ | OR: poss. Agnes LUMLEY  +
          |              |        /-- poss. Richard RADCLIFFE  +
          |              \-- Isabel RATCLIFFE
          /                       \-- poss. Agnes SCROPE  +

- Jane LAMBTON
          \                          /-- William (Sir) EURE  +
          |                          /-- Ralph (Sir; of Witton Castle) EURE (? - 1539)
          |                          /        \-- Margaret CONSTABLE  +
          |              /-- William (1st Baron de Wilton) EURE
          |              /        \-- Muriel HASTINGS  +
          /-- Ralph (Sir; of Witton) EURE (1508 - 6/3/1545)
          |       |        \           /-- Christopher (of Parham) WILLOUGHBY  +
          |       |        \-- Elizabeth WILLOUGHBY
          |       /                  \-- Margaret JENNEY  +
          \-- Frances (de) EURE (EVERS)
                  \                  /-- Ralph (Sir; of Streatlam) BOWES  +
                  |-- Ralph (Sir; of Streatlam) BOWES (? - 1516)
                  |        /        \-- Marjery (Margaret) CONYERS  +
                  \-- Margery (Margaret) BOWES (1506 - ?)
```

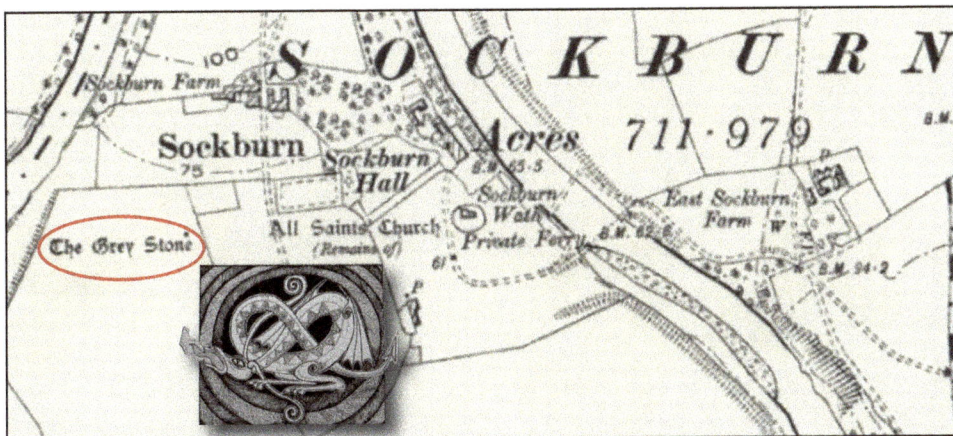

Kate's Conyers ancestors built their Sockburn estate in a loop of the River Tees in County Durham in the 1100s. According to legend, Sir John Conyers was interred in All Saints Church and the giant worm that he killed was buried nearby under a large grey stone (circled).

— 61 —

WIKIPEDIA

EDWARD IV'S ILLEGITIMACIES

THE Duchess of Cambridge has the dubious distinction of being descended from William the Bastard through Margaret Plantagenet, an illegitimate daughter of the allegedly illegitimate Edward IV (pictured above at his wedding) whose grandfather Richard of Conisburgh was almost certainly the illegitimate son of Peter the Cruel's illegitimate daughter Isabel Perez.

Edward IV's maternal line was also problematic because his grandmother Joan Beaufort was an illegitimate daughter of Katherine Swynford.

To make matters worse, Edward IV's legitimate children, including Henry VII's wife Elizabeth of York and the Princes in the Tower (See Page 106), were declared illegitimate by their uncle Richard III. (Edward's marriage to Elizabeth Woodville was allegedly bigamous because he had promised to marry another woman.)

There is no proof that Richard of York was cuckolded by a French archer named Blaybourne; however, it is likely that Edmund of Langley was cuckolded by John Holland KG (shown opposite) so, like Kate, the royal family almost certainly has no legitimate patrilineal bloodline from Edward IV to Edward III.

Note: Through Isabel Perez and Muslim princess Zaida of Seville (born c1070), Kate possibly descends from the Prophet Muhammad.

DNA tests may eventually determine if Richard of York was the father of Edward IV and the great-grandson of Edward III.

The PEDIGREE of
Elizabeth (Margaret) PLANTAGENET
Born: abt. 1460

HRH Charles's 14-Great Grandmother. Lady Diana's 14-Great Grandmother.

Husband/Partner: Thomas (Sir; de) LUMLEY
Children: Richard (4th Lord) LUMLEY ; Roger (Esq.; of Ludworth Tower) LUMLEY ; Anne LUMLEY ;
       Sibill LUMLEY

```
                              /-- Edward III (WINDSOR; King) of ENGLAND
                       /            \-- Isabella `the She-Wolf' of FRANCE  +
                  /-- Edmund of LANGLEY (PLANTAGENET) (1341 - 1402)
                  |        \ | OR: poss. John (K.G.) HOLLAND  +
                  /            \-- Philipa d' AVESNES of HAINAULT  +
             /-- Richard PLANTAGENET of CONISBURGH
             /          \-- Isabel PEREZ (Princess) of CASTILE  +
        /-- Richard PLANTAGENET-YORK
        |      \ | or: poss. BLAYBOURNE the Archer (cuckolder)
        |      |          /-- Roger de MORTIMER  +
        |      \-- Anne de MORTIMER  (1390 - 1411)
        /           \-- Alianore (Lady) HOLLAND  +
   /-- Edward IV `of Rouen' PLANTAGENET-YORK
   |    \           /-- John (III; de) NEVILL  +
   |    |     /-- Ralph I NEVILL (de NEVILLE)  (1363? - 1425)
   |    |     /      \-- Matilda (Maud Mary) de PERCY  +
   |    \-- Cecily (Lady) NEVILLE  (1415 - 1495)
   |         \         /-- John (BEAUFORT) of GAUNT  +
   |         \-- Joan (Lady; de) BEAUFORT  (1379? - 1440)
   |              \         /-- Paon (Sir; of GUIENNE) de ROET  +
   |              \-- Katherine ROELT
   |                   \-- poss. Catherine d' AVESNES  +
   /                        | or: prob. another of AVESNES family
- Elizabeth (Margaret) PLANTAGENET
   \                      /-- John WAITE
   |               /-- poss. John WAITE
   |         /-- Thomas WAYTE (WAITE)  (1413? - 1482)
   |         |    \         /-- William DISNEY
   |         /    \-- poss. Margaret DISNEY
   \-- Elizabeth WAYTE (WAITE)
        \ | or: (aka) Elizabeth LUCY
```

FABPEDIGREE.COM

THE CATHERINE CLARINGTON MYSTERY

BECAUSE nearly everything about Margaret Plantagenet is uncertain, it is remotely possible that her mother was Edward IV's mysterious mistress Catherine Clarington.

As shown above, it has long been assumed that Margaret's mother was either Elizabeth Wayte or Elizabeth Lucy (who may have been the same person).

In *The Private Life of Edward IV* (2016) John Ashdown-Hill, speculated about Edward having an affair with a young woman named Catherine 'of no social consequence' while staying at the royal hunting park in Clarendon, Wiltshire. Ashdown-Hill concluded: 'Obviously one alternative possibility is that, like Elizabeth Lucy, Catherine did not really exist at all.'

Kate's children are descended from Sibill Lumley (shown above) through Katherine Threlkeld and the first Earl of Harewood whose mother Katherine Hole may have been the daughter or granddaughter of an African slave (See Page 166).

DESCENDED FROM ADAM AND EVE?

SOON after overthrowing Catherine of Valois' son Henry VI, Katherine Swynford's great-grandson Edward IV used bogus genealogy to bolster his claim to the throne.

At the top of his 6.5-metre ancestry roll (shown opposite) is Kate's ancestor on his warhorse and a roundel depicting God — which supposedly meant Edward IV had a divine right to the throne — and another roundel depicting Adam and Eve. The roll also features the arms of mythological ancestors including St George, Brutus of Troy and the legendary Welsh kings Cadwallader and King Arthur.

Welsh bloodlines through the Mortimers were especially important because Edward IV claimed he was fulfilling an ancient prophecy about a victorious red dragon. Millions of people are descended from the Mortimers through Katherine Swynford's son-in-law and daughter-in-law.

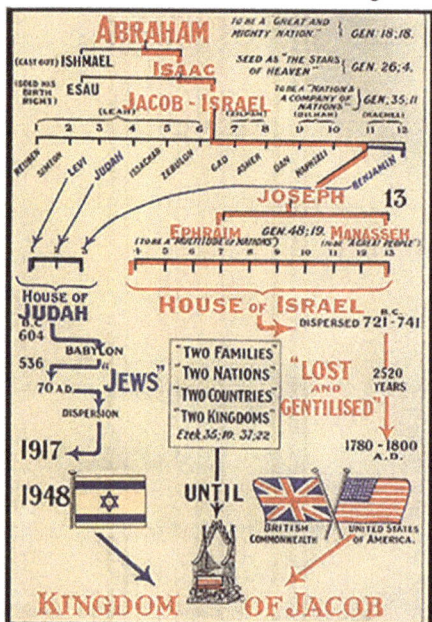

The doctrine of British Israelism, which was concocted in the 1840s, claimed that Queen Victoria and her subjects were descended from the Lost Tribes of Israel. This seemingly harmless mix of biblical prophecy and pseudo history (outlined left) morphed into imperialism and led to atrocities such as the Opium Wars with China.

References to King David were included in Elizabeth II's coronation service in 1953 and will probably be repeated when Prince William is crowned alongside Queen Catherine.

Some people believe that the so-called Stone of Destiny under Britain's coronation chair was once used by the biblical Jacob as a pillow.

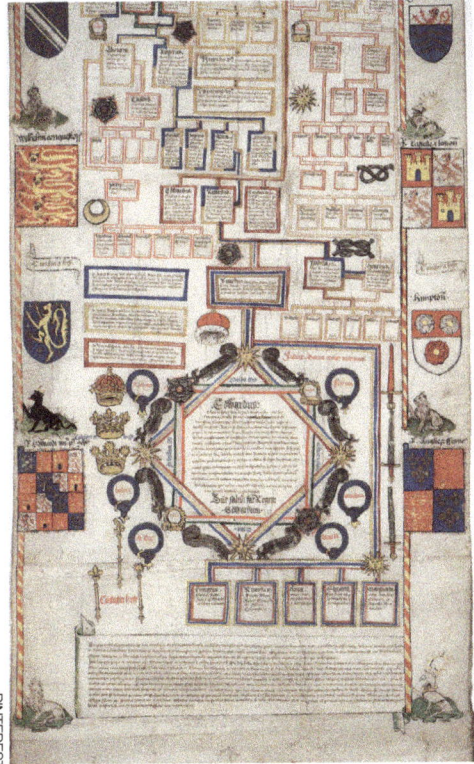

After the birth of Prince George in 2013, a BBC royal correspondent ruined his credibility by asserting that Kate is 'a Jew on her matriarchal side and therefore her baby will be a Jew, according to Jewish law and tradition'. Carole Goldsmith's parents, grandparents and great-grandparents were married in Christian churches.

Another bogus theory is that Kate's late mother-in-law Princess Diana was the love child of Jewish tycoon James Goldsmith (who was unrelated to Kate's mother).

However, it is true that Charles III was snipped by a Jewish mohel in 1948 and, based on Prince Harry's book *Spare,* it seems that he and Prince William (and most likely their sons) were circumcised soon after birth.

WHAT'S IN A NAME?

THE royal family has a long tradition of acknowledging its alleged King Arthur bloodline, starting with Henry VII's oldest son Prince Arthur who was Catherine of Aragon's first husband.

One of Queen Victoria's sons was named Prince Arthur and since then Arthur has been a middle name of George VI, Charles III, Prince William and Prince Louis.

KATE'S APHRODITE BLOODLINE

HYPOTHETICALLY, if Edward IV descended from Brutus of Troy, Kate has a bloodline from Brutus' even more mythical great-great-grandmother Aphrodite, the Greek equivalent of the Roman goddess immortalised in The Birth of Venus (above) held by Italy's renowned Uffizi Gallery.

Kate is very familiar with the gallery and Botticelli's masterpiece after spending several months in Florence before starting her art history course at St Andrews University.

While Maike Vogt-Lüerssen has claimed on kleio.org that the model for The Birth of Venus was Caterina Sforza, an illegitimate daughter of the Duke of Milan, most art historians believe that the goddess was inspired by another golden-haired beauty, Simonetta Vespucci.

According to Nigel Goodman, Kate's namesake is the goddess in Venus and Mars, a fresco painted by Botticelli in the Sistine Chapel. But, in The Birth of Venus, Caterina is the attendant (circled above).

Goodman also claims that Caterina Sforza inspired all of the graces in Primavera (inset) which hangs in the Uffizi Gallery not far from another Botticelli masterpiece featuring Caterina, Pallas and the Centaur.

The Viscontis, who claimed descent from Venus, are ancestors of Kate's children through Maria de Medici and illegitimate offspring of Charles II and James II.

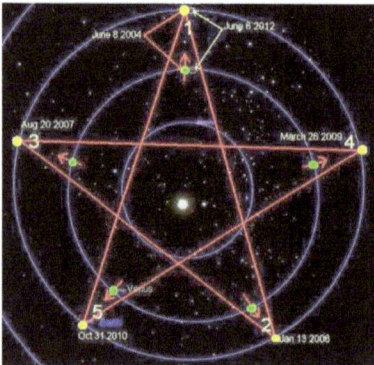

As explained in The Da Vinci Code, *the planet Venus traces a pentacle across our sky every eight years. But the claim that Botticelli preceded Leonardo da Vinci as the Priory of Sion's grand master is nonsense.*

THE PEDIGREE OF

Caterina SFORZA

Born: 1462   Died: 1509
Lady Diana's 14-Great Grandmother.

Husband/Partner: **Jean de MEDICIS**
Child: **Giovanni Ludovico dei MEDICI**

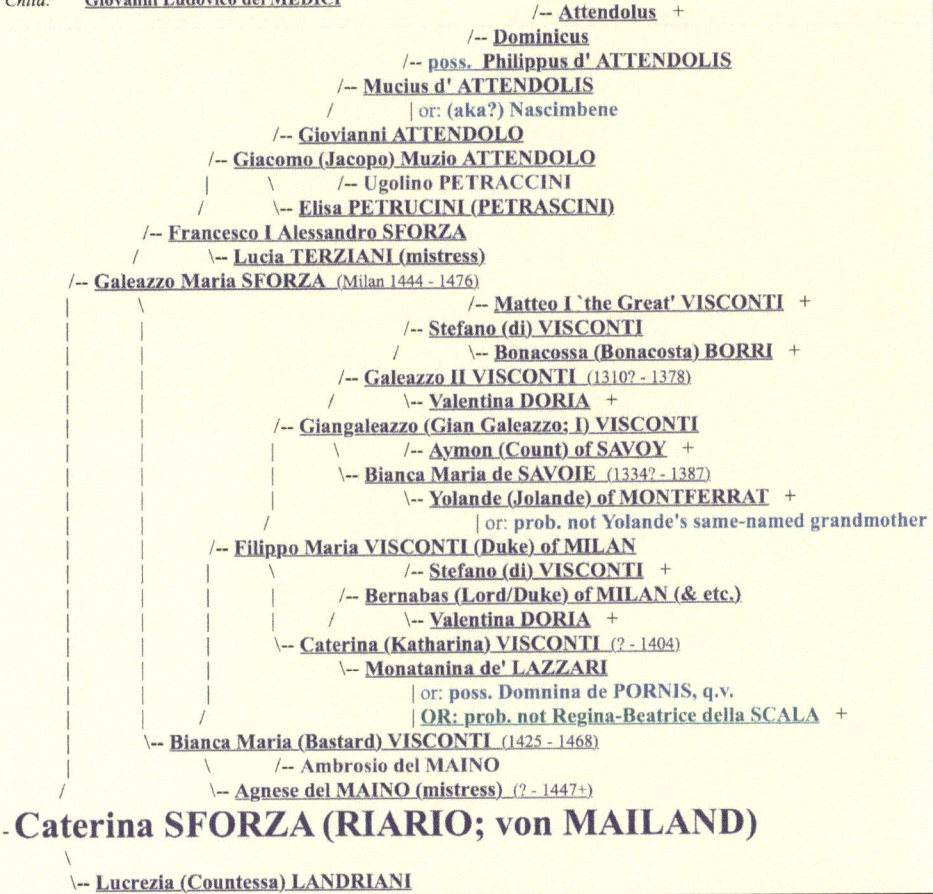

```
                                                    /-- Attendolus  +
                                          /-- Dominicus
                                    /-- poss. Philippus d' ATTENDOLIS
                               /-- Mucius d' ATTENDOLIS
                          /         | or: (aka?) Nascimbene
                     /-- Giovianni ATTENDOLO
               /-- Giacomo (Jacopo) Muzio ATTENDOLO
               |      \         /-- Ugolino PETRACCINI
               |       \-- Elisa PETRUCINI (PETRASCINI)
          /-- Francesco I Alessandro SFORZA
          /        \-- Lucia TERZIANI (mistress)
     /-- Galeazzo Maria SFORZA  (Milan 1444 - 1476)
     |   \                             /-- Matteo I `the Great' VISCONTI  +
     |    |                       /-- Stefano (di) VISCONTI
     |    |                       /         \-- Bonacossa (Bonacosta) BORRI  +
     |    |                 /-- Galeazzo II VISCONTI  (1310? - 1378)
     |    |                 /         \-- Valentina DORIA  +
     |    |           /-- Giangaleazzo (Gian Galeazzo; I) VISCONTI
     |    |           |      \         /-- Aymon (Count) of SAVOY  +
     |    |           |       \-- Bianca Maria de SAVOIE  (1334? - 1387)
     |    |           |             \-- Yolande (Jolande) of MONTFERRAT  +
     |    |           |             | or: prob. not Yolande's same-named grandmother
     |    |     /-- Filippo Maria VISCONTI (Duke) of MILAN
     |    |     |      \             /-- Stefano (di) VISCONTI  +
     |    |     |      |       /-- Bernabas (Lord/Duke) of MILAN (& etc.)
     |    |     |      |       /         \-- Valentina DORIA  +
     |    |     |       \-- Caterina (Katharina) VISCONTI  (? - 1404)
     |    |     |             \-- Monatanina de' LAZZARI
     |    |     |             | or: poss. Domnina de PORNIS, q.v.
     |    |     |             | OR: prob. not Regina-Beatrice della SCALA  +
     |    \-- Bianca Maria (Bastard) VISCONTI  (1425 - 1468)
     |           \         /-- Ambrosio del MAINO
     /           \-- Agnese del MAINO (mistress)  (? - 1447+)
```

- Caterina SFORZA (RIARIO; von MAILAND)

```
     \-- Lucrezia (Countessa) LANDRIANI
```

ST CATHERINE OF GENOA

THROUGH her great-great-grandmother Caterina Visconti (shown above), Caterina Sforza descended from the Fieschi family of St Catherine of Genoa (right) who was related to two popes, Innocent IV and Adrian V.

One of the Fieschis wrote a famous letter in which he claimed that Kate's ancestor Edward II escaped death after the invasion of his wife Isabella 'the She-Wolf' and spent his last days in an abbey in northern Italy.

St Catherine of Genoa is the patron saint of people who are victims of unfaithfulness.

THE MONA CATERINA CODE…

COULD Mona Lisa's smile, as Sigmund Freud famously suggested, be a recovered memory of Leonardo da Vinci's mother Caterina, who closely resembled Caterina Sforza and was often equated with the Madonna?

In 2011, Australian researcher Graeme Cameron claimed his Mona Lisa 've-gascan' (inset) was an image of da Vinci's 60-year-old mother Caterina which had been 'rejuvenated'. Meanwhile 'multispectral analysis' by Italian scientist Pascal Cotte has detected several hidden portraits, including one with a 'Madonna-style headdress' (above right). Note that there is no smile.

Leonardo was emotionally attached to three masterpieces in his possession when he died in France in 1519: the Louvre version of the Mona Lisa; one of his Madonna paintings, The Virgin and Child with St Anne (the Virgin's mother); and St John the Baptist. St John, St Anne and the Mona Lisa have similar smiles and some experts believe that all three were modelled on Leonardo's male lover Salai.

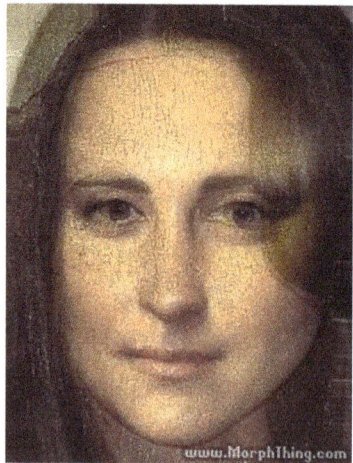

In 2002, German art historian Magdalena Soest claimed facial analysis suggested Caterina Sforza and Mona Lisa were 'one and the same person'. However, the 1487 Lorenzo di Credi portrait (above left) cited by Magdalena more closely resembles an unsmiling early version of da Vinci's portrait, featuring two columns, that Raphael copied around 1505.

This morphthing.com image shows that Kate, whose official 2012 portrait by Paul Emsley was unfavourably compared to the Mona Lisa, is a good match for da Vinci's masterpiece.

... AND THE LAST SUPPER

CONTRARY to Dan Brown's assertion that the feminine figure next to Jesus in The Last Supper is Mary Magdalene, it is much more likely that da Vinci used a female model, possibly his mother Caterina or Caterina Sforza, to depict the youthful St John the apostle.

Commissioning of the mural in a Milan monastery around 1493 coincided with the reunion of da Vinci and his mother after a long separation. Caterina died in his arms the following year, aged about 60.

It is therefore significant that Harvard art fellow James Constable discovered a subsurface image of an 'older woman', similar to Graeme Cameron's Mona Lisa 'vegascan', on a metalcut plate of The Last Supper dated around 1500 and apparently signed by da Vinci. In other words, a 'younger Caterina' could have inspired both the Mona Lisa and St John (businesswire.com article, August 2015).

The notion that Caterina Sforza was the model for St John is not farfetched because her uncle Ludovico, the Duke of Milan, was da Vinci's patron from 1482 to 1499. Note also that Maike Vogt-Luerssen claims Caterina was the model for Pietro Perugino's St Catherine of Alexandria (inset above). The resemblance to St John and some of da Vinci's Madonnas is undeniable.

In 2017, Martin Kemp claimed da Vinci's mother was an orphaned peasant girl named Caterina di Meo Lippi but, according to Carlo Vecce, author of *Caterina's Smile* (2023), she was a Circassian slave.

Note: Leonardo's muse in the 2021 TV series starring Aidan Turner is the entirely fictional Caterina da Cremona.

ST CATHERINE ART SECRETS

BEING patron of the National Portrait Gallery, and with access to the Royal Collection, Kate is uniquely positioned to curate an exhibition devoted to St Catherine of Alexandria. There are many masterpieces to choose from, including one that was hidden for hundreds of years and another which is still hidden under another painting.

As revealed on the BBC's *Fake or Fortune?* program in 2012, Anthony van Dyck's unfinished portrait of Charles I's wife Henrietta Maria as St Catherine (above left) was hidden under an unremarkable portrait of the queen (above right) which English art dealer Philip Mould purchased at a bargain price. Now restored to its original glory, the painting is probably worth several million pounds.

Artemisia Gentileschi, who painted several portraits of St Catherine, may have seen van Dyck working on his St Catherine because she was in London around 1639 to see her father Orazio Gentileschi, an accomplished artist who, like van Dyke, worked for Henrietta Maria.

Nobody knows why the St Catherine portrait was unfinished. However, Henrietta Maria was unpopular and a depiction of her as a Catholic saint would have made things worse. Henrietta Maria's daughter-in-law Catherine of Braganza was also unpopular but her portrait as St Catherine has survived intact.

Van Dyck painted this portrait of Prince William's ancestor Katherine Stanhope, Countess of Chesterfield, the governess and confidant of Henrietta Maria's oldest daughter Mary.

While frequenting the Uffizi gallery in Florence during her university gap year, Kate must have viewed Artemisia Gentileschi's magnificent portrait of St Catherine (above right).

The portrait supposedly depicts Caterina de Medici, Governor of Siena, a great-granddaughter of her namesake who was Queen of France and a first cousin once removed of Henrietta Maria, from whom Kate's children are descended through James II's illegitimate daughter Henrietta FitzJames.

However, the Uffizi portrait is strikingly similar to Artemisia's self-portrait as St Catherine (above left), now in the National Gallery in London, and it wasn't totally surprising when x-ray analysis of the Uffizi painting revealed a hidden self-portrait with a turban instead of a crown. The presence of a 'mysterious little face' suggests that Artemisia reused the canvas to save on materials.

While a lot has been written about Artemisia as a rape survivor depicting violence against men, most notably Judith Slaying Holofernes, she painted many other subjects and is now getting the recognition she deserves.

Note: A painting of St Catherine of Alexandria by Bernardino Luini, first recorded at Buckingham Palace in 1790 as a work by Leonardo da Vinci, was moved to Windsor Castle fifteen years later. Luini (died 1532) was greatly influenced by Leonardo and also by Raphael.

Caterina de Medici, Governor of Siena

MASSACRE OF THE HUGUENOTS

KATE'S Huguenot ancestors must have been terrified in the aftermath of the 1572 St Bartholomew's Day Massacre instigated by Catherine de Medici, pictured above viewing some of the dead in Paris. In the following days there were similar massacres throughout France, including in the Dordogne region where Kate's Martineau ancestors lived.

Catherine de Medici effectively ruled France as regent for nearly 30 years and had a fearsome reputation. On the day of the massacre she forced her goddaughter Catherine de Bourbon to convert to Catholicism.

A century of relative peace between Catholics and the Protestant Huguenots ended in 1685 with the Revocation of the Edict of Nantes. Many Huguenots fled France, including Kate's ancestor Gaston Martineau who settled in Norfolk where he worked as a surgeon.

Gaston's grandson David Martineau married Sarah Meadows whose great-grandfather Benjamin Fairfax was a non-conformist minister. Benjamin's sister, also named Sarah, married Bartholomew Allerton who was one of the Puritans who sailed to America on the *Mayflower*.

David Martineau's daughter Harriet was the famous sociologist and author Harriet Martineau who eventually became an atheist. Kate is descended from Harriet's Unitarian sister Elizabeth whose grandson Francis Martineau Lupton married Harriet Davis (See chart on Page 153).

Kate was secretly confirmed in 2011 to prevent any embarrassment when Prince William becomes Supreme Governor of the Church of England and, like every monarch since Henry VIII, Defender of the Faith.

The PEDIGREE of

Catherine (of FLORENCE) de MEDICI

Born: Florence 1519 Died: 1589 Blois

Husband/Partner: Henry II de VALOIS (King) of FRANCE
Children: Francis (Francois) II (King) of FRANCE ; Claudia de FRANCE ;
Elizabeth de FRANCE

```
                              /-- Cosimo (I) `the Elder' dei MEDICI +
                        /-- Piero I `the Gouty' de MEDICI (1416 - 1469)
                       /        \-- Lotta (Contessina) de' BARDI +
                /-- Laurent (Lorenzo) `le Magnifique' de MEDICIS
               /        \-- Lucrezia TORNABUONI +
        /-- Piero (Peter; II) de MEDICI (1471 - 1503)
       |    \              /-- Giocomo (di Monterotondo) ORSINI +
       |     \-- Clarissa (Clarice) ORSINI (1453 - 1488)
       |        \ | OR: prob. not Clarice ORSINI [alt ped] +
       |          \-- Maddalena ORSINI +
    /-- Lorenzo (II) de MEDICIS (1492? - 1519?)
   |    \              /-- Carlo ORSINI +
   |     |        /-- Roberto ORSINI (Conte) di TAGLIACOZZO (& d' Alba)
   |     |       /        \-- Paola Gironima ORSINI +
   |     \-- Alfonsina ORSINI (? - 1520)
   /          \-- Violante (Caterina?) SANSEVERINO
```

Catherine (of FLORENCE) de MEDICI

```
   \                  /-- Bertrand IV (Sn.) de la TOUR +
   |           /-- Bertrand V (I) de la TOUR D'AUVERGNE (? - 1461)
   |          /        \-- Marie d' AUVERGNE +
   |     /-- Bertrand II (VI) de la TOUR D'AUVERGNE (? - 1497)
   |    /        \-- Jacquette (Jaqueline) du PESCHIN +
   |   /-- Jean I de la TOUR D'AUVERGNE (1467?? - 1501?)
   |  |    \              /-- Georges (Sn.) de la TREMOILLE +
   |  |     \-- Louise de la TREMOILLE
   |  /          \-- Catherine de l' ISLE BOUCHARD +
   \-- Madeleine de la TOUR D'AUVERGNE (? - 1519?)
```

MEDICI BLACK MAGIC

CATHERINE DE MEDICI, a distant relative of Caterina Sforza through Lorenzo 'the Magnificent' (shown above), used cows' dung and sheeps' urine as fertility potions before delivering three French kings: Francis II, Charles IX and Henry III.

The talisman (right), made from a mixture of metals and goat's blood, was specially designed for Catherine de Medici by Nostradamus whose predictions have always been vague and meaningless. (It has been claimed that Nostradamus predicted that Prince Harry will be Britain's next monarch.)

PHILIP II'S MOTHERS-IN-LAW

A LITTLE-KNOWN fact about Philip II of Spain is that he had three mothers-in-law named Catherine (or variations thereof).

His first mother-in-law was Katherina Habsburg, pictured above with St Catherine of Alexandria, whose daughter Maria Manuela (shown opposite) was Philip II's double first cousin through Catherine of Aragon's sisters Maria Trastamara and Joanna (Juana), nicknamed 'the Mad'.

Catherine of Aragon was the mother of Philip II's second wife, and first cousin once removed, Mary I of England who died childless in 1558. Thirty years later Philip sent the Spanish Armada against Mary's half-sister Elizabeth I.

Philip II's third wife was Elizabeth de France, daughter of Catherine de Medici and mother of Catherine Michaela of Spain (See chart on Page 77).

Wife number four was Philip II's niece Anna of Austria; their grandson Philip IV married one of his nieces; and their son was the horribly deformed Charles II of Spain who had the same mitochondrial DNA as Charles II of England.

Philip II had the same mitochondrial DNA as three of his wives and their mothers: Katherina Habsburg, Catherine of Aragon, and his own sister Maria of Austria.

The PEDIGREE of
Katherina (Catalina) HABSBURG
Born: 1507   Died: 1578

Husband/Partner: **Joao III d' AVIZ (King) of PORTUGAL**
Child: **Joao IV d' AVIZ of PORTUGAL   Maria Manuela**

```
                    /-- Frederick V (III) HABSBURG von OESTERREICH
            |          \-- Cymbarka of CZERSK  +
            /              | OR: prob. not Cymburgis of MASOVIA [alt ...  +
    /-- Maximilian I HABSBURG von OESTERREICH  (1459 - 1519)
    |        \        /-- Duarte JOAEZ de PORTUGAL (the Algarves)  +
    |         \-- Eleonore Helena de PORTUGAL  (1434 - 1467)
    /              \-- Leonora de ARAGON  +
  /-- Philip I `le Beau' von HAPSBURG  (1478 - 1506)
  |     \              /-- Philippe III `the Good' (Duke) of BURGUNDY  +
  |      |        /-- Charles de VALOIS (Duke) of BURGUNDY
  |      |       /       \-- Isabella de PORTUGAL  +
  |      \-- Marie (de BOURGOGNE) de VALOIS  (1457 - 1482)
  |            \              /-- Charles I de BOURBON  +
  |             \-- Isabella de BOURBON  (1435? - 1465?)
  /                   \-- Agnes de BOURGOGNE  +
```

-Katherina (Catalina) HABSBURG

```
  \              /-- Juan I (King) de CASTILE (& Leon)  +
  |             /-- Fernando I of ARAGON & SICILY (Mallorca & Valencia)
  |            /      \-- Eleanor of ARAGON (& Valencia)  +
  |         /-- John II `the Great' (King) of ARAGON
  |        /      \-- Leonor Urraca Sancha (Princess) of CASTILE  +
  |     /-- Ferdinand V (King) of CASTILE (SPAIN)  (1452 - 1516)
  |     |     \       /-- Federigo (Count) of MELGAR  +
  |     |      \-- Juana (Princess) of MELGAR
  |     /            \-- Maria (Baroness) of AYOLY-CORDOVA  +
  \-- Juana (Queen) de ESPANA  (Toledo 1479 - 1555)
        \              /-- Enrique III (King) de CASTILE (& Leon)  +
        |        /-- Juan II (King) de CASTILE (& Leon)  (1405 - 1454)
        |       /      \-- Katherine (Lady) PLANTAGENET  +
        \-- Isabella (I; Queen) de CASTILE  (1451 - 1504)
```

ONLY SIX GREAT-GREAT-GRANDPARENTS

LIKE Kate's ancestor Peter the Cruel — grandfather of Catherine of Castile, shown above as Katherine Plantagenet —- Katherina Habsburg's grandson Don Carlos (right) had only four great-grandparents: sisters Joanna 'the Mad' and Maria Trastamara, and their husbands.

Don Carlos was even more inbred, with only six great-great-grandparents instead of 16, so it is no wonder that he was mentally unstable. He died in 1568 after being locked up by his father Philip II.

Kate's children are descended from Katherina Habsburg's brother Ferdinand I through Maria de Medici and Charles II.

CATHERINE OF ARAGON'S SISTERS

SOME OF Kate's Middleton ancestors had consanguineous relationships similar to those of Catherine of Aragon and her sisters: Joanna 'the Mad' (pictured above mourning her husband Philip I), Maria Trastamara and Isabella of Aragon.

As shown opposite, Joanna (Juana) and Maria were Philip II's grandmothers. Maria married Manuel I of Portugal after the death of his first wife, Maria's sister Isabella; and after Maria died in 1517 Manuel married Joanna's daughter Eleanor.

The grandmothers of Kate's great-grandfather Richard Noel Middleton were sisters Mary and Ellen Ward (See chart on Page146). After Mary died in 1859, her widowed husband William Middleton married Mary's sister Sarah. And another of Kate's ancestors married his daughter's sister-in-law (See Page 153).

Incredibly, William Middleton's second marriage was illegal based on the same biblical passage which supposedly justified Henry VIII's divorce of Catherine of Aragon, the widow of his brother Prince Arthur (See Black Catherine's Secret, Page 222).

Louis XVI, a matrilineal descendant of Catherine Michaela of Spain, was guillotined in 1793. Two centuries later a DNA test on his presumed blood identified a rare form of mitochondrial haplogroup N.

Maria Trastamara was the grandmother of Catarina of Portugal who was the great-grandmother of Catherine of Braganza.

The PEDIGREE of

Catherine Michaela (Princess) of SPAIN

Born: Madrid 1567   Died: 1597 Turin

Husband/Partner: Carlo-Emanuele I `il Grande' (Duke) of SAVOY
Children: Vittorio Amedeo I (Duke) of SAVOY ; Margaretha von SAVOYEN

```
                        /-- Philip I `le Beau' von HAPSBURG  (1478 - 1506)
                   /         \-- Marie (de BOURGOGNE) de VALOIS  +
            /-- Charles I (King) of SPAIN  (1500 - 1558)
            |        \          /-- Ferdinand V (King) of CASTILE (SPAIN)  +
            |         \-- Juana (Queen) de ESPANA  (Toledo 1479 - 1555)
           /                   \-- Isabella (I; Queen) de CASTILE  +
       /-- Philip II HAPSBURG (King) of SPAIN  (1527 - 1598)
       |        \                   /-- Fernando (Duke) de VISEU (VISEO)  +
       |        |          /-- Manuel I (King) de PORTUGAL
       |        |          /    \-- Beatriz de PORTUGAL  +
       |         \-- Isabella (AVIS) de PORTUGAL  (1503 - 1539)
       |                  \          /-- Ferdinand V (King) of CASTILE (SPAIN)  +
       |                   \-- Maria TRASTAMARA de ARAGON  (1482 - 1517)
      /                            \-- Isabella (I; Queen) de CASTILE  +
```

- Catherine Michaela (Princess) of SPAIN

```
       \                /-- Francois I de VALOIS (King) of FRANCE
       |          /         \-- Louise de SAVOY (SAVOIE)  +
       |     /-- Henry II de VALOIS (King) of FRANCE
       |     |        \          /-- Louis XII (King) of FRANCE  +
       |     |         \-- Claude I (Queen) de FRANCE  (1499 - 1524)
       |     /                   \-- Anne (Heiress of BRITTANY) de DREUX  +
        \-- Elizabeth de FRANCE  (1545 - 1568)
                 \                /-- Piero (Peter; II) de MEDICI  +
                 |          /-- Lorenzo (II) de MEDICIS  (1492? - 1519?)
                 |          /    \-- Alfonsina ORSINI  +
                  \-- Catherine (of FLORENCE) de MEDICI
```

THE LADY IN ERMINE

KATE is almost certainly familiar with this brilliant portrait, unsigned and sitter un-identified, which has been attributed to either El Greco or Alonso Sanchez Coello.

However, Donna DiGiuseppe — author of *Lady in Ermine: The Story of a Woman Who Painted the Renaissance* (2019) — claims the artist was Sofonisba Anguissola and the sitter was Catherine Michaela of Spain. Sofonisba painted Catherine Michaela as a child and also painted her parents, Philip II and Elizabeth de France.

— 77 —

FRANCO-SPANISH CATHERINES

CATHERINE was a popular name for French and Spanish royals during the Renaissance and many of them were closely related, genetically and geographically.

As shown opposite, Catalina of Navarre (died 1517) was the granddaughter of Charles VII of France, brother of Catherine of Valois who married Henry V of England. Charles VII had a daughter, also named Catherine of Valois, who was Catalina's aunt.

Another aunt of Catalina of Navarre was Catherine of Foix (died 1494) who, as mentioned previously, was the matrilineal ancestor of three monarchs from whom Kate's children are descended: Catherine the Great, Queen Victoria and Charles II.

Charles II's wife Catherine of Braganza was descended from Catherine of Castile and so was Henry VIII's first wife Catherine of Aragon, a first cousin of Catherine of Foix through John 'the Great' of Aragon.

Catalina of Navarre's great-granddaughter Catherine of Bourbon, who was born in Albret, was the regent of Bearn (circled above) in the late 1500s.

Kate, who is destined to be Britain's sixth Queen Catherine, is descended from Catherine of Castile's stepmother Katherine Swynford who was probably born in northern France around 1350.

Catalina of Navarre (left) was a niece of Catherine of Foix whose first cousin Catherine of Aragon was the great-granddaughter of Catherine of Castile.

— 78 —

Catalina de FOIX (Queen) of NAVARRE

Born: 1470   Died: 1517
HRH Charles's 12-Great Grandmother.   Lady Diana's 13-Great Grandmother.
Husband/Partner: __John III (King) of NAVARRE__
Children: __Isabelle d' ALBRET__ ; __Henry (Enrique) II d' ALBRET (King) of NAVARRE__

```
        /-- Gaston IV (Count) de FOIX  (1423 - 1472)
        |          \          /-- Charles (I) d' ALBRET  +
        |           \-- Jeanne d' ALBRET  (? - 1433?)
        /              \-- Marie de SULLY  +
    /-- Gaston de FOIX  (? - 1470)
    |        \                    /-- Fernando I of ARAGON & SICILY  +
    |         |        /-- John II `the Great' (King) of ARAGON
    |         |       /      \-- Leonor Urraca Sancha (Princess) of CASTILE  +
    |          \-- Eleanor (Leonor) (Queen) de NAVARRE  (1425 - 1479)
    |                   \        /-- Carlos III (King) de NAVARRE  +
    |                    \-- Blanca (Blanche II) (Queen) de NAVARRE
    /                            \-- Eleonore ENRIQUEZ (Infanta) de CASTILLE  +
```

Catalina de FOIX (Queen) of NAVARRE

```
    \                        /-- Jean (John) II `the Good' de VALOIS  +
    |                /-- Charles V `the Wise' de VALOIS
    |               /       \-- Jutte Bonne (Bona) of LUXEMBURG  +
    |       /-- Charles VI `the Beloved' de VALOIS
    |       |          \ | or: prob. not Louis (Charles VI 's brother)
    |      /            \-- Jeanne (Joan) de BOURBON  +
    /-- Charles VII de VALOIS (King) de FRANCE  (1403 - 1461)
    |      |          \         /-- Stefan III `the Magnificent' of BAVARIA  +
    |      |           \-- Isabelle of BAVARIA  (1371 - 1435)
    |     /                     \-- Taddea VISCONTI  +
    \-- Madelaine (Magdalen) de FRANCE  (1443 - 1485+)
```

KATE AND KING FELIPE

SPAIN'S Felipe VI, pictured with Kate in Belgium in 2014, is also Felipe VI of Castile, Felipe V of Aragon, and Felipe VIII of Navarre.

Like Sweden's Carl XVI Gustaf, Felipe VI has an all-female bloodline from Catherine of Foix but, unlike Carl Gustaf, Felipe descends from the French countess through all of his great-great-grandparents. Felipe VI also descends from Philip (Felipe) IV who sired the horribly inbred and infertile Charles II of Spain (another matrilineal descendant of Catherine of Foix).

The PEDIGREE of

Katharina of AUSTRIA

Born: Innsbruck 1533   Died: 1572 Linz

Lady Diana's 12-Great Aunt.
Husbands/Partners: Franz III GONZAGA von MANTUA-MONFERRAT ;
Sigismund II August (King) of POLAND

```
            /-- Philip I `le Beau' von HAPSBURG  (1478 - 1506)
        |        \           /-- Charles de VALOIS (Duke) of BURGUNDY  +
        |         \-- Marie (de BOURGOGNE) de VALOIS  (1457 - 1482)
        /                    \-- Isabella de BOURBON  +
    /-- Ferdinand I (EMPEROR) of GERMANY  (1503 - 1564)
    |        \                /-- John II `the Great' (King) of ARAGON  +
    |         |         /-- Ferdinand V (King) of CASTILE (SPAIN)
    |         |        /        \-- Juana (Princess) of MELGAR  +
    |         \-- Juana (Queen) de ESPANA  (Toledo 1479 - 1555)
    |                  \        /-- Juan II (King) de CASTILE (& Leon)  +
    |                   \-- Isabella (I; Queen) de CASTILE  (1451 - 1504)
    /                            \-- Isabella d' AVIZ de PORTUGAL  +
```

- Katharina of AUSTRIA

```
    |        /-- Vladislas II JAGELLON (King) of HUNGARY-BOHEMIA
    |        |        \           /-- Albert V von HAPSBURG  +
    |        |         \-- Elizabeth von HABSBURG (Princess) of AUSTRIA
    |        /                    \-- Eliska (Elisabeth) (Princess) of BOHEMIA  +
    \-- Anne JAGELLON (Queen) of BOHEMIA  (1503 - 1547)
             \                /-- Jean (I; Count) de FOIX (FOIX-CANDALE)  +
             |         /-- Gaston II de FOIX  (? - 1500)
             |        |        \-- Margaret de KERDESTON  +
             \-- Anne de FOIX  (1484? - 1506)
                      \        /-- Gaston IV (Count) de FOIX  +
                       \-- Catherine (Catalina Katharina) de FOIX
```

AUSTRO-POLISH CATHERINES

THE interconnectedness of Kate's Austrian and Polish royal namesakes and some of her own ancestors is evident in these two charts.

Katharina of Austria, who was a granddaughter of Catherine of Aragon's sister Joanna 'the Mad' (shown above) and a niece of Katharina Habsburg, had an all-female bloodline from Catherine of Foix and therefore had the same mitochondrial DNA as Catherine the Great and Queen Victoria.

And Katharina of Austria's grandfather Vladislas II, and his brother Sigismond I of Poland (shown opposite), had the same mitochondrial DNA as George I, III and V through all-female bloodlines from Katharina von Pfannberg.

Like Catherine of Aragon, Katharina of Austria (left) claimed her first marriage to Franz III of Mantua-Monferrat had not been consummated. Katharina later married Sigismond II of Poland whose first wife was her older sister

The PEDIGREE of
Catharine (Katarzyna) JAGIELLO of POLAND
Born: 1526   Died: 1583 Stockholm
HRH Charles's 13-Great Half-Aunt.

Husband/Partner: Johann III (King) of SWEDEN
Child: Sigismund III VASA (King) of POLAND

```
                    /-- Kazimierz IV (King) of POLAND (& Grand Duke of LITHUANIA)
            |        \        /-- Andrzej IWANOWITSCH von HOLSZANY  +
            |         \-- Sofia of HOLSZANY  (1405? - 1464)
            /              \-- Alexandra Dimitrijewna (Princess) of DRUCKA  +
   /-- Sigismond (Zygmunt) I JAGELLON (King) of POLAND
   |        \                    /-- Albert IV (von) HAPSBURG (Duke) of AUSTRIA  +
   |        |        /-- Albert V von HAPSBURG
   |        |       /        \-- Johanne (Jeanne) Sofie von WITTELSBACH  +
   |        \-- Elizabeth von HABSBURG (Princess) of AUSTRIA
   |                 \          /-- Zikmund of BOHEMIA (Holy Roman EMPEROR)  +
   |                  \-- Eliska (Elisabeth) (Princess) of BOHEMIA
   |                          \-- Barbara of CILLY  +
```

- Catharine (Katarzyna) JAGIELLO of POLAND

```
   \                        /-- Giacomo (Jacopo) Muzio ATTENDOLO  +
   |                /-- Francesco I Alessandro SFORZA
   |               /        \-- Lucia TERZIANI (mistress)
   |        /-- Galeazzo Maria SFORZA  (Milan 1444 - 1476)
   |        |       /        \-- Bianca Maria (Bastard) VISCONTI  +
   |   /-- Gian Galeazzo II Maria SFORZA  (1469 - 1494 Pavia)
   |   |        \          /-- Luigi (Ludovico) (Duke) of SAVOY  +
   |   |         \-- Bonne de SAVOIE  (1449 - 1485)
   |   /                   \-- Anne de LUSIGNAN (Princess) of CYPRUS  +
   \-- Bona (of MILAN) SFORZA  (1495 - 1558 Bari)
           \                /-- Ferdinand I d' ARAGON (King) of NAPLES  +
           |        /-- Alfonso II (King) of NAPLES  (1448 - 1495)
           |       /        \-- Isabel de CLERMONT  +
           \-- Isabella of ARAGON  (1470 - 1524)
```

Elisabeth. [Manuel I of Portugal and Kate's ancestor William Middleton also married sisters of their deceased wives.]

Kate's children are descended from Sigismond I's sister Barbara Jagellon through Catherine Vasa of Sweden and Catherine the Great's husband Peter III. Prince George and his siblings also have numerous bloodlines from both Catherine of Foix and Katharina von Pfannberg through George V.

Two of Kate's ancestors, Catherine Stafford and Catherine Mortimer, had the same mtDNA as Catherine of Foix' mother-in-law Margaret de Kerdeston (shown opposite).

Catherine Jagellon (Jagiello) of Poland, sister-in-law of Katharina of Austria, was a great-niece of Caterina Sforza who may have been the real Mona Lisa.

KATHERINA'S BOOK OF HOURS

THIS prayer book, commissioned in the 1400s for Katherina von Kleve (also known as Catherine of Cleves), is one of the world's most beautiful illuminated manuscripts.

The Book of Hours has more than 150 elaborate miniatures by a gifted unknown artist, including the one above showing the duchess kneeling before the Virgin Mary and baby Jesus. Of special interest is a rare depiction of the entrance to Hell.

Another famous Book of Hours, mostly commissioned by Katherine Swynford's grandson John Beaufort KG for his wife Margaret Beauchamp, was inherited by their daughter Margaret Beaufort, mother of Henry VII.

The deaths of Catherine of Valois (in 1437) and Catherine of Aragon (in 1536) were recorded in the Beaufort/Beauchamp book which is now held by the Morgan Library and Museum in New York. Images from Catherine of Aragon's alleged long-lost Book of Hours can be found on the internet.

Kate's children descend from James II of Scotland, nicknamed 'Fiery Face' because of a prominent birthmark, who was a nephew of John Beaufort KG and Margaret Beauchamp, and also a son-in-law of Katherina von Kleve. Like Marie Antoinette, Katherina inherited haplogroup H through an all-female bloodline from Bertha von Putelendorf who died in 1190.

Katherina von Kleve, who had daughter named Catharina (shown opposite) and a granddaughter named Katherine, descended from William the Bastard through all of her grandparents.

Note: Kleve, in north-western Germany near the Dutch border, was the home of Henry VIII's not-so-ugly fourth wife Anne of Cleves who he quickly replaced with the younger and more attractive Catherine Howard.

The PEDIGREE of
Katherina (Duchess) von KLEVE
aka Catherine de CLEVES
Born: 1417   Died: 1479

Lady Diana's 16-Great Grandmother.

Husband/Partner: **Arnold van EGMOND (Duke) of GUELDERS**
Children: **Catharina (Regent) van GUELDRES**

```
            /-- Adolphe III (I) de CLEVES  (1350? - 1394)
        |           \       /-- Thierry VIII de CLEVES  +
        |            \-- Marguerite de CLEVES  (by 1314 - 1348+)
        /                    \-- Marguerite de GUELDRE  +
    /-- Adolf (I; IV) von KLEVE  (1373 - 1448)
    |       \                    /-- William V (I; Duke) of JULICH  +
    |        |            /-- Gerhard VI (Count/Duke) of JULICH  (1321? - 1360)
    |        |           /       \-- Johanna of HOLLAND  +
    |        \-- Margareta of JULICH  (1350? - 1429 (or '25))
    |                     \            /-- Otto III (IV; Count) von RAVENSBERG  +
    |                      \-- Margarethe (Margareta) von RAVENSBERG
    /                                  \-- Margareta (of BERG) van LIMBURG  +
```

- Katherina (Duchess) von KLEVE

```
        \                            /-- Philip VI (King) of FRANCE  +
        |                    /-- Jean (John) II `the Good' de VALOIS
        |                   /       \-- Joanna (Queen?) of BURGUNDY  +
        |            /-- Philip (II) `The Bold' (Duke) of BURGUNDY
        |           /                 \-- Jutte Bonne (Bona) of LUXEMBURG  +
        |    /-- John `the Fearless' (Duke) of BURGUNDY
        |   |        \            /-- Louis I de MALE  +
        |   |         \-- Margaret II de MALE  (1350? - 1405)
        |   |        /            \-- Marguerite de BRABANT  +
        \-- Marie VALOIS of BURGUNDY  (1394? - 1463 (or '41))
```

Catherine of Aragon, presumably depicted in her Book of Hours with St Catherine, was a granddaughter-in-law of Margaret Beaufort who inherited a similar book from her mother Margaret Beauchamp (whose parents-in-law are possibly depicted above right).

KATHERINA OF POMERANIA…

THE FIRST pregnancy and childbirth manual in English, which was dedicated to Henry VIII's fifth wife Catherine Howard, was translated from a German book presented to Katherina of Pomerania (inset) in 1513.

Written by German physician Eucharius Rosslin, *The Rose Garden* was based on ancient Greek texts and included illustrations by a student of renowned German painter Albrecht Durer.

Retitled *The Birth of Mankind*, Rosslin's manual was almost certainly consulted by midwives attending Catherine Parr when she gave birth to her first child Mary Seymour on 30th August 1548.

Catherine died of 'childbed fever' six days later and her daughter, who was placed in the care of one of Catherine's best friends Catherine Willoughby, the Duchess of Suffolk, probably died before her third birthday.

Kate's children descend from Katherina of Pomerania through Catherine the Great who had a separate all-female bloodline from Catherine of Foix. Joachim Nestor (shown opposite) had an all-female bloodline from Katharina von Pfannberg.

The Birth of Mankind, which was in print for more than 100 years, included this advice: *'The Midwife her selfe shall sit before the labouring woman, and shall diligently observe and waite, how much, and after what meanes the child*

Advice to let the placenta 'putrifye' in the womb may have contributed to Catherine Parr's death.

Catherine (Margravine) of BRANDENBURG-KUSTRIN

Born: 1549 Died: 1602

HRH Charles's 10-Great Grandmother.

Husband/Partner: Joachim (III) Frederick (Elector) of BRANDENBURG
Children: Barbara Sophie von BRANDENBURG ; Anna Cathrine von BRANDENBURG

```
                        /-- Johann Cicero (Elector) von BRANDENBURG
                /             \-- Margaret ZEHRINGEN of BADEN  +
        /-- Joachim I Nestor (Elector) von BRANDENBURG
        |       \         /-- Wilhelm III `the Brave' (Duke) von SACHSEN  +
        |       \-- Margarethe von SACHSEN (THURINGEN)  (1449? - 1501)
        /                 \-- Anna von OESTERREICH  +
    /-- Johann I (Margrave) of BRANDENBURG-KUSTRIN
    |   \               /-- Christian I (King) of DENMARK  +
    |   |       /-- John (Hans) OLDENBURG (King) of DENMARK
    |   |       /         \-- Dorothea von BRANDENBURG-ANSBACH  +
    |   \-- Elisabeth OLDENBURG  (1485? - 1555)
    |           \         /-- Ernest (I) de WETTIN (Elector) of SAXONY  +
    |           \-- Christina (of SAXONY) WETTIN  (1461 - 1521)
    /               \-- Elizabeth WITTELSBACH of BAVARIA-MUNCHEN  +
```

- Catherine (Margravine) of BRANDENBURG-KUSTRIN

```
    \               /-- Wilhelm I `the Victorious' WELF  +
    |           /-- Wilhelm II WELF (Duke) of BRUNSWICK-LUNEBURG
    |           /         \-- Cecile de HOHENZOLLERN  +
    |       /-- Henry I (VIII; Duke) `the Bad' von BRAUNSCHWEIG-WOLFENBUETTEL
    |       /         \-- Elisabeth de STOLBERG  +
    |   /-- Heinrich II von BRUNSWICK-WOLFEN
    |   |   \         /-- Erich II of POMERANIA  +
    |   |   \-- Katherina of POMERANIA  (1465? - 1526)
    |   /               \-- Sofie of POMERANIA  +
    \-- Katherine von BRUNSWICK-WOLFENBUETTEL  (1518? - 1574)
        \               /-- Ulrich (V) von WURTTEMBERG  +
        |       /-- Heinrich (Duke) von WURTTEMBERG  (1448 - 1519)
        |       /         \-- Elisabeth de BAVIERE-LANDSHUT  +
        \-- Marie von WURTTEMBERG  (15/8/1496 - 1541)
```

stirreth itselfe: also shall with hands, first anoynted with the oyle of almonds or the oyle of those white lillies, rule and direct everything as shall seeme best.'

Catherine of Pomerania (died 1426) was a candidate to marry England's Henry V before he married Catherine of Valois. Note also that Katherina of Pomerania descended from Henry II.

...MOTHER KATE OF KUSTRIN

NICKNAMED 'Mother Kate' because of her good deeds, Katherina of Pomerania's granddaughter Katherine von Brunswick-Wolfenbuettel (right), should not be confused with her aunt Katharina von Braunschweig-Wolfenbuettel who died in 1563.

Mother Kate set up a pharmacy in Kustrin on the Polish border from which she distributed free medicine to the poor. Catherine of Brandenburg-Kustrin funded her philanthropy by selling milk at a Berlin market.

CATHERINES OF SWEDEN

WITH an all-female bloodline from Catherine of Foix; descents from Katharina von Pfannberg through all of his great-great-grandparents; descents from Katherine Swynford and Catherine of Valois through all of his great-grandparents; and bloodlines from Catherine the Great through both parents; Carl XVI Gustaf of Sweden (inset above) is living proof that the 'Catherine Code' has dominated Europe's royal families for hundreds of years.

Remarkably, one of Carl Gustaf's two bloodlines from Queen Victoria is through Prince Leopold whose haemophilia was transmitted to his grandson Prince Rupert of Teck, a first cousin once removed of Carl (Charles) Gustaf who, coincidentally, has the same mitochondrial DNA (haplogroup H) as the horribly inbred Charles II of Spain.

Through Catherine the Great's son, who also had haplogroup H, Carl Gustaf descends from Catherine Vasa of Sweden (died 1638) who was a matrilineal descendant of Katharina von Pfannberg and therefore had the same mitochondrial DNA (haplogroup T) as George I, George III and George V and also Charles I.

Catherine Vasa of Sweden, who had an all-female bloodline from Katharina von Pfannberg (haplogroup T), married Johann Casimir von Simmern who had an all-female bloodline from Catherine of Foix (haplogroup H).

The PEDIGREE of
Catherine (KARLSDOTTER) VASA (Princess) of SWEDEN
Born: 1584 Died: 1638
HRH Charles's 9-Great Grandmother.

Husband/Partner: Johann Casimir (Kasimir) von SIMMERN
Children: Carl X JOHANSSON (King) of SWEDEN ; Christina Magdalena von SIMMERN

```
                        /-- Erik (JOHANSSON) VASA (WASA)  (1470? - 1520)
                        |      \-- Birgitta GUSTAVSDOTTER (STURE)  +
                        /            / OR: Not! Ebba Eriksdotter KRUMMEDIGE  +
            /-- Gustaf I ERIKSSON (King) of SWEDEN  (1496 - 1560)
            |      \          /-- Magnus KARLSSON (EKA)  +
            |       \-- Cecilia (MANSDOTTER) EKA  (1476? - 1523?)
            /            \-- Sigrid ESKILSDOTTER (BANER) pa Lindholmen  +
    /-- Carl IX VASA (King) of SWEDEN  (1550 - 1611)
    |      \              /-- Abraham Kristiernsson LEIJONHUFVUD  +
    |      |       /-- Erik ABRAHAMSSON (LEIJONHUFVUD pa Loholmen)
    |      |      /       \-- Birgitta MAGNUSDOTTER NATT OCH DAG  +
    |      \-- Margareta ERIKSDOTTER  (1514 - 1551)
    |             \          /-- Erik KARLSSON (pa Norrby)  +
    |             |        / OR: Erik (JOHANSSON) VASA (WASA)  +
    |             \-- Ebba ERIKSDOTTER (VASA; WASA)  (1491? - 1549)
    /             .            \-- Anna KARLSDOTTER (VINSTORPAATTEN)  +
```

- Catherine (KARLSDOTTER) VASA (Princess) of SWEDEN

```
    \                   /-- John I WITTELSBACH of SIMMERN  +
    |             /-- John II WITTELSBACH (Landgrave) of SIMMERN
    |            /       \-- Johanna de NASSAU-SAARBRUCKEN  +
    |      /-- Frederick III WITTELSBACH (Elector) of PALATINE
    |      |      \-- Beatrix ZAHRINGEN of BADEN  +
    |      /-- Louis (Ludwig) VI (Elector) of PALATINE
    |      |      \          /-- Casimir de HOHENZOLLERN  +
    |      |      \-- Marie von BRANDENBURG-KULMBACH
    |      /            \-- Suzanne von WITTELSBACH  +
    \-- Anna Maria von der PFALZ  (1561 - 1589)
            \                /-- William II (Landgrave) von HESSEN  +
            |         /-- Philip `the Magnanimous' (Landgrave) of HESSE
            |        /       \-- Anna von MECKLENBURG-SCHWERIN  +
            \-- Elizabeth of HESSE  (1539 - 1582)
                    \          /-- Georg `the Bearded' (Duke) of SAXONY  +
                    \-- Christine (Christina; de) WETTIN
```

The cult of St Catherine of Alexandria was well established in Sweden when construction started on St Catherine's Church at Visby in the mid-1200s. Katarina Church in Stockholm, named after Catherine Vasa, has been rebuilt twice since the 1600s.

On her 2018 visit to Sweden, Kate was almost certainly unaware that her children descend from Catherine Vasa and her aunt Katarina Vasa (died 1610), and also from Katarina of Sweden (died c1289) and Katerina Ingesdottir (died c1140).

St Catherine of Sweden (born 1332), a close friend of St Catherine of Siena, is the patron saint of difficult pregnancies and, if Kate was a Catholic, she would probably have prayed to the Swedish saint while suffering from hyperemesis gravidarum.

Note: Carl XVI Gustaf is a first cousin of Princess Mary of Denmark's mother-in-law (See next page).

St Catherine of Sweden

KATE AND PRINCESS MARY

NICKNAMED the 'style twins' because of their similar fashion tastes, former commoners Catherine Elizabeth Middleton and Mary Elizabeth Donaldson have a connection that was almost unthinkable when Mary was born in Australia in 1972 and when Kate was born in Berkshire in 1982.

In short, Mary's husband Prince Frederik has the same mitochondrial DNA as the Duchess of Cambridge's great-grandfather-in-law George VI and his grandmother, nicknamed 'Fat Mary', whose mother was the last Duchess of Cambridge.

Surprisingly, there is a long tradition of commoners marrying Scandinavian royals. Prince Frederik's mother Margrethe II married an unofficial French count in 1967; Harald V of Norway married commoner Sonja Haraldsen in 1968; and Carl XVI Gustaf of Sweden married Silvia Sommerlath in 1976. However, things were rather different in Britain.

By 2000, when Mary met Crown Prince Frederik in a pub during the Sydney Olympics, there was no impediment to their marriage. Meanwhile, Kate was on the verge of meeting Prince William at St Andrews University and, after the death of Princess Diana, he could marry virtually anyone he wanted.

The need for new blood in Denmark's royal family is not immediately evident in Margrethe II's ancestry chart. But like Carl XVI Gustaf, her first cousin through Margaret of Connaught (shown opposite), Margrethe descends from Katharina von Pfannberg through all of her great-great-grandparents.

In June 2022, Vogue journalist Gladys Lai explained why Kate and Mary draw so many comparisons: 'There's their backgrounds, for one, both women who married into their respective royal families and quickly carved out reputations for their eloquence and dedication to social issues over the course of their career.

'But Kate and Mary's approach to dress is another common denominator. Style aside, the royals share a wry understanding of the relationship between fashion, image and diplomacy. Their reputation as trendsetters emerges from this nexus, which they occupy effortlessly.'

The PEDIGREE of

Margrethe II Alexandrine Thorhildur Ingrid of DENMARK

Born: 1940

Husband/Partner: Henri Marie Jean Andre (Comte) de LABORDE de MONPEZAT

```
                              /-- Wilhelm SCHLESWIG-HOLSTEIN-SONDERBURG-.  +
                    /-- Christian IX OLDENBURG (King) of DENMARK
                    /        \-- Luise Caroline von HESSE-CASSEL  +
          /-- Frederick VIII Wilhelm Carl (King) of DENMARK
          /         \-- Louise Wilhelmina Fredericka Caroline A.J.  +
     /-- Christian X (King) of DENMARK  (1870 - 1947)
     |         \        /-- Charles XV BERNADOTTE (King) of SWEDEN  +
     |         \-- Louise Josephine (Princess) of SWEDEN & Norway
     |                  \-- Louise von NASSAU  +
  /-- Frederik IX (King) of DENMARK  (1899 - 1972)
  |         \                /-- Friedrich Franz II Alexander of MECKLENBUR.  +
  |         |       /-- Friedrich Franz III Paul Nikolaus Ernst of MECKLENBURG-SCHWERIN
  |         |       /        \-- Auguste Mathilde Wilhelmine REUSS SCHLEIZ-.  +
  |         \-- Alexandrine Augusta of MECKLENBURG-SCHWERIN
  |                  \        /-- Mikhail Nicolaievitch ROMANOV of RUSSIA  +
  |                  \-- Anastasia Mikhailovna (Grand Duchess) of RUSSIA
  /                           \-- Cacilie Auguste of BADEN  +
```

-Margrethe II Alexandrine Thorhildur Ingrid of DENMARK

```
  \                          /-- Oscar I BERNADOTTE of SWEDEN (Norway)  +
  |                 /-- Oscar II (King) of SWEDEN (& Norway)
  |                 /        \-- Josephine de BEAUHARNAIS  +
  |        /-- Gustav V (King) of SWEDEN  (1858 - 1950)
  |        /        \-- Sophia Wilhelmina Marianne of NASSAU  +
  |    /-- Gustav VI Adolph (King) of SWEDEN  (1882 - 1973)
  |    |   \               /-- Frederick I (ZAHRINGEN) von BADEN-HOCHBERG  +
  |    |   \-- Victoria (Sophie) von BADEN  (1862 - 1930)
  |    /              \-- Louise (of PRUSSIA) von HOHENZOLLERN  +
  \-- Ingrid Victoria (Princess) of SWEDEN
           \               /-- Albert Augustus Charles of SAXE-COBURG-GOTHA  +
           |     /-- Arthur William Patrick Albert von SAXE-COBURG-GOTHA
           |     /        \-- Victoria of HANOVER (Queen) of ENGLAND  +
           \-- Margaret (of CONNAUGHT) von SAXE-COBURG-GOTHA
```

According to familytreedna.com Margrethe II, pictured above with son Frederik, has haplogroup H inherited from Katherina Polyxene of Solms-Rodelheim who died in 1765. Other matrilineal descendants have included monarchs of Britain, Germany, Russia, Sweden, Norway, Belgium and The Netherlands, plus the Grand Duke of Luxembourg (See Page 23).

THE LAST DUCHESS OF CAMBRIDGE

PRINCE GEORGE'S great-great-grandfather George VI had an all-female bloodline from Katherina Polyxene through 'Fat Mary' of Cambridge whose sister-in-law Sarah Fairbrother (inset) should have been the last Duchess of Cambridge before Kate, and not Mary's mother, the beautiful Augusta of Hesse-Cassel (above).

Mary's brother Prince George inherited the dukedom from his father Prince Adolphus in 1850, ten years after he met Sarah, a popular actress who was the mother of two illegitimate children with different fathers.

In 1847, having borne two of George's children and pregnant with another, Sarah pressured the prince into marriage without permission from his first cousin Queen Victoria. Sarah could not use her husband's title and was known simply as Mrs FitzGeorge. Meanwhile, her husband maintained his relationship with Louisa Beauclerk and chose to be buried close to her grave.

Mary, who descended from Katharina von Pfannberg through all of her great-great-grandparents, was the mother of Mary of Teck who married the future George V after previously being engaged to his brother Albert Victor who died during an influenza outbreak in 1892. Kate's great-great-grandmother Harriet Lupton died just five days later (See A Coronavirus Connection, Page 152).

Like Elizabeth II and Charles III, Princess Augusta was a strong supporter of homeopathy and was patron of the hospital, now The Royal London Hospital of Integrated Medicine, founded by Dr Frederick Quin in 1849.

Note: There have been eight dukes of Cambridge but only three duchesses (See The Dukes Who Died Young, Page 162).

Mary Adelaide (Princess) of CAMBRIDGE

Born: Hanover 1833   Died: 1897 Surrey

HRH Charles's Great-Great-Grandmother.

Husband/Partner: Franz (Francis) (1st Duke) of TECK
Children: Mary (Princess) of TECK

```
                              /-- George I Louis HANOVER of ENGLAND  +
                       /-- George II Augustus (King) of ENGLAND
                      /         \-- Sophia Dorothea von BRUNSWICK-CELLE  +
               /-- Frederick Louis (Lewes) (Prince) of ENGLAND
              /            \-- Wilhelmina Charlotte Caroline ANSPACH of B.  +
         /-- George III (King) of ENGLAND
        |       \          /-- Frederick II (Duke) of SAXE-GOTHA  +
        |        \-- Augusta (Princess) von SACHSEN-GOTHA-ALTENBURG
        |       /            \-- Magdalena Augusta of ANHALT-ZERBST  +
  /-- Adolphus Frederick (Prince) of GREAT BRITAIN & Ireland
  |      \              /-- Adolphus Frederick II of MECKLENBURG-STRE.  +
  |       \     /-- Karl I (Duke) of MECKLENBURG-STRELITZ
  |       |    /       \-- Christiane Emilie Antonie of SCHWARZBURG-.  +
  |       \-- Sophia Charlotte (Charlotte Sophia) von MECKLENBURG-STRELITZ
```

-Mary Adelaide (Princess) of CAMBRIDGE

```
  |                /-- Friedrich II (Landgrave) of HESSEN-KASSEL
  |               /        \-- Dorothea Wilhelmine of SACHSEN-ZEITZ  +
  |       /-- Friedrich (III; Landgrave) of HESSE-CASSEL
  |      |      \         /-- George II Augustus (King) of ENGLAND  +
  |      |       \-- Mary HANOVER (Princess) of ENGLAND  (1723 - 1772)
  |      |      /          \-- Wilhelmina Charlotte Caroline ANSPACH of B.  +
  \-- Augusta Wilhelmina Louisa (Landgravine) of HESSE-CASSEL
         \           /-- Karl (Fuerst) von NASSAU-USINGEN  +
          |    /-- Karl Wilhelm (Prince) of NASSAU-USINGEN
          |   /        \-- Christiane Wilhelmine of SACHSEN-EISENACH  +
          \-- Caroline (Princess) of NASSAU-USINGEN
                 \        /-- Christian Karl Reinhard von LEININGEN  +
                  \-- Karoline Felizitas (Grafin) zu LEININGEN
                          \-- Katherina Polyxene of SOLMS-RODELHEIM  +
```

George V's wife Mary of Teck (far left) commissioned a replica of the famous Cambridge Lover's Knot Tiara given to her grandmother Augusta as a wedding gift in 1818. The replica was passed down to Elizabeth II, gifted to Princess Diana, and is now worn by Kate on special occasions.

THE ORDER OF THE DRAGON

THROUGH Elizabeth II's grandfather George V, and also Prince Philip's grandfather George I of Greece, Prince George and his siblings descend from alleged vampire Barbara of Cilly (circled above) who co-founded the Order of the Dragon in 1408.

Another member of the Order of the Dragon, based on the Order of St George founded about 80 years earlier by Charles I of Hungary, was George VI's ancestor Vlad the Impaler (See opposite).

Catherine of Valois' first husband Henry V, who met Barbara of Cillys' husband Zikmund of Bohemia in London in 1416, joined the Order of the Dragon around the same time that Zikmund joined the Order of the Garter which has similar associations with the dragon-slaying St George.

Like other matrilineal descendants of Katharina von Pfannberg, George I and George V - and their Russian relative Nicholas II - had the same mitochondrial DNA (haplogroup T) as Barbara of Cilly who, as shown opposite, was a granddaughter of Katarina Kotromanic, a relative of Katalin of Hungary (See chart on Page 39).

Nicholas II and George I's son Prince George of Greece got dragon tattoos in Japan about ten years after George V of England did the same (See Page 97).

Insignia of the Order of the Dragon featured a serpent with a St George cross on its back and its tail looped around its neck.

The PEDIGREE of

Barbara of CILLY

Born: abt. 1391 Died: 1451 Bohemia

Lady Diana's 16-Great Grandmother.

Husband/Partner: **Zikmund of BOHEMIA (Holy Roman EMPEROR)**
Child: **Eliska (Elisabeth) (Princess) of BOHEMIA**

```
        /-- Hermann I (Count) von CILLI (? - 1385)
        |        \        /-- Ulrich von WALSEE  +
        |         \-- Diemut von WALDSEE (? - 1353?)
       /               \-- Diemut von ROHRAU  +
    /-- Hermann II (Count) of CILLY-ORTENBURG (? - 1435)
    |    \              /-- Stjepan I KOTROMANIC (Ban) of BOSNIA  +
    |    |         /-- Stjepan II KOTROMANIC (King/Ban) of BOSNIA
    |    |        /       \-- Jelisaveta NEMANJIC (Regent) of SERBIA  +
    |    \-- Katarina KOTROMANIC (? - 1396+)
    |          \ | OR: Katarina KOTROMANIC [alt ped]  +
    |          |        /-- Kazimierz III (Prince) of INOWROCLAW  +
    |          \-- Elzbieta (Princess) of INOWROCLAW (? - 1343+)
   /                   | or: Doroteja VIDINSKA, q.v.
```

Barbara of CILLY

```
    \                /-- Heinrich IV (Count) von SCHAUNBERG  +
    |            /-- Heinrich V von SCHAUNBERG (? - by 1357)
    |           /       \-- Agnes (Baroness) von NEUHAUS  +
    |        /-- Heinrich VII von SCHAUNBERG (? - 1390)
    |        |    \        /-- Ulrich (d.J.) von TRUHENDINGEN  +
    |        |     \-- Anna von TRUHENDINGEN (? - 1331+)
    |        /            \-- Imagina von ISENBURG  +
    \-- Anna Elisabeth von SCHAUNBERG (? - by 1396)
         \ | OR: poss. not Bearer of T mtdna-Haplogroup  +
         |              /-- Albert III (II) von GORZ-LIENZ  +
         |          /-- Meinhard VI (VII) von GORZ (? - 1385+)
         |         /       \-- Offmei Utehild von MATSCH  +
         \-- Ursula von GORZ (? - 1383+)
              \        /-- Ulrich V of PFANNBERG  +
               \-- Katharina von PFANNBERG (? - 1375?)
```

VLAD THE IMPALER

VLAD DRACUL, the original 'Dracula', joined the Order of the Dragon and so did his son Vlad the Impaler (right) who had a mistress named Katharina Siegel. Charles III, who descends from Vlad through Katalin Perenyi, has joked about his 'stake' in Transylvania where he owns property.

In 2013, when Pippa Middleton was a major celebrity, a Romanian tourism advertising campaign included the slogan: 'Half of our women look like Kate. The other half, like her sister.'

MAD KING GEORGE'S DNA

GENETIC causes of George III's madness could be somewhere in his bloodlines from Catherine of Valois and Katharina von Pfannberg. And, almost certainly, inbreeding was a contributing factor.

According to a popular theory, King George (pictured above as St George) inherited porphyria from Catherine of Valois with a bloodline through James I who, coincidentally, had a separate all-female bloodline from Catherine of Valois' father Charles 'the Mad' through Catherine de Vendome and Catherine d'Artois (See chart on Page 111).

George III descended from James I, whose mother Mary Queen of Scots married her half-first cousin, and also through George I who married his first cousin. Like George III and George V, George I had an all-female bloodline from Katharina von Pfannberg (haplogroup T) and he also descended from Georg Guelph (shown opposite) who had an all-female bloodline from Katherina of Pomerania.

Incredibly, George III had bloodlines from Katharina von Pfannberg through all of his great-grandparents, five of whom were matrilineal descendants. And, to make matters worse, his maternal parents were first

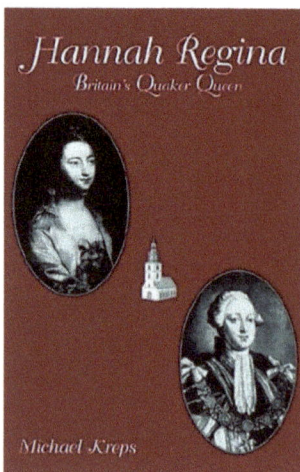

Hannah Regina
Britain's Quaker Queen

Michael Kreps

Did George III marry Hannah Lightfoot and have several children, including Catherine Ritso who married Dr James Dalton of the East India Company? If so, George III's marriage to Queen Charlotte was bigamous and all monarchs since him have been illegitimate.

George III (King) of ENGLAND

Born: Norfolk House 1738 **Died:** 1820 Windsor Castle

HRH Charles's 4-Great Grandfather.

Wife/Partner: Sophia Charlotte (Charlotte Sophia) von MECKLENBURG-STRELITZ

Children: Mary HANOVER (Princess) of GREAT BRITAIN & Ireland ; William IV Henry (King) of ENGLAND
Adolphus Frederick (Prince) of GREAT BRITAIN & Ireland ; Edward Augustus (Prince) of GREAT BRITAIN
Ernst August (King) von HANNOVER ; George IV (King) of ENGLAND ; Frederick (Duke) of YORK

```
                          /-- Georg GUELPH of BRUNSWICK (Calenberg) +
                      /-- Ernest Augustus I (1st Elector) of HANOVER
                      /          \-- Anna Eleonore of HESSE-DARMSTADT +
                  /-- George I Louis HANOVER (King) of ENGLAND
                  /          \-- Sophia WITTELSBACH +
              /-- George II Augustus (King) of ENGLAND  (1683 - 1760)
              |      \          /-- George William (Duke) von BRUNSWICK-LUNEBURG +
              |       \-- Sophia Dorothea von BRUNSWICK-CELLE  (1666 - 1726)
              /              \-- Eleonore DESMIER (Princess) d' OLBREUSE +
          /-- Frederick Louis (Lewes) (Prince) of ENGLAND
          |   \              /-- Albrecht V (Margrave) of BRANDENBURG-ANSBACH +
          |    |          /-- Johann Friedrich (Margrave) of BRANDENBURG-ANSBACH
          |    |      /          \-- Sophie Margarethe of OETTINGEN-OETTINGEN +
          |    \-- Wilhelmina Charlotte Caroline von ANSPACH of BRANDENBURG
          |         \          /-- Johann Georg I (Duke) of SACHSEN-EISENACH +
          |          \-- Eleonore (Princess) of SACHSEN-EISENACH
          /              \-- Johannette (Princess) of SAYN-WITTGENSTEIN +
```

- George III (King) of ENGLAND

```
          |              /-- Friedrich I (Duke) of SACHSEN-GOTHA  (1646 - 1691)
          |          /          \-- Elisabeth Sofie of SACHSEN-ALTENBURG +
          |      /-- Frederick II (Duke) of SAXE-GOTHA  (1676 - 1732)
          |      |   \          /-- August (Duke) of SACHSEN-WEISSENFELS +
          |      |    \-- Magdalena Sibylla (Princess) of SACHSEN-WEISSENFELS
          |      /              \-- Anna Marie Dorothea of MECKLENBURG-SCHWERIN +
          \-- Augusta (Princess) von SACHSEN-GOTHA-ALTENBURG
                  \          /-- Johann (VI; Fuerst) of ANHALT-ZERBST +
                  |      /-- Karl Wilhelm (Fuerst) of ANHALT-ZERBST
                  |      /          \-- Sophia Auguste of SCHLESWIG-HOLSTEIN +
                  \-- Magdalena Augusta (Princess) of ANHALT-ZERBST
```

cousins through all-female bloodlines from Anna Marie Dorothea of Mecklenburg-Schwerin whose parents were first cousins through all-female bloodlines from Christine of Hesse.

In an online article titled 'Mitochondrial dysfunction psychiatric morbidity' (2015), Dr Lilach Toker and Professor Galila Agam wrote: 'Numerous studies provide evidence for the involvement of mitochondrial dysfunction in psychiatric disorders... One possibility is that mitochondrial dysfunction induces vulnerability of brain cells to other disease-specific factors... Alternatively, mitochondrial dysfunction can be an epiphenomenon related to frequent characteristics of psychiatric patients such as smoking, drug abuse, and disturbed eating and sleeping.'

Tests on a sample of George III's hair revealed high levels of arsenic, a known trigger of porphyria, which probably contaminated the antimony administered by his doctors.

WIKIPEDIA

MITOCHONDRIAL MARRIAGES

THE HAPLOGROUPS of Catherine of Foix and Katharina von Pfannberg were united in 1863 when the future Edward VII (haplogroup H) married Alexandra of Denmark (haplogroup T) in St George's Chapel at Windsor Castle.

As shown above, Queen Victoria, still mourning the death of Prince Albert 16 months earlier, watched her son's wedding from the Oriel Window built by Henry VIII (haplogroup U) for his first wife Catherine of Aragon.

Beneath the Oriel Window is the tomb of Katherine Swynford's great-grandson Edward IV (haplogroup J) and Elizabeth Woodville (haplogroup U) who secretly married in 1464 (inset above). Edward IV's tomb may also hold the remains of the Princes in the Tower who were allegedly murdered on the orders of their uncle Richard III (See Page 106).

Edward IV's funeral was held in St George's Chapel in 1483, 22 years after he seized the throne from Catherine of Valois' son Henry VI (who was also buried in the chapel).

In 1547, Henry VIII's last wife Catherine Parr observed his funeral from the Oriel Window. Henry VIII's remains are in a vault under the chapel and so are those of George III (haplogroup T), whose madness may have been caused by porphyria transmitted from Catherine of Valois.

After Queen Victoria's funeral service in the chapel in 1901 she was buried alongside Prince Albert in the royal mausoleum on the nearby Frogmore estate.

The future William V and Queen Catherine will almost certainly be buried in St George's Chapel near her most recent royal ancestor, Edward IV, and many of William's relatives, including his great-great-great-grandparents, Edward VII and Alexandra.

The PEDIGREE of

George V WINDSOR (King) of ENGLAND

Born: London 1865 Died: 1936 Sandringham

HRH Charles's Great-Grandfather.

Wife/Partner: Mary (Princess) of TECK

Children: Mary (Princess) of GREAT BRITAIN & Ireland ; George (1st Duke) of KENT ; Edward VIII
George VI Albert WINDSOR (King) of ENGLAND ; Henry William Frederick Albert‚

```
                              /-- Ernest Frederick of SAXE-COBURG  +
                     /-- Francis (Franz) Frederick (Duke) of SAXE-COBURG
                     /       \-- Sophia Antonia of BRUNSWICK  +
            /-- Ernst I (Duke) of SAXE-SAALFELD-COBURG
            /       \-- Augusta Caroline Sophia of REUSS-EBERSDORF  +
      /-- Albert Augustus Charles (Prince) of SAXE-COBURG-GOTHA
      |     \       /-- Emil (Duke) of SACHSEN-GOTHA  +
      |      \-- Luise (Dorothea) (Duchess) of SAXE-GOTHA
      /              \-- Louise Charlotte of MECKLENBURG-SCHWERIN  +
/-- Edward VII of SAXE-COBURG-GOTHA (King) of ENGLAND
|      \              /-- George III (King) of ENGLAND
|      |     /-- Edward Augustus (Prince) of GREAT BRITAIN & Ireland
|      |     /       \-- Sophia Charlotte von MECKLENBURG-STRELITZ  +
|      \-- Victoria of HANOVER (Queen) of ENGLAND
|              \      /-- Francis Frederick (Duke) of SAXE-COBURG  +
|              \-- Victoria (Duchess) of SAXE-SAALFELD-COBURG
/                      \-- Augusta Caroline Sophia of REUSS-EBERSDORF  +
```

- George V WINDSOR (King) of ENGLAND

```
 \                    /-- Karl Anton of SCHLESWIG-HOLSTEIN  +
 |              /-- Friedrich Karl Ludwig (Duke) of SCHLESWIG
 |              /       \-- Friederike of DOHNA-SCHLOBITTEN  +
 |       /-- Wilhelm (Duke) von SCHLESWIG-HOLSTEIN-SONDERBURG-GLUCKSBURG
 |       /       \-- Friederike Amalie (Countess) von SCHLIEBEN  +
 /-- Christian IX OLDENBURG (King) of DENMARK
 |       |       \      /-- Karl (Charles) (Landgraf) von HESSE-CASSEL  +
 |       |       \-- Luise (Charlotte) Caroline (Landgravine) von HESSE-CASSEL
 |       |              \-- Louise OLDENBURG (Princess) of DENMARK  +
 \-- Alexandra Caroline Marie (Princess) of DENMARK
         \              /-- Friedrich (III; Landgrave) of HESSE-CASSEL  +
         |       /-- Wilhelm (X; Landgrave) of HESSE-CASSEL
         |       /      \-- Caroline (Princess) of NASSAU-USINGEN  +
         \-- Louise Wilhelmina Fredericka Caroline A. J. (Princess) of HESSE-CASSEL
```

THE KING WITH A DRAGON TATTOO

WHEN the future George V (haplogroup T) got a dragon tattoo (inset) in Japan in 1882 he was almost certainly unaware that nearly all of his great-great-great grandparents had bloodlines from his matrilineal ancestor Katharina von Pfannberg through Order of the Dragon co-founder Barbara of Cilly.

Russia's Nicholas II (haplogroup T) had a dragon tattoo and so did two of Prince Philip's relatives: his uncle Prince George of Greece and grandfather Prince Louis of Battenberg.

ON H.M. KING GEORGE V.

Descent of Mountbatten

Louis II Grand Duke of Hesse

Louis III Grand Duke of Hesse, 1st son

Countess Julia Hauke "Princess of Battenberg" — Morganatic marriage — Prince Alexander of Hesse, 3rd son

Prince Karl of Hesse, 2nd son

Queen Victoria

"Prince Louis of Battenberg" Louis Mountbatten 1st Marquess of Milford Haven

Louis IV Grand Duke of Hesse — Princess Alice, 3rd daughter

King Edward VII

1st cousin once removed

Princess Victoria of Hesse

King George V

George Mountbatten 2nd Marquess of Milford Haven

Louis Mountbatten, 1st Earl Mountbatten of Burma

Princess Alice of Battenberg — Prince Andrew of Greece

King George VI

Prince Philip, Duke of Edinburgh — 3rd cousins — Queen Elizabeth II

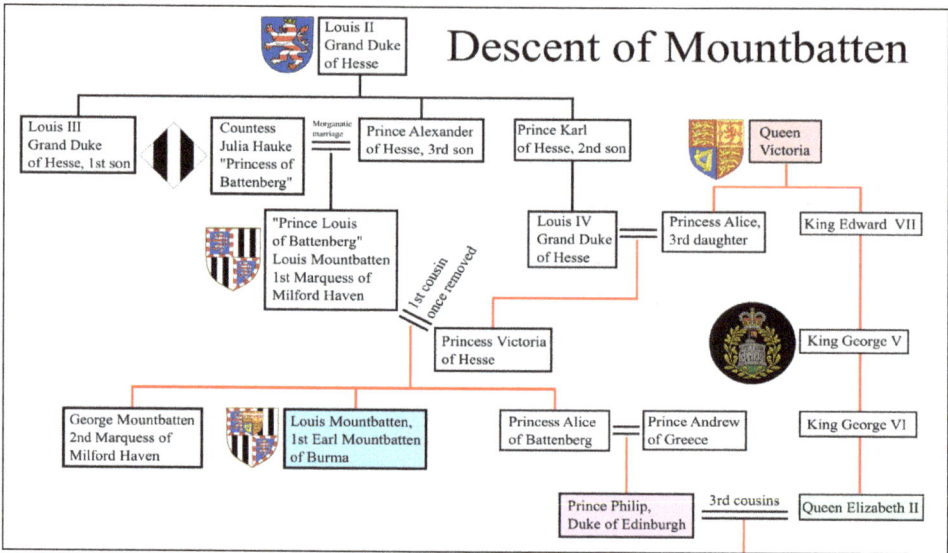

BADGES OF BASTARDY

OFFICIALLY, as shown above, Kate's children descend from Grand Duke Louis (Ludwig) II through Prince Alexander of Hesse and Prince Louis of Battenberg, not to be confused with his son Louis Mountbatten after whom Kate's youngest son was named. If so, as shown opposite, Prince Alexander's parents would have been first cousins through Ludwig IX and quadruple second cousins through Ludwig VIII.

The good news for Prince George and his siblings is that Prince Alexander was undoubtedly sired by Wilhelmine Louise's Swiss lover Auguste Louis von Senarclens-Grancy whose grandmother, great-grandmother and great-great-grandmother were named Catherine. The bad news is that Kate's children also descend from Alexander's legitimate half-brother Prince Karl (shown above) who did have the bloodlines shown opposite.

To make matters worse, Prince Karl married his quadruple second cousin Maria Elisabeth of Prussia; their son Louis IV of Hesse married Princess Alice, daughter of Queen Victoria and her first cousin Prince Albert; and Princess Alice's daughter Princess Irene married her first cousin Prince Henry of Prussia. Four of Princess Alice's descendants inherited haemophilia (See chart on Page 123).

Surprisingly, Ludwig IX, his father Ludwig VIII, and grandfather Ernst Ludwig (shown opposite),

While four of Prince Alexander's descendants inherited haemophilia from his daughter-in-law Princess Beatrice, he reduced the risk of further genetic disasters by being born illegitimate and marrying non-royal Julia Hauke.

THE PEDIGREE OF

Alexander (Prince) of HESSE AND BY RHINE

Born: Darmstadt 1823 **Died:** 1888 Darmstadt
HRH Charles's Great-Great-Grandfather.

Wife/Partner: Julie Therese Salomea (Grafin) von HAUCKE (HAUKE)
Children: Louis (Prince; H.S.H.) of BATTENBERG (MOUNTBATTEN) ; Henry Maurice (Prince) of BATTENBERG

```
                              /-- Ernst Ludwig of HESSE-DARMSTADT  +
                      /-- Ludwig VIII (Landgrave) of HESSE-DARMSTADT
                 /         \-- Dorothea Charlotte of BRANDENBURG-AN.  +
            /-- Ludwig IX (Landgrave) of HESSEN-DARMSTADT
           /          \-- Charlotte Christine Magdalene Johanna H.  +
     /-- Ludwig (Louis) I (Grand Duke) of HESSE AND BY RHINE
    |      \        /-- Christian III of (PFALZ) ZWEIBRUCKEN  +
    |       \-- Karoline Henriette Christine Louisa von der PFALZ-ZWEIBRUCKEN
    |            \-- Karoline (Princess) of NASSAU-SAARBRUCKEN  +
 /-- Ludwig (Louis) II (Grand Duke) of HESSE AND BY RHINE
 |     \ | or: Auguste Louis von SENARCLENS-GRANCY (q.v.)
 |      |                 /-- Ludwig VIII (Landgrave) of HESSE-DARMSTADT  +
 |      |      /-- Georg Wilhelm (Landgrave) of HESSEN-DARMSTADT
 |      |     /          \-- Charlotte Christine Magdalene Johanna H.  +
 |      \-- Louise (Landgravine) of HESSE-DARMSTADT
 |            \        /-- Christian Karl Reinhard von LEININGEN  +
 |             \-- Maria (Grafin) of LEININGEN-DAGSBURG
 |                  \-- Katherina Polyxene of SOLMS-RODELHEIM  +
```

Alexander (Prince) of HESSE AND BY RHINE

```
 \                    /-- Karl Wilhelm of BADEN-DURLOCH  +
 |          /-- Friedrich Magnus (Margrave of) BADEN-DURLOCH
 |         /         \-- Magdalene Wilhelmine WURTTEMBERG  +
 |      /-- Karl Friedrich ZAHRINGEN (Grand Duke) of BADEN
 |     /          \-- Anna Charlotte Amalie von NASSAU-DIETZ  +
 |  /-- Karl Ludwig (Hereditary Prince) of BADEN
 |  |      \         /-- Ludwig VIII (Landgrave) of HESSE-DARMSTADT  +
 |  |       \-- Carolina Louisa (Princess) of HESSE-DARMSTADT
 |  /          \-- Charlotte Christine Magdalene Johanna H.  +
 \-- Wilhelmine Louise (Margravine) von BADEN
       \                /-- Ludwig VIII (Landgrave) of HESSE-DARMSTADT  +
        |      /-- Ludwig IX (Landgrave) of HESSEN-DARMSTADT
        |     /          \-- Charlotte Christine Magdalene Johanna H.  +
        \-- Amalie Friederike (Landgravine) of HESSE-DARMSTADT
              \        /-- Christian III of (PFALZ) ZWEIBRUCKEN  +
               \-- Karoline Henriette Christine Louisa von der PFALZ-ZWEIBRUCKEN
```

had the same mitochondrial DNA (haplogroup T) through all-female bloodlines from Katharina von Pfannberg.

The Battenberg title created for Prince Alexander's morganatic wife Julia Hauke was changed to Mountbatten in 1917. Prince Philip's adopted surname passed to Prince Charles and Princess Anne but, after their mother ascended the throne in 1952, any future children had to be surnamed Windsor.

Eight years later, while Elizabeth II was pregnant with Prince Andrew, a lawyer named Edward Iwi claimed that Windsor would be a 'badge of bastardy' because only illegitimate children take their mother's name. (Ironically, Prince Philip had done exactly that.) It was quickly decided that future male descendants would be Mountbatten-Windsors.

In 2012, Kate used her Mountbatten-Windsor surname when she and Prince William sued a French newspaper which published topless photos of her.

THE MAN IN THE IRON MASK

LOUIS XIV, portrayed by Richard Chamberlain in the 1977 version of *The Man in the Iron Mask*, exemplifies the 'Catherine Code' because of his many matrilineal connections to Catherine of Foix, six children by his double first cousin, plus a dozen or more bastards by his many mistresses.

As shown opposite, the Sun King's oldest son had only two great-grandmothers, Maria de Medici and Margaret Habsburg. And because Maria and Margaret both had all-female bloodlines from Catherine of Foix, all of Louis de Viennois' grandparents — Louis XIII, Anne Habsburg, Philip IV and Elizabeth de Bourbon — had the same mitochondrial DNA.

Louis XIII, Louis XIV, Louis de Viennois, Louis of Burgundy and Louis XV had separate all-female bloodlines from Catherine of Foix. In other words, five consecutive namesakes had the same mtDNA (haplogroup H) and Y-DNA (haplogroup R), a sequence that is probably unique.

Alexander Dumas' classic novel was based on a true story. However, the unfortunate inmate was most likely a valet named Eustache Dauger and not an identical twin brother of Louis XIV. The real prisoner did not wear a mask all the time and when he did, it was made of velvet, not iron.

This sculpture on Paris' Hotel de Beauvais reputedly depicts one-eyed Catherine Bellier who deflowered Louis XIV when he was aged 15. Another mistress, Catherine Gramont, allegedly slept with Louis' first cousin Henrietta of England, sister of Charles II, who had the same mtDNA through Catherine of Foix.

The PEDIGREE of

Louis de VIENNOIS (Dauphin) of FRANCE

Born: 1661 Died: 1711

Wives/Partners: Marie Anna Christine (Princess) of BAVARIA
Children: Louis (Duke) of BURGUNDY ; Philip (Felipe) V de BOURBON (King) of SPAIN

```
                      /-- Antoine (Anton) de BOURBON  +
            /-- Henry IV BOURBON (King) of FRANCE  (1553 - 1610)
           /          \-- Jeanne d' ALBRET (Queen) de NAVARRE  +
    /-- Louis XIII BOURBON (King) of FRANCE  (1601 - 1643)
   |       \          /-- Francesco (Francis) I de MEDICI of ITALY  +
   |        \-- Maria de MEDICI (MEDICIS)
   |                  \-- Joanna HABSBURG (Archduchess) of AUSTRIA  +
/-- Louis XIV (King) of FRANCE  (1638 - 1715)
|  |                  /-- Philip II HAPSBURG (King) of SPAIN  +
|  |       /-- Philip III (King) of SPAIN
|  |      /           \-- Anna Maria HABSBURG von OESTERREICH  +
|  \-- Anne (HABSBURG) d' AUTRICHE
|          \          /-- Charles von STYRIA (Archduke) of AUSTRIA  +
|           \-- Margaret HABSBURG von OESTERREICH  (1584 - 1611)
/                     \-- Maria Anna von BAYERN  +
```

Louis de VIENNOIS (Dauphin) of FRANCE

```
   \                  /-- Philip II HAPSBURG (King) of SPAIN  +
   |       /-- Philip III (King) of SPAIN
   |      /           \-- Anna Maria HABSBURG von OESTERREICH  +
   |-- Philip IV HABSBURG (King) of SPAIN
   |  |   \           /-- Charles von STYRIA (Archduke) of AUSTRIA  +
   |  |    \-- Margaret HABSBURG von OESTERREICH  (1584 - 1611)
   |  /                \-- Maria Anna von BAYERN  +
   \-- Marie-Therese HABSBURG (Princess) of SPAIN
      \               /-- Antoine (Anton) de BOURBON  +
       |   /-- Henry IV BOURBON (King) of FRANCE  (1553 - 1610)
       |  /           \-- Jeanne d' ALBRET (Queen) de NAVARRE  +
       \-- Elizabeth de BOURBON  (1603 - 1663)
          \           /-- Francesco (Francis) I de MEDICI of ITALY  +
           \-- Maria de MEDICI (MEDICIS)
                      \-- Joanna HABSBURG (Archduchess) of AUSTRIA  +
```

Dubbed the 'Rose Line' in *The Da Vinci Code,* and wrongly conflated with the Saint-Sulpice sundial line, the Paris Meridian borders the Louvre, one of Louis XIV's royal residences. Coincidentally, the line also runs near the presumed birthplace of his matrilineal ancestor Catherine of Foix (See map on Page 78).

The Paris Meridian was replaced by Greenwich in 1884; William Glyn-Jones' online article The Meridian and the Hexagram (2008) has more.

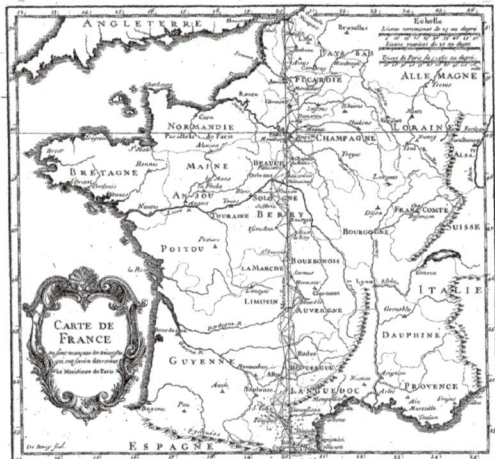

CARTE DE FRANCE

FABPEDIGREE.COM

CATHERINE THE GREAT'S BASTARD

P RINCESS CHARLOTTE probably knows by now that she shares her birthday (2nd May) with Catherine the Great, from whom she descends through Prince Philip, but Charlotte is almost certainly unaware that her great-grandfather had the same mitochondrial DNA as the Russian tsarina and her illegitimate son.

Catherine the Great's real first name was Sophie; she was Prussian, not Russian; and her parents were double second cousins through Marie Elizabeth of Saxony (shown opposite) who descended from Catherine of Lancaster through a sister of Catherine of Aragon. The most recent common ancestor of Kate and the tsarina is probably Catherine of Lancaster's grandfather Peter the Cruel who had only four great-grandparents (See chart on Page 35).

Through his philandering bisexual father Prince Andrew of Greece, Prince Philip descended from Catherine the Great's possibly illegitimate son Paul I whose bastard half-brother Alexey Bobrinski was sired by Catherine's lover Count Grigory Orlov. Paul I had a mistress named Catherine and so did his grandson Alexander II, whose illegitimate daughter Princess Catherine Yurievskaya died in 1959.

Prince Philip's mitochondrial DNA (haplogroup H) inherited from Catherine of Foix helped scientists to identify the skeletons of Nicholas II's wife and their children (See The Last of the Romanovs, Page 120).

The last kings of Romania and Greece, Michael I (died 2017) and his first cousin Constantine II (died 2023), descended from Catherine the Great and, like her and Prince Philip, they both had all-female bloodlines from Catherine of Foix.

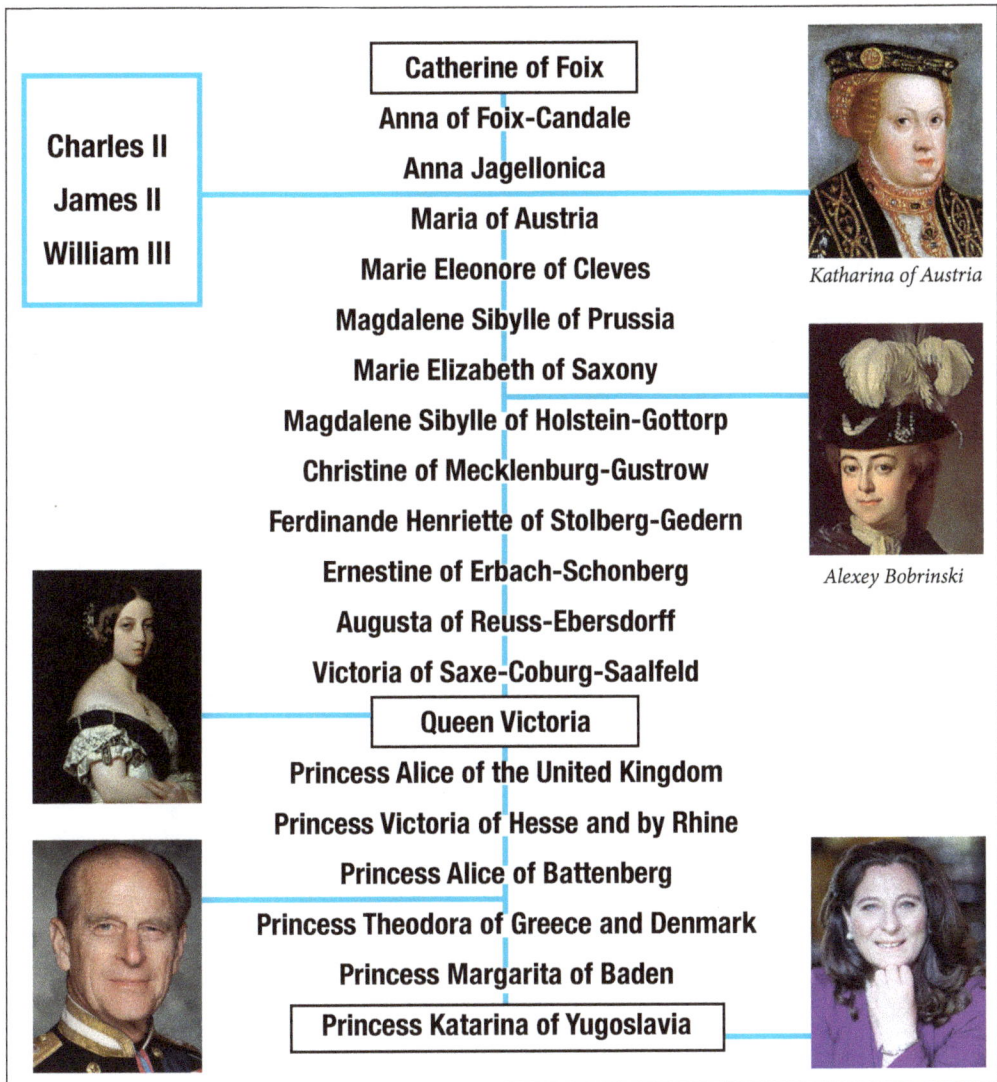

Charles II
James II
William III

Catherine of Foix
Anna of Foix-Candale
Anna Jagellonica
Maria of Austria
Marie Eleonore of Cleves
Magdalene Sibylle of Prussia
Marie Elizabeth of Saxony
Magdalene Sibylle of Holstein-Gottorp
Christine of Mecklenburg-Gustrow
Ferdinande Henriette of Stolberg-Gedern
Ernestine of Erbach-Schonberg
Augusta of Reuss-Ebersdorff
Victoria of Saxe-Coburg-Saalfeld
Queen Victoria
Princess Alice of the United Kingdom
Princess Victoria of Hesse and by Rhine
Princess Alice of Battenberg
Princess Theodora of Greece and Denmark
Princess Margarita of Baden
Princess Katarina of Yugoslavia

Katharina of Austria

Alexey Bobrinski

(Michael's bloodline was through Queen Victoria and Constantine's bloodline was through Victoria's half-sister Feodora.)

Michael I and Constantine II attended Kate's wedding in 2011. So did Crown Princess Katherine of Yugoslavia, not to be confused with Princess Katarina of Yugoslavia who is a matrilineal descendant of Catherine of Foix through Prince Philip's sister Princess Theodora. In 2013, Katarina succeeded Prince Michael of Kent as patron of the Society of Genealogists.

Edward VII's wife Queen Alexandra (haplogroup T) and Prince Philip's mother Princess Alice of Battenberg (haplogroup H) both received Russia's prestigious Order of St Catherine (inset opposite) which was founded for Catherine the Great's grandmother-in-law Catherine I.

Note: Catherine the Great's imperialism inspired Vladimir Putin's annexation of Crimea and his subsequent invasion of Ukraine so it was not surprising that her statue in Odessa was torn down in late December 2022.

RICHARD III'S REMAINS

DNA tests on the remains of Richard III, pictured above on his white courser at the Battle of Bosworth, confirmed his all-female bloodline from Katherine Swynford but they also cast doubt on his all-male bloodline from Katherine's father-in-law Edward III.

Y-DNA from relatives of the current Duke of Beaufort, who claims an all-male bloodline from Edward III, did not match Richard III's remains. It is well known that Charles Somerset KG was illegitimate. However, that did not affect the all-male bloodline so there must have been at least one other 'false paternity event', most likely between Edward III and Richard III.

As mentioned previously, the prime candidate is Richard III's grandfather Richard of Conisburgh (shown opposite) from whom Kate is descended through an illegitimate daughter of Edward IV.

Prince William and Kate have nothing to worry about because the line of succession has been secure since the 1701 Act of Settlement. However, Richard III's dubious bloodline is embarrassing for the royal family which claims direct descent from William the Conqueror through Edward IV's legitimate daughter Elizabeth of York who married Henry VII. (Note Henry's dragon banner in the picture above).

Based on research by Susan Fern, and analysis of Richard III's skull found under a Leicester car park in 2012, the fatal blow was probably delivered with a poleaxe, which was the favourite weapon of Welsh nobleman Rhys ap Thomas.

Kate's children have a possible bloodline from ap

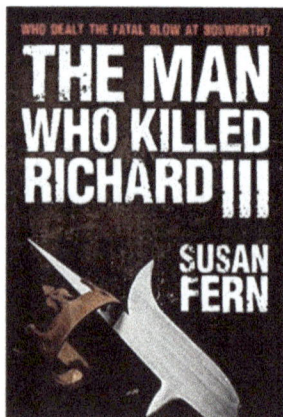

WHO DEALT THE FATAL BLOW AT BOSWORTH?

THE MAN WHO KILLED RICHARD III

SUSAN FERN

Katherine MANNERS

HRH Charles's 14-Great Aunt. Lady Diana's 12-Great Grandmother.

Husband/Partner: <u>Robert (Sir; of Everingham) CONSTABLE</u>
Children: <u>Everilda CONSTABLE</u> ; <u>Marmaduke CONSTABLE</u> ; <u>Barbara CONSTABLE</u>

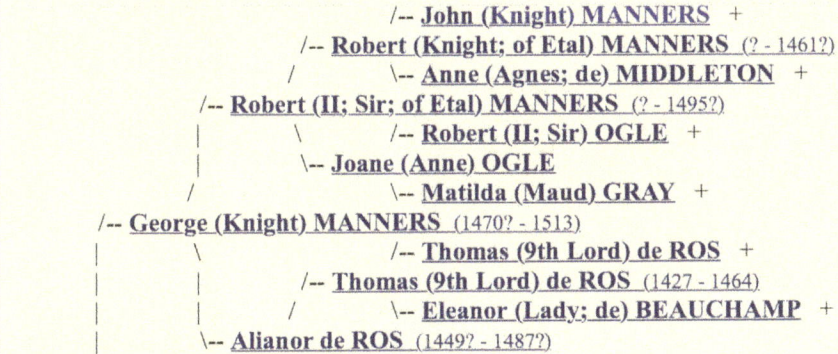

```
                             /-- John (Knight) MANNERS  +
                    /-- Robert (Knight; of Etal) MANNERS  (? - 1461?)
                   /            \-- Anne (Agnes; de) MIDDLETON  +
        /-- Robert (II; Sir; of Etal) MANNERS  (? - 1495?)
        |          \            /-- Robert (II; Sir) OGLE  +
        |           \-- Joane (Anne) OGLE
        |          /            \-- Matilda (Maud) GRAY  +
   /-- George (Knight) MANNERS  (1470? - 1513)
   |       \                    /-- Thomas (9th Lord) de ROS  +
   |       |            /-- Thomas (9th Lord) de ROS  (1427 - 1464)
   |       |           /            \-- Eleanor (Lady; de) BEAUCHAMP  +
   |       \-- Alianor de ROS  (1449? - 1487?)
   |
```

Katherine MANNERS

```
   |      /-- Thomas (Sir) ST. LEGER  (Kent 1419? - 1483 Devon)
   |      |          \            /-- James (of Rainham) DONNET  +
   |      |           \-- Margery DONNETT  (? - 1442+)
   |      |          /            \-- Margery CHEYNE  +
   \-- Anne ST. LEGER  (1476 - 1526)
           \                    /-- Richard PLANTAGENET of CONISBURGH
           |            /-- Richard PLANTAGENET-YORK
           |           /            \-- Anne de MORTIMER  +
           \-- Anne PLANTAGENET  (1439 - 1476)
                   \                    /-- Ralph I NEVILL (de NEVILLE)  +
                    \-- Cecily (Lady) NEVILLE  (1415 - 1495)
                            \-- Joan (Lady; de) BEAUFORT  +
```

Thomas through Katherine Wiriot and an illegitimate daughter of Charles II.

In 2016 the London *Daily Telegraph* gleefully reported that Benedict Cumberbatch, who played Richard III in *The Hollow Crown* TV series, was the king's third cousin 16 times removed, neglecting to mention that many millions of people around the world have closer cousinships through Katherine Swynford's illegitimate offspring.

MATCHING MITOCHONDRIA

THE all-female bloodline from Katherine Swynford to Wendy Duldig (right) helped scientists to identify Richard III's rare mitochondrial DNA (haplogroup J1c2c). Wendy's bloodline is through Richard III's sister Anne Plantagenet and Katherine Manners' granddaughter Katherine Crathorne.

Through Anne Middleton (shown above), Prince William has a bloodline from a brother-in-law of Kate's ancestor Sir William Plumpton (See chart on Page 143).

UNIVERSITY OF LEICESTER

FABPEDIGREE.COM

THE PRINCES IN THE TOWER

CATHERINE WOODVILLE (Wydeville), daughter-in-law of Catherine of Valois and sister-in-law of Edward IV, probably knew a lot of royal secrets, including the identity of one of Britain's most infamous murderers.

As well as being an aunt of the so-called Princes in the Tower, Edward V and Richard of Shrewsbury, Catherine Woodville's first husband Henry Stafford, the Duke of Buckingham, was one of the prime suspects in their murder. (Another suspect was Prince William's ancestor John Howard, the Duke of Norfolk, husband of Catherine Moleyns.)

Henry Stafford, who allegedly acted on Richard III's orders, was executed for treason in November 1483, just five months after Catherine's brother Anthony Woodville suffered the same fate at Pontefract Castle. Fourteen years earlier, Anthony's brother John Woodville, best known for his 'diabolical' marriage to the much older Catherine Neville (See Page 194), was executed with their father Richard Woodville after the Battle of Edgecote.

Catherine Woodville's second husband was Catherine of Valois' son Jasper Tudor who, like his brother Edmund (father of Henry VII), was illegitimate because their mother's marriage to Owen Tudor was illegal. Jasper and Edmund were raised by Katherine de la Pole at Barking Abbey (See Page 216).

Another Catherine connected to the Princes in the Tower was Katherine Swynford's great-great-grand-

Kate's children are descended from Catherine Woodville through Katherine Pole's great-granddaughter Catherine Hastings (See Hypothetical Queen Catherines, Page 46).

Catherine WYDEVILLE (WYDVILLE)

Born: by 1458   Died: 1497 (or 1525+)

HRH Charles's 14-Great Grandmother. Lady Diana's 13-Great Grandmother.

Husbands/Partners: Henry (K.G.) STAFFORD ; Jasper (of HATFIELD) TUDOR ;
Richard (K.G.) WINGFIELD

Children: Elizabeth (Lady) STAFFORD ; Henry (K.G.) STAFFORD ;
Anne (Lady of Buckingham) STAFFORD ; Edward (K.G.) STAFFORD

```
                        /-- John (of Grafton) de WYDEVILLE (1341? - 1403+)
                   /         \-- Elizabeth LYONS  +
           /-- Richard (Sir; of Grafton) WOODVILLE
           /         \-- Isabel GODARD
     /-- Richard (K.G.) WYDEVILLE (1408? - 1469 Kenilworth)
     |     \             /-- John BODULGATE  +
     |     |        /-- Thomas BODULGATE (BITTLESGATE) (Devon ? - 1390?)
     |     |        |       \ | (skip this generation?)
     |     |        /       \-- Mary (de) BEAUCHAMP  +
     |     \-- Elizabeth (Mary Joan) BEDLISGATE (1385? - 1448+)
     |            \        /-- John (Sir; de) BEAUCHAMP  +
     |            \-- Joan (Mary) BEAUCHAMP (Somersets. ? - 1385?)  (skip?)
     |                     \-- Joan de BRUDEPORT  +
```

- Catherine WYDEVILLE (WYDVILLE)

```
     \                       /-- Jean (I; Count) de LUXEMBOURG  +
     |                  /-- Guy (Count) de LUXEMBOURG
     |                  /       \-- Alice (Countess?) de FLANDERS  +
     |            /-- Jean II (John) de LUXEMBOURG
     |            /       \-- Maude (Mathilde) de CHATILLON  +
     |      /-- Pierre I (Peter) de LUXEMBOURG (1390? - 1433)
     |      |     \        /-- Louis d' ENGHIEN  +
     |      |      \-- Marguerite d' ENGHIEN (ENGHIEN) (1357? - 1393)
     |      /                \-- Giovanna di SAN SEVERINO  +
     \-- Jacquette de LUXEMBOURG (1416? - 1472)
```

daughter Catherine Gordon, wife of Perkin Warbeck who inspired an uprising against Henry VII after claiming he was Richard of Shrewsbury. Kate's children have a bloodline from Catherine Gordon's namesake niece through Katherine Forbes of Echt.

Frustratingly, the late John Ashdown-Hill, whose genealogical research helped scientists to identify Richard III's skeleton, was prevented from DNA testing the remains of two children found under a staircase in the Tower of London in 1674. The remains are currently inside a monument in Westminster Abbey.

Ashdown-Hill had a DNA sample from opera singer Elizabeth Roberts (right) who, like the princes, has an all-female bloodline from Jacquette de Luxembourg (haplogroup U). Elizabeth's bloodline is through Katherine Pole and Margaret Woodville.

PONTEFRACT CONNECTIONS

RICHARD II, brother-in-law of Catherine of Valois, was allegedly murdered at Pontefract Castle (above) in 1400 by Katherine Swynford's son Thomas Swynford (haplogroup J) on the orders of Katherine's stepson Henry IV who was Catherine of Valois' father-in-law.

The headless bodies of Kate's ancestor Richard of York and his brother-in-law Richard Neville (haplogroup J) were held at the castle in 1460 (See Vengeance at Wakefield, Page 190). And in 1483, Catherine Woodville's brother Anthony Woodville (haplogroup U) — uncle and guardian of the Princes in the Tower who had the same mitochondrial DNA — was executed at Pontefract on the orders of Richard III (haplogroup J) whose illegitimate children John and Katherine may have been born there.

Catherine Howard, fifth wife of Henry VIII (haplogroup U), committed adultery with her distant cousin Thomas Culpepper at Pontefract in 1541 and she was executed the following year. The castle inspired Harrenhall in *Game of Thrones*.

The Catherine Code

Part II

PRINCESS KATHERINE'S DNA

BRITAIN'S first Princess Katherine (above far right), whose deafness may have been congenital, had the same mitochondrial DNA as James I and also Charles 'the Mad', father of Britain's first Queen Catherine who may have transmitted porphyria to James I through a sister of Henry VIII.

On fabpedigree.com James I has an all-female bloodline through Catherine de Vendome, Catherine d'Artois and Catherine de Courtenay. However, according to wikitree.com and geni.com Catherine d'Artois was the daughter of Blanche de Bretagne (shown opposite) and not her granddaughter.

Blanche was a daughter of Princess Katherine's sister Beatrice Plantagenet and so was Marie de Dreux who was Charles the Mad's matrilineal ancestor. Arthur de Dreux (shown opposite) was Marie's and Blanche's brother.

After Princess Katherine died aged three, her grief-stricken father Henry III commissioned an elaborate shrine in Westminster Abbey. Katherine's brother Edward I (above far left) went to even greater lengths to commemorate his wife Eleanor of Provence, erecting twelve large stone crosses across England, including one at St Katherine's Priory outside Lincoln.

Edward I, Henry VII and Charles I had short-lived daughters named Catherine and James II had two (See Page 162).

Mary Queen of Scots and her son James I, who may both have suffered from porphyria or some other genetic disorder, had the same mitochondrial DNA as Catherine of Valois' father Charles 'the Mad'.

The PEDIGREE of

Catherine de VENDOME

Died: 1412

Lady Diana's 16-Great Grandmother.

Husband/Partner: John I (Count) de la MARCHE
Children: Louis II de VENDOME ; Charlotte of BOURBON-VENDOME ; Jean de BOURBON

```
      /-- Bouchard V (VI; Comte) de VENDOME  (? - 1354)
      |        \         /-- Philippe II de MONTFORT-L'AMAURY  +
      |        |        /       / or: poss. Simon de MONTFORT
      |        \-- Eleanore de MONTFORT-L'AMAURY  (? - 1338+)
      /                 \-- Jeanne de LEVIS  +
  /-- Jean VI (Comte) de VENDOME  (? - 1364)
  |        \              /-- Jean II de DREUX  +
  |        |        /-- Arthur de DREUX  (1262 - 1312)
  |        |        /       \-- Beatrice PLANTAGENET of ENGLAND  +
  |        \-- Alix de BRETAGNE  (1297? - 1377)
  |                 \         /-- Robert IV (I) de DREUX  +
  |                 \-- Jolanta MONTEFORTE  (1263? - 1322)
  /                          \-- Beatrice de MONTFORT  +
```

-Catherine de VENDOME

```
  |                 /-- Jean (I) de PONTHIEU (Comte) d' AUMALE
  |                /        \-- Laure de MONTFORT  +
  |        /-- Jean II de PONTHIEU  (? - 1341?)
  |        |        \         /-- Amaury II de MEULAN  +
  |        |        \-- Ide de MEULLENT (de BEAUMONT)  (? - 1324)
  |        /                  \-- Marguerite (de BEAUMONT; Dame) de NEUFBOURG  +
  \-- Jeanne de PONTHIEU  (? - 1376)
           \              /-- Phillipe I (Count) d' ARTOIS  +
           |        /-- Robert III d' ARTOIS  (1287? - 1342)
           |        |      \ / (skip this generation!)
           |        /       \-- Blanche de BRETAGNE  +
           \-- Catherine d' ARTOIS  (1292+ - 1368?)
                    \         /-- Charles III de VALOIS  +
                    \-- Jeanne de VALOIS  (1304? - 1363?)  (skip!)
                             \-- Catherine I de COURTENAY  +
```

CATHERINES OF CONSTANTINOPLE

SUPPOSEDLY born on St Catherine's feast day in 1274, Catherine de Courtenay was titular empress of Constantinople but spent most of life in exile, as did her daughter Catherine of Valois (right), not to be confused with Charles the Mad's daughter. Both Catherines had the same mtDNA as Princess Katherine through all-female bloodlines from Beatrice de Savoie (died 1266).

Kate's children descend from Catherine de Courtenay through Katharine von Waldeck-Eiseberg, a matrilineal ancestor of Queen Victoria's father Prince Edward.

CATHERINE OF VALOIS' CURSES

BRITAIN'S royal family may have been doubly cursed by the first Queen Catherine, pictured above with Henry V at their wedding. The first curse seemingly had almost immediate consequences, but the second curse possibly lasted more than 500 years (See Prince William's Porphyria, Page 114).

It started in December 1421 when Catherine of Valois gave birth to the future Henry VI (inset above) at Windsor Castle, allegedly defying her superstitious husband who apparently believed a famous 'prophecy': 'Henry born at Monmouth shall small time reign and much get, but Henry born at Windsor shall long reign and lose all.'

The Monmouth-born Henry V died aged 35 in August 1422, less than seven years after his famous victory at Agincourt, and Henry VI's long reign was blighted by the loss of his French kingdom and the Wars of the Roses. The younger Henry was allegedly murdered in 1471 after Edward IV won the Battle of Tewkesbury.

From August 1453, Henry VI was catatonic for nearly 18 months and it seems obvious that he inherited something bad from his French grandfather Charles VI, nicknamed 'the Mad'. Charles' insane

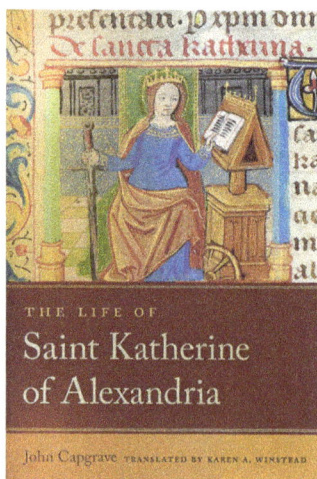

According to Michael M Baker's 2005 University of Tennessee thesis titled Piety and Politics, John Capgrave's fictional biography of St Catherine of Alexandria (c1445) was 'Yorkist propaganda' because it criticised Catherine of Valois' son Henry VI.

The PEDIGREE of

Catherine de VALOIS

Born: Paris 1401 Died: 1437 London

Lady Diana's 14-Great Grandmother.

Husbands/Partners: Owen (Sir) TUDOR ; Henry V PLANTAGENET (King) of ENGLAND
Children: Edmund TUDOR ; Jasper (of HATFIELD) TUDOR ; Henry VI PLANTAGENET

```
                            /-- Philip VI (King) of FRANCE  +
                    /-- Jean (John) II `the Good' de VALOIS  (1319 - 1364)
                   /            \-- Joanna (Queen?) of BURGUNDY  +
           /-- Charles V `the Wise' de VALOIS
          |         \            /-- Jan de LUXEMBOURG (King) of BOHEMIA  +
          |          \-- Jutte Bonne (Bona) of LUXEMBURG
          |                      \-- Eliska (Elisabeth) (Princess) of BOHEMIA  +
      /-- Charles VI `the Beloved' de VALOIS
     |    |         \            /-- Louis (I) `le Boiteux' de CLERMONT  +
     |    |          /-- Pierre (Peter) I (Duke) de BOURBON
     |    |         /            \-- Marie de HAINAULT  +
     |    \-- Jeanne (Joan) de BOURBON  (1338 - 1377)
     |              \            /-- Charles III de VALOIS  +
     |               \-- Isabelle de VALOIS  (1313? - 1383)
```

- Catherine de VALOIS

```
     \            /-- Ludwig IV `der Bayrisch' von WITTELSBACH  +
     |    /-- Stephen II `mit der Hafte' von WITTELSBACH
     |    |         \-- Beatrix von SCHLESIEN-GLOGAU  +
     |    |         / OR: poss. Beatrix SCHLESIEN-GLOGAU [alt ...  +
     |    /-- Stefan III `the Magnificent' (Duke) of BAVARIA
     |    |    \         /-- Frederick (I; II; III; King) of SICILY  +
     |    |     \-- Elizabeth (Princess) of SICILY  (1309? - 1349)
     |    |              \-- Eleanor (d' ANJOU) of SICILY & NAPLES  +
     \-- Isabelle of BAVARIA  (1371 - 1435)
          \         /-- Stefano (di) VISCONTI  +
          |    /-- Bernabas (Lord/Duke) of MILAN (& etc.)
          |    /         \-- Valentina DORIA  +
          \-- Taddea VISCONTI  (Milan 1351? - 1381 Munich)
```

relatives included his mother Jeanne; one of her brothers; their father Pierre de Bourbon; and his father Louis 'le Boiteux' de Clermont (shown above), from whom Kate's children have bloodlines through Catherine de Bourbon (died 1427) and Katherina de Bourbon (died 1469).

According to medical experts, the madnesses of Charles VI and Henry VI were quite different. Charles weirdly believed he was made of glass and had well-documented violent episodes, unlike his pious grandson whose breakdown may have been caused by stress. It is possible that both monarchs had schizophrenia; another theory is that they had familial sarcoidosis.

Catherine of Valois died in 1437 soon after giving birth to a short-lived daughter reportedly named Margaret Catherine. The Queen's body lay in state at St Katherine's by the Tower and, bizarrely, her remains were later exposed to the public for several centuries in Westminster Abbey.

Note: Catherine of Valois was related to Caterina Sforza through her great-aunt CaterinaVisconti (See chart on Page 67).

PRINCE WILLIAM'S PORPHYRIA

WHILE the likelihood that Kate's children have inherited porphyria from Catherine of Valois is almost zero, the notion is not completely ludicrous because Prince William of Gloucester (above) was diagnosed with the disorder in 1968. He died in a plane crash four years later and it has been speculated that he lost control of his plane while having a seizure.

Prince William, after whom Kate's husband was named, descended from Catherine of Valois through all of his great-grandparents, including Edward VII, who had a bloodline through George III, and Franz of Teck who had a bloodline through Frederick William I (father of Frederick the Great).

Given that both King George and Frederick William had porphyria-like symptoms, including violent stomach pains and erratic behaviour, it is noteworthy that they had the same mitochondrial DNA (haplogroup T) through all-female bloodlines from Katharina von Pfannberg.

Through Katalin Perenyi and Katalin Forgach de Ghymes, Prince William's grandmother Mary of Teck descended from Vlad the Impaler who may have had porphyria because it was common in Transylvania. Symptoms of the disorder possibly explain folklore about avoiding sunlight, drinking blood and eating garlic for protection. Vampirism has also been linked to rabies and tuberculosis.

This 'penny dreadful' published in 1845 introduced several tropes of vampire fiction including sharpened teeth, hypnotic powers and supernatural strength.

THE PEDIGREE OF

Prince William of GLOUCESTER

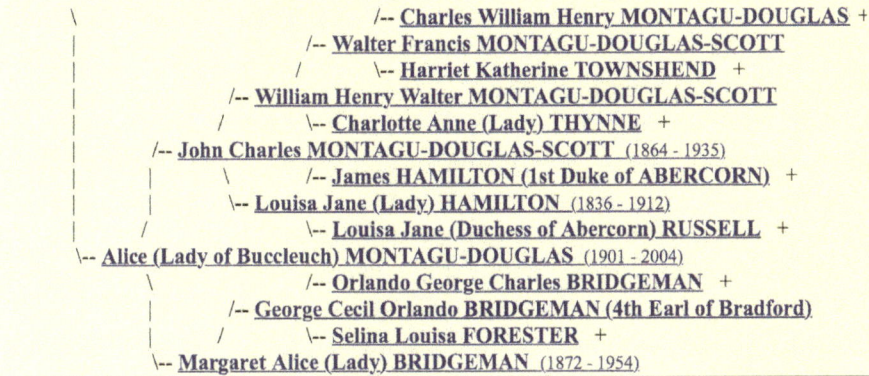

Born: 1941 Died: 1972

HRH Charles' First Cousin 1x removed

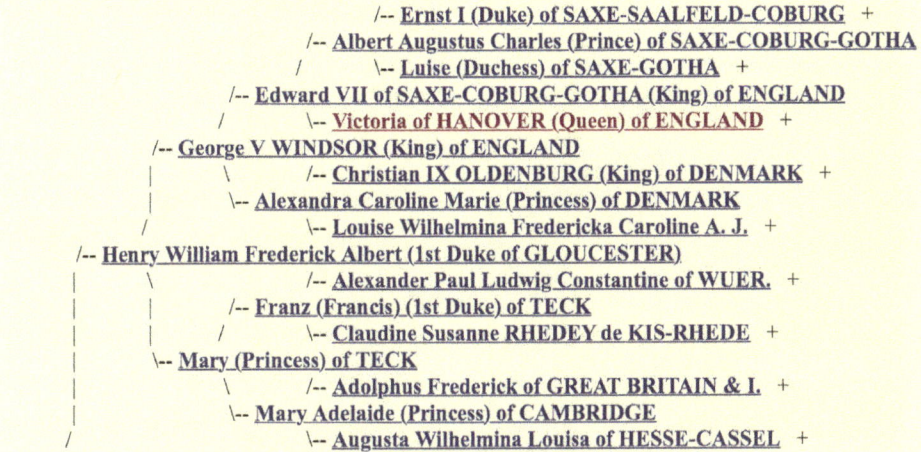

```
                              /-- Ernst I (Duke) of SAXE-SAALFELD-COBURG  +
                  /-- Albert Augustus Charles (Prince) of SAXE-COBURG-GOTHA
                  /         \-- Luise (Duchess) of SAXE-GOTHA  +
        /-- Edward VII of SAXE-COBURG-GOTHA (King) of ENGLAND
        /         \-- Victoria of HANOVER (Queen) of ENGLAND  +
    /-- George V WINDSOR (King) of ENGLAND
    |    \              /-- Christian IX OLDENBURG (King) of DENMARK  +
    |     \-- Alexandra Caroline Marie (Princess) of DENMARK
    /              \-- Louise Wilhelmina Fredericka Caroline A. J.  +
/-- Henry William Frederick Albert (1st Duke of GLOUCESTER)
|    \                        /-- Alexander Paul Ludwig Constantine of WUER.  +
|     |            /-- Franz (Francis) (1st Duke) of TECK
|     |            /    \-- Claudine Susanne RHEDEY de KIS-RHEDE  +
|     \-- Mary (Princess) of TECK
|              \           /-- Adolphus Frederick of GREAT BRITAIN & I.  +
|               \-- Mary Adelaide (Princess) of CAMBRIDGE
/                          \-- Augusta Wilhelmina Louisa of HESSE-CASSEL  +
```

Prince William of GLOUCESTER

```
    \                        /-- Charles William Henry MONTAGU-DOUGLAS  +
    |            /-- Walter Francis MONTAGU-DOUGLAS-SCOTT
    |            /    \-- Harriet Katherine TOWNSHEND  +
    |    /-- William Henry Walter MONTAGU-DOUGLAS-SCOTT
    |    /        \-- Charlotte Anne (Lady) THYNNE  +
    /-- John Charles MONTAGU-DOUGLAS-SCOTT  (1864 - 1935)
    |    |            /-- James HAMILTON (1st Duke of ABERCORN)  +
    |    |    \-- Louisa Jane (Lady) HAMILTON  (1836 - 1912)
    |    /        \-- Louisa Jane (Duchess of Abercorn) RUSSELL  +
\-- Alice (Lady of Buccleuch) MONTAGU-DOUGLAS  (1901 - 2004)
         \                /-- Orlando George Charles BRIDGEMAN  +
          |    /-- George Cecil Orlando BRIDGEMAN (4th Earl of Bradford)
          |    /    \-- Selina Louisa FORESTER  +
          \-- Margaret Alice (Lady) BRIDGEMAN  (1872 - 1954)
```

CATHERINE CONNECTIONS

THROUGH Margaret Bridgeman (shown above) and Lady Catherine Grey (right), Prince William of Gloucester was descended from Mary Tudor whose sister Margaret may have transmitted a genetic disorder from Catherine of Valois (See chart on Page 13).

It is possible that Henry VII, Mary Tudor, two of her sons (both named Henry), and Catherine Grey all died from tuberculosis. As well, one of Mary's brothers and two of her nephews may have had cystic fibrosis.

During the 1890s, when many Americans linked tuberculosis to vampirism, the body of Mercy Brown of Rhode island was exhumed so that rituals could be performed. Around the same time, four of Kate's Harrison ancestors died from tuberculosis (See Page 157).

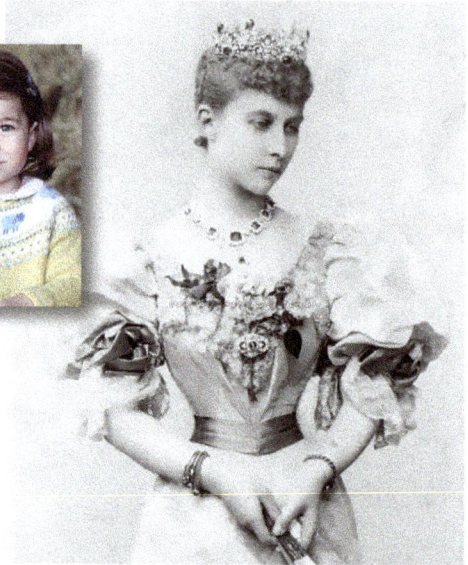

DOUBLY CURSED CHARLOTTES?

TWO of Princess Charlotte's namesakes, who may have inherited porphyria from Catherine of Valois, were descended from Katharina von Pfannberg through all of their great-great-great-grandparents.

And, like Prince William of Gloucester, Princess Charlotte of Wales (above left) and Princess Charlotte of Prussia (above right) may have been doubly cursed because of their bloodlines through two suspected sufferers, George III and Frederick William I (shown opposite as Friedrich Wilhelm I).

In a 1999 article, Claus A Pierach of the University of Minnesota described Frederick William I's symptoms — abdominal pains, erratic behaviour and discoloured urine — and concluded: 'We propose that (he) suffered from an inducible porphyria.'

Like his uncle and father-in-law George I, Frederick William I married one of his first cousins; so did George III's maternal grandmother Magdalena Augusta; and so did George IV, father of the charismatic Princess Charlotte of Wales who married Queen Victoria's uncle Leopold. Porphyria may have contributed to Charlotte death after she delivered a stillborn boy.

Queen Victoria and her first cousin Prince Albert were the maternal grandparents of Princess Charlotte of Prussia and Kaiser Wilhelm II, leader of Germany during World War I, who

The notoriously bad-tempered Frederick William I (left) was a great-great-grandson of James I and a nephew of George I.

Charlotte Augusta GUELPH (Princess of WALES)

Born: 1796   Died: 1817   d. in childbirth

Husbands/Partners: Leopold I (1st King) of the BELGIANS

```
                                    /-- George I Louis HANOVER of ENGLAND  +
                            /-- George II Augustus (King) of ENGLAND
                           /           \-- Sophia Dorothea von BRUNSWICK-CELLE  +
                    /-- Frederick Louis (Lewes) (Prince) of ENGLAND
                   /           \-- Wilhelmina Charlotte Caroline ANSPACH of B.  +
            /-- George III (King) of ENGLAND
           |       \            /-- Frederick II (Duke) of SAXE-GOTHA  +
           |        \-- Augusta (Princess) von SACHSEN-GOTHA-ALTENBURG
           |                    \-- Magdalena Augusta of ANHALT-ZERBST  +
     /-- George IV (King) of ENGLAND  (1762 - 1830)
    |      \                /-- Adolphus Frederick II of MECKLENBURG-STRE.  +
    |       |       /-- Karl I (Duke) of MECKLENBURG-STRELITZ
    |       |      /           \-- Christiane Emilie Antonie of SCHWARZBURG-.  +
    |       \-- Sophia Charlotte (Charlotte Sophia) von MECKLENBURG-STRELITZ
    |                \          /-- Ernst Frederick of SACHSEN-HILDBURGHAUSEN  +
    |                 |      /    / OR: Ibrahim HANNIBAL (Prince) of ETHIOPIA
    |                 \-- Elizabeth-Albertine of SAXE-HILDBURGAUSEN
    /                           \-- Sofie Albertine (Countess) of ERBACH  +
```

- Charlotte Augusta GUELPH (Princess of WALES)

```
    |                 /-- Charles BEVERN (Duke) of BRUNSWICK-WOLFENBUTTEL
    |                /           \-- Antoinette Amelia of BRAUNSCHWEIG-BLANKEN.  +
    |       /-- Charles II William Ferdinand BEVERN (Duke) of BRUNSWICK-WOLFENBUTTEL
    |      |       \            /-- Friedrich Wilhelm I HOHENZOLLERN of PRUSSIA  +
    |      |        \-- Philippine Charlotte of PRUSSIA
    |      /                    \-- Sophia Dorothea von HANOVER  +
    \-- Caroline Amelia Elizabeth BEVERN of BRUNSWICK
            \                /-- George II Augustus (King) of ENGLAND  +
            |       /-- Frederick Louis (Lewes) (Prince) of ENGLAND
            |      /           \-- Wilhelmina Charlotte Caroline ANSPACH of B.  +
            \-- Augusta Friederike GUELPH (von HANNOVER)
```

had an all-male bloodline from Frederick William I (See next page).

In 1996, DNA tests on the remains of Princess Charlotte and her daughter Feodora showed they probably had a rare form of porphyria. After years of ill health, Feodora committed suicide in 1945.

Another descendant of Charles 'the Mad' through Frederick William I was Mad King Ludwig of Bavaria whose maternal grandmother Maria married her first cousin. Ludwig was also descended from Joanna 'the Mad' and may have inherited a predisposition to schizophrenia.

Kate's children have a bloodline through Prince Philip's schizophrenic mother Princess Alice of Battenberg who was descended from Frederick William I's son Augustus, not to be confused with his brother August who married his niece.

Princess Charlotte of Wales inherited haplogroup T from Katharina von Pfannberg; her Prussian namesake inherited haplogroup H from Catherine of Foix (See next page); and George III's allegedly black wife Queen Charlotte was a matrilineal descendant of Katharine von Waldeck-Eiseberg (See Page 248).

Note: The current Princess Charlotte is the first British princess to maintain her place in the line of succession after the birth of a younger brother.

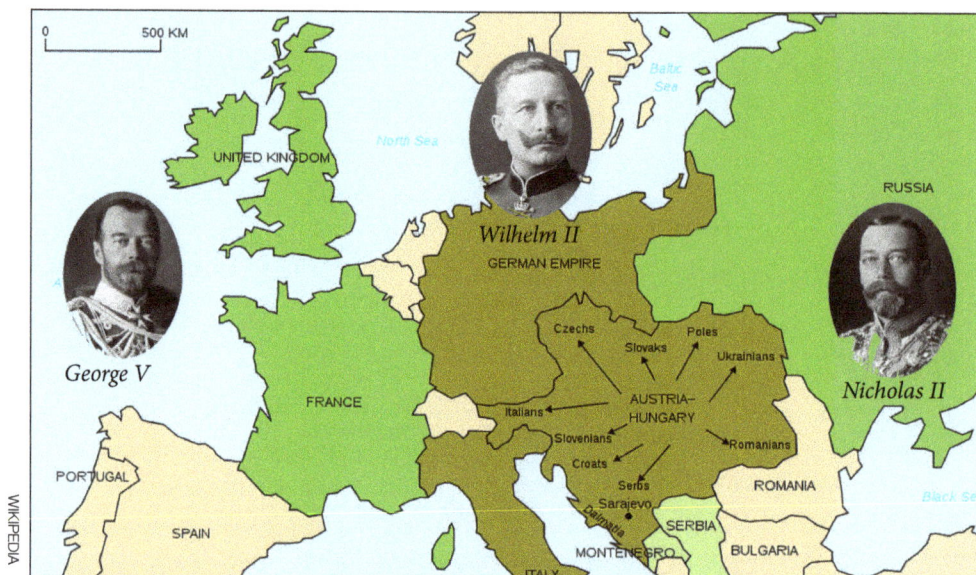

WILLY, NICKY AND GEORGE

THE ancestry chart of Kaiser Wilhelm II, brother of Princess Charlotte of Prussia, is remarkable because every single person shown opposite had an astonishing number of bloodlines from Katharina von Pfannberg.

Unlike their first cousin George V, and his first cousin Nicholas II, Wilhelm and Charlotte did not have an all-female bloodline from Katharina von Pfannberg (haplogroup T). But, through Queen Victoria, Wilhelm and his sister were matrilineal descendants of Catherine of Foix (haplogroup H), and so was their first cousin Alexandra who was Nicholas II's wife.

These cousinships were hugely significant during World War I which, as Miranda Carter has detailed in several books, sometimes resembled a family feud.

As mentioned previously, Princess Charlotte and Wilhelm II were descended from Katharina von Pfannberg through all of their great-great-great-grandparents; George V had Pfannberg bloodlines through all of his great-great-grandparents; and Nicholas II would have been similarly connected if his grandmother Maria von Hessen had not been illegitimate. (Kate's children are descended from Maria's illegitimate brother Prince Alexander of Hesse and by Rhine.)

Regardless of whether Wilhelm II inherited something bad from Catherine of Valois through George III and/or Frederick William I, from whom Wilhelm had an all-male bloodline, there is no doubt that the kaiser had several disorders. He probably did not have porphyria like his sister, but he was apparently bipolar and definitely a malignant narcissist.

Shortly before the start of World War I, Wilhelm II accused his dead uncle Edward VII of launching the conflict to humiliate and destroy him. 'Even after his death, Edward VII is still stronger than I,' Wilhelm wrote.

Several years later, after George V changed the name of the royal house to

The PEDIGREE of

Wilhelm II (EMPEROR) of the GERMAN REICH

Born: 1859   Died: 1941

Wife/Partner: Augusta Victoria of SCHLESWIG-HOLSTEIN
Children: Viktoria Luise (Princess) of PRUSSIA ; Wilhelm (Crown Prince) of PRUSSIA

```
                              /-- Augustus William HOHENZOLLERN  +
                      /-- Friedrich Wilhelm II (King) of PRUSSIA
                     /        \-- Louise Amelia of BRAUNSCHWEIG-WOLFEN.  +
              /-- Friedrich Wilhelm III (King) of PRUSSIA
             /        \-- Friederike (Princess) of HESSEN-DARMSTADT  +
      /-- Wilhelm I (EMPEROR) of the GERMAN REICH
     |        \        /-- Karl II of MECKLENBURG-STRELITZ  +
     |         \-- Luise Augusta (Duchess) of MECKLENBURG-STRELITZ
     /              \-- Friederike Karoline Luise of HESSEN-DARMS.  +
  /-- Friedrich III (EMPEROR) of the GERMAN REICH
 |        \              /-- Karl August (Grand Duke) von SACHSEN-WEIMAR  +
 |         |      /-- Karl Friedrich (Grand Duke) von SACHSEN-WEIMAR
 |         |     /        \-- Luise von HESSEN-DARMSTADT  +
 |          \-- Marie Luise Augusta Catharina von SACHSEN-WEIMAR
 |                     \        /-- Paul I ROMANOV (CZAR) of All The RUSSIAS  +
 |                      \-- Maria Pawlowna ROMANOWA  (1786 - 1859)
 /                              \-- Sophie Dorothea (Duchess) of WUERTTEMBERG  +
```

- Wilhelm II (EMPEROR) of the GERMAN REICH

```
 |                      /-- Ernst I (Duke) of SAXE-SAALFELD-COBURG
 |              /        \-- Augusta Caroline Sophia of REUSS-EBERSDORF  +
 |      /-- Albert Augustus Charles (Prince) of SAXE-COBURG-GOTHA
 |     |        \        /-- Emil (Duke) of SACHSEN-GOTHA  +
 |     |         \-- Luise (Dorothea) (Duchess) of SAXE-GOTHA
 |     /              \-- Louise Charlotte of MECKLENBURG-SCHWERIN  +
  \-- Victoria Adelaide Marie Luise von SACHSEN-COBURG-GOTHA
           \              /-- George III (King) of ENGLAND  +
           |      /-- Edward Augustus (Prince) of GREAT BRITAIN & Ireland
           |     /        \-- Sophia Charlotte von MECKLENBURG-STRELITZ  +
            \-- Victoria of HANOVER (Queen) of ENGLAND
                    \        /-- Francis Frederick (Duke) of SAXE-COBURG  +
                     \-- Victoria (Duchess) of SAXE-SAALFELD-COBURG
                              \-- Augusta Caroline Sophia of REUSS-EBERSDORF  +
```

Windsor, Wilhelm II jokingly referred to Shakespeare's play as *The Merry Wives of Saxe-Coburg-Gotha.*

Like George V and Nicholas II, who both had dragon tattoos, Wilhelm II had numerous bloodlines from Barbara of Cilly who co-founded the Order of the Dragon (See Page 92). And until Wilhelm's appointment was annulled in 1915, the three cousins belonged to Britain's Order of the Garter.

Kate's maternal great-grandfather Stephen Goldsmith survived World War I but three of Kate's Lupton great-great uncles died on the Western Front.

THE LAST OF THE ROMANOVS

THE REMAINS of Nicholas II and his family could not have been identified without DNA samples from matrilineal descendants of Catherine of Foix and Katharina von Pfannberg.

A grave containing the skeletons of the tsar, his wife Alexandra, and three of their daughters, was found in Yekaterinburg in the late 1970s but there was no DNA testing until after the Soviet Union fell in 1991. The remains of Alexey Romanov and one of his sisters, possibly Anastasia, were found in a separate grave in 2007.

Identification of the tsarina's remains depended on a sample from Prince Philip who inherited the same mtDNA (haplogroup H) through an all-female bloodline from Queen Victoria. Nicholas II's remains were identified from a sample provided by Tatiana Sfiris' mother Xenia Sheremeteva who inherited haplogroup T from the tsar's sister, also named Xenia.

Officially, Anastasia and her siblings descended from Katharina von Pfannberg through nearly all of their great-great-grandparents, with two bloodlines though Ludwig II. However, Maria von Hessen (shown opposite) was, like Prince Philip's great-grandfather Prince Alexander of

The Church on the Blood in Yekaterinburg, named after Catherine I, was built on the site of the Ipatiev house in which the Romanovs were executed in 1918. Their remains are now in St Catherine's Chapel in Peter and Paul Cathedral in St Petersburg.

The PEDIGREE of

Anastasia ROMANOV (Grand Duchess) of RUSSIA

Born: 1901   Died: 16 Jul 1918 executed by Bolsheviks

```
                              /-- Paul I ROMANOV (CZAR) of All The RUSSIAS  +
                          /-- Nicholas (Nikolaj) I (CZAR) of All The RUSSIAS
                     /         \-- Sophie Dorothea of WUERTTEMBERG  +
                 /-- Alexander (Aleksandr) II ROMANOV (CZAR) of RUSSIA
                /              \-- Charlotte HOHENZOLLERN (Princess) of PRUSSIA  +
           /-- Alexander III ROMANOV (CZAR) of RUSSIA  (1845 - 1894)
           |     \            /-- prob. Auguste Louis von SENARCLENS-GRANCY  +
           |      |      /      / OR: poss. Ludwig II of HESSE AND BY RHINE  +
           |      |     /  \-- Maria von HESSEN  (1824 - 1880)
           /       \-- Wilhelmine Louise (Margravine) von BADEN  +
      /-- Nicholas (Nikolia) II Alexandrovich ROMANOV (last CZAR) of RUSSIA
      |     \                /-- Wilhelm SCHLESWIG-HOLSTEIN-SONDERBURG-GLUC.  +
      |      |          /-- Christian IX OLDENBURG (King) of DENMARK
      |      |     /      \-- Luise Caroline von HESSE-CASSEL  +
      |       \-- Maria Sophie Friederike Dagmar OLDENBURG
```

- Anastasia ROMANOV (Grand Duchess) of RUSSIA

```
      |                 /-- Karl Wilhelm Ludwig (Prince) of HESSE AND BY RHINE
      |           /       \-- Wilhelmine Louise (Margravine) von BADEN  +
      |      /-- Ludwig IV (Grand Duke) of HESSE AND BY RHINE
      |      |     \          /-- Frederick Wilhelm Karl (Prince) of PRUSSIA  +
      |      |      \-- Maria Elisabeth Karoline Victorie (Princess) of PRUSSIA
      |       /          \-- Maria Anna (Landgravine) of HESSE-HOMBURG  +
       \-- Alexandra Fedorovna von HESSEN  (1872 - 16/7/1918)
            \              /-- Ernst I (Duke) of SAXE-SAALFELD-COBURG  +
            |        /-- Albert Augustus Charles (Prince) of SAXE-COBURG-GOTHA
            |     /      \-- Luise (Dorothea) (Duchess) of SAXE-GOTHA  +
             \-- Alice Maud Mary (Princess) of GREAT BRITAIN & Ireland
                  \          /-- Edward Augustus of GREAT BRITAIN & I.  +
                   \-- Victoria of HANOVER (Queen) of ENGLAND
```

Hesse, undoubtedly sired by Auguste von Senarclens-Grancy. (It is also possible that Nicholas II's patrilineal ancestor Paul I was a bastard son of Catherine the Great.)

Like his first cousin George V, Nicholas II got a dragon tattoo, probably unaware that they both had the same mtDNA as Barbara of Cilly who co-founded the Order of the Dragon. Nicholas II, who was born in a Year of the Dragon (1868), also belonged to the Order of the Double Dragon which was founded by the Qing dynasty.

The 1956 film *Anastasia* starring Ingrid Bergman was inspired by Anna Anderson whose claim to be the youngest Romanov daughter was disproved by DNA evidence. (Coincidentally, Bergman was named after Sweden's Princess Ingrid who inherited haplogroup H from Katherina Polyxene.)

Note: Another mystery was solved in 2015 after a 72-year-old Russian man died alone in Katherine in Australia's Northern Territory. He was eventually identified as Leonid Kulikovsky, grandson of Nicholas II's sister Olga.

QUEEN VICTORIA'S BAD BLOOD

BECAUSE at least ten descendants of Queen Victoria and her first cousin Prince Albert inherited haemophilia, it has long been presumed that the so-called 'royal disease' is linked to inbreeding. While that may be partly true, about one third of cases result from spontaneous mutations.

Queen Victoria's mutation probably originated in her middle-aged father Prince Edward. He and his wife, also named Victoria, were not closely related but they were both descended from Katharina von Pfannberg through nearly all of their great-grandparents.

Haemophilia spread to other European royals through Victoria's offspring, including her granddaughter Alexandra who married Nicholas II of Russia. They and their children were executed by the Bolsheviks in Yekaterinburg (named after Catherine I) in 1918.

Ninety years later, DNA from Alexandra's cousin Prince Philip, both matrilineal descendants of Catherine of Foix (haplogroup H), enabled scientists to identify the remains of Alexey Romanov and one of his sisters.

As shown opposite, Queen Victoria's youngest son Prince Leopold had haemophilia and two his sisters, Alice and Beatrice, were carriers.

Queen Victoria's last surviving great-granddaughter with haplogroup H, Princess Katherine of Greece and Denmark (died 2007), was lucky to avoid the four genetic disorders — haemophilia, porphyria, schizophrenia and epilepsy — which afflicted her royal cousins.

Haemophilia in the descendants of Queen Victoria

Queen Victoria (1819-1901)

Princess Alice of the United Kingdom (1843-1878)

Prince Leopold, Duke of Albany (1853-1884)

Princess Beatrice of the United Kingdom (1857-1944)

Princess Irene of Hesse and by Rhine (1866-1953)

Prince Friedrich of Hesse and by Rhine (1870-1873)

Alexandra Feodorovna of Russia (1872-1918)

Princess Alice of Albany (1883-1981)

Victoria Eugenie of Battenberg queen of Spain (1887-1969)

Prince Waldemar of Prussia (1889-1945)

Prince Heinrich of Prussia (1900-1904)

Alexey Nikolaevich of Russia (1904-1918)

Prince Rupert of Teck (1907-1928)

Alfonso of Spain, Prince of Asturias (1907-1938)

Kate's children are descended from Princess Alice's daughter Victoria Alberta whose infant brother Friedrich bled to death in 1873. The last known royal victim Prince Waldemar of Prussia died in 1945 and presumably that mutation has disappeared.

Porphyria is still a remote possibility because Prince William of Gloucester was diagnosed in 1968, and so is schizophrenia which afflicted Prince Philip's mother Princess Alice of Battenberg who died in 1969.

Edward VII's oldest son Prince Albert Victor may have been genetically predisposed to a mild form of epilepsy. And George V's youngest son Prince John, who was severely epileptic, died aged 13. John was hidden from the public to avoid embarrassment, but at least he was not written off as dead like the Queen Mother's niece Katherine Bowes-Lyon (See Page 209).

WIKIPEDIA

THE REAL ALICE IN WONDERLAND...

HYPOTHETICALLY, the real Alice in Wonderland could have been the real Queen of Hearts' daughter-in-law.

Firstly, many people believe that Queen Victoria inspired the Queen of Hearts (pictured above ordering someone's head off), not to be confused with the Red Queen in *Through the Looking-Glass* who is quite different.

Secondly, it is well documented that Victoria's youngest son, Prince Leopold the haemophiliac, had a close friendship with Alice Liddell who inspired Lewis Carroll. Kate knows a great deal about Carroll (real name Charles Lutwidge Dodgson) because his photographs of children were the subject of her university honours thesis.

Some say that Queen Victoria prevented Leopold from marrying Alice Liddell because she was a commoner. Either way, he married a German princess and their daughter Princess Alice of Albany transmitted haemophilia to Prince Rupert of Teck who suffered a fatal brain haemorrhage in 1928.

Alice Liddell's son Leopold Reginald Hargreaves, who was killed in action during World War I, was named after Prince Leopold who was also his godfather. Alice died at Westerham in Kent in 1934 aged 82.

Kate's children are descended from Princess Alice of Battenberg, granddaughter of Prince Leopold's sister Princess Alice of the United Kingdom who transmitted haemophilia to several of her descendants (See chart on previous page).

The PEDIGREE of
Alice Pleasance LIDDELL
Born: 1852 Died: 1934

Husband/Partner: Reginald Gervis Hargreaves

```
                              /-- Thomas LIDDELL (1670 - 1715)
                             /           \-- Catherine BRIGHT  +
                         /-- Thomas LIDDELL (1710 - ?)
                         |        \           /-- James (of Greencroft) CLAVERING
                         /          \-- Jane CLAVERING (? - 1774)
                     /-- Henry George (5th Baronet) LIDDELL (1749 - 1791)
                     |        \                 /-- Thomas (of STREATLAM) BOWES  +
                     |         |       /-- William (Sir; of Streatlam Castle) BOWES
                     |         |      /          \-- Anne MAXTONE  +
                     |         \-- Margaret BOWES
                     |                  \              /-- Francis (of Gibside) BLAKISTON  +
                     |                   \-- Elizabeth (of Gibside) BLAKISTON (? - 1736)
                     /                          \-- Anne BOWES  +
                 /-- Henry George (Rev.) LIDDELL (1787 - 1872)
                 |        \          /-- Thomas STEELE
                 /          \-- Elizabeth STEELE
             /-- Henry George (Very. Rev.) LIDDELL (1811 - 1898)
             |        \                        /-- Patrick LYON  +
             |         |                /-- John LYON (Castle Huntly 1663 - 1712)
             |         |               /          \-- Helen (Lady) MIDDLETON  +
             |         |         /-- Thomas LYON
             |         |         |      \          /-- Philip STANHOPE  +
             |         |         |       \-- Elizabeth (Lady of Chesterfield) STANHOPE
             |         |         /                 \-- Elizabeth (Lady) BUTLER  +
             |         |     /-- Thomas LYON (1741? - 1796)
             |         |     |      \               /-- James NICHOLSON (? - 1681?)
             |         |     |       \       /-- James (of West Rainton) NICHOLSON (? - 1727)
             |         |     |        |     /          \-- Jane HESLOP  +
             |         |     |         \-- Jean NICHOLSON (1713 - 1778 Durham)
             |         |     /                \-- Anne ALLAN (? - 1719)
             |          \-- Charlotte LYON (1783 - 1871)
             /                   \-- Mary Elizabeth WREN
- Alice Pleasance LIDDELL
             \          /-- James REEVE
              \-- Lorina REEVE
```

... AND THE FIRST EARL OF MIDDLETON

SCOTTISH soldier John Middleton (left), made the first Earl of Middleton by Charles II, was the father of Alice Liddell's and Prince William's ancestor Helen Middleton (shown above). And Catherine Bright was descended from Prince William's ancestor Catherine (Anne) Mydelton (See chart on Page 145).

Kate's ancestor Jane Lambton was related to the Blackiston and Bowes families, and also to the Lyon family which owned the Hetton-le-Hole colliery which employed Kate's Harrison ancestors.

KATE AND LEWIS CARROLL

MOST people familiar with the four nude photographs opposite, especially the reclining study of Evelyn Hatch, fully understand why Kate's university honours thesis will almost certainly never be published.

The thesis, titled 'Angels from Heaven: Lewis Carroll's Photographic Interpretation of Childhood', must have considered his photos of Alice Liddell, pictured above with her sisters Edith (left) and Lorina (centre). But, to be intellectually honest, Kate must also have considered accusations that some of Carroll's photographs were, at the very least, inappropriate.

In 2015, the BBC broadcast *The Secret World of Lewis Carroll* which made sensational claims based on a dubious nude photograph. Four years later, an online article titled The Lewis Carroll Problem was much more nuanced:

'What he has left us with is scattered biographical details, signs of some stripe of mental illness, and childhood paraphernalia tainted by trauma. Much like Alice and, most probably, Carroll himself, we have been left to suffer the terrible ambiguities of life, logic, sexuality, and childhood. Ironically, it is all that we can be sure of in Wonderland or in any other setting.'

Fortunately for Kate, there were no difficult questions in 2018 when she curated an exhibition for the National Portrait Gallery which featured Lewis Carroll and three other Victorian photographers: Oscar Rejlander, Clementina Hawarden and Julia Margaret Cameron.

This suggestive image of Lewis Carroll and Alice Liddell combines two perfectly innocent photographs which can easily be found online.

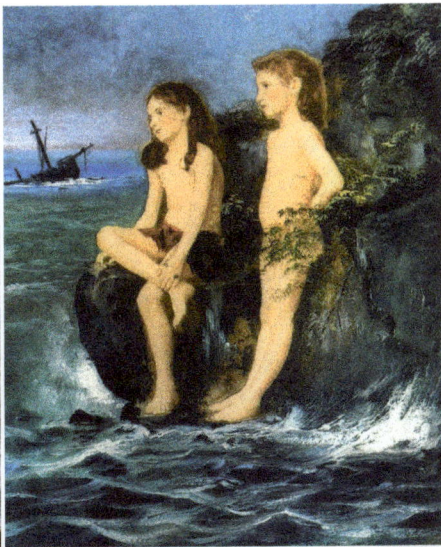

In her introduction to *Victorian Giants: The Birth of Art Photography*, Kate, who is patron of the NPG, wrote: 'These photographs allow us to reflect on the importance of preserving and appreciating childhood while it lasts… Children held a special place in the Victorian imagination and were celebrated for their seemingly boundless potential. This notion still rings true for us today.'

ART OR PORNOGRAPHY?

ANYONE discussing Lewis Carroll's nude photographs of children should bear in mind that such images were commonplace at that time and considered both innocent and beautiful. A good example is Julia Margaret Cameron's 'Love in Idleness' (right) dated around 1867.

It is also worth nothing that Queen Victoria and Prince Alfred had a large collection of nude paintings and sculptures at Osborne House on the Isle of Wight.

THREE FAMOUS STUTTERERS

WHILE *The King's Speech* (2010) implied that strict parenting was primarily responsible for the stutter which afflicted George VI (above), the family histories of Charles Dodgson (Lewis Carroll) and Charles Darwin strongly suggest a genetic cause for the disorder.

The author of *Alice in Wonderland* and nine of his siblings, including three girls, stuttered through and beyond their happy childhoods. It is also significant that their parents Charles Dodgson and Frances Lutwidge (shown opposite) were first cousins.

George VI may not have been dangerously inbred but his great-grandparents Queen Victoria and Prince Albert were first cousins with numerous bloodlines from Katharina von Pfannberg. Coincidentally, James II had a stammer and so did his father Charles I who had the same mtDNA (haplogroup T) as George VI's father George V.

According to one of Carroll's biographers, failure to correct his speech impediment was the overarching symbol of his entire life. '(Carroll) learned to live with his stammering', wrote John Pudney. 'He knew what it permitted him to do, what not, where it would snare him and destroy the effects he sought to achieve.'

Charles Darwin undoubtedly inherited a predisposition for stuttering because his grandfather, father and one of his uncles had the disorder. However, Darwin's well-documented bad health was inherited from his mother.

Nobody knows for certain if Kate's children have a predisposition to stuttering — or haemophilia, porphyria, schizophrenia or epilepsy — so it is remotely possible that their offspring could inherit one of more of these disorders.

The PEDIGREE of

Lewis CARROLL
Born: Cheshire 1832   Died: 1898

```
                              /-- Christopher Charles DODGSON (1696 - 1750)
                          /        \-- poss. Agnes BROWNE (1670? - ?)
                     /-- Charles (Rt. Rev.) DODGSON
                   /        \-- Elizabeth COULTON (? - 1744)
              /-- Charles (Capt.) DODGSON (1769? - 1803 Eire)
              |      \        /-- poss. William SMITH (Dublin)
              /        \-- Mary Frances SMYTH (Dublin, Eire 1749 - 1796)
         /-- Charles (Rev.) DODGSON (1800? - 1868?)
        /
```

- Lewis CARROLL

```
        \                     /-- Thomas (of Whitehaven) LUTWIDGE
        |               /-- Henry LUTWIDGE (Lancas. 1724 - 1798)
        |               |      \                 /-- Richard (3rd Baronet) HOUGHTON +
        |               |      |          /-- Charles (4th Baronet) HOUGHTON
        |               |      |          /      \-- Sarah (Lady) STANHOPE +
        |               |      \-- Lucy HOGHTON (Lancas. 1694 - 1780)
        |               |               \             /-- John SKEFFINGTON +
        |               |                \-- Mary SKEFFINGTON
        |               |                         \         /-- John CLOTWORTHY +
        |               |                          \-- Mary CLOTWORTHY (? - 1686)
        |               /                                 \-- Margaret JONES +
        |        /-- Charles (Major) LUTWIDGE
        |        |      \          /-- Rigby MOLINEUX
        |        /       \-- poss. Jane MOLINEUX (? - 1791)
        \-- Frances Jane LUTWIDGE (Cumberland 1803 - 1851)
                 \                     /-- Robert DODGSON (1605? - ?)
                 |               /-- poss. Robert DODGSON (1652 - ?)
                 |               |      \ / or: poss. Christopher John DODGSON
                 |               /        \-- Ellen BROWN +
                 |         /-- Christopher Charles DODGSON (1696 - 1750)
                 |         /        \-- poss. Agnes BROWNE (1670? - ?)
                 |      /-- Charles (Rt. Rev.) DODGSON
                 |      /        \-- Elizabeth COULTON (? - 1744)
                 \-- Elizabeth Anne DODGSON (1770 - 1836)
```

DARWINIAN INBREEDING

IF KATE'S great-great-grandparents, John William Middleton and his first cousin Mary Asquith, had met Charles Darwin (right) prior to 1863, the famous scientist may well have advised the couple not to get married (See chart on Page 146).

Darwin had rightly deduced that his marriage to first cousin Emma Wedgwood contributed to three of their children dying young and another three having childless marriages.

WIKIPEDIA

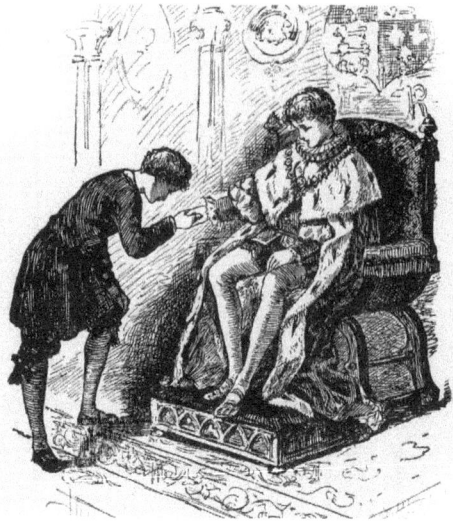

WIKIPEDIA

THE PRINCESS AND THE PAUPER

IN NOVEMBER 1819, less than six months after the future Queen Victoria was born in Kensington Palace, Kate's ancestor James Dorsett was born not far away in Hammersmith. He was the son of a labourer and surrounded by poverty.

When Mark Twain (above left) starting writing *The Prince and the Pauper* (1881), the novel was based on Queen Victoria's oldest son, the future Edward VII. That premise was unworkable so the novel was reset in the 1500s and based on Henry VIII's son, the future Edward VI, who changes places with Tom Canty (above right).

After working as a labourer for more than fifty years, James Dorsett was listed

in the 1891 census as a 'road sweeper'. Some sweepers, like young Jo in Charles Dickens' novel *Bleak House,* were virtual beggars. However, the majority were paid very low wages to remove never-ending piles of horse manure.

James Dorsett died in Hammersmith in 1893 and his wife Charlotte, who reportedly gave birth to 17 children, died six years later. Queen Victoria died in January 1901.

William Stanford Powell (shown opposite) was a labourer; so were the fathers, both named John, of Esther Jones and Eliza Jenkins; and so were the father and grandfather, both named John, of Stephen Goldsmith. Stephen was a labourer for much of his working life but his son Ronald escaped poverty by becoming a lorry driver and builder.

Sweepers had the unenviable task of removing hundreds of tons of horse manure dropped on London's streets each day.

Ronald John James GOLDSMITH

Born: Middlesex 1931   Died: 2003 Berks.

Wife/Partner: **Dorothy HARRISON**
Child: **Carole Elizabeth GOLDSMITH**

```
                         /-- John GOLDSMITH (1827? - 1888)
                        /           \-- Rebecca TUFFEE
            /-- John GOLDSMITH (1852? - 1901+)
           |        \        /-- John JONES
           |         \-- Esther JONES
           |              \-- Sarah
      /-- Stephen Charles GOLDSMITH (Middlesex 1886 - 1938)
      |    |    \                    /-- James DORSETT
      |    |    |    /-- Michael James DORSETT (1789? - ?)
      |    |    |   /         \-- Sarah
      |    |    /-- James DORSETT (1821? - 1893)
      |    |   /         \-- Ann HUGHES (1802? - ?)
      |    \-- Jane DORSETT (1861 - 1895)
      |              \    /-- William Stanford (of Turnham Green) POWELL
      |               \-- Charlotte Mercy POWELL (1821? - 1899)
      /                    \-- Charlotte SMITH
```

Ronald John James GOLDSMITH

```
      \                 /-- Miles Tugwell CHANDLER
      |    /-- Theophilus Benjamin CHANDLER
      |   /         \-- Eliza JENKINS (1818? - 1896 Worcesters.)
      \-- Edith Eliza CHANDLER (Buckinghams. 1889 - 1971)
            \         /-- Uriah WHITE (Bath 1806? - 1867 Buckinghams.)
             \-- Amelia WHITE (Buckinghams. 1846 - ?)
```

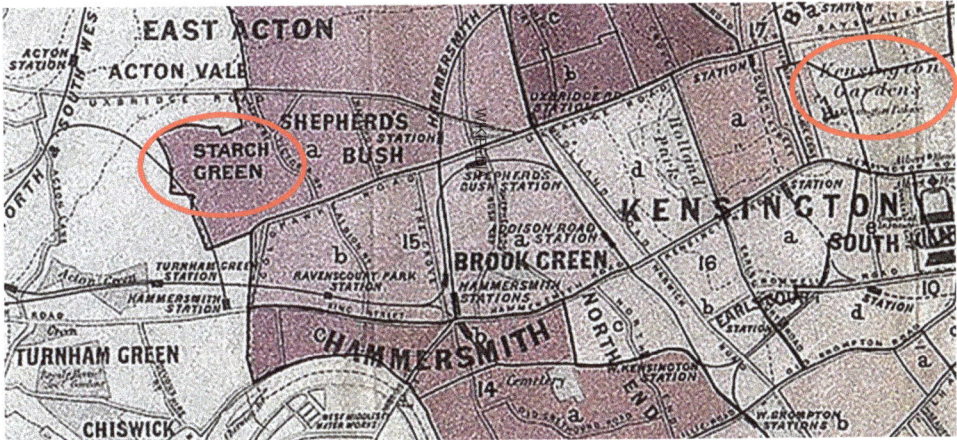

Charles Booth's famous poverty map published in 1889 shows a number of slums in London's West End. Kate's ancestor James Dorsett was born in Starch Green in 1819 and lived for many years in a cottage in Paradise Place (later Row) in Hammersmith. Like their ancestor Queen Victoria, Prince George and his siblings have been raised in Kensington Palace on the west side of Kensington Gardens (circled above).

THE PEASANT AND
THE PRINCE

BY

HARRIET MARTINEAU

A WOMAN FOR ALL SEASONS

THE MOST famous author in Kate's family tree is Harriet Martineau (above left) who at her peak outsold Charles Dickens, discussed important matters with Charles Darwin, and is now acclaimed as a proto-feminist and the first female sociologist. Her novel *The Peasant and the Prince*, about the young son of Louis XVI and Marie Antoinette, was published in 1841.

As shown opposite, Harriet was a sister of Kate's ancestor Elizabeth Martineau, wife of renowned epidemiologist Dr Thomas Michael Greenhow (See Page 153).

Princess Victoria was a big fan of Harriet's work, especially *Illustrations of Political Economy* published in 1832, and six years later the author was personally invited to Victoria's coronation.

Harriet met Charles Darwin after his famous voyage around the world and was a close friend of his older brother Erasmus. Charles admired Harriet's intellect but cruelly described her as 'little ugly'.

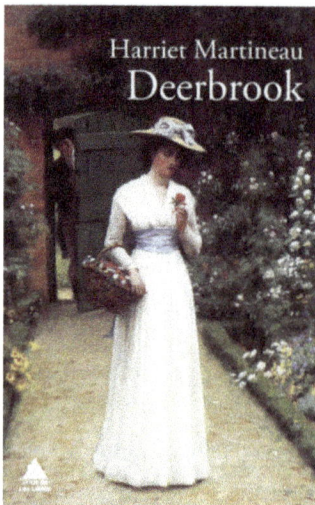

Harriet Martineau
Deerbrook

As depicted in the 2016 play *Harriet Martineau Dreams of Dancing*, the recuperating author amused herself at Tynemouth by watching beachgoers through a telescope. She also observed the ruined priory where Edward II's illegitimate teenage son Adam Fitzroy was buried in 1322.

The works of Harriet Martineau and her philosopher brother James are celebrated by members of the Martineau Society who may one day invite Kate to be their patron.

According to literary historians, Deerbrook *(1839) bridges the gap between two of Kate's favourite novels, Jane Austen's* Sense and Sensibility *(1811) and George Eliot's* Middlemarch *(1871).*

Thomas MARTINEAU

Born: 1764   Died: 1826

Wife/Partner: **Elizabeth RANKIN**
Children: **Elizabeth MARTINEAU** ;
Harriet (famous economist : novelist : etc.) ; James (famous theologian)

```
                        /-- Gaston MARTINEAU  (Dordogne 1654 - by 1726)
                    /          \-- Marguerite BARBESSON
                /-- David MARTINEAU  (1697 - 1729)
                |       \           /-- Guillaume PIERRE
                |        \-- Marie PIERRE
                |                   \-- Marie JOURDAIN  +
            /-- David MARTINEAU  (1726 - 1768)
            |       \                   /-- Peter FINCH  +
            |       |           /-- Henry FINCH  (Lancas. 1633 - 1704)
            |       |          /          \-- Katherine
            |       |       /-- Peter FINCH  (1661 - 1754)
            |       |      /            \-- Mary HAMMOND
            |       \-- Elizabeth FINCH  (1700 - 1748)
            /                   \-- Elizabeth MACKERELL
```

- Thomas MARTINEAU

```
            \                   /-- William MEADOWS (MEDOWE)  +
            |           /-- Daniel MEADOWS  (Rushmere 1577 - 1659)
            |          /            \-- Agnes (Margaret)  (? - 1678?)
            |       /-- John (Rev.) MEADOWS  (Suffolk 1622 - 1697)
            |      /            \-- Elizabeth SMITH  +
            |   /-- Philip MEADOWS  (1679 - 1752)
            |   |       \           /-- Benjamin (Rev.; of Halesworth) FAIRFAX  +
            |   |        \-- Sarah FAIRFAX  (1654 - 1688)
            |   /                   \-- Bridget STRINGER  +
            \-- Sarah MEADOWS  (Norfolk 1725 - 1800 Norfolk)
```

TELESCOPIC PHILANTHROPY

CHARLES DICKENS badly treated his wife Catherine (nee Hogarth) and unfairly satirised the profoundly deaf Harriet Martineau in *Bleak House* (1852). Mrs Jellyby, who inspired the Punch cartoon (right), neglected her own children while preoccupied with helping the natives in far-off Borrioboola-Gha.

During a bitter dispute about articles in *Household Words,* Dickens described Harriet's naming him as a 'humanity-monger' (like Mrs Jellyby) as a 'vomit of conceit'.

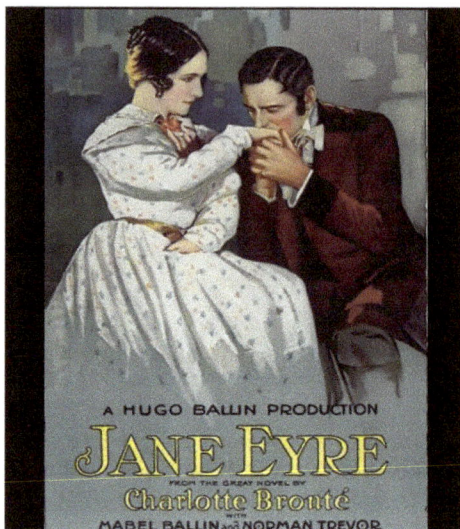

KATE'S BRONTË CONNECTIONS

WHEN she was pregnant with Princess Charlotte in early 2015, Kate suffered from the same severe morning sickness (hyperemesis gravidarum) that contributed to the death of Charlotte Brontë (above left) exactly 160 years earlier.

There are other connections between the two Charlottes, starting with Harriet Martineau who was one of the suspected authors of *Jane Eyre* when it was published under the pen name Currer Bell in 1847. Harriet and Charlotte Brontë, who were both short and plain like the fictional Jane, were friendly until Harriet's criticism of Charlotte's last novel *Villette* (1853) provoked a passionate response.

Through John Wilmot, the debauched Earl of Rochester who inspired his fictional namesake in *Jane Eyre*, Kate's children are descended from Walter Hungerford (beheaded 1540) — father of the Sir Walter Hungerford shown opposite — who inspired General Tilney in Jane Austen's *Northanger Abbey*.

Charlotte Brontë was not impressed by *Northanger Abbey*, claiming that Jane Austen 'ruffles her reader by nothing vehement, disturbs him by nothing profound: the passions are perfectly unknown to her.'

Kate's favourite Brontë novel is *Wuthering Heights,* written by Charlotte's sister Emily under the pen name Ellis Bell, which features Catherine Earnshaw and her daughter Cathy who marries Heathcliff's son Linton. It has long been speculated that Heathcliff was based on Emily's brother Branwell.

As shown opposite, John Wilmot (left), who inspired Edward Rochester in Jane Eyre, *was descended from Henry VIII's illegitimate daughter Catherine Carey (Katherine Cary).*

The PEDIGREE of

John WILMOT 2nd Earl of ROCHESTER;

Born: 1647   Died: 1680

Lady Diana's 8-Great Grandfather.

Wife/Partner: **Elizabeth MALLET (MALET)**
Children: **Elizabeth (Lady) WILMOT** ; **Malet (Lady) WILMOT** ; **Anne WILMOT**

```
                          /-- Edward (of Witney) WILMOT
                  /-- Edward (of Culham) WILMOT
          /-- Charles (1st Viscount of ATHLONE) WILMOT
         /          \-- Elizabeth STAFFORD
    /-- Henry (2nd Viscount) WILMOT  (1613? - 1658)
   |         \         /-- Henry (Sir) ANDERSON
   /          \-- Sarah ANDERSON
```

- John WILMOT

```
   |                      /-- John (Sir) ST. JOHN  (? - 11/9/1594)
   |              /           \-- Elizabeth (of Mapledurham) BLOUNT  +
   |          /-- John (Sir) ST. JOHN  (? - 1648)
   |         |         \         /-- Walter (Sir; of Farley) HUNGERFORD  +
   |         |          \-- Lucy HUNGERFORD  (? - 1598 (or 1627?))
   |         |                    \-- Anne DORMER  +
   |         /                       / or: poss. Anne BASSET
    \-- Anne (of Lydiard Tregoze) ST. JOHN  (1614 - 1696)
              \                 /-- John (of Watlesburgh) LEIGHTON  +
              |          /-- Thomas (Sir; of Feckenham) LEIGHTON  (? - 1611?)
              |         /         \-- Joyce (SUTTON) DUDLEY  +
              \-- Anne LEIGHTON  (? - 1628)
                        \                 /-- Francis (K.G.; of Rotherfield) KNOLLYS  +
                        \-- Elizabeth KNOLLYS  (1549 - ?)
                                  \         /-- Henry VIII TUDOR  +
                                  |        / OR: prob. not William (Esq.) CAREY  +
                                  \-- Katherine CARY  (1524? - 1569)
                                            \-- Mary BOLEYN  +
```

On her 1839 visit to Norton Conyers House (above) in North Yorkshire, Charlotte Brontë was told about a 'mad woman in the attic' who presumably descended from a former resident named Catherine Graham. There was great excitement in 2004 when a previously hidden staircase matched Brontë's description.

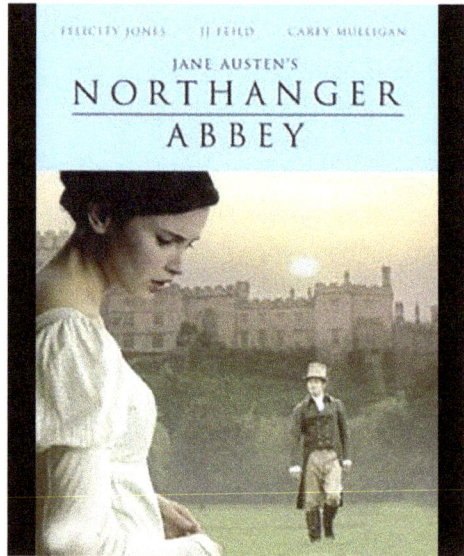

JANE AUSTEN'S CATHERINES

IF ONE of Kate's favourite Jane Austen novels had been published during the author's lifetime it would have been titled *Catherine*.

The manuscript for *Northanger Abbey*, then titled *Susan*, was sold in 1803 to a London bookseller who held on to it for thirteen years. Jane (above left) then re-wrote parts of the manuscript, renaming the main character Catherine because a novel titled *Susan* had been published in the interim. Henry Austen changed the title of his sister's novel from *Catherine* to *Northanger Abbey* after she died in 1817.

Catharine or The Bower, an unfinished novel probably written in the mid-1790s, has been described as a bridge between Jane's juvenilia and her most famous works. Another unfinished novel, *The Watsons*, was completed by Jane's niece Catherine Hubback.

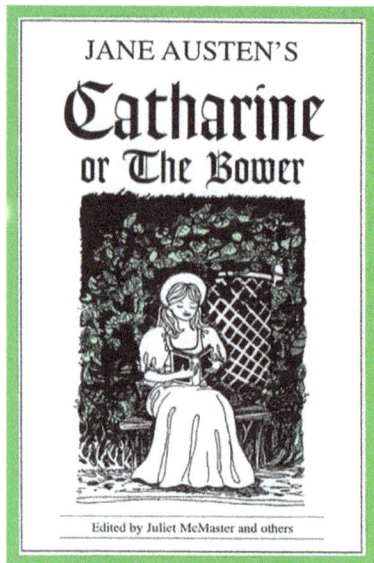

The 2007 film version of *Northanger Abbey*, starring Felicity Jones (poster above), was released twenty years after Katherine Schlesinger portrayed the naive Catherine Morland opposite Robert Hardy as General Tilney. (Hardy later played Sir John Middleton in a version of *Sense and Sensibility*.)

General Tilney was inspired by Prince William's ancestor Walter Hungerford who allegedly imprisoned his wife at Farleigh Castle which Jane visited while she was living in Bath.

In 2011, ancestry.com gleefully announced that the recently married Kate Middleton was

Katherine Percy	
Elizabeth Grey	**Anne Grey**
Elizabeth Greystoke	**Edmund Grey**
Mable Dacre	**Elizabeth Grey**
John Scrope	**Charles Brydges**
Margaret Scrope	**Gilbert Brydges**
Henry Constable	**John Brydges**
Dorothy Constable	**James Brydges**
Henry Lawson	**Mary Brydges**
Dorothy Lawson	**Thomas Leigh**
Ralph Blakiston	**Cassandra Leigh**
Jane Blakiston	**Jane Austen**

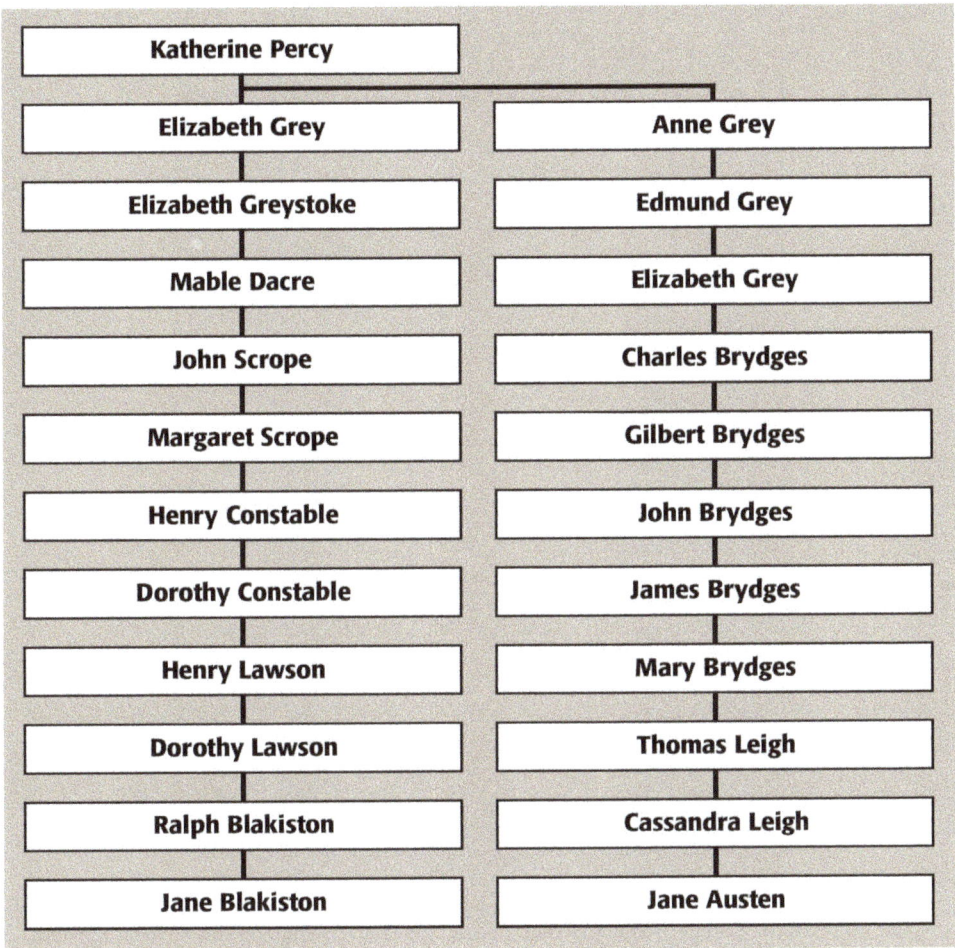

a 'distant relation' of Jane Austen. Very distant indeed because they are 11th cousins 6 times removed through a grandson of Katherine Swynford. For the record, Kate and Jane Austen are also 10th cousins 10 times removed through Katherine Percy and Jane Blakiston (shown above), mother of Sir Thomas Conyers (See chart on Page 57).

According to ancestry.com historian Anastasia Harman, Kate is 'the modern Jane Austen heroine: a middle-class girl marrying the future King of England.'

Note: The nobility of Mr Darcy's imperious aunt in *Pride and Prejudice* is revealed by her title, Lady Catherine de Bourgh. If her father was a mere knight she would be Lady de Bourgh.

WIKIPEDIA

Prince William's ancestor Walter Hungerford, who inspired General Tilney in Northanger Abbey, *was executed for sodomy in 1540 on the same day that Henry VIII married Catherine Howard.*

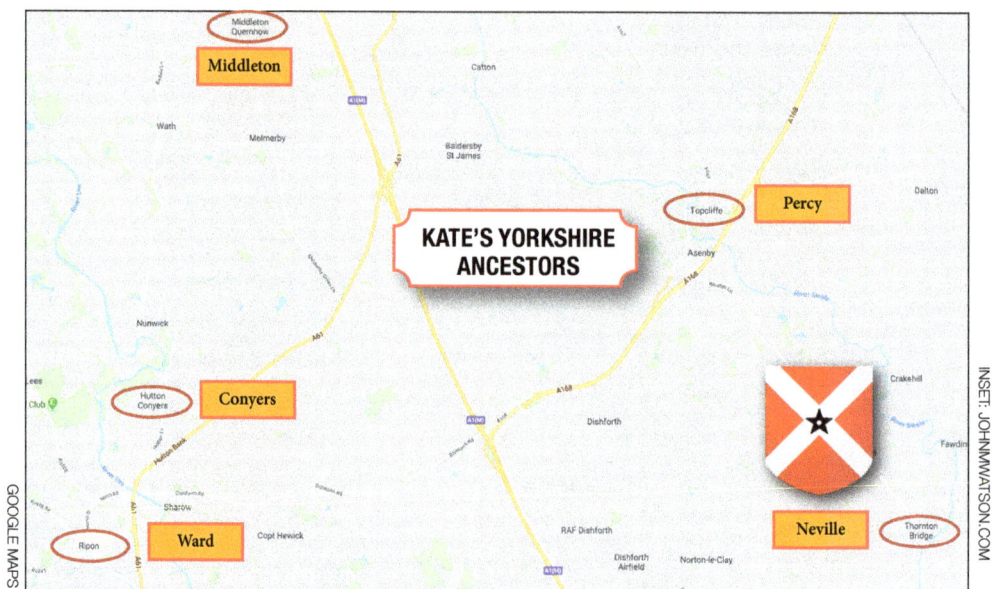

YORKSHIRE KITH AND KIN

LIKE Prince William, his and Kate's joint ancestor Sir Henry Constable of Burton was probably descended from Katherine of Flanders through all eight of his great-grandparents, most of whom lived in Yorkshire and were related to the Percys and Nevilles. These two powerful families intermarried for many years until a bloody feud erupted before the Wars of the Roses.

As shown above, Kate's Conyers and Ward ancestors lived near Ripon, not far from the Yorkshire homes of the Percys and Nevilles. There was a similar cluster of Kate's Gascoigne and Fairfax ancestors around the home of the Stockeld Middletons near Wetherby (See map on Page 140).

North of Hutton Conyers is the small hamlet of Middleton Quernhow which, like half a dozen other Middletons in Yorkshire, could be Kate's ancestral home. Not much is known about William de Middleton and his son Ranulph who were living there in the 1200s.

In 1393, the Scropes of Bolton Castle in North Yorkshire took over the manor at Middleton Quernhow from the Constables of Burton in East Yorkshire and, as shown opposite, it seems that the two families were close for many generations.

Many of Kate's Yorkshire ancestors were persecuted Catholics, including Henry Constable's wife Margaret Dormer who was imprisoned several times during the 1590s. Margaret's daughters Catherine and Dorothy Constable were recusants, and so was their great-grandmother Catherine Clifford who was descended from Katherine Swynford through Katherine Spencer (See chart on Page 189).

Kate is descended from Dorothy Constable through Thomas Conyers, and Prince William is descended from Dorothy's sister Catherine. Prince William is also descended from Catherine Constable's niece Katherine Constable who married William Middleton of Stockeld.

Henry (Sir; of Burton) CONSTABLE

Died: 1608 London

Lady Diana's 14-Great Grandfather.

Wife/Partner: **Margaret DORMER**

Children: **Catherine CONSTABLE** ; **Dorothy CONSTABLE**

```
                          /-- John (Sir; of Burton Constable) CONSTABLE
            /              \-- Anne EURE (EWER)  +
        /-- John (Sir; of Burton Constable) CONSTABLE  (? - 1542)
        |       \              /-- Thomas (Sir; of Metham) METHAM  +
        |        \-- Agnes METHAM
        |                      \-- Elizabeth (of Flamborough) CONSTABLE  +
    /-- John (Sir; of Kirkby Knowle) CONSTABLE  (1527 - 1579)
    |       \              /-- Ralph NEVILLE  +
    |        |         /-- Ralph (Sir; of Thornton Bridge) NEVILLE
    |        |        /      \-- Anne GASCOIGNE  +
    |        \-- Joan NEVILLE  (? - 1551+)
    |                 \              /-- Christopher (Knight; of Givendale) WARDE  +
    |                  \-- Anne WARDE (WARD)  (? - 1521)
    /                                \-- Margaret GASCOIGNE  +
```

Henry (Sir; of Burton) CONSTABLE

```
    |                      /-- Henry (7th Lord of Bolton) SCROPE  (? - 1533)
    |              /          \-- Elizabeth (Lady) PERCY  +
    |          /-- John (8th Lord of Bolton) SCROPE  (? - 1549)
    |          |        \              /-- Thomas (2nd Lord; of GILSLAND) DACRE  +
    |          |         \-- Mabel DACRE
    |          /                      \-- Elizabeth (Baroness) GREYSTOKE  +
    \-- Margaret SCROPE
            \              /-- Henry (9th/10th Lord) CLIFFORD  +
            |          /-- Henry CLIFFORD (1st Earl) of CUMBERLAND
            |         /      \-- Anne ST. JOHN  +
            \-- Catherine (Lady) CLIFFORD  (1518? - 1598)
                      \              /-- Henry Algernon (K.G.) PERCY  +
                       \-- Margaret (Lady) PERCY  (? - 1540)
                                      \-- Katherine SPENCER  +
```

Burton Constable Hall (above) in East Yorkshire, not to be confused with Constable Burton Hall in North Yorkshire, was a haven for Catholic recusants during Elizabeth I's reign. Prayer meetings were held in a remote room at the top of the south tower.

Map labels: en Harlow Carr · A661 · Plumpton · A661 · Little Ribston · Hunsingore · Cattal · Follifoot · North Deighton · Cowthorpe · T · ridge · Pannal · A61 · A58 · A661 · Spofforth · Percy · Stockeld Park · Middleton · Ingmanthorpe · Bickerton · gton · Swindon Ln · Kirkby Overblow · Sicklinghall · A661 · A661 · A1(M) · Wetherby · Wig · Vavasour · Netherby · Linton · A58 · Fairfax · Walton · Weeton · Dunkeswick · Collingham · A1(M) · Thorpe Arch Estate · Weardley · Harewood · Harewood House · East Keswick · Boston Spa · Newt · ton · Gascoigne · Bardsey

KATE'S YORKSHIRE ANCESTORS

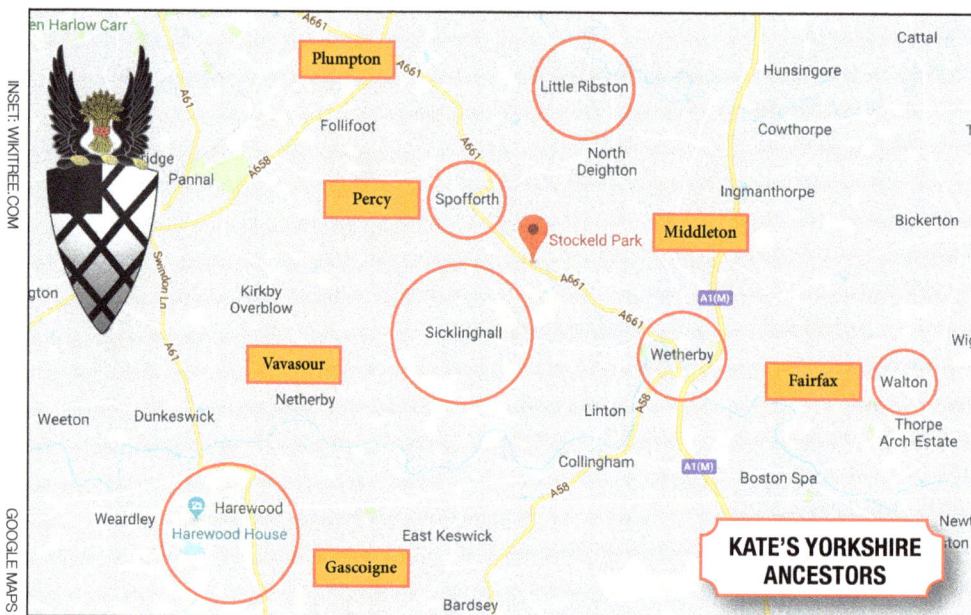

THE STOCKELD MIDDLETONS

KATHERINE CONSTABLE, granddaughter of Kate's ancestor Sir Henry Constable of Burton, had connections to Kate's Gascoigne ancestors and also to the Stockeld Middletons (arms inset).

As shown opposite, Katherine's husband William Middleton had a bloodline from Margaret Gascoigne, a niece of Agnes Gascoigne who is one of the most recent common ancestors of Kate and Prince William. William Middleton was also descended from Joan Gascoigne, mother of one of Kate's namesakes (See The Catherine Mydelton Mystery, Page 145).

The interrelatedness of the Stockeld Middletons and the Gascoignes of Gawthorpe is not surprising because the two families were almost neighbours. As shown above, Stockeld Park is not far from Harewood, home of Prince William's Lascelles ancestors (See Page 167), where Gawthorpe Hall stood until it was demolished in 1773.

Agnes Gascoigne's husband Sir Thomas Fairfax of Gilling owned Walton east of Wetherby. A branch of the powerful Percy family, which included Kate's ancestor Henry 'Hotspur' occupied Spofforth Castle; the Vavasours of Hazlewood had a country retreat near Sicklinghall; one of the Stockeld Middletons was living at Kirkby Overblow in the early 1400s; and Kate's Plumpton ancestors lived about halfway between Harrogate and Little Ribston. The Plumptons and Middletons were closely connected (See chart on Page 143).

According to geni.com and wikitree.com the Stockeld Middletons were related to the Middletons of Kirkby Lonsdale in Westmorland (now Cumbria), including Isabel Middleton (shown opposite) who married her distant cousin John Middleton of Stockeld in the 1500s.

Peter (of Stockeld Hall) MIDDLETON

Born: abt. 1654   Died: 1714
Wife/Partner: **Elizabeth LANGDALE**
Child: **Elizabeth MIDDLETON**

```
                                    /-- Thomas (Heir of Stockeld) MIDDLETON  +
                            /-- John (of Stockeld) MIDDLETON
                           /      \-- Margaret GASCOIGNE  +
                    /-- William (of Stockeld) MIDDLETON  (? - 1614)
                   /         \-- Isabel MIDDLETON
             /-- Peter (Sir) MIDDLETON
            /            \-- Mary ELTOFTS
      /-- William (of Stockeld Hall) MIDDLETON  (? - 1658)
      |        \                /-- William (Sir; of Ripley) INGLEBY  +
      |         |         /-- David INGLEBY
      |         |        /      \-- Anne MALLORY  +
      |         \-- Mary INGLEBY
      |              \              /-- Charles NEVILL  +
      |               \-- Anne (Lady) NEVILL
      /                    \-- Jane (Lady) HOWARD  +
```

Peter (of Stockeld Hall) MIDDLETON

```
      \                      /-- John (of Burton Constable) CONSTABLE  +
      |                /-- John (Sir; of Kirkby Knowle) CONSTABLE
      |               /          \-- Joan NEVILLE  +
      |         /-- Henry (Sir; of Burton) CONSTABLE
      |        /           \-- Margaret SCROPE  +
      |  /-- Henry CONSTABLE (1st Viscount DUNBAR)  (1588 - 1645)
      |  |        \          /-- William (Sir) DORMER  +
      |  |         \-- Margaret DORMER  (1562 - 1637)
      |  /                   \-- Dorothy CATESBY  +
      \-- Katherine CONSTABLE  (1621 - ?)
            \              /-- John TUFTON  +
             |       /-- John (1st Baronet of Hothfield) TUFTON
             |      /      \-- Mary BAKER  +
             \-- Mary TUFTON  (? - 1659)
```

Katherine Constable's descendant William Haggerston-Constable (died 1847), who changed his surname to Middleton after inheriting Stockeld Park (above), divorced his wife Clara after she had a notorious affair with a groom named John Rose. Stockeld Park features in Britain's second-oldest soap opera, Emmerdale.

KATE'S ANCESTRAL HOME?

GENEALOGISTS may eventually prove that Kate is directly descended from the builders of Myddelton Lodge (above) near the villages of Middleton and Ilkley in West Yorkshire.

In the meantime, through Sir Thomas Fairfax, Kate has a bloodline from Sir William de Plumpton whose sister Eustachia (shown opposite) married Sir Peter de Middleton. Like his brother-in-law, Sir Peter was a High Sheriff of Yorkshire.

The patriarch of the Stockeld Middletons, Hypolitus de Braham, settled near Ilkley in the late 1100s. His descendants moved to Stockeld near Wetherby in the early 1300s but they retained Myddelton Lodge. Like the Constables, the Middletons were Catholic recusants and the lodge became well-known for its prayer meetings.

Sir Thomas Middleton's wife Elizabeth Gramary (shown opposite) was related to William Gramary of Bickerton who was living at Middleton between Leeds and Wakefield in the early 1200s. That Middleton, famous for its coal mines, is another contender for Kate's ancestral home.

According to some sources, Elizabeth Gramary died at Middleton Hall near Kirkby Lonsdale in Westmorland (now Cambria) where a branch of the family lived for several centuries. The Stockeld Middletons may also have been related to their namesakes of Belsay Castle in Northumberland who rebelled against Edward II in 1317.

The presumed effigy of Sir Peter de Middleton (died 1336) is in All Saints church at Ilkley. Sir Peter's father may have been William de Middleton, one of Britain's last Templar knights who was tried in Edinburgh in 1309 after being initiated at Temple Newsam in Leeds.

Nicholas (Sir; of Midelton & Stockeld) MIDELTON

Lady Diana's 18-Great Grandfather.   HRH Charles's 16-Great Uncle.

poss. Wives/Partners: **Avice STAPLETON** ; Alice MIDDLETON ; (1st) Matilda
Child: **John (Sir; of Stockeld) MIDELTON**

```
                              /-- Hypolitus de BRAHAM
                        /-- Hugh de MIDDLETON
                  /-- Ralf (Sir) de MIDELTON
            /-- Peter (Sir) de MIDDLETON  (? - 1284+)
           /            \-- Aeneas
      /-- William de MIDDLETON  (? - 1327+?)
     /            \-- Agnes
  /-- Peter (Sir) de MIDDLETON  (? - 1336?)
  |        \                /-- Wm. le BOTELER (of Wemme; BOTILER)  +
  |        |               /          | or: brother Ralph
  |        |          /-- Nigel (Sir) BOTELER
  |        |         /          \-- Angharad verch GRIFFITH  +
  |        \-- Agnes (le) BOTELER
 /-- Thomas (Sir; de) MIDDLETON  (1321? - by 1393)
 |        \                      /-- Robert de PLUMPTON  +
 |        |               /-- Nigel de PLUMPTON  (Yorks. 1216? - 1271?)
 |        |              /          \-- (Miss) MOWBRAY
 |        |         /-- Robert de PLUMPTON  (1241? - 1298?)
 |        |        /          \-- Avicia de CLARE  +
 |        |   /-- Robert (Sir; of Plumpton) de PLUMPTON
 |        |  |        \          /-- Serlonis de WESTWICK  (1217? - ?)
 |        |  /          \-- Isabella (de) WESTWICK  (1243? - ?)
 |        \-- Eustachia de PLUMPTON
 |                \                /-- William (Sir) de ROS (ROOS)  +
 |                |         /-- William (Sir; of Ingmanthorpe) de ROS
 |                |        /          \-- Lucy (Lucia) FitzPIERS  +
 |                \-- Lucy (ROOS) de ROS  (1270? - 1332+)
```

Nicholas (Sir; of Midelton & Stockeld) MIDELTON

```
     \          /-- Robert (Sir) GRAMARY
     |         /          | or: Henry (Sir, of Bickerton) GRAMARY
     \-- Elizabeth (Eliza; de) GRAMARY  (1335? - ?)
```

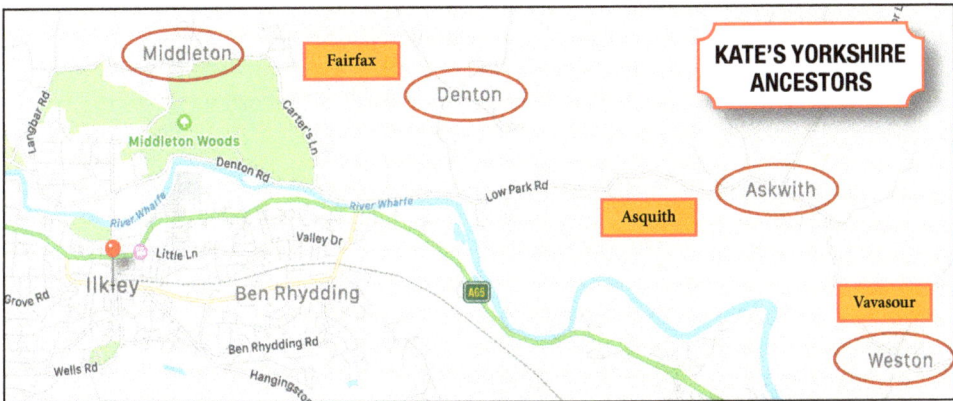

KATE'S YORKSHIRE ANCESTORS

Middleton · Fairfax · Denton · Askwith · Asquith · Vavasour · Weston
Middleton Woods · Langbar Rd · Carter's Ln · Denton Rd · Low Park Rd · River Wharfe · Valley Dr · Little Ln · Ilkley · Grove Rd · Ben Rhydding · Ben Rhydding Rd · Wells Rd · Hangingstone

Both Kate and Prince William descend from several families who lived near Middleton and Ilkley in West Yorkshire around 800 years ago. The most recent Asquith in Kate's family tree is Mary Asquith who married her first cousin John William Middleton in 1863.

WAKEFIELD CONNECTIONS

WAKEFIELD'S famous medieval bridge (above) must have been familiar to some of Kate's Middleton ancestors but, unfortunately, her paternal bloodline before 1800 is highly uncertain.

William Addams Reitwiesner traced Kate's pedigree to a cabinet maker named John Middleton whose son William was born in Wakefield in 1807. John Middleton's wife may have been named Mary or Ann (Beckett or Carrington), and his father may have been another John Middleton who married Martha Hampshire in 1781. According to geni.com the older John Middleton married Catherine File whose mother-in-law was named Katherin, but that is unlikely.

Elizabeth Ward who reportedly married Robert Middleton in Wakefield in 1749 may have been related to Richard Noel Middleton's grandmothers Mary and Ellen Ward (See chart on Page 147).

Prince William's ancestors Sir Peter Mydelton of Stockeld and Catherine (or Anne) Vavasour are especially interesting because they spent most of their lives in Wakefield, and so did their daughter Alice who married Richard Peck of Haselden Hall. One of Peck's ancestors married a Miss Middleton in the 1100s; and according to wikitree.com Richard Peck's namesake great-grandson married a Catherine Vavasour.

Edward IV's father Richard of York died during the Battle of Wakefield in 1460 and soon after the battle Edward's brother Edmund was allegedly murdered by Kate's ancestor John 'Blackfaced' Clifford (See Page 191).

Kate's ancestor William Middleton, who was baptised in Wakefield's All Saints parish church in 1807, spent most of his life in Leeds where he died in 1884.

— 144 —

William (Sir; of Stockeld) MIDDLETON

Born: ? **Died:** by 1553

Lady Diana's 13-Great Grandfather.

Wives/Partners: Isabella DIGHTON ; (1st) Jane Sutton ; (3rd) Jane Robynson
Children: Margaret MIDDLETON ; Elizabeth MIDDLETON

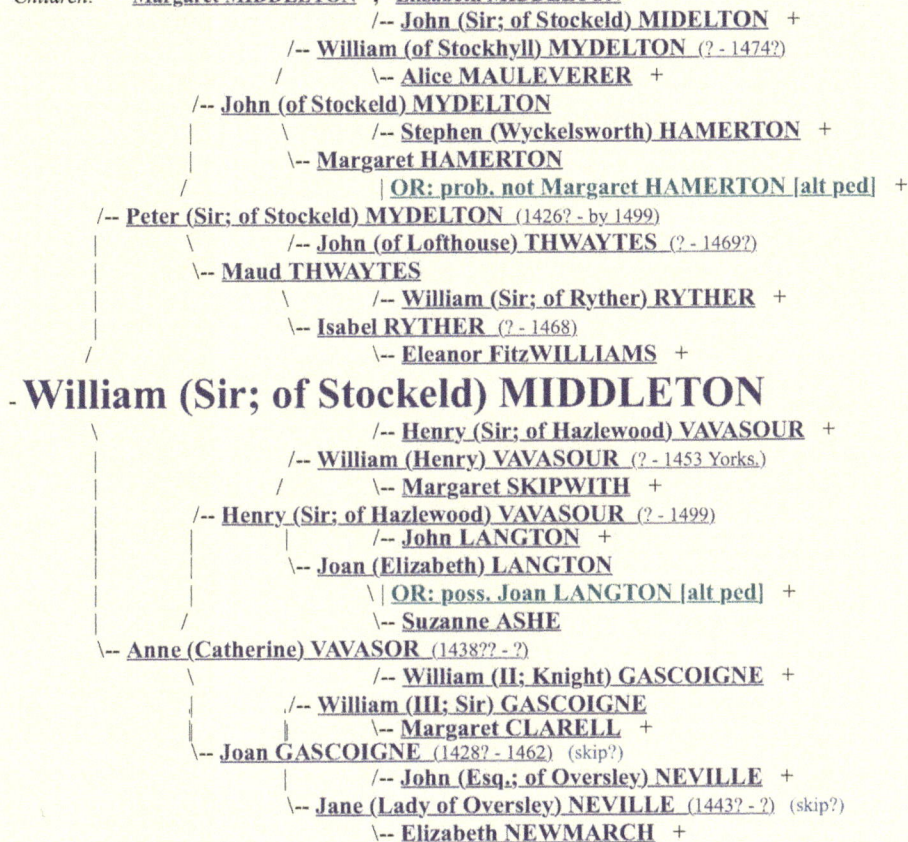

```
                                  /-- John (Sir; of Stockeld) MIDELTON   +
                       /-- William (of Stockhyll) MYDELTON  (? - 1474?)
                      /            \-- Alice MAULEVERER  +
           /-- John (of Stockeld) MYDELTON
           |          \          /-- Stephen (Wyckelsworth) HAMERTON  +
           |           \-- Margaret HAMERTON
           |                     | OR: prob. not Margaret HAMERTON [alt ped]  +
           /-- Peter (Sir; of Stockeld) MYDELTON  (1426? - by 1499)
           |          \          /-- John (of Lofthouse) THWAYTES  (? - 1469?)
           |           \-- Maud THWAYTES
           |                     \          /-- William (Sir; of Ryther) RYTHER  +
           |                      \-- Isabel RYTHER  (? - 1468)
           /                                 \-- Eleanor FitzWILLIAMS  +
```

William (Sir; of Stockeld) MIDDLETON

```
           \                     /-- Henry (Sir; of Hazlewood) VAVASOUR  +
           |          /-- William (Henry) VAVASOUR  (? - 1453 Yorks.)
           |         /           \-- Margaret SKIPWITH  +
           |        /-- Henry (Sir; of Hazlewood) VAVASOUR  (? - 1499)
           |        |            /-- John LANGTON  +
           |        |  \-- Joan (Elizabeth) LANGTON
           |        |            \ | OR: poss. Joan LANGTON [alt ped]  +
           |        /            \-- Suzanne ASHE
           \-- Anne (Catherine) VAVASOR  (1438?? - ?)
                    \             /-- William (II; Knight) GASCOIGNE  +
                    |   /-- William (III; Sir) GASCOIGNE
                    |   |         \-- Margaret CLARELL  +
                    \-- Joan GASCOIGNE  (1428? - 1462)  (skip?)
                        |         /-- John (Esq.; of Oversley) NEVILLE  +
                        \-- Jane (Lady of Oversley) NEVILLE  (1443? - ?)  (skip?)
                                  \-- Elizabeth NEWMARCH  +
```

THE CATHERINE MYDELTON MYSTERY

NOT MUCH is known about Sir Peter Mydelton and Catherine Vavasour — including her first name — but it seems that, like Romeo and Juliet, there was a blood feud between their families.

The feud started in 1333 when a previous Peter Middleton, possibly a first cousin of the Sir Peter Middleton buried at Ilkley, was murdered at the instigation of Thomas Vavasour. Twelve years later, Peter's son Richard Middleton mortally wounded Vavasour in his orchard at Denton.

Kate's ancestor Maud le Vavasour and her husband Fulk FitzWarine may have been the original Maid Marian and Robin Hood (See Page 175).

Note: Kate's children probably descend from Catherine Myddelton (née Meredydd) who lived in Wales during the 1400s. Her descendant Hugh Myddelton (born c1560), whose brother Thomas was Lord Mayor of London, built the New River which still supplies water to the city.

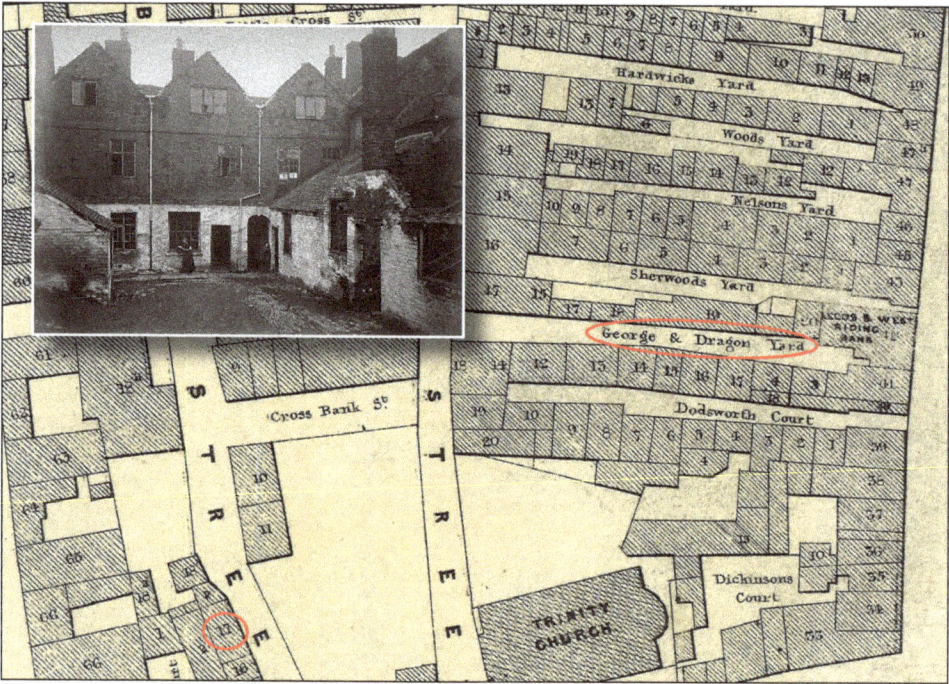

BACK-TO-BACK COUSINS

PREPOSTEROUS as it sounds, there was a time when Kate's Middleton ances-tors may have been more inbred than the royal family.

In 1830 William Middleton began working for a Leeds solicitor named William Ward at 17 Bank Street (circled above), not far from the back-to-back house in George and Dragon Yard occupied by John Ward. (His relationship to William Ward is unknown.)

William Middleton married John Ward's daughter Mary in February 1838 and eight months later Mary's sister Ellen Ward married a cloth dresser named Joseph Asquith. As shown opposite, Kate descends from the first cousin marriage of John William Middleton and Mary Asquith (whose brother John William Asquith married John William Middleton's younger sister Annie).

Adding to the confusion, William Middleton's second wife was Mary Ward's sister Sarah, and the second wife of Dr Thomas Michael Greenhow (shown opposite) was his daughter's sister-in-law Anne Lupton.

Through both Elizabeth II and Prince Philip, who were second cousins once removed, Kate's children descend from Queen Victoria who married her first cousin Prince Albert in 1840. The royal union was slightly less genetically risky than the Middleton marriage because Victoria's mother and Albert's father were brother and sister.

Mary Asquith was born in 1839 in George and Dragon Yard even though her parents were living in the suburb of Woodhouse. One year earlier, when Ellen Ward married Joseph Asquith, her address was Sterne's Building which backed on

Peter Francis (Capt.) MIDDLETON

Born: 1920 Died: 2010
Wife/Partner: **Valerie GLASSBOROW**
Child: **Michael Francis MIDDLETON**

```
                           /-- William MIDDLETON  (1807 - 1884)
                    /           \-- Ann CARRINGTON
              /-- John William MIDDLETON  (1839 - 1887)
              |       \        /-- John WARD
              |        \-- Mary WARD  (Leeds, Yorks. 1811? - ?)
              /                \-- Margaret
        /-- Richard Noel MIDDLETON  (Yorks. 1878 - 1951)
        |      \                  /-- John ASQUITH  (Yorks. 1785? - by 1851)
        |       |          /-- Joseph ASQUITH  (Leeds 1816? - 1874 Leeds)
        |       |          /      \-- Mary  (Yorks. 1784? - 1851+)
        |       \-- Mary ASQUITH
        |              \          /-- John WARD
        |               \-- Ellen WARD  (Leeds 1816? - 1888 Leeds)
        /                          \-- Margaret
```

-Peter Francis (Capt.) MIDDLETON

```
        \                    /-- Arthur LUPTON  +
        |             /-- William LUPTON  (Leeds 1777 - 1828)
        |             /      \-- Olive RIDER  +
        |      /-- Francis LUPTON  (Leeds 1813 - 1884 Yorks.)
        |      /      \-- Ann DARNTON  +
        |   /-- Francis Martineau LUPTON
        |   |      \          /-- Thomas Michael (Dr.) GREENHOW  +
        |   |       \-- Frances Elizabeth GREENHOW
        |   /                 \-- Elizabeth MARTINEAU  +
        \-- Olive Christiana LUPTON  (Yorks. 1881 - 1936 Leeds)
```

to the yard. John Ward and his wife Margaret (nee Bracewell) lived in No. 8 and presumably that is where he worked as a hatter.

Kate has several other Wards in her family tree, including Katherine Ward who died in Coventry in 1811 (See chart on Page 153), and Anne Warde of Givendale in Yorkshire whose daughter Katherine Neville was born in Thornton Bridge around 1500 (Details on wikitree.com). Possible ancestors include Elizabeth Ward, who married Robert Middleton in Wakefield in 1749, and William Ward who married Jane Middleton from Healaugh around 1780.

Note: As a Leeds councillor in the late 1800s, Kate's ancestor Francis Martineau Lupton oversaw the demolition of numerous back-to-back houses which were often badly built and with no sanitation.

Kate's ancestor John Ward may have suffered the same occupational hazard as the Mad Hatter in Alice in Wonderland: serious mental problems caused by mercury poisoning.

THE ILLEGAL MIDDLETON MARRIAGE

BURIED in the churchyard of Old St Matthew's (above) in Chapel Allerton in Leeds are several of Kate's ancestors, including John William Middleton (inset), who married his first cousin Mary Asquith, and John's father William Middleton who married Mary Ward and her sister Sarah. Nothing unseemly, except for the fact that William's second marriage was illegal. Not a good move for a solicitor.

For reasons explained opposite, William and Sarah tied the knot in a Protestant church in Neuchatel in Switzerland in September 1860, one year after Mary died. There were no inheritance issues and, as far as we know, the couple lived happily until William died after a long illness in December 1884.

The Leeds Times described William Middleton as an esteemed solicitor who had been 'articulated' to Mr W Ward. Interestingly, there was no mention of Mary or Sarah; the newspaper simply stated that he had married 'a daughter of the late Mr John Ward'. Sarah died soon after and, like her husband and sister, was buried in the cemetery next to St Matthew's church which was demolished in 1935.

The cause of William Middleton's marital dilemma was an 1835 Act of Parliament passed primarily to benefit Henry Somerset, the 7th Duke of Beaufort.

Somerset, a descendant of Katherine Swynford through Charles Somerset, married Georgiana Fitzroy who was descended from one of Charles II's bastards. Georgiana was also a niece of the Duke of Wellington whose wife and mother-in-law were both named Catherine.

After Georgiana died in 1821, Somerset married her younger half-sister Emily Smith, despite the duke's strong disapproval. Wellington was justifiably concerned

Henry Somerset (above) married his deceased wife's half-sister in 1822.

because the marriage contravened canon law and could be voided. (Somerset and Emily had a daughter named Katherine born in 1834).

The 1835 Act legitimated all previous marriages to deceased wives' sisters, protecting the Beaufort inheritance. However, reminiscent of Henry VIII's claim against Catherine of Aragon, such marriages were deemed incestuous and made illegal from then on.

After numerous couples defied the law by marrying in Europe, the House of Lords judgment in *Brook v Brook* 1858 clearly stated: 'The law of the country in which a marriage is solemnised cannot give validity to a marriage prohibited by the laws of the country of the domicile and allegiance of the contracting parties.'

William Middleton must have known that his second marriage was illegal. Fortunately there were no repercussions and, after decades of heated debate, the 1835 Act was repealed in 1907.

Artist William Holman Hunt was shunned after marrying his deceased wife's sister Edith Waugh (right) in Switzerland, probably in the same church in which the Middletons were married.

— 149 —

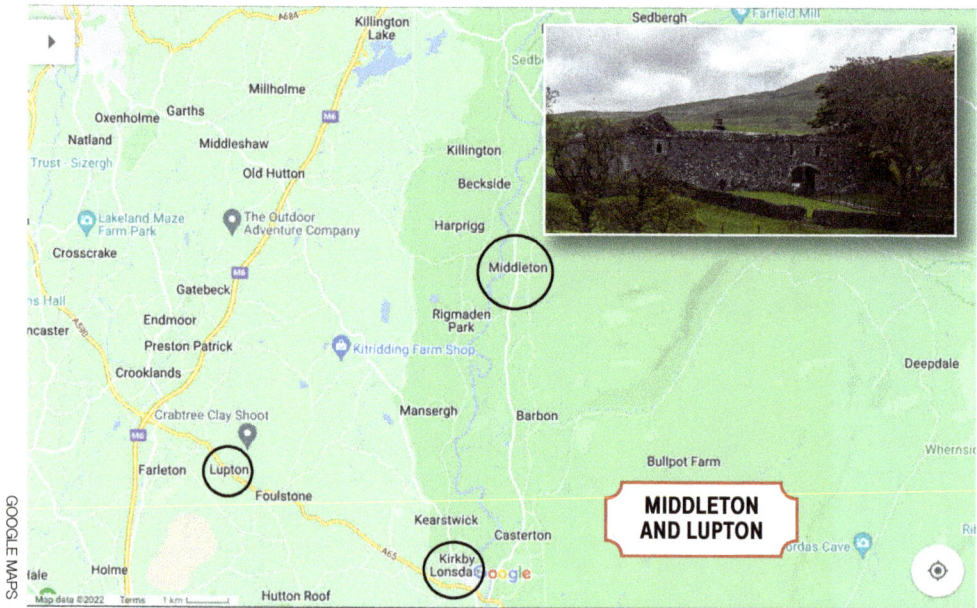

MIDDLETON
AND LUPTON

WHEREFORE THE LUPTON WOLF?

UNLIKE Kate's Middleton ancestors, the Luptons shown opposite knew exactly from whence their surname came because the only Lupton township in England is in Cumbria (formerly Westmorland). Conversely, England has more than 30 Middletons from which Kate's surname could have originated, including the one shown above which is not far from Lupton and Kirkby Lonsdale.

The exact relationship between the Middletons of Middleton Hall (inset) and their Stockeld namesakes is unknown but the two families were connected in the 1500s when John Middleton of Stockeld, a great-nephew of Kate's ancestor Agnes Gascoigne, married Isabel Middleton of Westmorland (See chart on Page 141).

Luptons from Cumbria were well established in neighbouring Yorkshire by the Middle Ages and Kate descends from those who settled in Leeds, including Francis Lupton's daughter Catherine who was born there in 1692. Olive Lupton, who married Richard Noel Middleton in 1914, came from a family of wealthy woollen merchants (See chart on Page 153).

There are no bloodlines on fabpedigree.com or any other website linking Kate's Lupton ancestors to their Cumbrian namesakes but apparently the connection was taken for granted, hence a wolf from the Lupton arms in the 1822 advertisement opposite.

Arms granted to Dr Roger Lupton in the 1500s had references to Eton College where he is commemorated each year on Threepenny Day (27th February). Prince William attended Eton and so might Prince George and Prince Louis.

The Lupton wolf on top of Michael Middleton's arms raises an interesting question: Why was a white hind chosen as the supporter in Kate's arms when a blue wolf was a better alternative? As J Paul Murdock pointed out in an online article

The PEDIGREE of
William LUPTON
Born: Leeds 1777 Died: 1828
Wife/Partner: **Ann DARNTON**
Children: **Francis LUPTON** ; Darnton (Mayor of Leeds : m. Sarah Darnton Luccock)

```
                    /-- Francis LUPTON  (Leeds 1658 - 1717 Leeds)
            /-- William LUPTON  (1700 - 1771)
        |       \                       /-- Edward (of Midgeley) MIDGELEY
        |       |                  /-- Richard (of Breragh) MIDGELEY
        |       |              /-- John MIDGELEY
        |       |          /-- Robert (of Breragh) MIDGELEY
        |       |      /-- Ralph (of Breragh) MIDGELEY
        |       |     /      \-- Mary SMITH
        |       \-- Ester MIDGELEY  (1669 - 1726)
        |             \            /-- George (of Potternewton) BURNISTON
        /                \-- Frances BURNISTON
    /-- Arthur LUPTON  (1748 - 1807)
    /       \-- Mary HIGSON  (Leeds 1715 - 1760)
```

William LUPTON

```
    \                       /-- Robert RIDER  (1633 - ?)
    |                  /-- Jonathon RYDER  (1684 - 1758 Yorks.)
    |          /-- David RIDER  (1716 - 1801)
    |         /      \-- Mary BERWICK  (1688 - 1758)
    \-- Olive RIDER  (Leeds, Yorks. 1753 - 1803)
        \                   /-- William AREY
        |          /-- William AREY  (1692 - 1736)
        |         /      \-- Sarah
        \-- Olive AREY  (1728? - 1753)
```

WM. LUPTON & CO.

WHITEHALL MILLS,
LEEDS

1773   1922

Reg. Trade Mark.

Telegrams :
" LUPTON, LEEDS."

Code :
A.B.C. (5th Edition).

in 2020, the Duchess of Cornwall's supporter is a blue boar from her father's arms.
Note: While the only connection between the Luptons and their animal symbol is
lupus, the Latin word for wolf, it is fitting because England's last wolf was purportedly killed at Humphrey Head in Cumbria in 1390.

A CORONAVIRUS CONNECTION?

KATE MIDDLETON'S life would have been completely different if Edward VII's oldest son had not died during an influenza outbreak less than a week before Kate's great-great-grandmother.

Scandal-prone Prince Albert Victor (above), who inherited haplogroup T from Katharina von Pfannberg, passed away at Sandringham on 14th January 1892 aged 28. And, according to her death certificate, 41-year-old Harriet Lupton (nee Davis) had influenza when she died on 19th January.

In a twist of fate reminiscent of Henry VIII and his deceased brother's wife Catherine of Aragon, the future George V married Prince Albert Victor's fiancée Mary of Teck.

Speculation that the outbreaks which began in 1889 may have been caused by a coronavirus was first raised in a 2005 article titled 'Complete Genomic Sequence of Human Coronavirus OC43' by Leen Vijgen and others. They wrote:

'Absolute evidence that an influenza virus was the causative agent of this epidemic was never obtained, due to the lack of tissue samples from that period...

However, it is tempting to speculate that the 1889-1890 pandemic may have been the result of interspecies transmission of bovine coronaviruses to humans... (One) argument is the fact that central nervous system symptoms were more pronounced than in other influenza outbreaks.'

Prince William tested positive to coronavirus in April 2020 but, reportedly, Kate and their children did not.

Two decades after Francis Martineau Lupton's wife Harriet died during an influenza outbreak, three of their sons died in World War I (See Page 41).

The PEDIGREE of

Olive Christiana LUPTON
Born: Yorks. 1881   Died: 1936 Leeds
Husband/Partner: **Richard Noel MIDDLETON**
Child: **Peter Francis (Capt.) MIDDLETON**

```
                              /-- Arthur LUPTON  (1748 - 1807)
                    /              \-- Mary HIGSON  (Leeds 1715 - 1760)
              /-- William LUPTON  (Leeds 1777 - 1828)
          /            \-- Olive RIDER  +
      /-- Francis LUPTON  (Leeds 1813 - 1884 Yorks.)
     |        \              /-- John DARNTON
     |         \-- Ann DARNTON  (Leeds 1784 - 1865)
  /-- Francis Martineau LUPTON
 |        \                    /-- Edward Martin GREENHOW  +
 |         |          /-- Thomas Michael (Dr.) GREENHOW
 |         |         /            \-- Mary POWDITCH  +
 |         \-- Frances Elizabeth GREENHOW
 |                  \              /-- Thomas MARTINEAU  +
 |                   \-- Elizabeth MARTINEAU  (1794 - 1850 Northumb.)
```

Olive Christiana LUPTON

```
     \                    /-- Thomas DAVIS  (1740 - 1820)
     |          /-- Richard Francis (Rev. Dr.) DAVIS
     |         /            \-- Jane SLADEN  (1742 - ?)
     |   /-- Thomas (Rev.) DAVIS
     |  |        \              /-- William STABLE  +
     |  |         \-- Sarah STABLE  (1778 - 1861)
     |  |                       \-- Judith DAWSON  (1756 - 1846)
     \-- Harriet Albina DAVIS  (Yorks. 1850 - 1892)
              \                 /-- Jonathan HOBBS  +
               |       /-- Robert HOBBES  (Oxon 1773 - 1817)
               |      /            \-- Katherine WARD  +
               \-- Christiana Maria HOBBES  (1810 - 1899)
```

THE DESPICABLE DR GREENHOW

IN MARCH 2020, *The Daily Telegraph* published a slightly ridiculous story headlined: 'The Duchess of Cambridge's ancestor would have led the fight against COVID-19'.

That ancestor was Dr Thomas Michael Greenhow (shown above) who was, as his Wikipedia entry attests, a distinguished epidemiologist who fought against cholera. However, he was on the wrong side of history because, as well as defending filthy conditions in hospitals, he supported the so-called miasma theory. The man who famously proved otherwise was Dr John Snow (see next page) who worked with Dr Greenhow in Newcastle.

Dr Greenhow (right) infuriated his sister-in-law and patient Harriet Martineau by releasing graphic gynae-cological information without her permission. After tuberculosis killed Elizabeth Martineau, Dr Greenhow married his son-in-law's sister Anne Lupton.

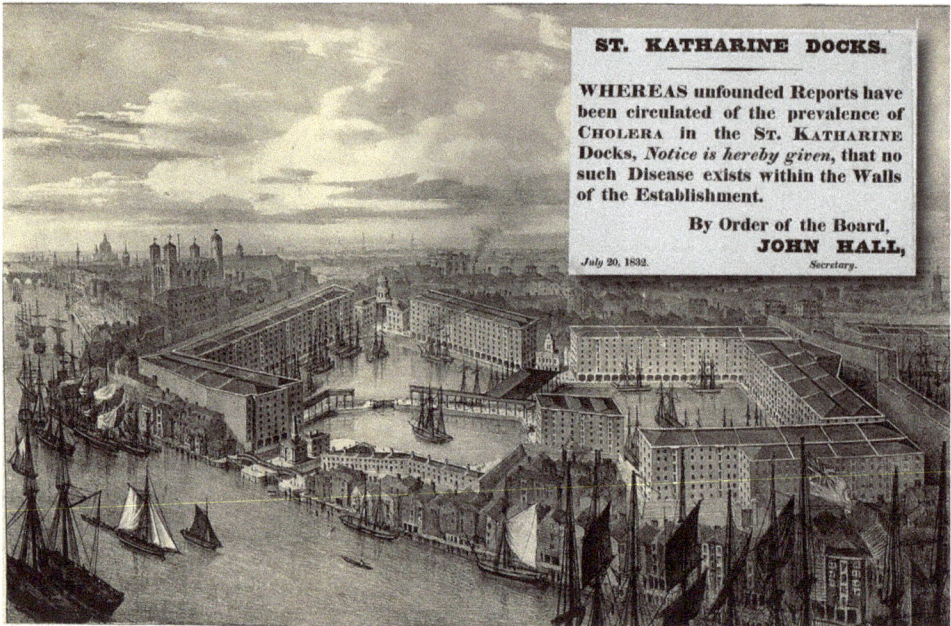

ST. KATHARINE DOCKS.

WHEREAS unfounded Reports have been circulated of the prevalence of CHOLERA in the ST. KATHARINE Docks, *Notice is hereby given*, that no such Disease exists within the Walls of the Establishment.

By Order of the Board,
JOHN HALL,
Secretary.

July 20, 1832.

'THE PESTILENCE IS AMONG US'

KATE'S paternal ancestor John Joseph Ablett died of cholera in 1847, fifteen years after London's first outbreak spread from the St Katharine docks. As shown above, the board issued a denial but *The Times* reported the grim truth: 'The pestilence is among us.'

Ablett was a farrier who lived in White Hart Street in Kennington, not far from where water was taken from the horribly polluted Thames. Relatively few people died of cholera in 1847 but the outbreak which started twelve months later claimed nearly 2000 lives.

The 1848 epidemic was studied by Dr John Snow who had previously noticed that coal workers contracted cholera deep underground. He concluded that the disease was most likely not caused by bad air, the so-called 'miasma theory' expounded in one of Kate's favourite Dickens novels, *Bleak House*.

Dr Snow, who was trained in Newcastle by Kate's ancestor Dr Thomas Michael Greenhow (see previous page), famously administered chloroform to Queen Victoria when she delivered her eighth child Prince Leopold in 1853.

John Ablett's wife Charlotte Grapes, and their son-in-law's father Thomas Glassborow (shown opposite), both died from tuberculosis, then known as phthisis.

London's Broad Street pump memorial commemorates Dr John Snow whose map of the 1854 cholera outbreak in Soho proved that the disease was water-borne.

— 154 —

The PEDIGREE of

Frederick George GLASSBOROW

Born: Essex 1889   **Died:** 1954 Folkestone

Wife/Partner: <u>Constance ROBISON</u>
Child: <u>Valerie GLASSBOROW</u>

```
                              /-- Richard GLASSBORROW  (1764 - ?)
                         /        \-- Sarah CRIPS
                    /-- Thomas GLASSBOROW  (London 1796? - 1860)
                   /         \-- Jane LEITH
              /-- Edward Thomas GLASSBOROW
             /         \-- Amy HARVEY  (Surrey 1788? - 1864)
        /-- Frederick John GLASSBOROW  (1859 - 1932)
        |      \         /-- John Joseph ABLETT  (1797? - 1847 Surrey)
        |       \-- Charlotte Elizabeth ABLETT
        |            \              /-- Joseph GRAPES
        |             |       /-- Joseph GRAPES  (London? 1760 - 1837)
        |             |      /      \-- Ann HUTTON
        |             \-- Charlotte GRAPES  (1799 - ?)
       /                        \-- Jane CELLSON
```

Frederick George GLASSBOROW

```
        \                /-- John ELLIOTT
        |       /-- John ELLIOTT
        |      /         \-- Sarah
        \-- Emily Jane ELLIOTT  (Mdsx. 1859 - 1901+)
```

During World War I, Kate's great-grandfather Frederick George Glassborow played rugby union with other sailors interned in the neutral Netherlands. As reported in the *Sunday Express* (30th October, 2016), Frederick probably played in an 'extraordinary' game between England and Scotland which was recreated a hundred years later in the city of Leeuwarden. Frederick's twin daughters Valerie and Mary served as code-breakers during World War II.

Note: In 1881, Frederick's grandfather Edward Glassborow (shown above) was an inmate, crime unknown, in London's Holloway Prison.

Sailors to celebrate WWI rugby game 100 years on

Scotland will face England in a replay of 1916 match-up

FABPEDIGREE.COM

TUDORS AND TUBERCULOSIS

CATHERINE of Aragon's first husband Prince Arthur was reportedly a victim of the mysterious 'sweating sickness' which first appeared in England after Henry VII defeated Richard III at Bosworth in 1485. However, Arthur may have had atypical cystic fibrosis which can cause severe lung damage in young people.

As Kyra Kramer, author of *Blood Will Tell* (2012), wrote in an online article: 'God knows that genetic conditions could flourish in a closed breeding population like the nobility. As many as 1 in 25 people of Northern European descent are carrying the recessive gene for cystic fibrosis, so it would not be very far-fetched for Henry VII and Elizabeth of York to both have the gene.' (Henry and Elizabeth were third cousins through Katherine Swynford.)

Two other possible victims were Edward VI, pictured above with his parents and grandparents, and Henry VIII's illegitimate son Henry Fitzroy (see opposite) who was descended from Katherine Swynford through Katherine Peshall.

Kate's children are descended from Fitzroy's half-sisters Catherine Clinton and Catherine Carey. And, coincidentally, through Alice FitzAlan (died 1416) Fitzroy had the same mtDNA as Edmund Beaufort who had an affair with Catherine of Valois.

Cystic fibrosis may have afflicted Henry VIII's nephew Henry Brandon (died 1534) whose

Prince Arthur (left) died soon after marrying Catherine of Aragon in November 1501.

— 156 —

The PEDIGREE of
Henry FitzROY
Born: Essex 1519   Died: 1536 London

HRH Charles's 13-Great Half-Uncle.   Lady Diana's 11-Great Half-Uncle.

Wife/Partner: **Mary (Lady) HOWARD**

```
                  /-- Edmund TUDOR  (1430? - 1456)
              /        \-- Catherine de VALOIS  +
          /-- Henry VII TUDOR (King) of ENGLAND
          |   \         /-- John (K.G.) BEAUFORT  +
          |    \-- Margaret BEAUFORT
          /         \-- Margaret (of BLETSOE) BEAUCHAMP  +
      /-- Henry VIII TUDOR  (London 1491 - 1547 London)
      |   \                 /-- Richard PLANTAGENET-YORK  +
      |   |                 |  / or: poss. BLAYBOURNE the Archer (cuckolder)
      |   |             /-- Edward IV `of Rouen' PLANTAGENET-YORK
      |   |             /      \-- Cecily (Lady) NEVILLE  +
      |   \-- Elizabeth (of YORK) PLANTAGENET
      |           \             /-- Richard (K.G.) WYDEVILLE  +
      |            \-- Elizabeth (Lady) WOODVILLE
      /                  \-- Jacquette de LUXEMBOURG  +
```

Henry FitzROY

```
      \                      /-- John (IV/III; Sir) BLOUNT  +
      |                  /-- Humphrey (Sir) BLOUNT
      |                  /      \-- Alicia de la BERE  +
      |              /-- Thomas (Sir; of Kinsel (Kinlet)) BLOUNT
      |              /        \-- Elizabeth WYNNINGTON  +
      |          /-- John (Sir) BLOUNT  (Shrops. 1484? - 1531)
      |          |   \             /-- prob. Richard (Sir; of Croft Castle) CROFT  +
      |          |    \-- Anne CROFT
      |          /         \-- prob. Eleanor CORNWALL  +
      \-- Elizabeth BLOUNT  (Shrops. 1502? - 1540?)
              \             /-- Humphrey (Esq.) PESHALL  +
              |             /  OR: poss. Humphrey PERSHALL  +
              |         /-- Hugh PESHALL  (1459?? - ?)
              \-- Katherine PESHALL  (1483? - 1540?)
```

mother Mary Tudor possibly died from tuberculosis, as did Henry VII in 1509.

In a cruel twist of fate, it seems that cystic fibrosis has persisted in humans because a single cystic fibrosis gene gives an evolutionary selective advantage against tuberculosis.

Tuberculosis, also known as phthisis or consumption, killed three of Kate's paternal ancestors: Elizabeth Martineau, Charlotte Grapes and Thomas Glassborow. And Kate's maternal ancestor John Harrison, pictured right with his wife Jane (née Hill), lost both parents and two of his siblings to tuberculosis in Hetton-le-Hole in Durham in the late 1800s.

— 157 —

CATHERINE OF ARAGON'S CURSES

AROUND 1527, after Catherine of Aragon had failed to produce a male heir, Henry VIII determined that their marriage was cursed because she had previously been married to his brother Prince Arthur. Despite having obtained a papal dispensation, Henry was obsessed with this passage from Leviticus: 'If a man takes his brother's wife, it is impurity; he has uncovered his brother's nakedness, they shall be childless.'

Queen Catherine is pictured above trying to convince her husband that she did not have sex with his brother (See Black Catherine's Secret, Page 222). Unfortunately, the truth was irrelevant because by this time Henry VIII was lusting after Anne Boleyn whose sister Mary was Catherine Carey's mother.

Cardinal Reginald Pole berated the hypocritical monarch: 'Are you ignorant of the law which certainly no less prohibits marriage with a sister of one with whom you have become one flesh, than with one with whom your brother was one flesh?'

According to Kyra Kramer, Catherine of Aragon's pregnancy problems resulted

from the blood which Henry VIII inherited from Jacquetta of Luxembourg (shown opposite). In an online article, Kyra wrote:

'If a foetus inherits the Kell positive blood type from the father, a Kell negative mother's body will develop a Kell alloimmunisation after the first Kell positive pregnancy... The mother's immune system

Cardinal Reginald Pole, a central character in Philippa Gregory's novel The King's Curse, *was an uncle of Katherine Pole (See Hypothetical Queen Catherines, Page 46).*

The PEDIGREE of

Mary I TUDOR (Queen) of ENGLAND

Born: London 18 Feb 1516   Died: 17 Nov 1558 London
Husband/Partner: Philip II HAPSBURG (King) of SPAIN

```
                    /-- Edmund TUDOR  (1430? - 1456)
                  /           \-- Catherine de VALOIS  +
                /-- Henry VII TUDOR (King) of ENGLAND
              |         \           /-- John (K.G.) BEAUFORT  +
              |          \-- Margaret BEAUFORT
              /               \-- Margaret (of BLETSOE) BEAUCHAMP  +
          /-- Henry VIII TUDOR  (London 1491 - 1547 London)
          |      \               /-- Richard PLANTAGENET-YORK  +
          |       |             /      / or: poss. BLAYBOURNE the Archer (cuckolder)
          |       |        /-- Edward IV `of Rouen' PLANTAGENET-YORK
          |       |       /        \-- Cecily (Lady) NEVILLE  +
          |        \-- Elizabeth (of YORK) PLANTAGENET
          |              \           /-- Richard (K.G.) WYDEVILLE  +
          |               \-- Elizabeth (Lady) WOODVILLE
          /                     \-- Jacquette de LUXEMBOURG  +
```

-Mary I TUDOR (Queen) of ENGLAND

```
          |                 /-- John II `the Great' (King) of ARAGON
          |               /          \-- Leonor Urraca Sancha (Princess) of CASTILE  +
          |        /-- Ferdinand V (King) of CASTILE (SPAIN)  (1452 - 1516)
          |       |         \           /-- Federigo (Count) of MELGAR  +
          |       |          \-- Juana (Princess) of MELGAR
          |       /               \-- Maria (Baroness) of AYOLY-CORDOVA  +
           \-- Catherine (Infanta) of ARAGON
                  \               /-- Enrique III (King) de CASTILE (& Leon)  +
                   |            /-- Juan II (King) de CASTILE (& Leon)  (1405 - 1454)
                   |           /        \-- Katherine (Lady) PLANTAGENET  +
                    \-- Isabella (I; Queen) de CASTILE  (1451 - 1504)
```

would attack a Kell positive foetus as foreign tissue, which would result in foetal or neonatal death.' Henry VIII's blood type would also explain his well-documented descent into irrational and tyrannical behaviour, traits consistent with McLeod Syndrome which impacts Kell positive men after the age of 30.

Note: If England had remained Catholic beyond the 1500s, Catherine of Aragon would probably have been canonised with many churches dedicated to her.

BLOODY MARY'S BLOOD

HENRY VIII allegedly wanted the future Queen Mary I, who was declared illegitimate after he married Anne Boleyn, to marry her illegitimate half-brother Henry Fitzroy. Mary instead married Philip II of Spain, her first cousin once removed who had the same mitochondrial DNA through Isabella of Castile (shown above). Catholic Mary was nicknamed 'Bloody Mary' because she ordered Protestants to be burned at the stake.

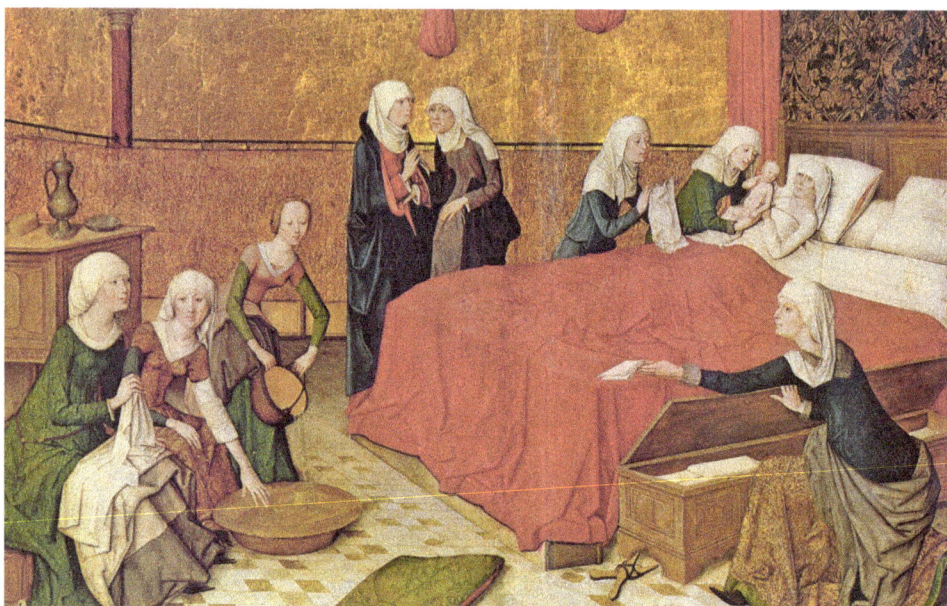

BACK-TO-BACK PREGNANCIES...

REGARDLESS of whether Henry VIII had Kell positive blood, Catherine of Aragon's gynaecological problems were exacerbated by 'disordered eating' and back-to-back pregnancies.

In April 1510, less than ten weeks after her first pregnancy had produced a stillborn daughter, Catherine was pregnant again with a boy named Henry who survived for just 52 days. She had at least four more pregnancies but only one surviving child, the future Mary I who died childless.

James II's oldest daughter Mary II was also childless after miscarrying two children in consecutive years. But the most obvious victim of back-to-back pregnancies is Mary's sister Queen Anne who had only five live births out of 17 pregnancies between 1683 and 1700, with none of her children surviving to adulthood.

In 2007, after studying Bedouin communities in which about half of all marriages are between first cousins, Suzanne E Joseph from the University of Massachusetts found that infants born to first cousins had more than double the odds of dying as infants born to other couples.

But Joseph also found that short birth intervals were a greater determinant of infant mortality than closely related parents. Crucially, for every additional month before the birth of the next child, the odds of infant death decreased by 3.7 per cent. Other studies have shown that babies conceived less than six months after their siblings have a 40 per cent increased risk of being born prematurely, plus a 60 per cent increased risk of low birth weight.

The births of Kate's three children were well spaced with nearly two years between George and Charlotte, and three years between Charlotte and Louis.

Catherine of Aragon's statue; Princess Diana at the White House; and Kate in Canada.

… AND ROYAL EATING DISORDERS

DESPITE concerns about Kate's 'unhealthy thinness', there is no proof that she has an eating disorder like Catherine of Aragon or St Catherine of Siena.

According to Giles Tremlett, author of *Catherine of Aragon: Henry's Spanish Queen* (2010), 'disordered eating' affected her menstrual cycles. The problem was so bad that Pope Julius warned that if fasting stood in the way of Catherine's 'physical health and the procreation of children' then her marriage could be annulled.

In *The Daily Mail,* Tremlett wrote: 'A disturbed menstrual cycle is one of the first symptoms to appear in modern eating disorders, and problems getting pregnant can be another knock-on effect… Stillbirths, miscarriages and infant deaths were a painfully repetitive part of (Catherine's) existence.'

As shown in *The Crown* TV series, Princess Diana suffered from bulimia which reportedly began when, while pregnant with Prince William, she learned that Prince Charles was involved with Camilla.

Unfounded claims that Kate is bulimic surfaced in 2017 after she was photographed several times with bandaged fingers.

St Catherine of Siena has been retrospectively diagnosed with anorexia mirabilis, a form of self-starvation that was common among devout Catholic girls in the 1300s. Catherine reportedly inserted sticks into her throat to induce vomiting.

THE DUKES WHO DIED YOUNG

AFTER SIRING four dukes of Cambridge who died in infancy, James II (above left) may well have believed that the title was cursed.

Anne Hydre (above right), one of the few commoners before Kate to marry an heir to the throne, was heavily pregnant with Charles Stuart when she exchanged vows with the then Duke of York in September 1660. Charles, the first Duke of Cambridge, died the following year aged six months.

The second duke was James Stuart (inset) who died before his fourth birthday in June 1667, one month after the death of his brother Charles, the Duke of Kendall, who lived for only ten months. The third Duke of Cambridge, Edgar Stuart, died four years later aged three.

Anne Hyde never recovered from the birth of Catherine in February 1671 and died the following month. Catherine died in December leaving two surviving sisters, the future queens Mary and Anne.

The short-lived fourth Duke of Cambridge, another Charles Stuart, was delivered by James II's second wife Mary of Moderna in 1677, two years after her daughter Catherine Laura died of convulsions aged less than nine months. James II's alleged illegitimate daughter Catherine Darnley died in 1743 aged about 62.

The Cambridge dukedom was recreated for the future George II. His wife Caroline was the first Duchess of Cambridge followed by Augusta, wife of George III's seventh son Prince Adolphus. Sarah Fairbrother, wife of Adolphus' son Prince George, should have been the third Cambridge duchess but was ineligible because of her illegitimate children.

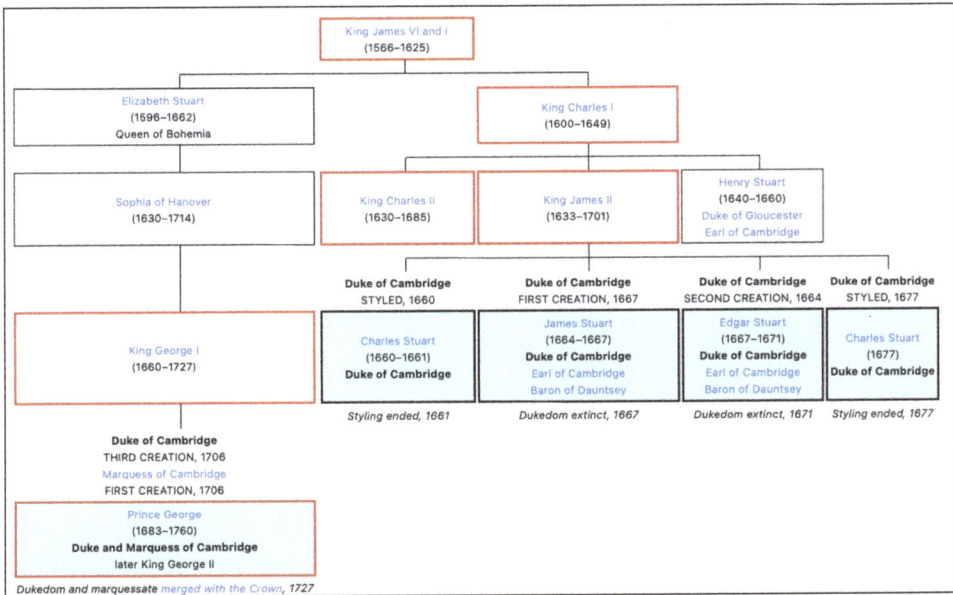

```
King James VI and I
(1566–1625)

Elizabeth Stuart                          King Charles I
(1596–1662)                               (1600–1649)
Queen of Bohemia

Sophia of Hanover      King Charles II    King James II     Henry Stuart
(1630–1714)            (1630–1685)        (1633–1701)       (1640–1660)
                                                            Duke of Gloucester
                                                            Earl of Cambridge

              Duke of Cambridge    Duke of Cambridge    Duke of Cambridge       Duke of Cambridge
              STYLED, 1660         FIRST CREATION, 1667 SECOND CREATION, 1664   STYLED, 1677

King George I      Charles Stuart    James Stuart      Edgar Stuart       Charles Stuart
(1660–1727)        (1660–1661)       (1664–1667)       (1667–1671)        (1677)
                   Duke of Cambridge Duke of Cambridge Duke of Cambridge  Duke of Cambridge
                                     Earl of Cambridge Earl of Cambridge
                                     Baron of Dauntsey Baron of Dauntsey

                   Styling ended, 1661  Dukedom extinct, 1667  Dukedom extinct, 1671  Styling ended, 1677

Duke of Cambridge
THIRD CREATION, 1706
Marquess of Cambridge
FIRST CREATION, 1706

Prince George
(1683–1760)
Duke and Marquess of Cambridge
later King George II

Dukedom and marquessate merged with the Crown, 1727
```

THE KENSINGTON PALACE CURSE

WHILE the Cambridge title is seemingly no longer cursed, the same may not be true for the palace where Kate raised her children.

The first Duchess of Cambridge, Caroline of Ansbach, died horribly at Kensington Palace in 1737 when her strangulated bowel burst. Her husband George II died 23 years later on one of the palace's toilets.

But the most ill-fated occupant was Anne Hyde's daughter Queen Anne who had 17 pregnancies but only one surviving child, Prince William, who died mysteriously aged 11.

Queen Victoria, whose daughter Louise designed the statue above, suffered under the Kensington System, a strict set of rules imposed by her mother's alleged lover John Conroy. Two other miserable residents were Princess Margaret and Princess Diana.

SLAVE-BRANDING.

SLAVE-TRADING ANCESTORS

ONE of Kate's paternal ancestors must have seen slaves branded with the initials of Prince William's ancestor James II whose ludicrous statue in Roman dress (above) still stands in London's Trafalgar Square.

British genealogist John Wintrip revealed this connection in an article (available online) titled 'The Ancestry of William Davenport of Reading'. It had previously been claimed that Kate is descended from Henry VIII's illegitimate daughter Catherine Carey through a William Davenport who was born in Shropshire. But Wintrip found that the husband of Grace Alloway (shown opposite) was born in Reading around 1682, exactly 300 years before Kate was born in the same city.

William Davenport's father Laurence was a surgeon employed by the Royal African Company (RAC) in Sierra Leone, probably on Bunce Island, from the mid-1680s until his death around 1693. During that time about 5000 slaves a year were being shipped from Africa to the Caribbean and nearly a quarter of them died en route.

The future James II co-founded the RAC in 1660 with his newly-crowned brother Charles II. James was governor of the company and thousands of slaves were branded with his initials (DY for Duke of York). The irons were dipped in palm oil so that flesh would not adhere to the metal.

Coincidentally, the Davenport arms feature a man with a rope around his neck to show the family's power over life and death.

Prince William is descended from George Smith (left) of Croydon whose family was compensated for 461 Jamaican slaves in 1833. Smith had a daughter named Catherine whose father-in-law Sir Robert Wigram, a surgeon in the East India Company, had a wife named Catherine.

THE PEDIGREE OF
Christiana Maria HOBBES
Born: 1810   Died: 1899

Husband/Partner: **Thomas (Rev.) DAVIS**
Child: **Harriet Albina DAVIS**

```
                              /-- Charles HOBBS  (? - 1700)
                    /-- Thomas HOBBS  (? - 1810 Gloucester)
          /-- Jonathan HOBBS  (Gloucester 1736 - 1787)
         /            \-- Mary MATTHEWS
    /-- Robert HOBBES  (Oxon 1773 - 1817)
   |    \                /-- William WARD  (Yardley?)
   |     |      /-- John WARD  (1707 - 1765)
   |     |     /            \-- Sarah GIBBONS
   |     \-- Katherine WARD  (1739 - 1811 Coventry)
   /                \-- Ann BILLINGSLEY  (1709 - 1782)
```

Christiana Maria HOBBES

```
    \           /-- Thomas ASHFORD  (1731 - 1797 Stratford)
    \-- Elizabeth Davenport ASHFORD  (1777 - 1825)
         \                      /-- Laurence DAVENPORT
         |          /-- William DAVENPORT  (Reading by 1682 - 1723)
         |         |      \ | OR: Not! William DAVENPORT  +
         |         /      \-- Elizabeth LEWIS  (? - 1712 Reading)
         |  /-- William DAVENPORT  (1713 - 1798 Berks.)
         | |      \        /-- Richard ALLOWAY  (? - 1713)
         | |       \-- Grace ALLOWAY  (Oxfords.? 1681 - 1757)
         | /                \-- Jane
         \-- Sarah DAVENPORT  (1741 - 1805 Stratford)
             \-- Elizabeth MARSHALL  (1714 - 1799 Berks.)
```

THE STATUE THAT NEVER WAS

TWO decades before Black Lives Matter protests led to statues of slave traders being pulled down, controversy erupted in New York over plans for a giant statue of Charles II's wife Catherine of Braganza in the district of Queens, which was supposedly named after her.

Supporters of the statue, including Donald Trump, claimed that Catherine set aside money to free slaves. However, the project became mired in protest and the nearly-completed statue by artist Audrey Flack was melted down in 1998. Soon after, a scale model (right) was erected in a Lisbon park.

By popularising tea drinking in Britain, Catherine inadvertently boosted the trans-Atlantic slave trade and also the Chinese opium trade (See From Braganza to Bridgerton, Page 248).

Note: Nobody knows if Katherine Ward (shown above) was related to Kate's other Ward ancestors.

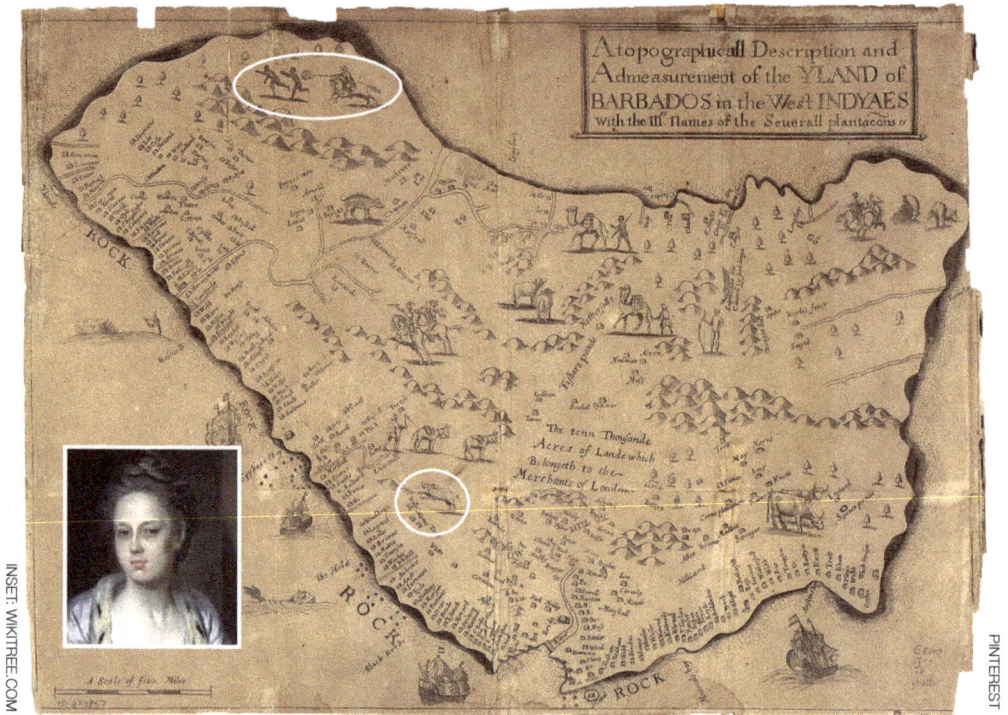

A topographicall Description and Admeasurement of the YLAND of BARBADOS in the West INDYAES with the III flames of the Seuerall plantacons

SUGAR IN THE ROYAL BLOOD?

GIVEN that rumours about a slave ancestor in Prince William's pedigree have been circulating inside the Lascelles family for hundreds of years, it is remarkable that the matter has received no attention from genealogists or historians.

In *Slavery, Family, and Gentry Capitalism in the British Atlantic* (2006), Dr Simon Smith revealed that Frances Ball (inset above and shown opposite) was allegedly a 'throwback'. That could explain why her father Guy Ball, who owned the Barbados plantation circled above, omitted Frances from his will.

Frances' descendant Ian Rankin pointedly referred to 'the mistake in the sugar plantation', clearly implying that one of his ancestors was a female slave. According to Andrea Stuart, author of *Sugar in the Blood* (2012), it was 'completely common' for planters to breed their own slaves because it lessened their dependence on the Royal African Company.

Ball's wife Catherine Dubois, shown opposite as Katherine Hole, was born in Barbados around 1688. According to ancestry.com her mother was Katherine Gilhampton; her father was Thomas Dubois (Duboys) who died in 1699; and Joseph Hole was her step-father.

Catherine Dubois had six children, including Catherine Ball who was born in 1709. Kate's children are descended from Frances Ball through Frances Lascelles (shown opposite), step-daughter of Edward Lascelles' first wife Catherine Mary Lloyd of Coedmore.

The royal family has never apologised for its historical involvement in slavery and that task may befall the future William V and Queen Catherine.

The PEDIGREE of

Edward (1st Earl of HAREWOOD) LASCELLES

Born: Barbados 1740   Died: 1820

Lady Diana's 6-Great Grandfather.

Wife/Partner: **Anne CHALONER**
Children: **Frances (Lady of Harewood) LASCELLES ; Henry (2nd Earl of Harewood) LASCELLES**

```
                                        /-- Robert (of Ganthorpe & Eyholme Grange) LASCELLES
                              /-- Francis (of Stank Hall & Northallerton) LASCELLES
                         /        \-- Dorothy NEWPORT
                  /-- William LASCELLES  (? - 1624)
                  |         \        /-- John (of Northallerton) CHARTER
                  |         /        \-- Elizabeth CHARTER
             /-- Francis (Colonel) LASCELLES  (1612 - ?)
             |        \        /-- Robert (of Yafforth) WADESON
             |        /        \-- Elizabeth WADESON
        /-- Daniel (of STANK & Northallerton) LASCELLES
        |        \                        /-- William (Sir) ST. QUINTON  +
        |        |                   /-- Gabriel ST. QUINTON  (? - by 1577)
        |        |                   /        \-- Dorothy HASTINGS  +
        |        |              /-- George ST. QUINTON  (? - 1584+)
        |        |              /        \-- Dorothy GRIFFITH  +
        |        |         /-- William (1st Baronet of HARPHAM) ST. QUINTON
        |        |         |        \        /-- William CREYKE  +
        |        |         |        \-- Agnes CREYKE
        |        |         |                 \-- Frances BABTHORPE  +
        |        \-- Frances ST. QUINTON  (? - 1658)
        |                 \        /-- Robert LACY  (? - by 1589)
        |                 \-- Mary LACY  (by 1590 - 1649)
        |                          \        /-- Marmaduke (of Esthorpe) THRELKELD  +
        |                          \-- Katherine THRELKELD  (? - by 1637)
        /                                   \-- Elizabeth HILTON  +
   /-- Edward LASCELLES
   |         \        /-- Edward LASCELLES  (? - 1690?)
   |         \-- Mary LASCELLES  (1662? - 1734)
```

-Edward (1st Earl of HAREWOOD) LASCELLES

```
        \        /-- Guy (of BARBADOS) BALL  (1673? - by 1722)
        \-- Frances BALL  (Barbados 1714? - 1761)
                 \        /-- Joseph (of Bridgetown) HOLE  (? - 1735)
                 \-- Katherine (of Barbados) HOLE  (1687? - ?)
```

Huge profits from slavery funded Harewood House (above) which replaced Gawthorpe Hall, home of Kate's Gascoigne ancestors (See map on Page 140). DNA tests on the remains of Edward Lascelles, who was buried at Harewood in 1820, would determine if he descended from an African slave.

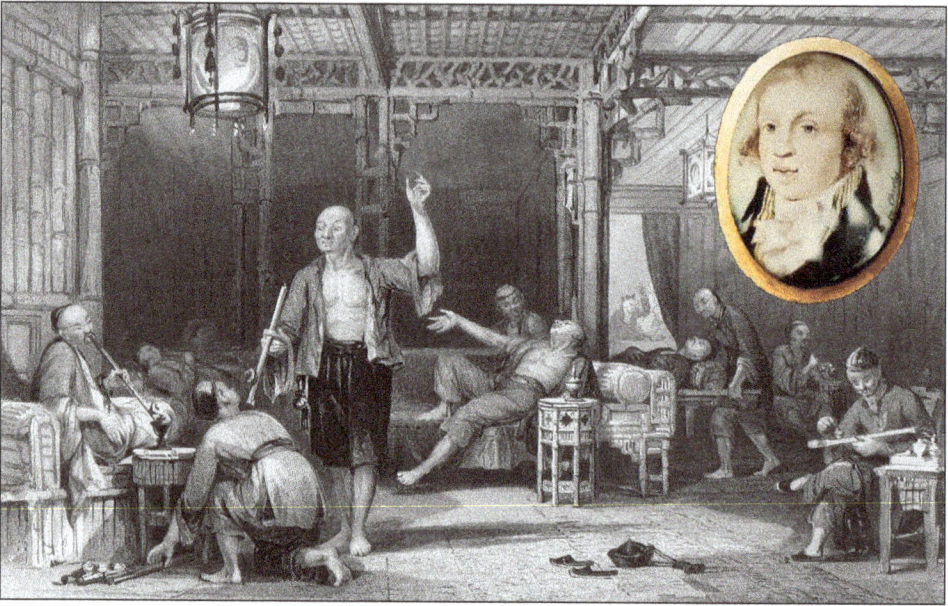

INSET: FINDAGRAVE.COM

WIKIWAND.COM

OPIUM APOLOGY OVERDUE

IF the royal family ever apologises for its historic involvement in slavery it should also apologise for the East India Company's opium shipments to China.

As Hong Kong University professor Jean-Pierre Lehmann wrote in the *Financial Times* in June 2014, shortly before the Queen met the Chinese Premier, a sincere apology would 'serve to remind us Europeans that while we admonish the Chinese today to be 'responsible stakeholders', when we were on top we did not play by the rules, because there were no rules, except for the rule of sheer brute force.'

The East India Company (EIC) employed many Scots, including Prince William's ancestor Theodore Forbes (inset above), father of Katherine Scott Forbes and her half-brother Frederick. As shown opposite, Theodore's parents were second cousins John Forbes of Boyndlie and Katherine Morison of Bognie, daughter of Catherine Duff and great-granddaughter of Katherine Duff.

Theodore Forbes worked in Bombay which Britain obtained from Portugal as part of Catherine of Braganza's dowry in 1661. The EIC had been founded 60 years earlier with help from several Middleton sea captains who were probably related to Prince William's ancestors.

William's fifth great-grandfather, George Smith the slave owner, was an EIC director prior to the First Opium War which started in 1839.

Prince William inherited extremely rare R30b mitochondrial DNA from Eliza Kevork, the Armenian-Indian mother of Katherine Scott Forbes (right) who had an aunt named Katherine and a niece named Catherine.

GENI.COM

THE PEDIGREE OF
Katherine Scott FORBES

Born: India 1812   Died: 1893 Aberdeen

Lady Diana's 3-Great Grandmother.

Husband/Partner: **James CROMBIE**
Child: **Jane CROMBIE**

```
                    /-- George (4th of Boyndlie) FORBES (1715 - 1794)
                    |        \        /-- George (2nd of Bognie) MORISON  +
                    |         \-- Susannah MORISON
                    /              \-- Christian URQUHART  +
          /-- John (5th of Boyndlie) FORBES (1758 - 1824)
          |         \        /-- William (of Bruxie) KEITH
          |          \-- Janet (of Bruxie) KEITH (1715 - 1763)
          |                  \        /-- Alexander (4th of Blackton) FORBES  +
          |                   \-- Helen (of Blackton) FORBES
          /                           \-- Isabel HACKETT
   /-- Theodore FORBES (1788 - 1820)
   |      \                   /-- George (2nd of Bognie) MORISON  +
   |       |          /-- Theodore MORISON (1685 - 1766)
   |       |          /       \-- Christian URQUHART  +
   |       |   /-- Alexander (4th of BOGNIE) MORISON (1727? - 1801)
   |       |   |      \        /-- Charles (of Pitrichie) MAITLAND  +
   |       |   |       \-- Catharine MAITLAND (? - 1743? (or '48?))
   |       |   /                \-- Jane (Jean) FORBES  +
   |       \-- Katherine (of Bognie) MORISON (1757 - 1832)
   |                  \        /-- Alexander (3rd of Drummuir) DUFF  +
   |                   /-- John (of Cubben) DUFF (1701? - 1743?)
   |                   |    /-- Katherine DUFF  +
   |                   \-- Catharine DUFF (1732 - 1803)
   |                         \        /-- James GORDON  +
   |                          \-- Helen GORDON (? - 1767?)
   /                                 \-- Helen (Hon.) FRASER  +
```

-Katherine Scott FORBES

```
          \        /-- Jakob KEVORK (KEVORKIAN) (Armenia?)
           \-- Eliza KEVORK (KEWARK) (Bombay?, India)
```

As a clerk for the East and West India Dock Company in London, Kate's Scottish-born great-great-great-grandfather James Cockburn Robison probably handled shipments of Chinese tea and Caribbean sugar during the early 1840s. His son was Gavin Fullarton Robison (See chart on Page 4).

KATE'S SCOTTISH CONNECTIONS

THROUGH seven of his wife's namesakes — Katherine Scott Forbes, Katherine Morison, Catherine Duff, Katherine Duff, Katherine Gordon, Katherine Forbes and Katherine Seton — the current Earl of Strathearn is descended from the first titleholder, Malise (shown opposite), whose wife may have been named Rosabella. Kate has a possible bloodline through Henry Constable's Scottish ancestors (See chart on Page 139).

There is no proof that legendary Templar knight Hugh de Payen (above left and shown opposite) married Catherine St Clair but he did visit Scotland in 1128 and was granted land at Temple, west of North Middleton and not far from the mysterious Rosslyn Chapel at Roslin (See map opposite).

Intriguingly, there is a local legend about the Temple church (above) which states: 'Twixt the oak and the elm tree you will find buried the millions free.'

While Henri St Clair may not have had a daughter named Catherine, he was a crusader and his father William 'the Seemly' accompanied St Margaret and an alleged piece of the True Cross. And, according to another legend, the Holy Grail was taken to Scotland after the Templars were outlawed in France.

Prince William's possible ancestor William de Middleton, who spent time at Temple (also known as Ballantrodoch) after his initiation at Temple Newsam near Leeds, was one of the last Templar knights tried at Holyrood in Edinburgh in 1309.

In 2016, the Countess of Strathearn, who often wears a Strathearn tartan scarf, visited St Catherine's Roman Catholic primary school which is not far from St Catherine's Well at Liberton, south of Edinburgh.

The PEDIGREE of

Catherine ST. CLAIR

poss. Husbands/Partners: Hugh (Sir) de PAYEN ; Hugues II de GISORS
Children: poss. Edmund ; poss. Theobald

```
                              /-- Mauger `the Young' of NORMANDY  (986? - 1040?)
                          |        \-- Poppa de ENVERMEU  (skip?)
                       /            | OR: prob. not Judith of BRITTANY  +
                   /-- Walderne (Earl) de ST. CLAIR  (1006? - 1047?)
                   |        \-- Germaine of CORBEIL  +
                   /            | or: (Miss) de ST. CLAIR-EN-AUGE (of BASSENVILLE)
               /-- William `the Seemly' de ST. CLAIR  (1028? - ?)
               |      \         /-- Richard II `the Good' of NORMANDY  +
               |        \-- Margaret (Helen) of NORMANDY
               |              \-- Judith (Princess) of BRITTANY  +
           /-- poss. Henri `the Crusader' de ST. CLAIR  (1100? - ?)
           |    \ | or: poss. (NN), Henri's brother
           |    |                /-- Maldred (FitzCRINAN) of SCOTLAND  +
           |    |      /-- Gospatrick I MacCRINAN (1st Earl) of DUNBAR
           |    |      /      \-- Ealdgyth (Edith) of NORTHUMBRIA  +
           |    \-- Dorothy (Doratha; of Raby) DUNBAR
           |          \       /-- Edred (Prince) of ENGLAND  +
           |            \-- poss. Aethelreda (Princess) of ENGLAND  (1042? - ?)
           |                  \ | OR: prob. not Aethelreda of WESSEX  +
           /
```

Catherine ST. CLAIR
```
           \
           |          /-- Forteith  (? - 1150?)
           |    /-- Malise (1st Earl) of STRATHEARN  (? - 1141+)
           \-- poss. Rosabel FORTEITH of STRATHEARN  (1082?? - ?)
```

ST CATHERINE
CONNECTIONS

Spilled holy oil from Mt Sinai allegedly created St Catherine's Well (inset) which was visited annually by nuns from St Catherine of Scienna (sic) convent near Edinburgh. Under Glencorse Reservoir is St Catherine's chapel which may have been visited by Kate's Newbigging ancestors from South Lanarkshire

DEBUNKING *THE DA VINCI CODE*

ROSSLYN CHAPEL, which features in Dan Brown's bestselling novel, was built by Catherine Stewart's grandfather long after the Templars were disbanded. There is no evidence that William St Clair (shown opposite) was a Templar knight and, significantly, two of his ancestors gave evidence against William de Middleton in Edinburgh in 1309.

However, the St Clairs (Sinclairs) were associated with Freemasonry. Another William St Clair became Scotland's first grand master in 1736, and a known Freemason carved many of the chapel's weird carvings in the mid-1800s.

Pierre Plantard de Saint-Clair, no relation to the Scottish clan, perpetrated the Priory of Sion hoax in the 1950s; the Jesus bloodline was invented by the authors of *Holy Blood, Holy Grail* (1982); and Dan Brown stole their pseudohistory.

There is zero proof that Jesus had any children and, even if he did, there are only two alternatives: countless millions of descendants (including Kate Middleton) through the Merovingian kings, or none at all.

Note: William St Clair's namesake great-great-grandfather and the legendary Black Douglas were both killed fighting Moors in Spain in 1330 while taking Robert the Bruce's heart to the Holy Land. Sir William Douglas of Nithsdale (shown opposite), was the bastard son of the Black Douglas' bastard son Archibald.

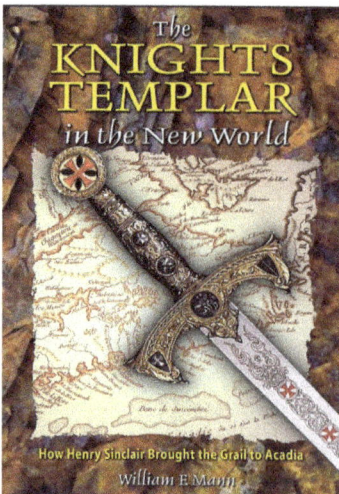

This is one of many books alleging that Henry St Clair of Roslin, grandfather of William St Clair who built Rosslyn Chapel, voyaged to North America long before Columbus sailed in 1492.

The PEDIGREE of

Catherine (Lady) STEWART

Lady Diana's 15-Great Grandmother.

Husband/Partner: <u>John (6th Lord) FORBES</u>
Child: <u>Elizabeth FORBES</u>

```
     /-- James (Sir) `Black Knight' STEWART
     |         \           /-- John MacALAN de ERGARDIA  +
     |          \-- Isabel (MacDOUGALL; of LORN) de ERGARDIA
     /                      \-- Joanna (Jonet Joan; de) ISAAC  +
 /-- John (of BALVENY) STEWART  (1441 - 1512)
 |        \                  /-- John (BEAUFORT) of GAUNT  +
 |         |          /-- John `Fairborn' (K.G.; de) BEAUFORT
 |         |         /     \-- Katherine ROELT  +
 |         \-- Joan (Joanna) BEAUFORT  (1407? - 1445)
 |                   \           /-- Thomas (II; de) HOLLAND  +
 |                    \-- Margaret (of Kent) HOLAND  (1384? - 1439)
 /                              \-- Alice (Lady of Arundel) FitzALAN  +
```

- Catherine (Lady) STEWART

```
     \                  /-- William (II) ST. CLAIR  +
     |                 /     | OR: source: R1b-S5246 y-Haplogroup  +
     |          /-- Henry (of Roslin) ST. CLAIR (SINCLAIR)
     |         /     \-- Isabel of STRATHEARN  +
     |   /-- Henry II SINCLAIR (ST. CLAIR)  (? - 1422)
     |  /     \-- Jean (of Dirleton Castle) HALIBURTON  +
     /-- William SINCLAIR (ST. CLAIR)  (? - 1480?)
     |  |         \           /-- William (Knight; of Nithsdale) DOUGLAS  +
     |  |          \-- Egidia (Jill) DOUGLAS  (? - 1438?)
     |  /                     \-- Egidia (Princess) STEWART  +
     \-- Eleanor (Lady) SINCLAIR  (by 1457 - 1518)
```

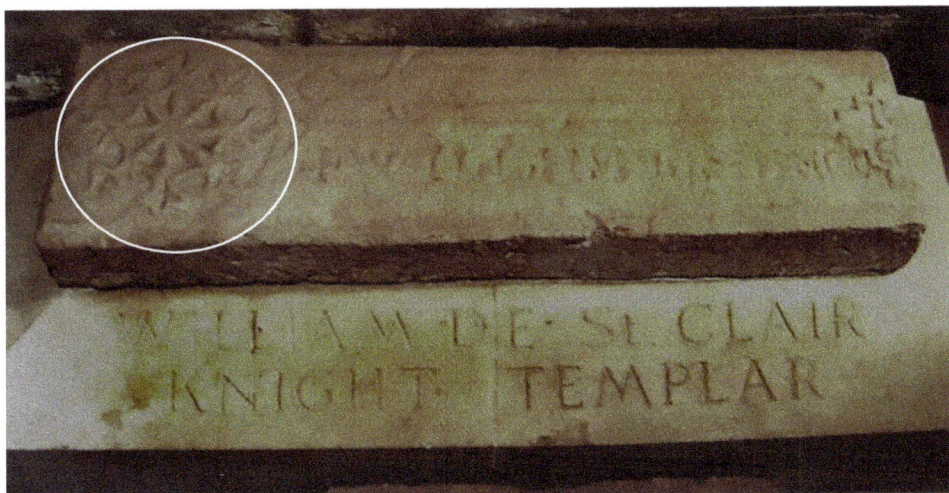

The 'Templar rose' on William St Clair's tomb is more likely a Catherine wheel venerating the family's patron saint. As shown above, William's son-in-law John Stewart of Balveny was Katherine Swynford's great-grandson. Note also that the St Clairs were related to the earls of Strathearn

LEGENDS OF THE WHITE CASTLE

WHITTINGTON CASTLE (above) in northern Shropshire was built by the Peverells and FitzWarines who reputedly had connections to both Robin Hood and King Arthur.

According to one story, Merlin spent time at Whittington and prophesied about a hero who would oppose tyranny. That hero was Fulk FitzWarine, often conflated with his namesake son, who features in Elizabeth Chadwick's novel *Lords of the White Castle* (2000).

Another story concerns one of many alleged Holy Grails guarded by the Peverells and FitzWarines at Whittington Castle for several centuries. The tiny cup (shown opposite) did not impress Tony Robinson in one of his TV programs. 'We can do much better than this,' he said, and kept searching at Rosslyn Chapel in Scotland and elsewhere.

Whittington Castle is supposedly haunted by the ghosts of two children who opened a cursed Elizabethan chest, against the instructions of their father, and died in a fire soon after. The grieving father sealed the chest and threw the keys in the moat.

The legendary Dick Whittington, Lord Mayor of London in the early 1400s, has long been associated with the castle even though he and his cat hailed from Whittington in Gloucestershire. Kate's children are descended from Dick's brother; and Kate, who played Dick in a school play (left), is descended from the FitzWarines through Katherine Percy and Katherine Grandison (See chart on Page 219).

— 174 —

The PEDIGREE of

Fulk (IV; Sir) FitzWARIN

Born: poss. abt. 1202 Died: abt. 14 May 1264

Lady Diana's 19-Great Grandfather.

poss. Wives/Partners: Clarice d' AUBERVILLE ; Constance de TOENI
Children: Fulk V FitzWARIN ; Eugenia FitzWARIN (FitzWARREN)

```
         /-- Fulk FitzWARINE  (? - 1195?)
         |          \          /-- Pagan (Payn) PEVERELL  +
         |           \-- poss. Mallet PEVERELL  (skip?)
         |              \| OR: poss. Miletta (Malet) WHITTINGTON  +
         |              \-- poss. Adelicia  (1082? - ?)
  /-- prob. Fulk (III; of Whittington) FitzWARINE
  |      \                  /-- Geoffrey (Geoffroy) (II; Sn.) de DINAN  +
  |      |        /-- Josceline (Sir) de DINANT  (1106? - 1154+)
  |      |        |         \-- Radegonde ORIELDIS (poss. de CHATEAU-GIRON)
  |      \-- Hawise de DINANT  (? - 1226+)
  |         \            /-- Hugh (3rd Lord of Weobley) de LACY  +
  |        '  \-- Sybil de LACY
  |            \| OR: prob. not Sybil TALBOT  +
  |            \-- Adeline TALBOT  +
  /
```

-Fulk (IV; Sir) FitzWARIN

```
  \                  /-- Mauger (II; Sir) (le) VASASOUR  +
  |                 /      | or: William (Mauger's son)
  |         /-- William (Sir; le) VAVASOUR  (1135? - 29/6/1191)
  |      /-- Robert (Sir) le VAVASOUR  (? - 1227?)
  |      |     \       /-- Thomas de MULTON  +
  |      |      \-- Julian de MULTON
  |      |         | or: (NN), if Julian was instead daughter-in-law
  |      /         | OR: poss. Nichola WALLIS  +
  \-- prob. Maud le VAVASOUR  (Yorks. 1176 - by 1226)
```

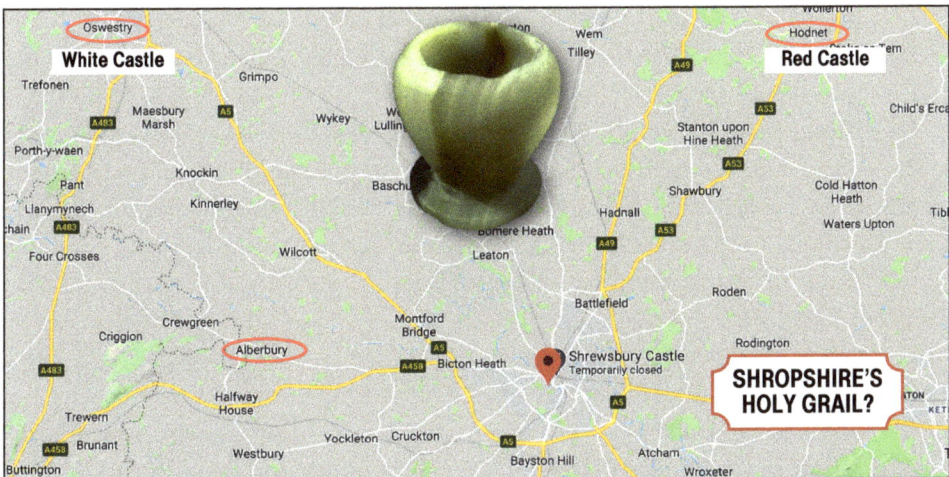

Graham Phillips, author of *The Chalice of Magdalene* (2004), tracked the alleged relic from Whittington Castle near Oswestry to the Red Castle near Hodnet. Fulk FitzWarine III and Maud le Vavasour, who may have been the original Robin Hood and Maid Marian, were buried at Alberbury (circled).

ROBIN HOOD CONTENDERS

KATE has bloodlines from several possible Robin Hoods, including Katherine of Flanders' great-great-grandson Robert de Vere, the third Earl of Oxford, and Fulk FitzWarine, a great-great-grandfather of Lady Katherine Grandison who may have inspired the Order of the Garter (See Page 218).

Robert de Vere, one of the barons who forced King John to sign Magna Carta, did not live in Sherwood Forest but he did spend several years as an outlaw. Kate is descended from de Vere through Catherine of Valois' lover Edmund Beaufort and Alice de Warenne (See chart on Page 15).

A medieval ballad titled 'Robin Hood and Queen Catherin' (sic) has references to King Henry so presumably the queen was either Catherine of Valois, wife of Henry V, or one of Henry VIII's wives, most likely Catherine of Aragon. The archery tournament in the ballad became an essential part of the legend.

Kate descends from two other Robin Hood contenders: John Conyers KG, sheriff of Yorkshire, and his namesake son who died in the Battle of Edgcote in 1469. Known collectively as Robin of Redesdale, the two Johns were manipulated by Richard 'the Kingmaker' Neville after he turned on Edward IV.

According to famouskin.com Olivia de Havilland (inset above), who played Maid Marian opposite Errol Flynn, was Kate's fourteenth cousin four times removed. Olivia died in 2020 aged 104.

There is a town named Robin Hood in West Yorkshire near Middleton, which may have been Kate's ancestral home because her third great-grandfather William Middleton was born in nearby Wakefield in 1807.

The PEDIGREE of

Robert de VERE

Born: abt. 1165   Died: 1221
Lady Diana's 21-Great Grandfather.

Wife/Partner: **Isabel de BOLEBEC**
Children: **Hugh de VERE** ; **Henry (Sir; of Great Addington) de VERE** ; **Alice (Alicia) de VERE**

```
                    /-- Alberic (I) `the Monk' de VERE  (1033? - 1088?)
           /              \-- Katherine of FLANDERS  +
       /-- Aubrey (Alberic; II) de VERE
       |       \           /-- poss.  Henry CASTELLAN (GAND)  (1005? - ?)
       |        \-- Beatrice (poss. de GAND; GHENT)  (1040? - ?)
       |                   \ | OR: poss. Beatrice de GHISNES  +
       /                    \-- poss.  Sibilla MANASSES of GHISNES  +
   /-- Aubrey (Alberic) III de VERE  (1115? - 24/12/1194)
   |       \                   /-- Richard FitzGILBERT (de) CLARE  +
   |        |          /-- Gilbert FitzRICHARD de CLARE
   |        |         /          \-- Rohese GIFFARD (GIFFORD)  +
   |        \-- Adeliza (Alice) de CLARE (CLAIR)  (1092 - 1163)
   |                 \          /-- Hugh (I) de CREIL (de CLERMONT)  +
   |                  \-- Adeliza (Adelaide) CLAREMONT  (1066? - 1117+)
   /                             \-- Marguerite de ROUCY (ROUCI)  +
```

Robert de VERE

```
   \                       /-- Robert (Sheriff) de ESSEX  +
   |                  /-- Suain (Suein Sweyne Sweyn) (Lord/Sheriff) de ESSEX
   |              /-- Robert (de ESSEX) FitzSUAIN  (1085 - ?)
   |         /-- Henry of ESSEX (de ABRINCIS ?)  (1110?? - 1163?)
   |         |      \             /-- Roger (II; le) BIGOD  +
   |         |       \-- Gunnor (Gunnora) (le) BIGOD  (1093 - ?)
   |         |                    \-- Adeliza GRANTSMESNIL  +
   |         /                     | OR: Adeliza de TONY  +
   \-- Lucia (Lucy Agnes) of ESSEX (de ABRINCIS ?)
```

A KNIGHTS TEMPLAR CONNECTION?

BASED ON symbols which have disappeared from Robin Hood's alleged grave at Kirklees Priory in West Yorkshire, John Paul Davis has claimed that the legendary hero was a Templar knight named Robert, Earl of Huntington (sic). Almost nothing is known about Huntington but Kate's children are descended from David de Huntingdon who was Robert the Bruce's great-great-grandfather (See Bannockburn Bloodlines, Page 192).

As shown above, Robert de Vere was descended from Richard FitzGilbert de Clare, a great-grandfather of the legendary Anglo-Norman knight Richard 'Strongbow' de Clare who married Irish princess Aoife.

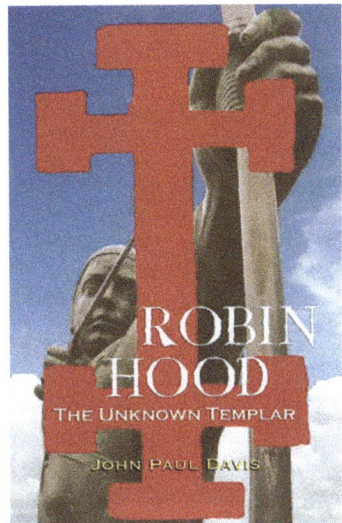

ROBIN HOOD
THE UNKNOWN TEMPLAR
JOHN PAUL DAVIS

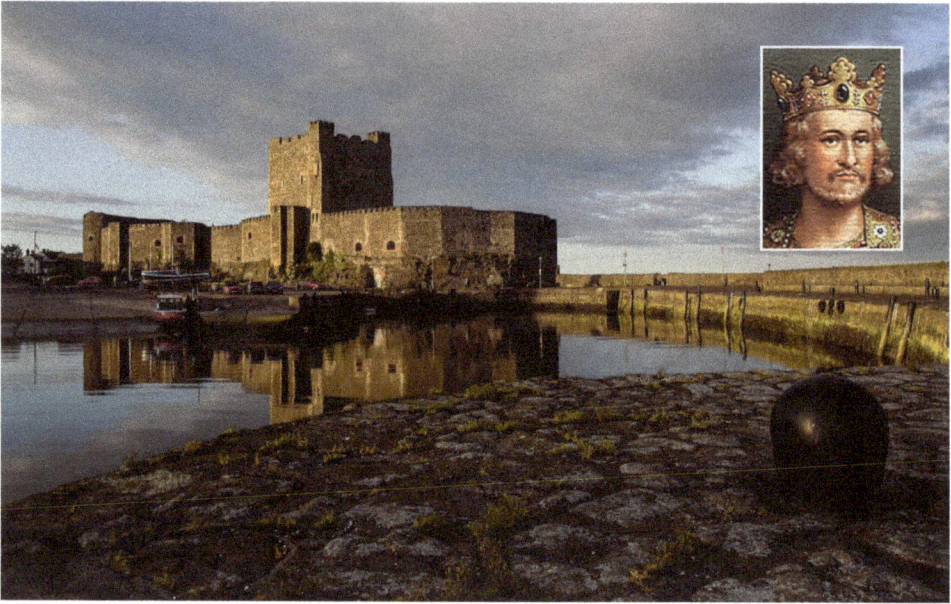

CARRICKFERGUS CONNECTIONS

GENEALOGISTS may eventually confirm that Kate, the current Baroness of Carrickfergus, is descended from John de Courcy (inset) who built Carrickfergus Castle (above) near Belfast in Northern Ireland in the late 1100s.

According to fabpedigree.com Kate has a bloodline from John (Miles) de Courcy, son of John de Courcy and Aufrick Godfredsdottir, but other websites claim they had no children and that the younger de Courcy (shown opposite) was illegitimate. Either way, Kate's bloodline through Katherine Percy and a daughter of Katherine Grandison is dubious because there is no proof that Aufrick de Courcy (died c1287) was John (Miles) de Courcy's granddaughter.

Also disputed is the claim on wikitree.com that John de Courcy, born in Middleton Cheney in Northamptonshire, had a granddaughter named Katherine, from whom Kate's children are descended through Katherine Carew (died 1546).

John de Courcy conquered much of Ulster with a small number of knights, taking advantage of a prophecy about an invincible English warrior riding a white horse with three birds on his shield. He was eventually captured by King John, the arch rival of Robin Hood contenders Robert de Vere and Fulk FitzWarine.

As shown opposite, Aufrick's paternal great-grandmother was Elizabeth of Gloucester, an illegitimate daughter of Henry I. And Aufrick's

Clad in a dark green Catherine Walker coat, Kate celebrated St Patrick's Day 2017 with a pint of Guinness.

The PEDIGREE of

Aufrick GODFREDSDOTTIR

Born: abt. 1162
HRH Charles's 23-Great Grandmother.   Lady Diana's 24-Great Grandmother.
Husband/Partner: John de COURCY
Children: John (Miles) de COURCY ; Patrick de COURCY

```
                    /-- Godfrey (Godred) `Crovan' of MAN
                   /        \-- poss. (Miss) RAGNFREDSDATTER +
            /-- Olaf I Bitling (King) of MAN (& the ISLES)
           |         \        /-- Harald III HARDRAADA (King) of NORWAY +
           |          \-- poss. Maria (Ragnhild; HARDRATA) HAROLDSDOTTIR
           |              \-- Ellisif JAROSLAVNA of KIEV +
      /-- Godfred `the Black' OLAFSSON  (? - 1187)
     |         \          /-- prob. Gospatrick I MacCRINAN of DUNBAR +
     |         |         |      | or: Dolfin Maldred de CARLYLE (Gospatrick's brother)
     |         |        /       | or: prob. not Godfrey Crovan of MAN,
     |         \-- Fergus (Lord/Prince) of GALLOWAY  (1078?? - 1166)
     |         |   |     \-- poss. Aethelreda (Princess) of ENGLAND +
     |         |   |         | or: Dolfin's wife
     |         |  /          | OR: prob. not Aethelreda of WESSEX +
     |          \-- Aufrick of GALLOWAY (Queen of MAN)  (1100? - ?)
     |               \         /-- Henry I BEAUCLERC (King) of ENGLAND +
     |                \-- Elizabeth (Joan) of GLOUCESTER
```

- Aufrick GODFREDSDOTTIR

```
     \                   /-- Domnall MacLOCHLAINN +
     |                 /-- Niall MacLOCHLAINN  (1091? - 1119)
     |                |      \-- Bean Midi ingen CONCHOBUIR +
     |                /          | or: Babhion O'BRIEN
     |          /-- Muirchertach MacLOCHLAINN  (1110? - 1166?)
     |        /-- Mael Sechnaill MacLOCHLAINN  (? - 1185?)
      \-- Findguala MacLOCHLAINN
```

maternal great-grandmother was probably descended from the legendary Irish king Brian Boru (See Page 183).

Because of his legendary exploits, John de Courcy was given the rare privilege of not having to doff his hat to English monarchs. Some of de Courcy's Kinsale descendants were still claiming that privilege hundreds of years later.

Regardless of whether Kate is directly descended from John de Courcy, she has an accepted bloodline from Elizabeth de Burgh, Countess of Ulster, who was born at Carrickfergus Castle in 1332 (See Katherine Percy's chart on Page 211).

Elizabeth was an aunt of Katherine Swynford's illegitimate children. And because she had an all-female bloodline from Aoife, wife of Richard 'Strongbow' de Clare, Elizabeth de Burgh (right) had the same mitochondrial DNA as Catherine of Valois' husband Henry V and her lover Edmund Beaufort (See chart on Page 185).

ST CATHERINE'S WELLS

THE MANNEQUIN of Aufrick Godfredsdottir (inset) at Carrickfergus Castle faces her birthplace, the Isle of Man, where St Catherine's Well at Port Erin has been dispensing water from ancient times. Young women who drank from a bucket containing three nails would supposedly marry within the year.

Scotland has several wells named after St Catherine of Alexandria, including the one in Edinburgh not far from Rosslyn Chapel, but Kate's Well in North Lanarkshire was dedicated to St Catherine of Siena.

In Yorkshire, there was a St Catherine's well near St Katherine's church at Loversall, a tiny village south of Doncaster. Water still flows from St Catherine's well near St Catherine's church at Eskdale in Cumbria, but St Catherine's well in the Coundon area of Coventry has long run dry.

Throughout Britain there are many hills named after St Catherine, including one in Leeds not far from where Kate's ancestors lived.

The Catherine Code

Part III

STRONGBOW AND AOIFE

IRISH princess Aoife MacMorrough, pictured above marrying the legendary Richard 'Strongbow' de Clare, was a matrilineal ancestor of many nobles who fought for and against Catherine of Valois' son Henry VI during the Wars of the Roses.

Strongbow, who married the teenaged Aoife soon after he arrived in Ireland around 1170, was supported by John de Courcy who married Aufrick Godfreds-dottir in 1180. Through Richard FitzGilbert de Clare (shown opposite), Strongbow was related to Robin Hood contender Robert de Vere.

Coincidentally, Catherine of Valois' first husband Henry V had an all-female bloodline from Aoife and so did two of Kates' ancestors: Catherine of Valois' lover Edmund Beaufort and his arch-rival Richard of York.

Henry VIII and three of his wives, Catherine of Aragon, Catherine Howard and Catherine Parr, were descended from Aoife. Catherine Carey's mother Mary Boleyn had an Aoife bloodline through Catherine Molines; and Henry VIII's illegitimate son Henry Fitzroy had a bloodline through Katherine Peshall (See chart on Page 157).

Kate has numerous bloodlines from Aoife, including one through Catherine Clifford and Katherine Spencer, and another through Katherine Clifford and Catherine Mortimer. Prince William has bloodlines through Catherine Mortimer and another ten of Kate's namesakes (See chart on Page 49).

Prince William reportedly drank ten pints of cider during a 'Strongbow marathon' while at St Andrews University. Bulmers has had a royal warrant since 1911.

FABPEDIGREE.COM

The PEDIGREE of

Isabel FitzGILBERT de CLARE

Countess of STRIGOIL; Heiress of PEMBROKE

Born: Wales 1172   Died: 1220 Eire or Wales

Husband/Partner: **William (the) MARSHALL (the PROTECTOR)**
Children: **Margaret MARSHALL ; Eve (Eva) MARSHALL ; Joan (Johanna) MARSHALL**
Eva(?) MARSHALL ; William MARSHAL (2nd Earl of PEMBROKE)

```
                              /-- Gilbert `Crispin' (Count) de BRIENNE  +
                     /-- Richard FitzGILBERT (de) CLARE  (1035? - 1089)
                     |        \-- poss. Gunnora d' AUNOU  +
                  /              / OR: poss. Gunnora de COURCY  +
            /-- Gilbert FitzRICHARD de CLARE
            /           \-- Rohese GIFFARD (GIFFORD)  +
      /-- Gilbert FitzGilbert de CLARE  (1100? - 1148)
      /            \-- Adeliza (Adelaide) CLAREMONT  +
   /-- Richard (STRONGBOW) FitzGILBERT de CLARE
   |      \               /-- Roger (Sn.) de BEAUMONT  +
   |      |        /-- Robert de BEAUMONT (1st Earl of LEICESTER)
   |      |        /      \-- Adeline de MEULAN (MEULENT)  +
   |      \-- Isabel (Elizabeth) de BEAUMONT
   |               \ / or: Mabel de BELLOMENT
   /                \-- Isabelle (de) VERMANDOIS  +
```

-Isabel FitzGILBERT de CLARE

```
   \              /-- Donnchad (V) MacMURCHADA  +
   |              /      / or: Enna (King) of LEINSTER
   |      /-- Dermod (IV; na Gall) MacMORROUGH  (1100? - 1171)
   |      |        \-- Orlaith ingen O'BRAENAIN  +
   |      /               / OR: Darfargila O'BRIEN  +
   \-- Eva (Aoife) MacMORROUGH (MURCHADA)
```

In 2013, Tourism Ireland trumpeted a convoluted connection between Kate and the legendary Brian Boru, obviously unaware that nearly everyone with British heritage has bloodlines through Katherine Swynford's grandchildren and Aoife. Boru, who supposedly died aged 88 fighting a Viking army at Clontarf in 1014, may have descended from the mythical Niall of the Nine Hostages.

ENGLAND'S GREATEST KNIGHT

LONDON'S historic Temple Church, visited by Robert Langdon and Sophie Neveu in *The Da Vinci Code,* is the burial place of Aoife's renowned son-in-law William Marshall (right) who served five English kings, including Princess Katherine's father Henry III who commissioned the Cosmati Pavement in Westminster Abbey (which also features in Dan Brown's novel).

Marshall, nicknamed 'The Protector', had five sons who died without issue after the Bishop of Ferns cursed them for refusing to restore church properties.

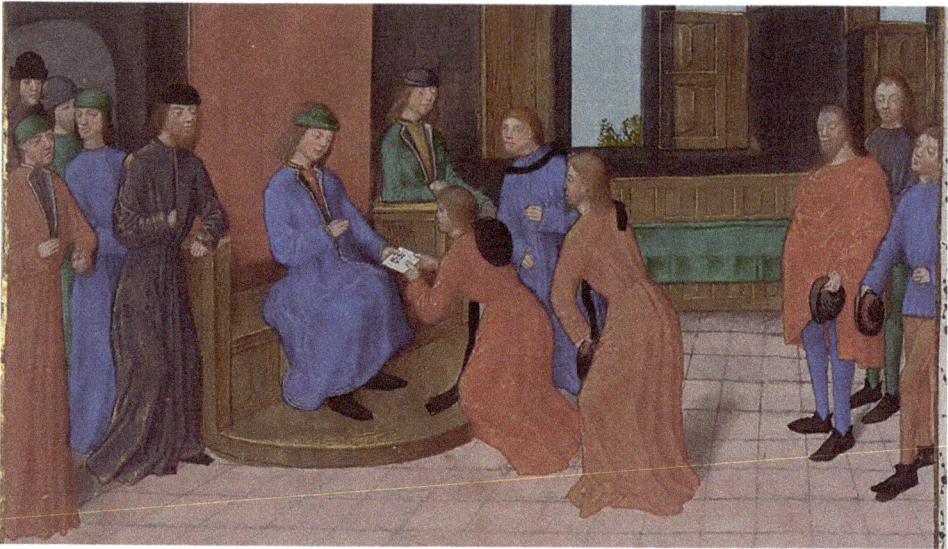

CATHERINE OF VALOIS' LOVER

IF AOIFE has living matrilineal descendants, which is not implausible, then her haplogroup may eventually be identified.

In the meantime, it is worth noting some of the royals who inherited her mitochondrial DNA, starting with Catherine of Valois' first husband Henry V, who was Katherine Swynford's step-grandson through Henry IV, and Katherine's grandson Edmund Beaufort, the Duke of Somerset, who had an affair with Catherine of Valois after Henry V died in 1422.

Edmund Beaufort is pictured above kneeling before Catherine of Valois' brother Charles VII who did not inherit the mental problems of their father Charles VI. Catherine's son Henry VI was not so fortunate (See Catherine of Valois' Curses, Page 112).

As shown opposite, Henry V and Edmund Beaufort had all-female bloodlines from Aoife through their grandmothers, Joan and Alice FitzAlan. Henry and Edmund also had all-male bloodlines through John of Gaunt, Edward III, Edward

II, Edward I, Henry III, King John and Henry II (who supported Aoife's husband Richard 'Strongbow' de Clare).

Hypothetically, if Catherine of Valois' second son was sired by Edmund Beaufort, Henry VII's parents (Edmund Tudor and Margaret Beaufort) would have been first cousins through Katherine Swynford's oldest son John 'Fairborn' Beaufort who, according to Richard III, was

According to a famous prophecy, alleged war criminal Henry V died young after Catherine of Valois defied him by giving birth to the future Henry VI at Windsor Castle while he was fighting in France.

— 184 —

Aoife MacMorrough	
Isabel FitzGilbert	
Maud Marshall	
Isabella Bigod	
Maud FitzJohn	
Isabel Beauchamp	
Maud Chaworth	
Eleanor Plantagenet	
Joan FitzAlan	Alice FitzAlan
Marie de Bohun	Margaret Holland
Henry V	Edmund Beaufort

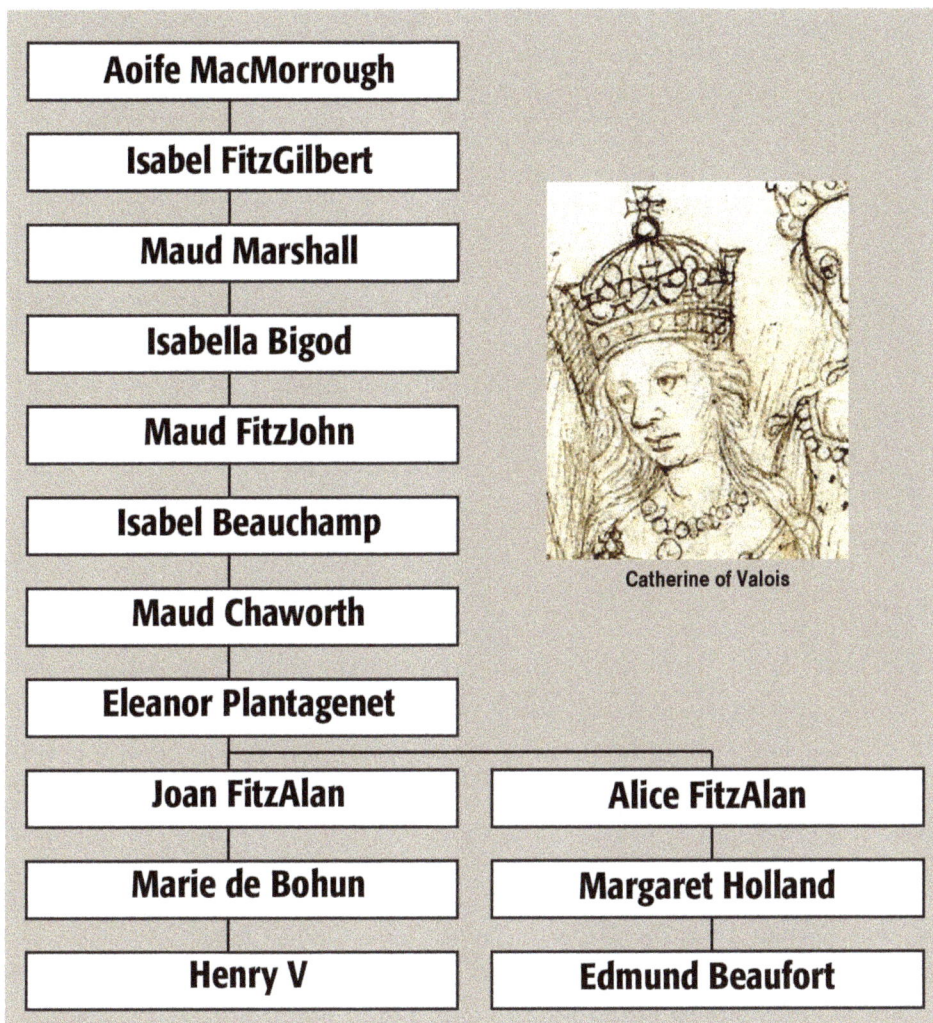

Catherine of Valois

'begotten in double adultery' (See Beaufort Bastard Bloodlines, Page 238).

It is also possible that Edmund Beaufort sired Catherine of Valois' grandson Edward of Westminster while Henry VI was incapacitated. Beaufort was a close advisor of Henry's formidable wife Margaret of Anjou and it was rumoured that they slept together.

Edward of Westminster, who inspired the despicable Joffrey Baratheon in *Game of Thrones,* was allegedly murdered in front of Edward IV after the Battle of Tewkesbury in 1471.

Kate is descended from Edmund Beaufort through Catherine Clifford and Katherine Spencer (See chart on Page 199), and Kate's children are descended from Catherine of Valois through Henry VIII's alleged illegitimate daughter Catherine Carey (See chart on Page 33).

Note: Richard of York should have had the same mtDNA and Y-DNA as Henry V and Edmund Beaufort but almost certainly did not (See next page).

GAMES OF THRONES AND ROSES

KATE'S combative ancestors Richard of York (above left) and Edmund Beaufort (right) almost certainly had the same mitochondrial DNA but different Y-DNA.

York, who inspired Ned Stark in *Game of Thrones,* had an all-female bloodline from Aoife through Alianore Holland (shown opposite), a sister of Edmund Beaufort's mother Margaret (See chart on previous page). But, while Beaufort had a probable all-male bloodline from Edward III, York's father was most likely sired by John Holland (See chart on Page 63).

Regardless of who sired Richard of Conisburgh, Edward IV and his brother Richard III inherited Katherine Swynford's haplogroup J. And Edward's daughters, including Katherine of York and her sister Elizabeth (wife of Henry VII), had the same mtDNA as Catherine Woodville and Catherine of Luxembourg (haplogroup U).

Edmund Beaufort, who supported Catherine of Valois' mentally unstable son Henry VI, was killed during the first Battle of St Albans in 1455; and Richard of York died five years later at the Battle of Wakefield. Richard 'the Kingmaker' Neville, who switched his allegiance from the Yorkists to the Lancastrians, was another matrilineal descendant of Aoife.

The so-called Wars of the Roses officially ended in 1485 when Catherine of Valois' grandson Henry VII defeated Katherine Swynford's great-grandson Richard III at Bosworth.

[Not many people know that Henry VII merged the non-historic Lancastrian red rose and the Yorkist white rose into the Tudor Rose (inset above) for

The PEDIGREE of

Katherine (of YORK) PLANTAGENET

Born: 1479   Died: abt. 1528 Tiverton
Lady Diana's 13-Great Aunt.
Husband/Partner: **William COURTENAY**
Children: **Henry (K.G.) COURTENAY** ; **Margaret COURTENAY**

```
                        /-- Richard PLANTAGENET of CONISBURGH
                       /        \-- Isabel PEREZ (Princess) of CASTILE  +
            /-- Richard PLANTAGENET-YORK
           |        \ I or: poss. BLAYBOURNE the Archer (cuckolder)
           |        |        /-- Roger de MORTIMER  +
           |        \-- Anne de MORTIMER  (1390 - 1411)
           /                \-- Alianore (Lady) HOLLAND  +
     /-- Edward IV `of Rouen' PLANTAGENET-YORK
    |        \        /-- John (III; de) NEVILL  +
    |        |    /-- Ralph I NEVILL (de NEVILLE)  (1363? - 1425)
    |        |   /        \-- Matilda (Maud Mary) de PERCY  +
    |        \-- Cecily (Lady) NEVILLE  (1415 - 1495)
    |                \        /-- John (BEAUFORT) of GAUNT  +
    |                \-- Joan (Lady; de) BEAUFORT  (1379? - 1440)
    /                        \-- Katherine ROELT  +
```

- Katherine (of YORK) PLANTAGENET

```
    \                        /-- Richard (of Grafton) de WYDVIL  +
    |                /-- John (of Grafton Regis) de WYDEVILLE
    |               /        \-- Elizabeth LYONS  +
    |        /-- Richard (Sir; of Grafton; of the Mote) WOODVILLE
    |       |        \-- Isabel GODARD (GOBION)  (? - 1401+)
    |   /-- Richard (K.G.) WYDEVILLE
    |  |        \        /-- Thomas BODULGATE (BITTLESGATE)  +
    |  |        |       |   /     I (skip this generation?)
    |  |        \-- Elizabeth (Mary Joan) BEDLISGATE  (1385? - 1448+)
    |  /                \-- Joan (Mary) BEAUCHAMP  (skip?)  +
    \-- Elizabeth (Lady) WOODVILLE
```

propaganda purposes, and that the term 'Wars of the Roses' was rarely used before it was popularised by Sir Walter Scott in the early 1800s.]

On a visit to Poland in 2017, Kate toured the *Game of Thrones* film set and asked for spoilers from cast members. By then she probably knew that, like millions of other fans, she descends from people who inspired some of the major characters.

According to famouskin.com Kit Harington, who played Jon Snow (half-brother of Robb Stark who equates to Kate's ancestor Edward IV), is Kate's fifteenth cousin once removed through a son of John 'Black-faced' Clifford. Clifford murdered Edward IV's brother Edmund and may also have beheaded their father's corpse (See *Vengeance at Wakefield*, Page 190).

Note: *Game of Thrones* creator George R R Martin was inspired by some of Shakespeare's historical plays and also by *The Accursed Kings*, a series of novels by Maurice Druon about Philip IV and his descendants.

Robb Stark's mother Catelyn (an Irish form of Catherine) was based on Cecily Neville, granddaughter of Katherine Swynford (Roelt) and grandmother of Katherine of York

— 187 —

SLAUGHTER IN ST ALBANS

FOUR OF Kate's noble ancestors who fought in the first Battle of St Albans on 22nd May 1455 had all-female bloodlines from Aoife. But while Richard of York had a decisive victory, his arch rival Edmund Beaufort, and two of Beaufort's commanders with the same mitochondrial DNA, were killed in close proximity in just half an hour.

Beaufort (middle circle) and Thomas Clifford (big circle) are pictured above fighting in support of Henry VI. The third noble who died in the battle was Catherine Clifford's great-great-great-grandfather Henry Percy (small circle), father of Henry Algernon Percy (shown opposite) and son of Henry 'Hotspur' Percy who died during the Battle of Shrewsbury in 1403. Kate has another bloodline from Hotspur and son through Katherine Percy (See chart on Page 211).

Like Henry V, who believed he was doomed after Catherine of Valois gave birth to the future Henry VI at Windsor, Edmund Beaufort was deeply superstitious. Told by a soothsayer that he would die in the shadow of a castle, Beaufort — who had an affair with Catherine of Valois after Henry V's death — panicked when he was cornered in the Castle Inn and made a suicidal charge into the enemy.

Through Aoife's matrilineal descendant Maud Chaworth (died c1322), Beaufort, Clifford and Percy had the same mtDNA as two of their opponents: Kate's ancestor Richard of York and Prince William's ancestor Richard Neville, later nicknamed 'the Kingmaker'. [Neville's namesake father and Richard of York were beheaded after the Battle of Wakefield in 1460.]

THE PEDIGREE OF
Catherine (Lady) CLIFFORD
Born: abt. 1518   Died: 1598

Lady Diana's 11-Great Grandmother.

Husbands/Partners: John (8th Lord of Bolton) SCROPE ; Richard (Sir; of Roxby) CHOMLEY
Children: Margaret SCROPE ; Catherine le SCROPE ; Henry (9th Lord of Bolton) SCROPE

```
                           /-- Thomas (8th Baron) CLIFFORD  +
             /-- John `Black faced' (8th/9th Lord) CLIFFORD
            /              \-- prob. Joan DACRE  +
      /-- Henry (9th/10th Lord) CLIFFORD  (1454? - 23/4/1523)
      |            \            /-- Henry (Sir; de) BROMFLETE  +
      |             \-- Margaret BROMFLETE  (1436? - 1493)
      |                         \-- Eleanor FitzHUGH  +
      |                         | OR: poss. Eleanor FitzHUGH  +
      |            /
  /-- Henry CLIFFORD (1st Earl) of CUMBERLAND  (1493 - 1542)
  |           \                  /-- Oliver (Sir; of Bletsho) ST. JOHN  +
  |            |                /  | OR: poss. Oliver (Sir) ST. JOHN [alt ped]  +
  |            |      /-- John (Sir; of Bletsoe) ST. JOHN
  |            |     /            \-- Margaret (of BLETSOE) BEAUCHAMP  +
  |            \-- Anne ST. JOHN  (? - by 1511)
```

Catherine (Lady) CLIFFORD

```
            \                  /-- Henry Algernon PERCY  +
            |         /-- Henry (K.G.) PERCY  (1449? - 1489)
            |        /         \-- Eleanor (Countess) POYNINGS  +
            |  /-- Henry Algernon (K.G.) PERCY  (1479 - 1528)
            |  |       \         /-- William (1st Baron) HERBERT  +
            |  |        \-- prob. Maud (Lady) HERBERT
            |  /                 \-- Anne DEVEREAUX  +
            \-- Margaret (Lady) PERCY  (? - 1540)
               \                  /-- Henry (Esq.; of Badby) SPENCER  +
               |         /-- Robert (Sir; of Spencercombe) SPENCER
               |        /         \-- Isabella LINCOLN  +
               \-- Katherine SPENCER  (? - 1542)
                  \                /-- Edmund (K.G.) BEAUFORT  +
                   \-- Eleanor (Countess of WILTSHIRE) BEAUFORT
                       \-- Eleanor (Lady; de) BEAUCHAMP  +
```

A sixth St Albans commander with Aoife's mitochondrial DNA was Catherine Mortimer's great-grandson Humphrey Stafford KG, Duke of Buckingham, from whom Kate's children are descended through his daughter Catherine.

Beaufort, Clifford and Percy (who was Clifford's uncle) were buried in St Alban's cathedral near the grave of Catherine of Valois' brother-in-law Humphrey, Duke of Gloucester, who prevented her from marrying Edmund Beaufort. ***Note:*** Like Henry Constable of Burton, Thomas Clifford was probably descended from Katherine of Flanders through all eight of his great-grandparents.

Catherine Clifford (right) was a Catholic recusant who spent her last years at Abbey House in Whitby, an alleged way station for fugitive priests. Her uncle Thomas Percy (son of Katherine Spencer) was executed after joining a Catholic uprising against Henry VIII (See Page 199).

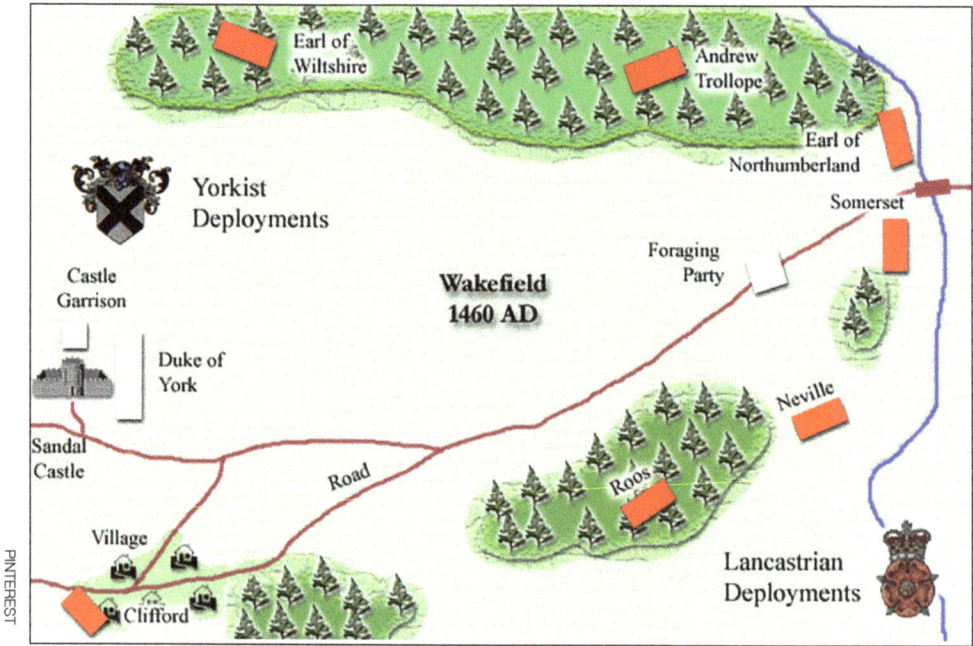

Yorkist Deployments

Castle Garrison

Duke of York

Sandal Castle

Earl of Wiltshire

Andrew Trollope

Earl of Northumberland

Somerset

Foraging Party

Wakefield 1460 AD

Road

Neville

Roos

Lancastrian Deployments

Village

Clifford

PINTEREST

VENGEANCE AT WAKEFIELD

FIVE YEARS after the first Battle of St Albans, the deaths of three of Kate's noble ancestors were avenged by their sons at the Battle of Wakefield.

As shown above, Richard of York left Sandal Castle unaware that he was surrounded by Lancastrians including Edmund Beaufort's son Henry, third Duke of Somerset; Henry Percy's son, also named Henry, third Earl of Northumberland; and Thomas Clifford's son John 'Black-faced' Clifford (See opposite).

Another Lancastrian commander was John Neville whose half-uncle Richard Neville supported his brother-in-law Richard of York. After the battle, the heads of the two Richards and York's son Edmund were displayed on the Micklegate at the entrance to York.

For the record, Richard of York and John Neville had all-female bloodlines from Aoife; Richard Neville, Edmund and the younger Henry Percy (brother of Katherine Percy) had all-female bloodlines from Katherine Swynford (haplogroup J); and John 'Black-faced' Clifford had an all-female bloodline from Catherine Mortimer.

Prince William is descended from Catherine Mydelton (nee Vavasour), who lived in Wakefield during the 1400s, and Kate's ancestor William Middleton was baptised in Wakefield in 1807 (See chart on Page 146).

PINTEREST

Richard Duke of York.

Kate's ancestor inspired the mnemonic ROYGBIV (Richard of York Gave Battle in Vain) which lists the colours of the rainbow.

The PEDIGREE of

John `Black faced' (8th/9th Lord) CLIFFORD

Born: 1435   Died: 28 Mar 1461 Battle of Towton

HRH Charles's 15-Great Grandfather.   Lady Diana's 14-Great Grandfather.

Wife/Partner: **Margaret BROMFLETE**
Children: **Henry (9th/10th Lord) CLIFFORD** ; **Elizabeth CLIFFORD**

```
                          /-- Thomas (6th Baron; de) CLIFFORD (1363 - 1391)
                        /          \-- Maud de BEAUCHAMP +
                  /-- John (7th Lord of; de) CLIFFORD
                  |       \          /-- Thomas de ROS (ROOS) +
                  |        \-- Elizabeth (de) ROS (1367? - 1424)
                  /                   \-- Beatrice de STAFFORD +
            /-- Thomas (8th Baron) CLIFFORD (1414 - 22/5/1455)
            |     \                  /-- Henry (K.G.) PERCY +
            |      |       /-- Henry `Hotspur' (K.G.) PERCY
            |      |      /          \-- Margaret (de) NEVILLE +
            |      \-- Elizabeth (de) PERCY (1390? - 1437)
            |             \          /-- Edmund `the Good' de MORTIMER +
            |              \-- Elizabeth (de) MORTIMER (Monmouth 1371 - 1417)
            /                         \-- Philippa of CLARENCE (PLANTAGENET) +
```

- John `Black faced' (8th/9th Lord) CLIFFORD

```
            |                  /-- William (5th Baron) de DACRE (& Multon)
            |                 /          \-- Ela MAXWELL +
            |       /-- Thomas (6th Baron; de) DACRE
            |       |      \          /-- James (2nd Earl of; de) DOUGLAS +
            |       |       \-- Joan (Mary) DOUGLAS
            |       |             \ / OR: prob. Joan DOUGLAS +
            |       /                   \-- Isabel Eupheme STEWART +
            \-- prob. Joan DACRE (1418? - ?)
                    \                 /-- John (III; de) NEVILL +
                    |       /-- Ralph I NEVILL (de NEVILLE) (1363? - 1425)
                    |      /          \-- Matilda (Maud Mary) de PERCY +
                    \-- Phillippa (Lady; de) NEVILLE (1386? - 1453+)
                          \          /-- Hugh (2nd Earl; de) STAFFORD +
                           \-- Margaret de STAFFORD (Durham ? - 1396)
                                     \-- Philipa (Philippa; de) BEAUCHAMP +
```

'YOUR FATHER SLEW MINE'

JOHN 'Black-faced' Clifford, pictured right murdering Edward IV's brother Edmund near Wakefield bridge, died in a skirmish before the Battle of Towton in 1461 and so did John Neville.

Henry Beaufort, who inexplicably had an intimate relationship with Edward IV, was beheaded after the Battle of Hexham in 1464. Seven years later, Beaufort's younger brother Edmund suffered the same fate after the Battle of Tewkesbury.

BANNOCKBURN BLOODLINES

THROUGH Catherine Clifford's great-grandfather John 'Black-faced' Clifford, who died before the Battle of Towton; and his father Thomas Clifford, who died at the first Battle of St Albans; Kate is descended from Robert de Clifford (shown opposite) who died at the Battle of Bannockburn in 1314.

While the three Cliffords had the same Y-DNA, Thomas and Robert (and Robert's son-in-law Henry Percy) were matrilineal descendants of Irish princess Aoife.

Kate is descended from Robert de Clifford through Katherine Clifford (died 1413) and also through Catherine de Aton, Catherine Eure and Catherine Neville (See chart on Page 45).

One of the English nobles who died fighting Robert the Bruce at Bannockburn was Gilbert de Clare (circled above), a first cousin of Robert de Clifford's wife Maud and a great-grandson of another Gilbert de Clare who married Aoife's granddaughter Isabella Marshall.

According to fabpedigree.com Kate is possibly descended from Robert the Bruce — whose father had an all-female bloodline from Aoife — through Joan Douglas, an illegitimate daughter of James, Earl of Douglas. And Kate's children have a probable bloodline from the Bruce's illegitimate daughter Margaret through Katherine Scott Forbes, Katherine Morison, Catherine Duff and Katherine Duff.

Robert de Clifford (left), who died fighting Robert the Bruce and the Black Douglas at Bannockburn, was descended from Robert of Gloucester, an illegitimate son of Henry I.

WHOBEGATWHOM.COM

— 192 —

Catherine de ATON (AYTON)

HRH Charles's 17-Great Grandmother.   Lady Diana's 17-Great Grandmother.

Husband/Partner: **Ralph (Sir; of Witton Castle; de) EURE**
Children: **Robert EURE** ; **William (Sir; of Witton) EURE** ; **Elizabeth EURE**

```
                                        /-- Gilbert (Knight) d' ATON (de ATON)  +
                            /-- William d' ATON (de ATON)
                           /            \-- Margerie de VESCY  +
                    /-- William (II; Sir?) d' ATON (de ATON)
            /-- Gilbert (1st Baron) de ATON  (by 1288 - 1350)
           |          \          /-- Simon (Sir; VEER) de VERE  +
           |           \-- Isabel de VERE
           /                     \-- Ada (de) BERTRAM  +
    /-- William (2nd Baron) de ATON  (1299? - by 1389)
   /
```

Catherine de ATON (AYTON)

```
           \                        /-- William (III; IV) de PERCY  +
           |                /-- Henry (II) de PERCY
           |               /         \-- Ellen de BALIOL  +
           |        /-- Henry (III; 1st Lord; de) PERCY
           |       /                  \-- Eleanor (PLANTAGENET) de WARRENNE  +
           |   /-- Henry (IV; III; 2nd Lord; de) PERCY
           |  |        \          /-- John (III) FitzALAN  +
           |  |         \-- Eleanor FitzALAN de ARUNDEL
           |  /                   \-- Isabella (de) MORTIMER  +
    \-- Isabel PERCY  (1326? - by 1368)
           \                        /-- Roger (III; Sir) de CLIFFORD  +
           |                /-- Robert de CLIFFORD  (1274 - 24/6/1314)
           |   /                    \-- Isabel de VIPONT (VESPONT)  +
           \-- Idonea (Idoine de) CLIFFORD
                  \          /-- Thomas de CLARE  +
                   \-- Maud (Matilda) de CLARE  (1279? - 1325)
                              \-- Juliane FitzMAURICE  +
```

In 1330, the renowned Black Douglas, whose lands were awarded to Robert de Clifford by Edward I, died fighting Moors in Spain while taking Robert the Bruce's heart to the Holy Land. Kate's children and their cousin Archie descend from Douglas' illegitimate son Archibald.

After William de Vescy's namesake bastard son died at Bannockburn his estates devolved to Margerie de Vescy (shown above). Through Katherine Ellis, Kate has a bloodline from Margerie's aunt Margaret FitzWilliam, an illegitimate daughter of William I (See Scottish Bastard Bloodlines, Page 240).

Claims that Templar knights helped Robert the Bruce to win the Battle of Bannockburn have been dismissed as 'rubbish' by Helen Nicholson, history professor at Cardiff University.

Note: Catherine de Aton was a first cousin once removed of Katherine Swynford's granddaughter Catherine Neville (See next page).

NEVERENDING NEVILLES

A FTER more than twenty generations there could be millions of people with bloodlines from the siblings and half-siblings of Katherine Swynford's grand-daughter Catherine Neville who, like Catherine Parr, was married four times.

As shown opposite, Catherine Neville's parents were Ralph Neville, first Earl of Westmorland, and his second wife Joan Beaufort (pictured above with some of her daughters). Ralph and Joan had 14 children; he had another eight with his first wife Margaret Stafford, a granddaughter of Catherine Mortimer; and Joan had two daughters with her first husband Robert Ferrers.

With a higher than normal growth rate, there could have been more than a thousand Neville offspring living in England in 1580 (See A Hundred Million Descendants, Page 36).

Kate descends from Catherine Neville's sisters Cecily (mother of Edward IV) and Eleanor (mother of Katherine Percy), and from five of Catherine's half-siblings: Margaret and Philippa Neville, and Elizabeth and Mary Ferrers (who married her step-brother Sir Ralph Neville).

A bitter inheritance dispute between the Stafford and Beaufort Nevilles was evident at the Battle of Wakefield when Catherine Neville's half-nephew John Neville opposed her brother Richard, the fifth Earl of Salisbury. Meanwhile, some of the Beaufort Nevilles were feuding with Katherine Percy's brothers.

John Mowbray (shown opposite) swung the Battle of Towton in Edward IV's favour in 1461, one year after Catherine Neville's third husband John Beaumont died at the Battle of Northampton. The 'diabolical' fourth marriage of 65-year-old Catherine to 19-year-old John Woodville ended with his execution at the Battle of Edgecote in 1469.

While Catherine Neville's daughter Katherine Strangeways inherited Katherine Swynford's mtDNA (haplogroup J), Catherine's niece Catherine Neville (died 1504) had an all-female bloodline from Aoife, and so did Prince William's ancestor Katherine Neville of Latimer who died in 1596 (See chart on Page 196).

Catherine NEVILLE

Born: abt. 1397   Died: 1478

Lady Diana's 15-Great Grandmother. HRH Charles's 17-Great Grandmother.

Husbands/Partners: Thomas (Sir) STRANGEWAYS ; John (de) MOWBRAY
Children: Jane STRANGEWAYS ; John MOWBRAY (4th Duke of NORFOLK)

```
                    /-- Ralph (2nd Baron of RABY; de) NEVILL
              /            \-- Euphemia (FitzROBERT; de) CLAVERING  +
         /-- John (III; de) NEVILL  (1327+ - 1388)
         |            \        /-- Hugh (Baron; de) AUDLEY  +
         |             \-- Alice (de) AUDLEY  (1303? - 1373?)
         |                          \-- prob. Isolda le ROUS  +
         /                          | OR: prob. not Isolda de BOHUN  +
    /-- Ralph I NEVILL (de NEVILLE)  (1363? - 1425)
    |         \                /-- Henry (III; 1st Lord; de) PERCY  +
    |          |        /-- Henry (IV; III; 2nd Lord; de) PERCY
    |          |         /         \-- Eleanor FitzALAN de ARUNDEL  +
    |          \-- Matilda (Maud Mary) de PERCY  (1342? - 1379)
    |                    \        /-- Robert de CLIFFORD  +
    |                     \-- Idonea (Idoine de) CLIFFORD
    /                              \-- Maud (Matilda) de CLARE  +
```

- Catherine NEVILLE

```
    \                          /-- Edward I (King) of ENGLAND  +
    |                    /-- Edward II (King) of ENGLAND
    |                    /         \-- Eleanor of CASTILE (& Leon)  +
    |         /-- Edward III (WINDSOR; King) of ENGLAND
    |         /              \-- Isabella `the She-Wolf' of FRANCE  +
    |    /-- John (BEAUFORT) of GAUNT
    |    |         \        /-- William (Guillaume) III d' AVESNES  +
    |    |          \-- Philipa d' AVESNES (Countess) of HAINAULT
    |    /                  \-- Jeanne de VALOIS  +
    \-- Joan (Lady; de) BEAUFORT  (1379? - 1440)
         \                /-- poss. Paon (Comte) de ROET  +
          |        /-- Paon (Sir; of GUIENNE) de ROET
          \-- Katherine ROELT
```

Catherine Neville, Duchess of Norfolk, was born at Raby Castle (above) in County Durham around 1397 and Kate's ancestor Cecily Neville, nicknamed 'the Rose of Raby', was born there in 1415. The castle was painted by JMW Turner in 1817.

The PEDIGREE of

Katherine PURCELL

Lady Diana's 8-Great Grandmother.

Husband/Partner: Godfrey (2nd Baronet) COPLEY
Child: Catherine COPLEY

```
/-- John (of Nantcribba) PURCELL  (Mongomery, Wales)
/
```

- Katherine PURCELL

```
|                /-- Owen (ap JOHN) VAUGHAN
|                |        \         /-- Hywel Fychan ap DAFYDD LLWYD  +
|                |        \-- Dorothy verch HYWEL FYCHAN
|                /                  \-- Margred verch ELISE  +
|      /-- Robert (Sir; of Llwydiarth) VAUGHAN
|      |        \              /-- Robert ap MORUS
|      |        |        /-- Morus (of Llangedwyn) ap ROBERT
|      |        |        /         \-- Margred verch RHEINALLT
|      |        \-- Catrin verch MORUS
|      |                \         /-- Elise ap MORUS  +
|      |                \-- Mary verch ELISE
|      /                          \-- Jonet BOWEN  +
\-- Eleanor (of Llwydiarth) VAUGHAN
       \                  /-- William (K.G.) HERBERT  +
       |        /-- Edward (Earl? of POWIS) HERBERT
       |        /         \-- Ann PARR  +
       |-- prob. William HERBERT  (1572? - 1655)
       |        |        \         /-- Thomas STANLEY
       |        /         \-- Mary STANLEY  (1550? - 1597+)
       \-- Katharine HERBERT
                \                  /-- Thomas (Sir) PERCY  +
                |        /-- Henry PERCY (8th Earl) of NORTHUMBERLAND
                |        /         \-- Eleanor HARBOTTLE (HARBOTTEL)  +
                \-- prob. Eleanor (Lady) PERCY  (? - 1650)
                         \         /-- John (Sir) NEVILLE  +
                         \-- Katherine (of LATIMER) NEVILLE  (1544? - 1596)
                                  \-- Lucy (Lady of Worcester) SOMERSET  +
```

AOIFE BLOODLINES

THE LONGEST matrilineal bloodline from Aoife in Prince William's family tree is through Katherine Neville of Latimer, Katherine Herbert and Katherine Purcell (left) to Catherine Copley who is shown above.

Catrin (Catherine) verch Morus descended from Llewelyn the Great; Ann Parr was a sister of Henry VIII's last wife Catherine Parr; and Lucy Somerset descended from Katherine Swynford through Charles Somerset KG (See Beaufort Bastard Bloodlines, Page 238).

The PEDIGREE of
Catherine SHORTER
Born: abt. 1682   Died: 1737
Lady Diana's 7-Great Grandmother.
Husband/Partner: **Robert (K.G.) WALPOLE**
Children: **Mary (Lady of Orford) WALPOLE** ; **Edward (K.B.) WALPOLE**

```
            /-- John (Sir) SHORTER  (1625? - 1688 London)
      |           \              /-- Richard (of Send) FORBIS  (Surrey)
      |            \-- Susanna FOREBANK (FORBIS)  (Surrey 1599? - ?)
      /                  \-- Isabel
  /-- John (of Bybrook) SHORTER  (Kent 1660? - ?)
  |        \                   /-- John BIRKETT
  |         |         /-- John BIRKET (BIRKETT)  (1600? - ?)
  |         |        /      \-- Isabel BIRKETT
  |         \-- Isabella BIRKET  (by 1633 - 1704)
  /                  \-- Elizabeth ROBINSON
```

Catherine SHORTER
```
  |                   /-- Richard (2nd Baronet of Picton Castle) PHILIPPS
  |           /        \-- Anne PERROT  +
  |    /-- Erasmus (3rd Baronet of Picton Castle) PHILIPPS
  |    |       \         /-- Erasmus DRYDEN  +
  |    |        \-- Elizabeth DRYDEN  (1597? - 1658+)
  |    /                 \-- Frances WILKES  +
  \-- Elizabeth PHILIPPS
       \                 /-- Robert (Sir; of Newhall) DARCY  +
       |        /-- Edward (of Newhall) DARCY  (Derbys.)
       |       /         \-- Grace REDDISH
       \-- Catherine d' ARCY  (1641? - 1713?)
               \                /-- John (Sir; of Elvaston) STANHOPE  +
               |      /-- Philip (Sir) STANHOPE  (1584 - 1656)
               |     /         \-- Cordell ALINGTON  +
               \-- Elizabeth (Lady) STANHOPE
                     \                /-- Francis (Lord) HASTINGS  +
                      \-- Catherine HASTINGS  (? - 1636)
                            \-- Sarah HARINGTON  +
```

Like Katherine Purcell, Catherine Shorter — wife of Britain's first Prime Minister Robert Walpole — descended from Aoife through all of her maternal great-grandparents, with one bloodline through Catherine d'Arcy, Catherine Hastings, Katherine Pole, Catherine Stafford and Catherine Mortimer. Catherine Shorter had a daughter named Katherine and an alleged illegitimate son named Horace.

Both Catherine Shorter (right) and Katherine Purcell descended from Kate's Despencer ancestors (See next page).

THE NOT-SO-NOBLE SPENCERS

THE HUMBLE origins of Princess Diana's family were exposed long ago during a heated exchange in the House of Lords.

When the upstart Spencer referred to his 'great ancestors', the distinguished Earl of Arundel cut him off with an unforgettable put down: 'My Lord, when these things you speak of were doing, your ancestors were keeping sheep'.

Based on research by historian J Horace Round, *The Complete Peerage* has dismissed the Spencers' fabricated Despencer bloodline as an 'elaborate imposture' which is 'incapable of deceiving the most credulous.' However, both Prince William and Kate are descended from Edward II's alleged lover Hugh Despencer through Elizabeth Despencer (shown opposite).

The sheep-farming Spencers established themselves at Althorp (above) in the early 1500s and Robert Spencer, the first Baron Spencer of Wormleighton, joined the Order of the Garter in 1601. Kate has a bloodline from Sir Robert Spencer of Spencercombe, shown opposite, through Katherine Spencer and Catherine Clifford (See chart on Page 139).

One of Katherine Spencer's nephews was William Carey, putative father of Henry VIII's illegitimate daughter Catherine Carey.

Note: Because of primogeniture, Althorp will not be inherited by Lady Kitty Spencer, eldest child of the current earl and his first wife Catherine Victoria Lockwood.

Through Elizabeth Despencer (shown opposite), Kate has a bloodline from Hugh Despencer the Younger, a matrilineal descendant of Aoife who was hanged, drawn and quartered in 1326 on the orders of Isabella the She-Wolf of France (See Page 204).

THE PEDIGREE OF

Katherine SPENCER

Died: 1542

HRH Charles's 14-Great Grandmother.   Lady Diana's 13-Great Grandmother.

Husband/Partner: Henry Algernon (K.G.) PERCY
Children: Ingelram (Sir) PERCY ; Margaret (Lady) PERCY ; Thomas (Sir) PERCY ; Anne PERCY ;
Henry Algernon PERCY (6th Earl of Northumberland)

```
                                        /-- poss. William (Sir) le DESPENCER
                            /-- John le SPENCER  (? - 1386??)
                          /           \-- poss. Anne
                  /-- Nicholas le SPENCER
                  /        \-- Alice DEVERELL  +
          /-- prob. Thomas SPENCER  (by 1335 - ?)
          /        \-- Joan POLLARD  +
      /-- Henry (Esq.; of Badby) SPENCER
      /        \-- Dorothy
  /-- Robert (Sir; of Spencercombe) SPENCER
  |      \        /-- Henry LINCOLN  (1338? - ?)
  |       \-- Isabella LINCOLN  (Northampts.)
```

- Katherine SPENCER

```
  \                       /-- Edward III (WINDSOR; King) of ENGLAND
  |                   /-- John (BEAUFORT) of GAUNT
  |                   /       \-- Philipa d' AVESNES of HAINAULT  +
  |               /-- John `Fairborn' (K.G.; de) BEAUFORT
  |               |        \-- Katherine ROELT  +
  |           /-- Edmund (K.G.) BEAUFORT  (Midx. 1406? - 22/5/1455)
  |           |   \        /-- Thomas (II; de) HOLLAND  +
  |           |    \-- Margaret (of Kent) HOLAND  (1384? - 1439)
  |           |    /        \-- Alice (Lady of Arundel) FitzALAN  +
  \-- Eleanor (Countess of WILTSHIRE) BEAUFORT  (1425? - 1501)
          \                /-- Thomas de BEAUCHAMP  +
          |        /-- Richard (de) BEAUCHAMP  (1382 - 1439 Normandy)
          |        |   \-- Margaret (de) FERRERS  +
          \-- Eleanor (Lady; de) BEAUCHAMP  (1408 - 1468 London)
                  \                /-- Maurice (4th Baron) de BERKELEY  +
                  |        /-- Thomas (Lord) de BERKELEY  (1351? - 1417)
                  |        /        \-- Elizabeth (le) DESPENCER  +
                  \-- Elizabeth de BERKELEY  (1386? - 1422)
```

Katherine Spencer's son Sir Thomas Percy (circled), who had a daughter named Catherine, was hanged, drawn and quartered in 1537 after a Catholic uprising against Henry VIII. Kate's children descend from co-conspirator Sir Robert Constable's daughter Catherine.

CAVENDISH CONNECTIONS

ONE OF Katherine Spencer's descendants was Georgiana Spencer, the beautiful and charismatic Duchess of Devonshire who was famous for her love affairs and gambling.

Georgiana, born at Althorp and mistress of Chatsworth House (above), married William Cavendish, the fifth Duke of Devonshire, grandson of the third duke (also named William) who married the vulgar Catherine Hoskins (See opposite). Through Catherine Preston (born c1514), Catherine Hoskins' husband was descended from the Stockeld Middletons and Kate's Plumpton ancestors (See chart on Page 143).

Kate's children have a bloodline from Georgiana Spencer's brother George Spencer KG and, as shown opposite, they also descend from Catherine Ogle, wife of Sir Charles Cavendish of Welbeck Abbey. Charles' father was yet another William Cavendish who died in 1557.

Chatsworth House, where Prince William worked during his university gap year, probably inspired Pemberley in *Pride and Prejudice* because Jane Austen wrote the novel while staying at nearby Bakewell.

Catherine Ogle's parents, Catherine Carnaby and Cuthbert Ogle, were second cousins through Margaret Gascoigne (shown opposite), sister of Kate's and Prince William's common ancestor Agnes Gascoigne and a first cousin of Katherine Spencer's husband Henry Algernon Percy.

Like Kate, Catherine Ogle had Lumley bloodlines from Edward IV's illegitimate daughter Margaret Plantagenet. Note also that Catherine was descended from Aoife through all of her grandparents.

Georgiana Spencer who sat for this Gainsborough portrait around 1786, had bloodlines from Katherine Grandison, Katherine Percy, Catherine Carey and Lady Catherine Grey.

Catherine (Baroness) OGLE

Born: 1569   Died: 1629
HRH Charles's 10-Great Grandmother.   Lady Diana's 11-Great Grandmother.
Husband/Partner: Charles (Sir; of Welbeck Abbey) CAVENDISH
Child: William (K.G.) CAVENDISH

```
                                    /-- Owen (2nd Lord) OGLE  +
                            /-- Ralph (3rd Lord) OGLE  (1468? - 1513)
                           /          \-- Eleanor HILTON  +
                    /-- Robert (4th Lord) OGLE  (? - by 1532)
                   /           \-- Margaret GASCOIGNE  +
            /-- Robert (5th Lord) OGLE  (? - 1545)
           |       \           /-- Thomas (Sir; de) LUMLEY  +
           |        \-- Anne LUMLEY  (1488? - ?)
           /                    \-- Elizabeth (Margaret) PLANTAGENET  +
    /-- Cuthbert (7th Lord) OGLE  (1545? - 1597)
   |       \                    /-- Edward (Sir; of Cartington) RADCLIFFE  +
   |        |          /-- Cuthbert (Knight; of Dilston) RADCLIFFE
   |        |         /          \-- Anne CARTINGTON  +
   |        \-- Jane RADCLIFFE  (? - 1564+)
   |                  \          /-- Henry (9th/10th Lord) CLIFFORD  +
   |                   \-- Margaret CLIFFORD  (1497? - 1550?)
   /                              \-- Anne ST. JOHN  +
```

- Catherine (Baroness) OGLE

```
   |        /-- Reynold (Sir; of Halton) CARNABY  (? - 1543)
   |       |            \          /-- Thomas (Sir; of Derwentwater) RADCLYFFE  +
   |       |             \-- Thomasine (Katherine?) RADCLIFFE
   |       |                       \-- Margaret PARR  +
   |       /                        / OR: prob. not Katherine BOOTH  +
   \-- Catherine CARNABY  (? - 1622?)
           \                    /-- Thomas (IV; of Adderston) FORSTER  +
           |          /-- Thomas (Sir) FORSTER  (? - 1526+ (or '34+))
           |         |          \-- Jane Anne de HILTON  +
           |         /            / or: poss. Margaret FETHERSTONEHAUGH
           \-- Dorothy (of Adderstone) FORSTER  (1517? - 1565+)
                    \          /-- Ralph (3rd Lord) OGLE  +
                     \-- Dorothy OGLE  (? - 1541)
                              \-- Margaret GASCOIGNE  +
```

THE 'DELIGHTFULLY VULGAR' DUCHESS

CATHERINE HOSKINS, pictured right as St Catherine of Alexandria, was the most recent common ancestor of Princess Diana and Prince Charles.

The daughter of a wealthy merchant, Catherine was the wife of the third Duke of Devonshire, mother of the fourth duke, and grandmother of the fifth duke who married Georgiana Spencer.

Mistress of Chatsworth House for more than 50 years, Catherine Hoskins was described by Hugh Walpole as 'more delightfully vulgar than one can imagine'.

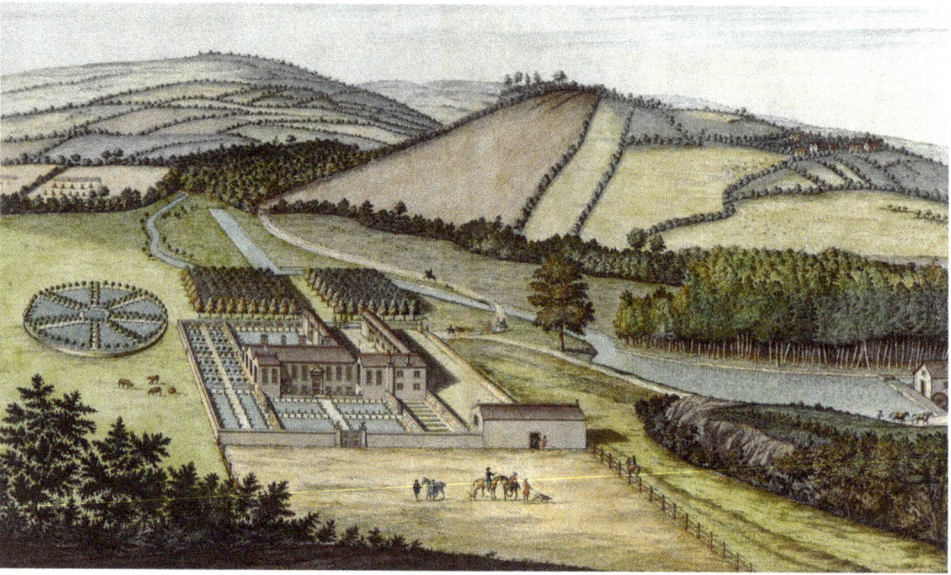

THE KATE TANFIELD MYSTERY

FURTHER research may confirm that Kate Middleton is descended from Kate Tanfield, daughter-in-law of Agnes Gascoigne of Gawthorpe Hall (above).

The families of Agnes (or Anne) and Sir Thomas Fairfax lived in Yorkshire, not far from the Stockeld Middletons (See map on Page 140). And according to fabpedigree.com and many other genealogical websites, Kate is descended from the William Fairfax shown opposite. Prince William descends from his namesake's possible twin Nicholas Fairfax.

The problem with William Fairfax was neatly summed up on narkive.com in 2011, before discovery of Kate's descent from Thomas Conyers: '(As) it stands today, Kate Middleton's descent from Edward III rests on the mid 17th-century belief among the Fairfaxes of Yorkshire and the Fairfaxes of East Anglia, that they were related, and their attempts to establish how. Yet apparently even they weren't able to give William Fairfax… a wife or any birth or death dates, nor any other details other than that his family settled in Norfolk.'

[Similar confusion between two William Davenports resulted in Kate's alleged bloodline from Catherine Carey (See Page 33).]

In *Pedigrees of the County Families of Yorkshire* (1874), Joseph Foster stated that William Fairfax (son of Sir Thomas Fairfax and Agnes Gascoigne) married Anne Baker and then had four children with his second wife Kate Tanfield.

Nothing else is known about Kate Tanfield, apart from the fact that her father was named Robert. That could be significant because Agnes Gascoigne was a first cousin twice removed of Catherine Neville of Raby Castle who married Robert Tanfield of Gayton in Northamptonshire.

William Fairfax's namesake son of Bury and Walsingham married Lucy Goodman, from whom Kate is descended through two Benjamin Fairfaxes who

The PEDIGREE of

Agnes (Anne) GASCOIGNE

Born: by 1484

Lady Diana's 13-Great Grandmother.

Husband/Partner: **Thomas (Sir; of Gilling Castle) FAIRFAX**
Children: **Nicholas (Sir; of Walton & Gilling) FAIRFAX** ; **William FAIRFAX**

```
                     /-- William (II; Knight) GASCOIGNE  (1398? - by 1466)
                  /        \-- Jane (Joan) WYMAN  (skip?)  +
            /-- William (III; Sir) GASCOIGNE
            |        \            /-- Thomas (Knight; of Aldwark) CLARELL  +
            |         \-- Margaret CLARELL  (1397? - 1466)
            |               \| OR: prob. not Margaret CLARELL [alt ped]  +
            |         /        \-- Matilda MONTGOMERY  +
      /-- William (IV; Sir) GASCOIGNE  (? - 1487)
      |     \                  /-- Ralph (Sir) NEVILLE  +
      |      |        /-- John (Esq.; of Oversley) NEVILLE  (1416? - 1482)
      |      |        /        \-- Mary de FERRERS  +
      |      \-- Jane (Lady of Oversley) NEVILLE  (1443? - ?)
      |               \         /-- Robert NEWMARCH  +
      |                \-- Elizabeth NEWMARCH
      |                     \-- prob. Joan SHIRLEY  +
      /                        | or: Anne ROLSTON
```

Agnes (Anne) GASCOIGNE

```
      \                       /-- Henry `Hotspur' (K.G.) PERCY  +
      |               /-- Henry (5th Lord) PERCY
      |               /        \-- Elizabeth (de) MORTIMER  +
      |        /-- Henry Algernon PERCY  (1421 - 29/3/1461)
      |        |     \            /-- Ralph I NEVILL (de NEVILLE)  +
      |        |      \-- Eleanor (Lady) NEVILLE  (1407? - 1472 (or '63))
      |        /         \-- Joan (Lady; de) BEAUFORT  +
      \-- Margaret (Lady) PERCY  (1447? - 1486)
               \            /-- Robert (Lord of) POYNINGS  +
               |     /-- Richard (Lord of) POYNINGS  (? - 10/6/1429)
               |     /        \-- Elizabeth (Eleanor Isabel) GREY  +
               \-- Eleanor (Countess) POYNINGS  (1422 - 1484)
```

were both Nonconformist ministers in the Church of England.

Even if she is not descended from William Fairfax and Kate Tanfield (or Anne Baker), the Duchess of Cambridge has bloodlines from the Gascoignes of Gawthorpe — as well as from Henry 'Hotspur' Percy and Elizabeth Mortimer — through Thomas Conyers, Henry Constable of Burton and Jane Lambton.

Agnes Gascoigne had bloodlines from Katherine Swynford through both parents, and from Katherine of Flanders and Aoife through most of her great-grandparents. And through Elizabeth Mortimer (shown above), Agnes descended from Roger Mortimer, the alleged lover of Isabella 'the She-Wolf of France' (See next page.)

Note: Before Kate's wedding in 2011, it was speculated that Kate's father Michael Middleton could be made Earl of Fairfax.

MORTIMER AND THE SHE-WOLF

GIVEN that they emulated their joint ancestor William the Bastard by conquering England, Kate's ancestors Roger Mortimer and his lover Queen Isabella (above) have not received the credit that they deserve.

In the film *Braveheart*, Isabella has an affair with William Wallace which could never have happened because she was aged about ten and living in France when he died in 1305. And while Isabella's husband did have an intimate relationship with Piers Gaveston, the depiction of Edward II is based on homophobic stereotypes. Edward was allegedly murdered in 1327 by having a red hot poker inserted in his anus but some historians believe he spent his last years in northern Italy.

After effectively ruling England for several years, Mortimer was executed by Isabella's teenaged son Edward III who was furious when Mortimer dressed up as King Arthur. Both Edward IV and Henry VII claimed Arthurian descent to bolster their claims to the throne.

Isabella spent her last three decades in captivity while her brothers Louis X, Philip V and Charles IV all died young, seemingly fulfilling the curse placed on their father Philip IV by Jacques de Molay while he was being burnt to death.

Many millions of people descend from Isabella through Katherine Swynford's illegitimate offspring, and there must be quite a few bloodlines from the bastard children of Isabella's grandson Reginald 'the Fat' of Guelders. According to legend, he was trapped for ten years in a room at Nijenbeek Castle because he couldn't fit through the door.

Roger Mortimer has millions of descendants through the fifteen children of Catherine Mortimer whose husband Thomas Beauchamp and grandfathers, Edmund Mortimer and Peter de Geneville, were matrilineal descendants of Aoife.

THE PEDIGREE OF

Catherine (de) MORTIMER

Born: Shrops. abt. 1314   Died: 1369

HRH Charles's 17-Great Grandmother.   Lady Diana's 16-Great Grandmother.
Husband/Partner: __Thomas (de) BEAUCHAMP__

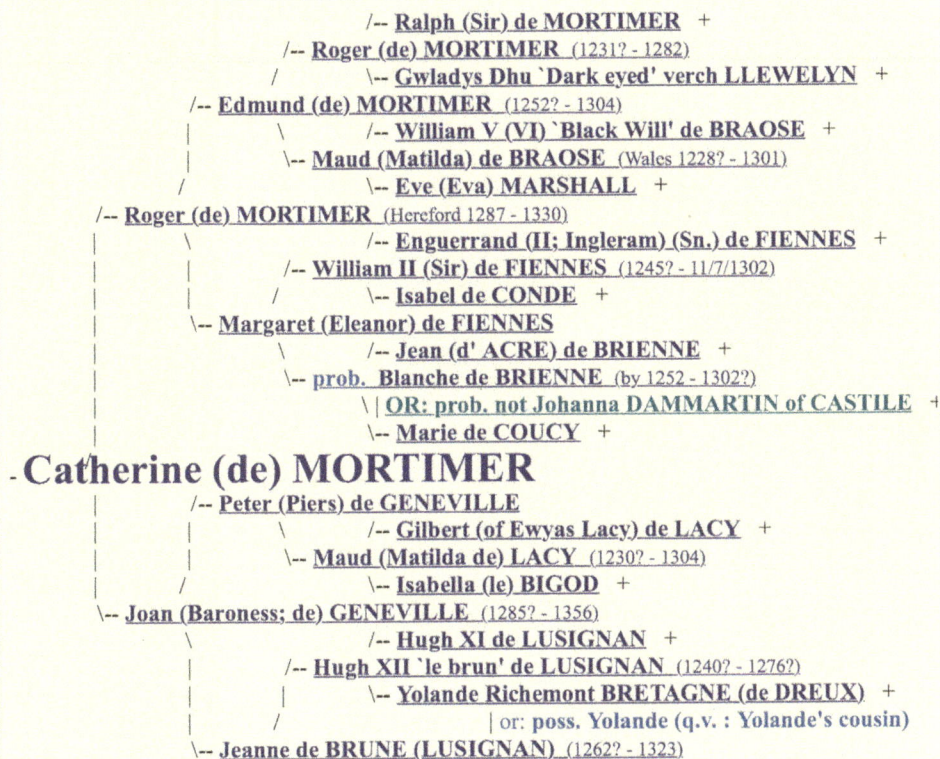

```
                              /-- Ralph (Sir) de MORTIMER  +
                      /-- Roger (de) MORTIMER  (1231? - 1282)
                     /           \-- Gwladys Dhu `Dark eyed' verch LLEWELYN  +
              /-- Edmund (de) MORTIMER  (1252? - 1304)
              |      \           /-- William V (VI) `Black Will' de BRAOSE  +
              |       \-- Maud (Matilda) de BRAOSE  (Wales 1228? - 1301)
              /                  \-- Eve (Eva) MARSHALL  +
       /-- Roger (de) MORTIMER  (Hereford 1287 - 1330)
       |      \                  /-- Enguerrand (II; Ingleram) (Sn.) de FIENNES  +
       |       |         /-- William II (Sir) de FIENNES  (1245? - 11/7/1302)
       |       |        /          \-- Isabel de CONDE  +
       |       \-- Margaret (Eleanor) de FIENNES
       |                 \          /-- Jean (d' ACRE) de BRIENNE  +
       |                  \-- prob. Blanche de BRIENNE  (by 1252 - 1302?)
       |                       \ | OR: prob. not Johanna DAMMARTIN of CASTILE  +
       |                        \-- Marie de COUCY  +
```

Catherine (de) MORTIMER

```
       |         /-- Peter (Piers) de GENEVILLE
       |         |      \          /-- Gilbert (of Ewyas Lacy) de LACY  +
       |         |       \-- Maud (Matilda de) LACY  (1230? - 1304)
       |         /                 \-- Isabella (le) BIGOD  +
       \-- Joan (Baroness; de) GENEVILLE  (1285? - 1356)
                 \                 /-- Hugh XI de LUSIGNAN  +
                 |         /-- Hugh XII `le brun' de LUSIGNAN  (1240? - 1276?)
                 |        |          \-- Yolande Richemont BRETAGNE (de DREUX)  +
                 |        /                | or: poss. Yolande (q.v. : Yolande's cousin)
                 \-- Jeanne de BRUNE (LUSIGNAN)  (1262? - 1323)
```

Kate descends from Catherine Mortimer through her granddaughter Katherine Clifford, and also through Katherine Spencer's granddaughter Catherine Clifford. Kate's children have Mortimer bloodlines through ten of their mother's namesakes (See chart on Page 49).

MORE MIDDLETON CONNECTIONS

THERE IS an all-female bloodline from Catherine Mortimer to Thomas Middleton of Stockeld (died c1549) through Matilda Clifford, sister of Kate's ancestor John 'Black-faced' Clifford, and Jane Dudley (or Sutton). Kate's children descend from Thomas Middleton's grandmother Catherine (Anne) Vavasour, who married Sir Peter Mydelton (sic), and some of Kate's Plumpton and Constable ancestors were closely related to Sir Peter's ancestors.

David Carpenter's book about the decline of the Stockeld Middletons was published in 1999.

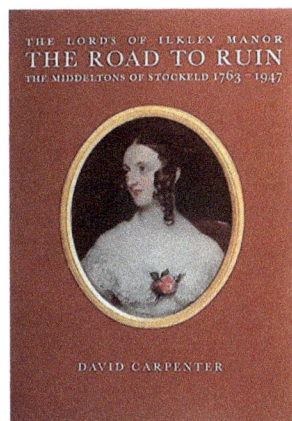

THE LORDS OF ILKLEY MANOR
THE ROAD TO RUIN
THE MIDDLETONS OF STOCKELD 1763 - 1947

DAVID CARPENTER

ELEANOR AND ROSAMUND

COUNTLESS millions of people in Britain and France unknowingly descend from Henry II's wife Eleanor of Aquitaine, pictured above menacing her arch-rival Rosamund Clifford.

Queen Eleanor supposedly found her way through an elaborate maze at Woodstock Castle and forced the fair Rosamund to drink poison. In reality, Rosamund's death at Godstow Abbey in Oxfordshire around 1176 was unsuspicious.

Eleanor had ten children, two with Louis VII and eight with Henry II, and there were nearly 40 grandchildren. So, if Edward III has about 100 million living descendants, his great-great-great-grandmother must have many more.

Both Kate and Prince William descend from Katherine Swynford's husband John of Gaunt who had bloodlines from Eleanor of Aquitaine through all but one of his great-grandparents. And through Jane Lambton and Katherine Clifford, Kate descends from Rosamund's father Walter Clifford (died 1190) of Clifford Castle in Herefordshire.

Bloodlines on fabpedigree.com and geni.com from Rosamund Clifford's alleged daughter (Miss FitzHenry), including a descent through Kate's ancestors Catherine Clifford and Katherine Spencer, should be disregarded.

Katherine Clifford's father Roger Clifford had an all-female bloodline from Aoife, and so did

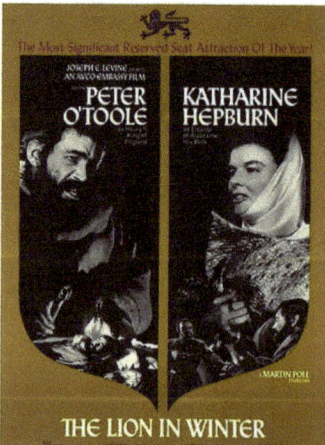

According to famouskin.com Katharine Hepburn, who played Eleanor of Aquitaine in The Lion in Winter, *was Kate's fourteenth cousin four times removed through two sisters of Katherine Constable (born c1453).*

The PEDIGREE of
Katherine (de) CLIFFORD
Born: by 1369   Died: 1413
Lady Diana's 17-Great Grandmother.   HRH Charles's 17-Great Grandmother.

Husband/Partner: Ralph (V; 3rd Baron) de GREYSTOKE
Children: John (4th/6th Baron) de GREYSTOKE (GREYSTOCK)

```
                /-- Robert II (III; 3rd Lord) de CLIFFORD  (1305 - 1344)
        |       \           /-- Thomas de CLARE  +
        |        \-- Maud (Matilda) de CLARE  (1279? - 1325)
        /                   \-- Juliane FitzMAURICE  +
    /-- Roger (5th Lord; de) CLIFFORD  (1333 - 1389)
    |       \                   /-- Thomas `the Wise' (1st Lord) de BERKELEY  +
    |       |           /-- Maurice (2nd Lord) de BERKELEY
    |       |           /       \-- Joan (Margaret) de FERRERS  +
    |       \-- Isabel (de) BERKELEY  (1307? - 1362)
    |               \           /-- Eudo (of HARRINGWORTH) la ZOUCHE  +
    |                \-- Eve la ZOUCHE
    /                           \-- Milicent de CANTILUPE  +
```

- Katherine (de) CLIFFORD

```
    \                       /-- William de BEAUCHAMP  +
    |                   /-- William (de ALCASTER) de BEAUCHAMP  (? -
    |                   /       \-- Isabel MAUDIT (de MAUDUIT)  +
    |           /-- Guy (de) BEAUCHAMP  (1278 - 1315)
    |           /           \-- Maud FitzJOHN  +
    |       /-- Thomas (de) BEAUCHAMP  (1314 - 1369)
    |       |       \           /-- Ralph (Roger) VII de TOENI  +
    |       |       \-- Alice (Countess) de TOENI  (1284? - 1324?)
    |       /                   \-- Mary (Clarissa) (poss. de BOHUN)  +
    \-- Maud de BEAUCHAMP  (? - 1403)
            \                   /-- Edmund (de) MORTIMER  +
            |           /-- Roger (de) MORTIMER  (Hereford 1287 - 1330)
            |           /       \-- Margaret (Eleanor) de FIENNES  +
            \-- Catherine (de) MORTIMER  (Shrops. 1314? - 1369)
```

his grandfather Robert de Clifford who fought at Bannockburn (See chart on Page 193). Other matrilineal descendants of Aoife were Katherine's maternal grandfather Thomas Beauchamp; his father Guy Beauchamp; and Catherine Mortimer's grandfather Edmund Mortimer, a great-grandson of King John's illegitimate daughter Joan of North Wales.

In *Parallel Alices* (2012), Christopher Tyler compared the adventures of the fictional Alice with the travails of Eleanor of Aquitaine's daughter Alice Capet, from whom Kate's children descend through Catherine of Valois.

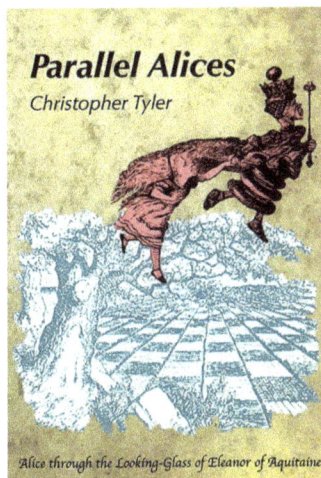

Parallel Alices
Christopher Tyler

Alice through the Looking-Glass of Eleanor of Aquitaine

Ralph BOWES
(1480–1516)
of Streatlam, Co Durham
High Sheriff

GRANDCHILDREN

Sir George BOWES	**Bridget BOWES**
Loyal to Queen Elizabeth I during the rising of the North, 1596	Married John Hussey of Dorking

GRANDSON

GREAT-GRANDSON

Sir William BOWES MP	**Captain Christopher HUSSEY**
(1657–1707) During reign of Charles II Royalist	(1598/9–1686) A founder of Nantucket, Massachusetts
Sir George BOWES MP (1701–1760)	**Huldah HUSSEY** (1643–1740) Married Lieutenant John SMITH
Mary Eleanor BOWES (1749–1800) Married John, 9th Earl of Strathmore	**Captain John SMITH** (1669–1752) Married Abigail SHAW, descended from the Bruce & Stewart Kings of Scotland

FOUR GENERATIONS | FOUR GENERATIONS

Claude George BOWES LYON (1854–1944) 14th Earl of Strathmore	**Mary SMITH** (1823–1908) Married Jacob Lee MERRILL
	George David MERRILL (1861–1924)
Lady Elizabeth BOWES LYON (1900–2001) HM Queen Elizabeth The Queen Mother	**Gertrude May MERRILL** (1887–1938) Married Frederick George SANDERS
	Doris SANDERS (1921–) Married Gordon Arnold Markle
HM The Queen (1926–)	

Lady Diana Spencer (1961–1997)	**HRH Prince of Wales** (1948–)	**Thomas Wayne Markle** (1944–)	**Doria L. Ragland** (1956–)

PRINCE HARRY	**(RACHEL) MEGHAN MARKLE**

15th Cousins

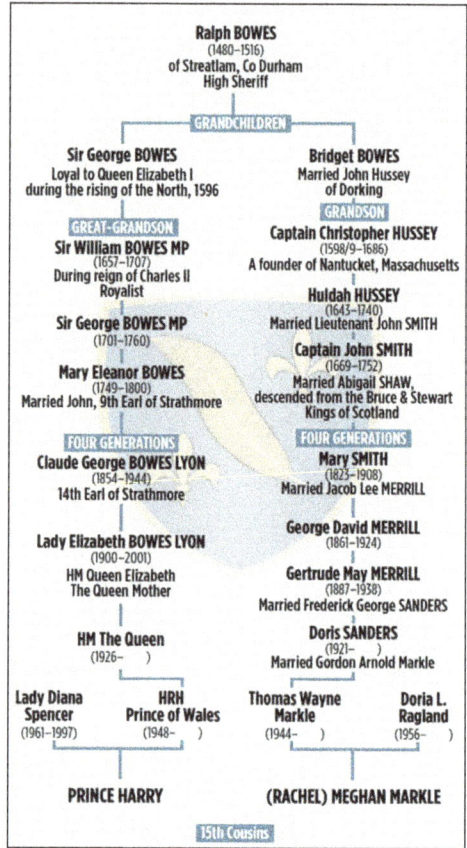

KATE AND MEGHAN CONNECTIONS

WHOEVER compiled the chart above confused Katherine Clifford's great-grandson Ralph Bowes with his namesake son who died in 1516, and made several other elementary mistakes.

More importantly, according to famouskin.com Meghan's bloodline from the older Ralph Bowes' son Richard is 'speculation and unproven' so we will probably never know if Meghan and Kate are 16th cousins once removed through Bridget and her first cousin Margery Bowes.

The most recent common ancestor of Kate and Meghan (and their husbands) is probably Sir John Hastings (died 1477), through whom the duchesses are 17th cousins once removed. And they are 18th cousins once removed through three other knights: Sir Roger Wentworth, Sir John Clifford, and Clifford's father-in-law Sir Henry 'Hotspur' Percy.

Katherine Collingwood descended from Hastings, Wentworth, Clifford and Percy through three of her great-great-great-grandparents shown opposite: Sir Hugh de Hastings, Margaret Constable and John 'Black-faced' Clifford.

Note: The legendary Monster of Glamis was reputedly the Queen Mother's great-uncle Thomas Lyon-Bowes (born 1821), a descendant of the Stockeld Middletons and also the first Earl of Middleton.

The PEDIGREE of
Katherine COLLINGWOOD
Husband/Partner: Lancelot (of Halton Castle) CARNABY
Child: Anne CARNABY

```
        /-- Cuthbert (Sir; of Eslington) COLLINGWOOD  (1538? - 1596)
      /
- Katherine COLLINGWOOD
      \                          /-- William (Sir; of Streatlam) BOWES  +
      |                  /-- Ralph (Sir; of Streatlam) BOWES  (? - 1482+)
      |                /        \-- Maud FitzHUGH  +
      |          /-- Ralph (Sir; of Streatlam) BOWES  (? - 1516)
      |          |      \          /-- Richard (Sir; of South Cowton) CONYERS  +
      |          |      \-- Marjery (Margaret) CONYERS  (? - 1532)
      |        /            \-- Alice WYCLIFFE  +
      |     /-- George (Sir) BOWES  (? - 1545)
      |     |    \                 /-- John `Black faced' CLIFFORD  +
      |     |    |          /-- Henry (9th/10th Lord) CLIFFORD
      |     |    |        /        \-- Margaret BROMFLETE  +
      |     |    \-- Elizabeth CLIFFORD
      |     |         \          /-- John (Sir; of Bletsoe) ST. JOHN  +
      |     |         \-- Anne ST. JOHN  (? - by 1511)
      |    /              \-- Alice BRADSHAW (of Haigh; BRADSHAIGH)  +
      \-- Dorothy BOWES
            \                    /-- William (Sir) EURE  +
            |            /-- Ralph (Sir; of Witton Castle) EURE  (? - 1539)
            |          /        \-- Margaret CONSTABLE  +
            |    /-- William (1st Baron de Wilton) EURE
            |    |    \             /-- Hugh (Sir; of Gressenhall) de HASTINGS  +
            |    |    \-- Muriel HASTINGS  (? - by 1499)
            |   /          \-- Anne GASCOIGNE  +
            \-- Muriel EURE  (? - 1557 Yorks.)
```

KATHERINE BOWES-LYON

FIRST REVEALED in 1987 was the truly shocking story of Katherine Bowes-Lyon (right) and her sister Nerissa who, despite being listed as dead in *Burke's Peerage*, had been confined in a mental hospital since 1941.

The Queen Mother, patron of the Mencap charity, never visited her nieces, reportedly worried about any hint of tainted royal blood. In fact, Katherine, Nerissa and three cousins inherited a genetic disorder through their Hepburn-Stuart-Forbes-Trefusis bloodlines.

Only hospital staff attended Nerissa's 1986 funeral and her grave had no headstone until her fate was revealed in the media. Katherine, born in the same year as her first cousin Elizabeth II, died in 2014.

In 2020, the tragic story of Katherine and Nerissa was told in the fourth season of *The Crown* TV series.

FROM HOTSPUR TO HOGWARTS

THROUGH Henry Constable of Burton and Katherine Swynford's great-grand-daughter Katherine Percy, Kate is descended from three Henry Percys who had the same mitochondrial and Y-DNA.

Katherine's father, namesake son of Henry 'Hotspur' Percy (above), had an all-female bloodline from Irish princess Aoife (See Slaughter in St Albans, Page 188). So did Hotspur's father Henry Percy KG, who was killed at the Battle of Bramham Moor in 1408, and so did the Henry Percy who died of natural causes in 1352.

Hotspur conspired with Edmund Mortimer and Welsh rebel Owen Glendower to form the so-called Tripartite Indenture which would have split England into three kingdoms, fulfilling an ancient prophecy involving a Dragon from the North, a Wolf from the West and a Lion out of Ireland. (Edmund Mortimer was the husband of Glendower's daughter Catherine and the brother of Hotspur's wife Elizabeth.)

According to Shakespeare, Hotspur was killed at Shrewsbury by the future Henry V (another matrilineal descendant of Aoife) but it is much more likely that Hotspur was killed by an arrow while charging Henry IV's army. After the death of his mother, Henry IV was raised by Katherine Swynford; and, after Catherine of Valois' death, her sons were raised by Katherine de la Pole (See The Abbesses of Barking, Page 216).

During the Battle of Shrewsbury, Hotspur's army shouted 'Henry Percy king', suggesting he had his eye on the throne. Hotspur descended from Henry III through Mary of Lancaster (shown opposite) and Hotspur's wife Elizabeth Mortimer had a stronger claim through Edward III.

Hotspur descended from several royal bastards,

Henry Percy KG inspired the character Lord Percy Percy in Blackadder *which, like the Harry Potter films, was partly shot at Alnwick Castle (above), home of Kate's close friend Lady Katie Percy.*

THE PEDIGREE OF

Katherine PERCY

Born: Leconfield 1423   Died: abt. 1504

HRH Charles's 16-Great Grandmother.   Lady Diana's 14-Great Grandmother.

Husband/Partner: **Edmund (Sir) GREY**
Children: **George (2nd Earl of KENT) GREY** ;   **Anne GREY** ;   **Elizabeth (Lady) GREY**

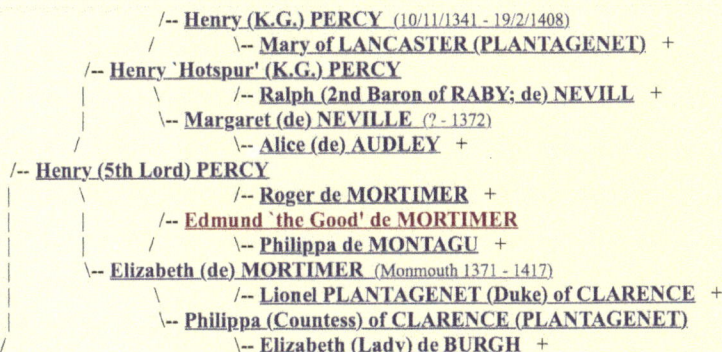

```
                    /-- Henry (K.G.) PERCY  (10/11/1341 - 19/2/1408)
                /           \-- Mary of LANCASTER (PLANTAGENET)  +
        /-- Henry `Hotspur' (K.G.) PERCY
        |       \           /-- Ralph (2nd Baron of RABY; de) NEVILL  +
        |        \-- Margaret (de) NEVILLE  (? - 1372)
        /                   \-- Alice (de) AUDLEY  +
    /-- Henry (5th Lord) PERCY
    |       \               /-- Roger de MORTIMER  +
    |        |      /-- Edmund `the Good' de MORTIMER
    |        |     /         \-- Philippa de MONTAGU  +
    |        \-- Elizabeth (de) MORTIMER  (Monmouth 1371 - 1417)
    |               \       /-- Lionel PLANTAGENET (Duke) of CLARENCE  +
    |                \-- Philippa (Countess) of CLARENCE (PLANTAGENET)
    /                       \-- Elizabeth (Lady) de BURGH  +
```

- Katherine PERCY

```
    \                       /-- Randolph (Ranulph; Ralph) de NEVILLE  +
    |                   /-- Ralph (2nd Baron of RABY; de) NEVILL
    |                  /        \-- Euphemia (FitzROBERT; de) CLAVERING  +
    |        /-- John (III; de) NEVILL  (1327+ - 1388)
    |       /           \-- Alice (de) AUDLEY  +
    |    /-- Ralph I NEVILL (de NEVILLE)  (1363? - 1425)
    |   |       \           /-- Henry (IV; III; 2nd Lord; de) PERCY  +
    |   |        \-- Matilda (Maud Mary) de PERCY  (1342? - 1379)
    |   /                   \-- Idonea (Idoine de) CLIFFORD  +
    \-- Eleanor (Lady) NEVILLE  (1407? - 1472 (or '63))
        \                   /-- Edward III (WINDSOR; King) of ENGLAND  +
        |           /-- John (BEAUFORT) of GAUNT
        |          /        \-- Philipa d' AVESNES (Countess) of HAINAULT  +
        \-- Joan (Lady; de) BEAUFORT  (1379? - 1440)
            \               /-- Paon (Sir; of GUIENNE) de ROET  +
             \-- Katherine ROELT
```

including Robert of Gloucester and William Longespee, and also from Joscelin de Louvain, the bastard son of Godfrey 'the Bearded' of Brabant who married a daughter of William de Percy of Topcliffe (See map on Page 138).

Katherine Percy, who inherited Katherine Swynford's haplogroup J, may not have been dangerously inbred but, as shown above, her parents had multiple cousinships through Alice Audley, Idonea Clifford and Edward III.

According to famouskin.com Kate and Meghan Markle are eighteenth cousins one removed through Katherine Percy's aunt Elizabeth Percy, grandmother of John 'Black-faced' Clifford (See Vengeance at Wakefield, Page 190).

The photoshopped image (right) appeared in 2013 after Kate toured the Harry Potter studio in Hertfordshire.

SHAKESPEAREAN CATHERINES

PERTAINING to Katherine Percy, there is one significant difference between the chart on the previous page and the one opposite, which raises the question: Why did Shakespeare change the name of Hotspur's wife from Elizabeth (nee Mortimer) to Kate?

One possible explanation is that Shakespeare was comparing Lady Percy to the tempestuous Kate Minola in *The Taming of the Shrew,* which he wrote several years before *Henry IV Part I.* Elizabeth Taylor played Kate opposite her real-life husband Richard Burton in the 1967 film version that implied Kate only pretended to obey Petruchio. However, many people agree with George Bernard Shaw who said *The Taming of the Shrew* was 'altogether disgusting to modern sensibility'.

Much has been written about Kate Percy even though she only appears in three scenes across two plays. In the most famous scene, depicted above, Kate complains about Hotspur's neglect.

As Carley Becker wrote in an online article titled 'Not Just a Pretty Face': 'At first glance, a reader may assume that Kate is a slave to her husband…(but) when studied in a deeper historical context, Kate's first lines show less of a woman fawning over her husband, and more of an intelligent, politically-savvy female figure.'

There is a memorable line in Shakespeare's play *Henry V* after the maid of a

Characters in Shakespeare's
Henry IV Part I

Philip IV of France — Charles, Count of Valois

Edward II of England — Isabella — Philip VI of France

Edward III — John II of France

Edward, the Black Prince — Lionel, Duke of Clarence — Blanche of Lancaster — John of Gaunt, Duke of Lancaster — Katherine Swynford — Edmund, Duke of York — Thomas of Woodstock, Duke of Gloucester — Charles V of France

Richard II — Philippa — Edmund Mortimer, Earl of March — Henry Bolingbroke (Henry IV) — Thomas Beaufort, Duke of Exeter — Joan Beaufort — Ralph Neville, Earl of Westmorland — Charles VI of France

Roger Mortimer, Earl of March — Henry V — John of Lancaster, Duke of Bedford — Humphrey, Duke of Gloucester — Edward, Duke of Aumerle (later Duke of York) — Louis the Dauphin — Katherine

Kate Percy (married to Hotspur in Henry IV) — Edmund Mortimer, Earl of March — Anne Mortimer — Richard, Earl of Cambridge

THE MOTION PICTURE THEY WERE MADE FOR!

A motion picture for every man who ever gave the back of his hand to his beloved... and for every woman who deserved it. Which takes in a lot of people!

COLUMBIA PICTURES PRESENTS

ELIZABETH TAYLOR · RICHARD BURTON

IN THE BURTON–ZEFFIRELLI PRODUCTION OF

THE TAMING OF THE SHREW

Selected for the 1967 British Royal Performance!

also starring CYRIL CUSACK · MICHAEL HORDERN · ALFRED LYNCH · ALAN WEBB with VICTOR SPINETTI
MICHAEL YORK · NATASHA PYNE Screenplay by PAUL DEHN, SUSO CECCHI D'AMICO, FRANCO ZEFFIRELLI · RICHARD McWHORTER · FRANCO ZEFFIRELLI
A ROYAL FILMS INTERNATIONAL/F.A.I. PRODUCTION TECHNICOLOR

LA VIDA DE UN GRAN REY...
FAMOSO POR SU ESPADA
Y POR SUS AMORES

J. ARTHUR RANK presenta
la máxima creación de
LAURENCE OLIVIER
en
"ENRIQUE V"
de WILLIAM SHAKESPEARE
en TECHNICOLOR
con
Robert   Renee   Leslie   Esmond
NEWTON · ASHERSON · BANKS · KNIGHT

young Catherine of Valois tells the English king that French girls do not kiss before marriage. He responds: 'O Kate, nice customs curtsy to great kings.'

However, the real relationship between Henry V and Queen Catherine may have been very different (See Catherine of Valois' Curses, Page 112). Author Anne O'Brien was likeminded, stating in an online article titled 'The Love Affair that Never Was' (2013): 'Shakespeare has a lot to answer for.'

There is no doubt that Queen Catherine and Owen Tudor, like Katherine Swynford and John of Gaunt, had a true romance (See next page).

THE SUN IN SPLENDOUR…

WHEN a parhelion appeared before the Battle of Mortimer's Cross in 1461, Edward IV's assurance that it was a good omen helped his army defeat Catherine of Valois' second husband Owen Tudor and their second son Jasper (second husband of Catherine Woodville).

Owen, derided in France as the 'bastard son of an alehouse keeper', lamented that his soon-to-be severed head previously laid on Queen Catherine's lap. He had no memorial until his illegitimate son David Owen paid for a tomb at Greyfriar's Church in Hereford.

One of the Yorkist commanders at Mortimer's Cross was Kate's ancestor William Herbert KG who replaced Jasper Tudor as Earl of Pembroke after the Battle of Towton in 1461. Six years earlier, Herbert, father-in-law of Richard III's illegitimate daughter Katherine, supported Edward IV's father Richard of York at the first Battle of St Albans.

Both Edward IV and Henry VII descended from Katherine Swynford, and both had daughters named Catherine. As well, Edward IV's father (Richard of York) and Henry VII's grandfather (John Beaufort KG) both had all-female bloodlines from Aoife.

Note: One of Edward IV's royal badges combined a blazing sun and the white rose of York.

All British monarchs since Henry VII have directly descended from illegitimate offspring of Katherine Swynford (left) and Catherine of Valois, daughter-in-law of Katherine's stepson Henry IV.

The PEDIGREE of

Henry VII TUDOR (King) of ENGLAND

Born: Wales 1457   Died: 1509 Surrey
HM George I's 5-Great Grandfather. Lady Diana's 12-Great Grandfather.

Wives/Partners: Elizabeth (of YORK) PLANTAGENET ; (NN), a Breton lady
Children: Henry VIII TUDOR ; Margaret TUDOR ; Mary Rose TUDOR (Princess) of ENGLAND
Arthur TUDOR (Prince) of WALES

Possible Child: Rowland (Sir) de VIELLEVILLE

```
                                      /-- Goronwy (Gronwy) ap TUDOR  +
                              /-- Tudor Hen FYCHAN (Lord) of PENMYNYDD  (? - 1367)
                      /              \-- Gwervyl verch MADOG  +
              /-- Maredudd (Meredith Meridith) ap TUDOR  (? - 1406)
      /              \-- Margred verch THOMAS  +
   /-- Owen (Sir) TUDOR
   |              \-- Margaret (LLWYD) verch DAFYDD  +
   /                   | OR: prob. not Margred verch THOMAS  +
/-- Edmund TUDOR  (1430? - 1456)
|     \                    /-- Charles V `the Wise' de VALOIS  +
|      |           /-- Charles VI `the Beloved' de VALOIS
|      |          /            \-- Jeanne (Joan) de BOURBON  +
|      \-- Catherine de VALOIS  (Paris 1401 - 1437 London)
/                \-- Isabelle of BAVARIA  +
```

-Henry VII TUDOR (King) of ENGLAND

```
\                    /-- John `Fairborn' (K.G.; de) BEAUFORT  +
|           /-- John (K.G.) BEAUFORT  (by 1404 - 1444)
|          /            \-- Margaret (of Kent) HOLAND  +
\-- Margaret BEAUFORT
         \              /-- John (Knight; de) BEAUCHAMP  +
          \-- Margaret (of BLETSOE) BEAUCHAMP  (? - 1482)
                   \              /-- John (Knight; of Stourton; de) STOURTON  +
                    \-- Edith (de) STOURTON
                             \-- Katherine (de) BEAUMONT  +
```

...AND THE SON OF DESTINY

THE Welsh-born Henry VII used Owen Tudor's alleged descent from Llewelyn the Great through Catherine verch Llewelyn to insinuate that he was the so-called 'Son of Destiny' and rallied support by flying the Welsh red dragon banner.

Katheryn of Berain, nicknamed the 'Mother of Wales', allegedly descended from Henry VII's illegitimate son Sir Rowland de Vielleville. And because Catherine of Valois married the allegedly illegitimate Owen Tudor illegally, or not at all, their sons Jasper (right) and Edmund were, like Katherine Swynford's Beaufort children, technically bastards. Jasper and Edmund were raised by Katherine de la Pole (See next page).

Note: Nobody knows if Katherine Beaumont (shown above) was Henry VII's maternal great-great-grandmother.

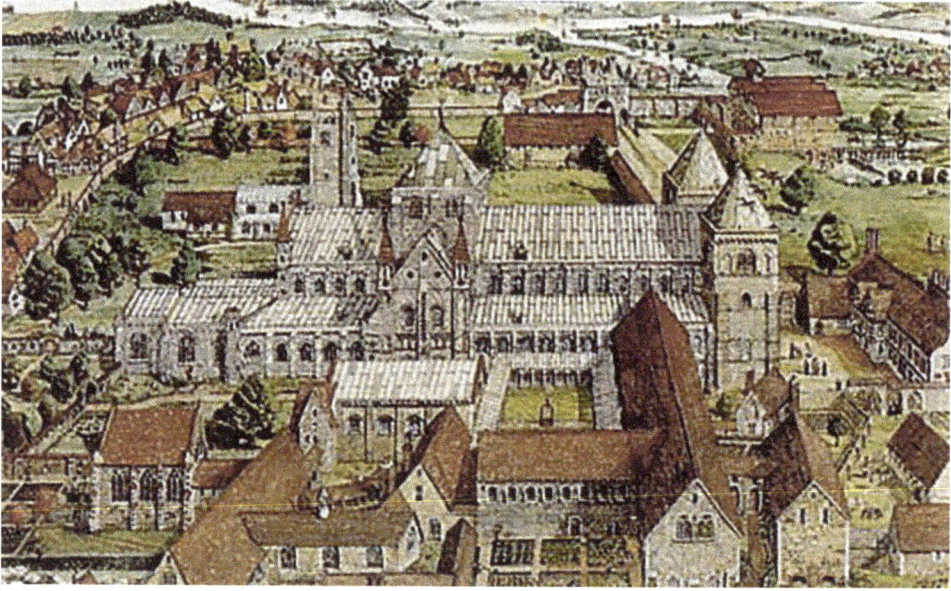

THE ABBESSES OF BARKING...

AFTER Catherine of Valois died in 1437, her sons Edmund and Jasper Tudor were raised by Katherine de la Pole, the Abbess of Barking whose predecessor was a daughter of Katherine Swynford who raised Catherine of Valois' father-in-law Henry IV after the death of his mother Blanche of Lancaster.

Barking Abbey (above) dominated East London from the seventh century. In the 1100s, Clemence of Barking wrote a 'feminist' biography of St Catherine of Alexandria, and two hundred years later an abbess named Katherine of Sutton became Britain's first female playwright.

While Margaret Swynford was abbess between 1419 and 1433, one of the nuns was her first cousin Elizabeth Chaucer whose father wrote *The Canterbury Tales.*

It has been speculated that some of Chaucer's children were sired by Katherine Swynford's husband John of Gaunt.

Katherine de la Pole and her sister Isabel, from whom Kate is descended through Katherine Hastings' sister Muriel, were matrilineal descendants of Catherine Mortimer. So was Katherine's and Isabel's brother William de la Pole, nicknamed Jackanapes, who was a close ally of Katherine Swynford's illegitimate son Cardinal Henry Beaufort (See Page 238). Both Jackanapes and the cardinal had dealings with Joan of Arc.

Katherine Hastings' father was descended from Katherine of Flanders through all of his grandparents.

Catherine Stafford was the mother of Katherine de la Pole, Abbess of Barking; grandmother of Catherine de la Pole (born 1410), a nun at Bruisyard in Suffolk; and niece of Katherine de Beauchamp, a nun at Shouldham Priory in Norfolk.

The PEDIGREE of

Katherine HASTINGS

Born: ? Died: 1557

HRH Charles's 15-Great Aunt.   Lady Diana's 14-Great Aunt.

Husband/Partner: John (Sir; of Aston) MELTON
Child: Dorothy MELTON

```
                              /-- Hugh (of Elsing & Gressenhall) HASTINGS  +
                   /-- Edward (8th Lord; de) HASTINGS  (1382? - 1438)
                  /            \-- Anne (le) DESPENCER  +
          /-- John (9th Lord; de) HASTINGS  (? - 1477)
          |          \          /-- John (III; Sir) DINHAM  +
          |           \-- Muriel (de) DINHAM
          |                     \-- Ellen (Alianore) de MONTAGU  +
          |                       | or: Ellen BROWNINGTON
          /                       | OR: prob. not Philippa LOVELL  +
    /-- Hugh (Sir; of Gressenhall) de HASTINGS  (? - 1488)
    |          \                /-- Robert MORLEY  +
    |          |          /-- Thomas (5th Baron) MORLEY  (1393? - 1435)
    |          |         /            \-- Isabel de MOLINES  +
    |          \-- Anne MORLEY  (? - 1471)
    |                     \          /-- Michael (II) de la POLE  +
    |                      \-- Isabel de la POLE  (? - 1467)
    /                                 \-- Catherine (de) STAFFORD  +
```

·Katherine HASTINGS

```
    \                      /-- William (Sir) GASCOIGNE  +
    |          /-- William (Sir; of GAWTHORP) GASCOIGNE
    |          |       \ | (skip this generation?)
    |          |        \-- Elizabeth (de) MOWBRAY  +
    |          /                  | OR: prob. not Elizabeth MOWBRAY [alt ped]
    |    /-- William (II; Knight) GASCOIGNE  (1398? - by 1466)
    |    |      \          /-- Henry WYMAN  (? - 1411)
    |    |       \-- Jane (Joan) WYMAN  (1375?? - by 1426)  (skip?)
    |    /                 \-- Agnes de BARDEN  +
    \-- Anne GASCOIGNE  (1436 - 1488)
```

…AND THE MONUMENTAL KNIGHT

KATHERINE HASTINGS' father, who had an all-female bloodline from Catherine Mortimer, had an all-male bloodline from his namesake ancestor Sir Hugh de Hastings (right) who, like his father, had an all-female bloodline from Aoife.

Following his death in 1347, Sir Hugh was immortalised in a famous monumental brass at Elsing Church in Norfolk. The original monument included images of Edward III and seven knights, including two of Kate's ancestors: Catherine Mortimer's husband Thomas Beauchamp and Katherine Spencer's ancestor Hugh Despencer the Younger, who were both matrilineal descendants of Aoife.

This group may have been a precursor to the Order of the Garter (See next page).

WIKIPEDIA

LADIES OF THE GARTER

EDWARD III supposedly founded the Order of the Garter in 1348 after picking up a dropped garter and uttering the famous motto: 'Honi soit qui mal y pense' ('Shame on him who thinks evil of it'). According to another story, Edward III raped the lady in question at Wark Castle in Northumberland.

Either way, it is generally agreed that the lady who dropped the garter was one of Kate's ancestors: either Katherine Grandison or her daughter-in-law Joan 'the Fair Maid of Kent' who was also Edward III's daughter-in-law while married to Edward, the Black Prince. Adding to the confusion, Joan's son Richard II married Catherine of Valois' sister Isabella.

Through Katherine Percy and Katherine Grandison, Kate is descended from Robin Hood contender Fulk FitzWarine (shown opposite). And through Katherine Grandison's husband William de Montagu, Kate is descended from Henry I's illegitimate son Robert of Gloucester.

The thrice-married Joan 'the Fair Maid of Kent', who was Kate's ancestor through Catherine Clifford and Katherine Spencer, became a Lady of the Garter in 1378. Joan's son John Holland allegedly sired Richard of Conisburgh, from whom Kate is descended through Edward IV.

The first of Kate's royal namesakes to join the order was Catherine of Lancaster, a direct ancestor of Catherine of Aragon and Catherine of Braganza, followed by Catherine of Lancaster's step-mother Katherine Swynford and Catherine of Valois. Katherine Swynford was appointed by her step-son Henry IV who was Catherine of Valois' father-in-law.

Katherine (Lady) de GRANDISON

Born: Hertfords. abt. 1304   Died: 1349 Berkshire

Lady Diana's 17-Great Grandmother.

Husband/Partner: William (MONTECUTE) de MONTAGU
Children: John (Knight; 1st Baron) de MONTAGU ; Philippa de MONTAGU

```
                              /-- Ebal (IV) von GRANDISON  +
                   /-- Pierre I (Sire) de GRANDISON  (1195? - 1263?)
                   |        \-- Beatrix de GENEVA  +
                   /            | OR: poss. Beatrix of GENEVA  +
          /-- Amadeus (Sire) de GRANDISON  (1229? - ?)
          |        |        /-- Ulric III (Comte) de NEUCHATEL  +
          |        \-- Agnes (de) NEUCHATEL
          /            \-- Yolande (d' URACH) ARBERG  +
    /-- William (1st Baron) de GRANDISON  (1260? - 1335)
    /        \-- Banoile (Benoite) de la TOUR de GERENSTEIN  (skip?)
```

Katherine (Lady) de GRANDISON

```
    \                   /-- Robert (I; Sir) de TREGOZ  +
    |        /-- Robert (II) de TREGOS (TREGOZ)
    |        |        \-- Sybilla (Sibyl) de EWYAS  +
    |        |            | OR: prob. Sybilla (Sibyl) de EWYAS  +
    |        /            | OR: poss. Sybilla de TREGOZ  +
    |   /-- John (1st Baron) de TREGOZ  (1233? - 1300)
    |   |        \        /-- William (II) de CANTILUPE (CAUNTELO)  +
    |   |        \-- Juliana de CANTILUPE  (? - 1285+)
    |   /            \-- Melicent de GOURNAY  +
    \-- Sybil de TREGOS  (1270? - 1334)
        \ | or: poss. Blanche de SAVOIE
        |                   /-- prob. Fulk (III; of Whittington) FitzWARINE  +
        |        /-- Fulk (IV; Sir) FitzWARIN  (1202?? - 14/5/1264?)
        |        |        \-- prob. Maud le VAVASOUR  +
        |        /            | or: Not! Clarice DAUBERVILLE, q.v.
        \-- Mabel FitzWARIN  (? - by 1297)
```

THE LADY IN WAITING

KATE WAS greatly amused when Prince William became the thousandth Knight of the Garter so it will be interesting to see how she behaves in the same ridiculous regalia. Queens consort are members ex officio.

In the meantime, Kate can watch rituals in St George's Chapel from Catherine of Aragon's closet where Queen Victoria stood when the future Edward VII exchanged vows with Alexandra of Denmark, the first Lady of the Garter appointed since 1488 (See Mitochondrial Marriages, Page 96).

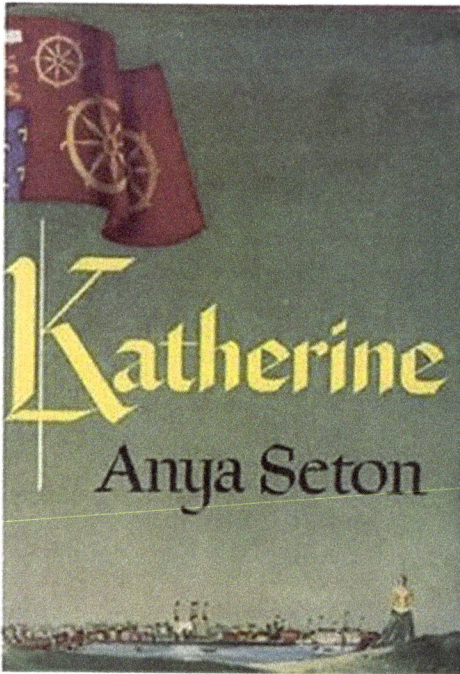

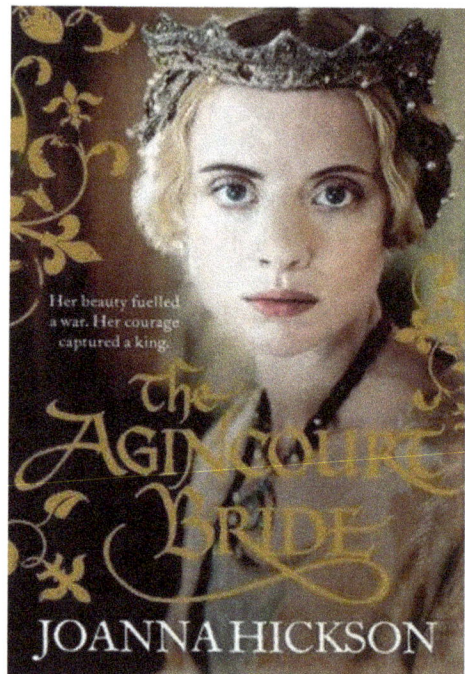

Her beauty fuelled a war. Her courage captured a king.

ROMANCES OF THE CATHERINES

KATE'S royal namesakes have provided rich fodder for novelists since 1954 when *Katherine*, Anya Seton's carefully researched study of Katherine Swynford, set a benchmark that has rarely been matched.

The Agincourt Bride (2013) by Joanna Hickson tells the story of England's first Queen Catherine — daughter of Charles the Mad, wife of Henry V, and founder of the Tudor dynasty — through the eyes of her nursemaid. Kate's children are descended from Catherine of Valois through Henry VIII's illegitimate daughter Catherine Carey.

Katharine, the Virgin Widow (1961) by Jean Plaidy poses the fundamental question: was Katharine/Catherine of Aragon a virgin when she married Henry VIII? She solemnly swore that her marriage to Prince Arthur was not consummated, but Henry, in lust with Anne Boleyn, discarded Catherine and changed the course of English history. Kate's children are descended from Katharine's sister Joanna the Mad through Charles II.

The Catherine Howard Conspiracy (2019) by Alexandra Walsh is a 'timeshift thriller' which jumps from the 1500s, when an ageing Henry VIII takes a fancy to the teenaged Catherine, to 2018 when Dr Perdita Rivers is trying to unravel a mystery involving her grandmother, a renowned Tudor historian. Kate's children are possibly descended from Catherine's aunt Katherine Howard through an illegitimate daughter of Charles II.

Catherine Parr (2010) by Elizabeth Norton. After outliving three husbands, including the obese and obnoxious Henry VIII, Catherine Parr finally marries her true love Thomas Seymour, brother of Henry's third wife Jane Seymour. Thomas

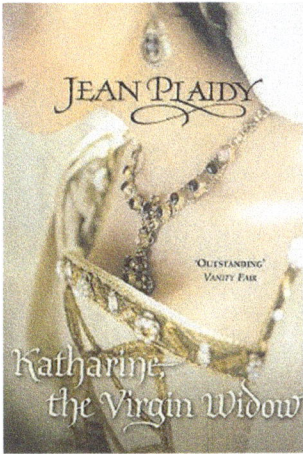

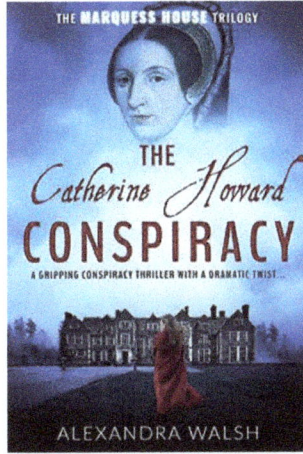

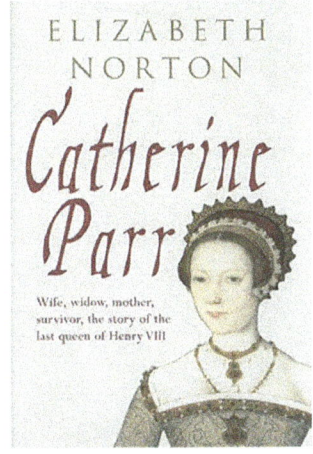

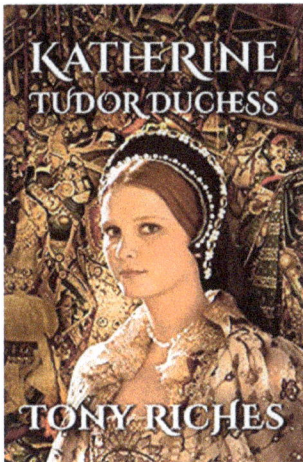

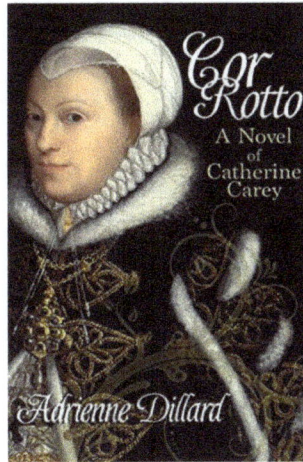

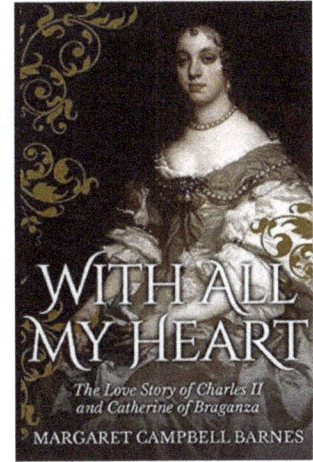

betrays Catherine who dies soon after delivering her only child. Kate's children are descended from Catherine Parr's nephew Edward Seymour and his wife Lady Catherine Grey.

Katherine: Tudor Duchess (2019) by Tony Riches. Katherine Willoughby, daughter of one of Catherine of Aragon's confidants, nearly became Henry VIII's seventh wife, replacing her best friend Catherine Parr. Kate's children are descended from Katherine's step-granddaughter Lady Catherine Grey.

Cor Rotto (2014) by Adrienne Dillard. Young Catherine Carey has nightmares about the execution of her aunt Anne Boleyn, unaware that the king is her real father. Catherine somehow survives and becomes a close confidant of her half-sister Elizabeth I.

With All My Heart (1951), by Margaret Campbell Barnes, tells how Catherine of Braganza captivated Charles II despite failing to produce an heir. Prince William will be the first monarch descended from him, albeit through two of his bastards.

Books about Kate include *William and Kate: A Royal Love Story* (2010), by Christopher Andersen; *Prince William & Kate: A Royal Romance* (2011), by Matt Doeden; and *The Making of a Royal Romance* (2011), by Katie Nicholl.

BLACK CATHERINE'S SECRET

THE PERSON best-placed to know Britain's biggest sex secret was a Moorish slave named Catalina who served as Catherine of Aragon's chief bedmaker.

Catalina handled the sheets on the mornings after Catherine slept with Prince Arthur and would have noticed any signs of sexual activity. Apparently, Catalina did the same after Catherine's first night with Henry VIII in 1509.

In *The Spanish Princess* TV series, the character played by Stephanie Levi-John was a composite of Catalina the slave and a high-born namesake who was a lady in waiting. As far as we know, neither Catalina ever revealed what they knew and Catherine of Aragon always insisted that her marriage to Prince Arthur was not consummated.

Another namesake with intimate knowledge of Catherine and Prince Arthur was Katherine St John who served the newlyweds at Ludlow Castle. Katherine was the mother-in-law of Katherine Howard whose niece Catherine Howard was Henry VIII's fifth wife.

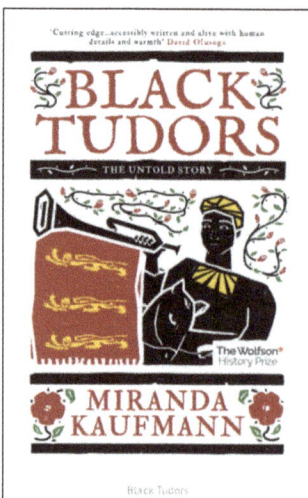

Catalina the bedmaker was eventually granted her freedom, married a Moorish crossbow maker with whom she had two children, and spent her last years in her hometown of Motril in Granada. Coincidentally, Motril was a sugar growing region which suffered from competition with the West Indian slave plantations.

The stories of Catalina and other 'black Tudors' have been documented by Miranda Kaufmann and also by Onyeka Nubia in his 2013 book titled Blackamoores.

— 222 —

Catherine (Infanta) of ARAGON

Born: Madrid 15 Dec 1485   Died: 7 Jan 1536 England

Husbands/Partners: Henry VIII TUDOR ; Arthur TUDOR (Prince) of WALES
Children: Mary I TUDOR (Queen) of ENGLAND ; 5 other children who died young

```
                                    /-- Henry II de CASTILE (& Leon)  +
                            /-- Juan I (King) de CASTILE (& Leon)
                           /        \-- Juana Manuel de CASTILLA  +
                    /-- Fernando I of ARAGON & SICILY (& Mallorca & Valencia)
                   /        \-- Eleanor of ARAGON (& Valencia)  +
            /-- John II 'the Great' (King) of ARAGON
           |        \          /-- Sancho ALFONSO (Prince) of CASTILE  +
           |         \-- Leonor Urraca Sancha (Princess) of CASTILE
           |                    \-- Brites de BORGONHA (Princess) of PORTUGAL  +
        /-- Ferdinand V (King) of CASTILE (SPAIN)  (1452 - 1516)
       |    \                   /-- Afonso ENRIQUEZ of MEDINA de Rio Seco  +
       |     |          /-- Federigo (Count) of MELGAR  (1396? - 1473)
       |     |         /        \-- Juana (Baroness) of GONZALES-MENDOZA  +
       |     \-- Juana (Princess) of MELGAR
```

Catherine (Infanta) of ARAGON

```
       \                            /-- Henry II de CASTILE (& Leon)  +
       |                    /-- Juan I (King) de CASTILE (& Leon)
       |                   /        \-- Juana Manuel de CASTILLA  +
       |            /-- Enrique III (King) de CASTILE (& Leon)
       |           /        \-- Eleanor of ARAGON (& Valencia)  +
       |        /-- Juan II (King) de CASTILE (& Leon)  (1405 - 1454)
       |       |    \          /-- John (BEAUFORT) of GAUNT  +
       |       |     \-- Katherine (Lady) PLANTAGENET  (1372 - 1418)
       |       |              \-- Constance Pedra (Princess) of CASTILE  +
       \-- Isabella (I; Queen) de CASTILE  (1451 - 1504)
           \                   /-- Joao I (King) of PORTUGAL  +
           |           /-- Joao II de BORGONHA de PORTUGAL  (1400 - 1442)
           |          /        \-- Philippe of LANCASTER  +
           \-- Isabella d' AVIZ de PORTUGAL  (1428? - 1496)
```

Catherine of Aragon's parents Ferdinand and Isabella conquered Granada in 1492, the same year that Columbus reached the New World and started making huge profits from slavery. In 2020, several of Columbus' statues were torn down during Black Lives Matter protests.

Isabella descended from two of Katherine Swynford's step-daughters (shown above): Catherine of Lancaster (Katherine Plantagenet) and her half-sister Philippa of Lancaster. As well, Isabella and her husband Ferdinand were second cousins through Juan I of Castile.

Unable to get a papal dispensation, Isabella and Ferdinand produced a forged letter from Pope Pius II who died five years previously. So, strictly speaking, the marriage was illegal; Catherine of Aragon was illegitimate; and so was her sister Joanna the Mad, from whom Kate's children are descended through the bastard offspring of Charles II and James II.

'LIKE A COMMON HARLOT'

WHY was Henry VIII's fifth wife Catherine Howard beheaded with an axe (above) while his second wife, and Catherine's first cousin, Anne Boleyn was dispatched with a sword (inset) for allegedly committing the same crime.

One possible explanation is that Henry knew that Anne did not commit treason by having sex with her brother, or anyone else. His main grievance, as with Catherine of Aragon, was Anne's failure to deliver a male heir.

Anne's beheading by an expert swordsman was compassionate because executions with an axe were often botched. (In 1541, it reportedly took several blows to sever the head of Katherine Pole's grandmother Margaret Plantagenet.)

It has also been claimed that having Anne Boleyn's head severed with a sword was somehow in keeping with Henry VIII's twisted ideas about chivalry connected to his alleged descent from King Arthur.

Middle-aged Henry was unmerciful towards the teenaged Catherine Howard because she admitted her indiscretions, most significantly with Francis Dereham whose marriage pre-contract, if confirmed, would have made all of Catherine's royal children illegitimate.

Damning evidence about Catherine's adulterous relationship with distant cousin Thomas Culpepper was given by another distant relative, Catherine's childhood companion Katherine Tilney.

The PEDIGREE of
Catherine HOWARD
Born: Surrey 1521   Died: 13 Feb 1542

Husband/Partner: Henry VIII TUDOR

```
                       /-- John (K.G.; 1st Baron) HOWARD
              /              \-- Margaret (Lady; de) MOWBRAY  +
       /-- Thomas HOWARD (Earl of SURREY)
      |        \              /-- William (4th Lord; MOLEYNS; de) MOLINES  +
      |        |        /        | (skip this generation!)
      |        |       /
      |        \-- Catherine MOLINES (MOLEYNS)
      /                \-- Anne WHALESBOROUGH  (skip!)  +
  /-- Edmund (Sir) HOWARD  (1477 - 1539)
 |        \              /-- Philip (Sir) TILNEY  +
 |        |        /-- Frederick (Knight) TILNEY
 |        |       /        \-- Isabel (de) THORPE  +
 |        \-- Elizabeth (Heiress) TILNEY (TYLNEY)
 |                \              /-- Lawrence (Sir; of Fen Ditton) CHEYNE  +
 |                \-- Elizabeth CHEYNE (CHENEY)
 /                        \-- Elizabeth COCKAYNE  +
```

- Catherine HOWARD

```
  \                    /-- Thomas CULPEPER  (1356 - 1429)
 |              /-- William (Sir; of Oxen Hoath) CULPEPPER
 |             |        \ | OR: Wm. (of Oxen Hoath) CULPEPPER [alt ped]  +
 |             /        \-- Joyce BAYNARD  +
 |        /-- Richard (Sir; of Oxen Hoath) CULPEPPER
 |       |        \              /-- prob. William VII (Lord) de FERRERS  +
 |       |        \-- Elizabeth (de) FERRERS  (1392? - 1460?)
 |       /                \-- poss. Philippa de CLIFFORD  +
 \-- Joyce CULPEPPER  (? - 1531 Wilts.)
         \              /-- Richard (de) WORSLEY  +
         |        /-- Otewell (Sir; of Calais) WORSLEY
         |       |        \ | OR: Otewell (of Calais) WORSLEY [alt ped]  +
         |       /        \-- Catherine CLARK  +
         \-- Isabel (Joyce) WORSLEY  (? - 1527)
```

For the record, Catherine Howard was charged with leading an 'abominable, base, carnal, voluptuous and vicious life, like a common harlot, with divers persons'.

Kate's children are possibly descended from Catherine Howard's sister Margaret, and reliably descended from several of Catherine's namesakes, including an aunt who married the grandson of reputed Richard III killer Rhys ap Thomas.

Catherine Howard had multiple descents from Aoife and Katherine of Flanders, with bloodlines through Catherine Molines and Catherine Clark. And Sir Richard Culpepper (shown above) had a possible all-female bloodline from Catherine Mortimer.

According to legend, Catherine's last words were: 'I die a queen but would rather die the wife of Culpepper.' Her ghost has allegedly been seen at Hampton Court Palace, and Henry VIII's last wife Catherine Parr supposedly haunts Sudeley Castle in Gloucestershire.

BONAIRE AND BUXOM IN BED

UNLIKE her royal namesakes, the future Queen Catherine did not promise her husband to be 'bonaire and buxom in bed'.

This quaint expression first appeared after the Norman Conquest and was uttered by English brides for hundreds of years. The exact words spoken by Henry VIII's last wife Catherine Parr in 1543 were: 'I, Catherine, take thee Henry to my wedded husband, to have and to hold from this day forward, for better, for worse, for richer, for poorer, in sickness and in health, to be *bonaire and buxom in bed and at board*, till death do us part.'

'Bonaire' derived from the French word for good humour and 'buxom' was an old English word for obedience.

Kate famously followed Princess Diana by not promising to obey her husband. The words to which Kate responded were: 'Catherine Elizabeth, wilt thou have this man to thy wedded husband, to live together according to God's law in the holy estate of matrimony? Wilt thou love him, comfort him, honour and keep him, in sickness and in health… so long as ye both shall live?'

Like the twice-widowed Catherine Parr, 29-year-old Kate was not a virgin when she became a royal. In the unforgettable words of the Archbishop of York, Kate had been 'testing the milk before buying the cow'.

Henry VIII, who contemplated Catherine Parr's execution after she argued about religious matters, died in 1547. Catherine then married her true love Thomas Seymour but died soon after delivering her only child from four

THE PEDIGREE OF

Catherine PARR

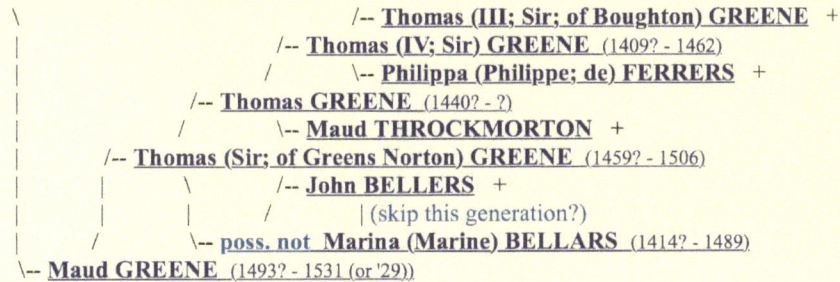

Born: Kendal Castle 1512   Died: 1548 Gloucesters.

Lady Diana's 13-Great Aunt.

Husbands/Partners: Henry VIII TUDOR ; Thomas (K.G.) SEYMOUR ; Edward de Burgh ;
John Neville

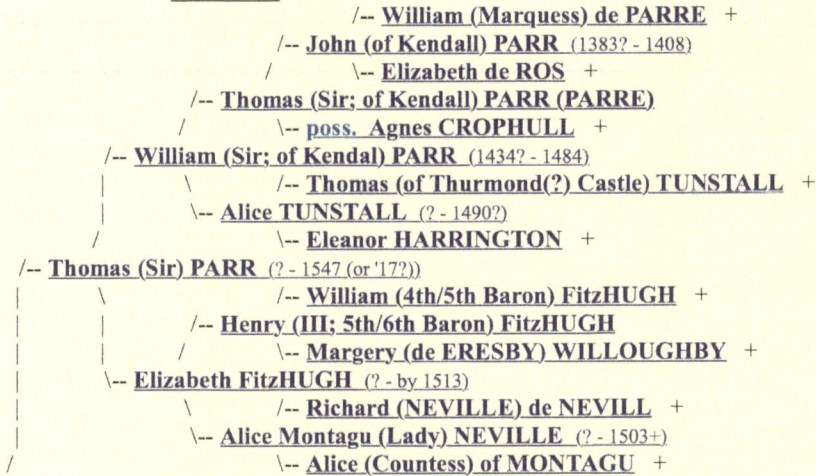

```
                                    /-- William (Marquess) de PARRE  +
                         /-- John (of Kendall) PARR  (1383? - 1408)
                     /            \-- Elizabeth de ROS  +
                 /-- Thomas (Sir; of Kendall) PARR (PARRE)
                 /            \-- poss. Agnes CROPHULL  +
           /-- William (Sir; of Kendal) PARR  (1434? - 1484)
           |            \            /-- Thomas (of Thurmond(?) Castle) TUNSTALL  +
           |             \-- Alice TUNSTALL  (? - 1490?)
           /                         \-- Eleanor HARRINGTON  +
       /-- Thomas (Sir) PARR  (? - 1547 (or '17?))
       |            \            /-- William (4th/5th Baron) FitzHUGH  +
       |             \            /-- Henry (III; 5th/6th Baron) FitzHUGH
       |             |           /            \-- Margery (de ERESBY) WILLOUGHBY  +
       |             \-- Elizabeth FitzHUGH  (? - by 1513)
       |                          \            /-- Richard (NEVILLE) de NEVILL  +
       |                           \-- Alice Montagu (Lady) NEVILLE  (? - 1503+)
       /                                        \-- Alice (Countess) of MONTAGU  +
```

-Catherine PARR

```
           \                      /-- Thomas (III; Sir; of Boughton) GREENE  +
           |                   /-- Thomas (IV; Sir) GREENE  (1409? - 1462)
           |                /            \-- Philippa (Philippe; de) FERRERS  +
           |            /-- Thomas GREENE  (1440? - ?)
           |            /            \-- Maud THROCKMORTON  +
           |       /-- Thomas (Sir; of Greens Norton) GREENE  (1459? - 1506)
           |       |            \            /-- John BELLERS  +
           |       |            |           /  | (skip this generation?)
           |       /             \-- poss. not  Marina (Marine) BELLARS  (1414? - 1489)
           \-- Maud GREENE  (1493? - 1531 (or '29))
```

marriages. Mary Seymour was placed in the care of Catherine Willoughby and presumably died in infancy. Thomas Seymour, who flirted with the young Elizabeth I, was executed for treason in 1549 (See Page 232).

Catherine Parr, whose father had an all-female bloodline from Aoife, was Henry VIII's third cousin once removed through Katherine Swynford's daughter Joan Beaufort. And like Catherine Howard, Catherine Parr descended from Katherine of Flanders through most of her great-grandparents.

Note: Like Catherine of Valois, Catherine Parr (named after Catherine of Aragon) suffered many posthumous indignities, most notably in 1792 when her coffin was reburied upside down.

The Dutchess of Suffolk

Catherine Parr's close friend Catherine Willoughby, the Duchess of Suffolk, nearly became Henry VIII's seventh wife.

WIPING THE KING'S BOTTOM

A S WELL AS being descended from Henry VIII through his illegitimate daughter Catherine Carey, Kate's children are descended from the man with the seemingly unenviable job of wiping the royal bottom. In fact, Sir Anthony Denny (shown opposite) was envied because he had privileged access to the monarch and was richly rewarded.

Prince William has bloodlines from quite a few Grooms of the Stool, including Catherine Carey's great-grandson Henry Rich and Catherine Grey's grandson William Seymour. Elizabeth I had no equivalent position but she did have 'first ladies of the bedchamber', including Katherine (Kat) Ashley (nee Champernowne) who was related to Sir Anthony Denny.

Sir John Harington, rumoured to be one of Elizabeth I's illegitimate sons, invented a flushing toilet but for several centuries the population made do with chamber pots and outside privies.

The Hanoverian kings reportedly wiped their own bottoms and so did Edward VII who abolished the position of Groom of the Stool. The legendary Thomas Crapper, who installed toilets in Edward VII's house, died in 1910 from bowel cancer.

Note: Kate developed a 'mischievous streak' at boarding school, earning the nickname 'Middlebum' after constantly flashing her bottom at male students.

Sir Anthony Denny married Joan Champernowne who was a close friend of Henry VIII's last wife Catherine Parr.

The PEDIGREE of

Catherine DENNY

Lady Diana's 12-Great Grandmother.

Husband/Partner: George (Sir) FLEETWOOD
Child: Honora FLEETWOOD

```
                          /-- Edmund (Sir; of Cheshunt) DENNY  (? - 1520)
                   /          \-- Agnes TROUTBECK  +
              /-- Anthony (Sir; of Cheshunt) DENNY  (1501 - 1549)
              |        \          /-- Robert TROUTBECK  +
              |        |      /      / (skip this generation?)
              |        \-- Mary TROUTBECK  (? - 1507)
              /                / OR: Mary COKE  +
         /-- Henry DENNY  (1540 - ?)
         |       \                /-- John (Sir; of Modbury) CHAMPERNON  +
         |       |        /-- Philip (Sir; of Modbury) CHAMPERNOWNE  (? - 1545)
         |       |        /       \-- Margaret COURTENAY  +
         |       \-- Jane (Joan) CHAMPERNOWNE
         |                \          /-- Edmund (Sir; of Mohun's Ottery) CAREW  +
         |                \-- Katherine CAREW
         /                     \-- Catherine HUDDLESFIELD  +
```

Catherine DENNY

```
         \                      /-- Reynold GREY  +
         |              /-- John (Sir) GREY  (? - 1499)
         |              |       \-- Tacine of SOMERSET  +
         |              /              / OR: Tacina TUDOR  +
         |          /-- Edmund (9th Lord; de WILTON) GREY  (1469? - 1511)
         |          /       \-- Anne (of Ruthin) GREY  +
         |      /-- William (13th Lord of Wilton) GREY  (1509? - 1562)
         |      |       \          /-- Ralph (Knight) HASTINGS  +
         |      |       \-- Florence HASTINGS  (? - 1511+)
         |      /               \-- Anne TATTERSHALL  +
         \-- Honora (of Wilton) GREY
                \                  /-- Henry (Sir) BEAUFORT  +
                |        /-- Charles (K.G.) SOMERSET  (1460? - 1526)
                |        /         \-- Joane HILL  +
                \-- Mary (Lady) SOMERSET
```

ROYAL TOILET TRIVIA

KATE'S mother reportedly breached etiquette in 2007 by saying 'toilet' in the presence of Queen Elizabeth II and was quickly informed that the correct word is lavatory.

Her Majesty took rolls of Andrex toilet paper when she travelled, but Charles III says the claim that he takes his own toilet seat is a 'load of crap'. As far as we know, Kate and Prince William make no special arrangements in this regard. Pictured right is a 2011 wedding souvenir.

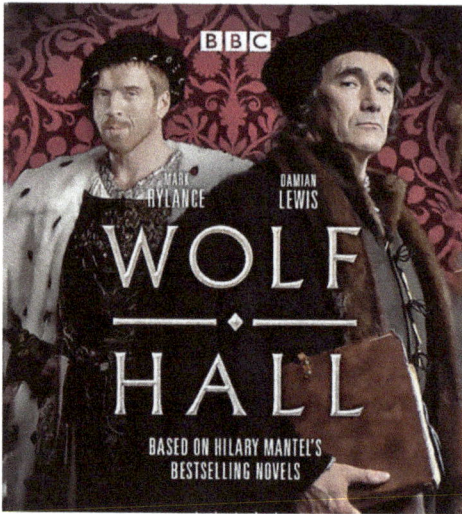

CROMWELL CONNECTIONS

WHILE Kate's opinions on the Booker Prize-winning novel *Wolf Hall* and the acclaimed TV series are unknown, we can safely assume that she was not kindly disposed towards author Hilary Mantel who died in 2022.

In 2013, Mantel was widely condemned after describing Kate as 'a shop-window mannequin, with no personality of her own, entirely defined by what she wore... her only point and purpose being to give birth.'

The real Thomas Cromwell (above right) never lived at Wolf Hall in Wiltshire, the ancestral home of the Seymours. Cromwell's son Gregory married Jane Seymour's sister Elizabeth, and Cromwell may have been at the house when Henry VIII first saw Jane, but the title of Mantel's book is misleading and somewhat ridiculous.

Thomas Cromwell increased his power by engineering Henry VIII's separation from Catherine of Aragon but had a dramatic fall after bungling the king's fourth marriage to the unattractive Anne of Cleves. The despised chief minister was beheaded on Tower Hill on 28th July 1540, the same day that Henry married his fifth wife Catherine Howard at Oatlands Palace.

Not much is known about Katherine Elizabeth Cromwell's mother Katherine Glossop (or Meverell) whose parents-in-law (shown opposite) may have been closer than first cousins. Note all the Cromwell/Smyth marriages.

Thomas Cromwell had a granddaughter named Katherine who married John Strode. And, through his illegitimate daughter Jane, Cromwell was an

In 1994, the Duchess of Kent (now known as Katherine Kent) became the first royal since 1701 to convert to Catholicism, an ironic move considering her direct descent from anti-Catholic dictator Oliver Cromwell.

The PEDIGREE of

Katherine Elizabeth CROMWELL

Born: abt. 1476   Died: abt. 1517

Lady Diana's 13-Great Grandmother.

Husband/Partner: **Morgan (ap) WILLIAMS**
Children: **Richard WILLIAMS (Knight) CROMWELL**
Possible Children: **(NN) GUILLIMS** ; **Walter WILLIAMS** ; **John(?) WILLIAMS**

```
                                  /-- Ralph (IV; V; Lord) de CROMWELL
                                 /      \-- Joan de la MARE  +
                             /-- Ralph (V; VI; 1st Baron) CROMWELL
                            /      \-- Amice (Anice) de BELLERS  +
                        /-- Ralph VII (VI) de CROMWELL (1368 - 1417)
                        |    \       /-- John (of Tattershall; de) BERNAKE  +
                        |     \-- Maud BERNACKE (1346 - 1419)
                       /              \-- Joan MARMION  +
                 /-- William de CROMWELL (1395? - ?)
                 |     \/ OR: prob. William CROMWELL  +
                /       \-- Joan SMYTH (1368 - ?)
           /-- John de CROMWELL (1442? - 1480?)
           |    \       /-- John SMYTH
           |     \-- Margaret SMYTH (1415? - ?)
          /              \-- Joan
     /-- Walter Smyth CROMWELL (1458?? - 1516??)
     |     \            /-- John SMYTH
     |      |     /-- William I SMYTH (1412? - ?)
     |      |    /      \-- Joan
     |      \-- Joan SMYTH (1442? - ?)
     |            \                   /-- Ulker CROMWELL  +
     |             |         /-- Richard (de; of Hucknall Torkard) CROMWELL
     |             |    /-- John (de; of Cromwell House) CROMWELL
     |             |   /-- Robert CROMWELL (1388? - 1461)
     |             \-- Margaret de CROMWELL (1418? - ?)
    /                   \-- poss. Joan SMYTH (1368 - ?)
```

- Katherine Elizabeth CROMWELL

```
     \         /-- (NN) GLOSSOP
      \-- Katherine GLOSSOP (1456? - ?)
```

ancestor of Elizabeth Langdale who married Katherine Constable's son Peter Middleton of Stockeld (See chart on Page 141).

Some ancestry charts wrongly show Katherine Elizabeth Cromwell's husband Morgan Williams with a bloodline from Joan Tudor, an alleged illegitimate daughter of Catherine of Valois' son Jasper. According to fabedigree.com this is a 'genealogical fraud', apparently done to give Oliver Cromwell a royal ancestor.

Prince William has a bloodline from Katherine Elizabeth Cromwell through Oliver Cromwell of Hinchinbrooke (not to be confused with his name-sake nephew) who supported Charles I and II during the Civil War and suffered accordingly. Prince William descends from Thomas Cromwell through his great-granddaughter Katherine Tollemache (née Cromwell) (right) who had an all-female bloodline from Irish princess Aoife.

SEYMOUR SEX SECRETS

CONTROVERSIES swirled around Catherine Parr's fourth husband Thomas Seymour (right) and his brother Edward (left), the first Duke of Somerset, and it wasn't surprising that both were executed for treason.

It was bad enough that Edward's and Thomas' father allegedly sired Edward's oldest sons (See opposite). But even more sensational was the claim that Thomas Seymour sired an illegitimate son with the future Elizabeth I.

Thomas Seymour flirted outrageously with the princess, sometimes in the presence of Catherine Parr who was Elizabeth's guardian. On one occasion, Elizabeth's governess Kat Ashley told Seymour to 'go away for shame'. After Catherine's death, Thomas sealed his fate by foolishly planning to marry Elizabeth without proper permission.

According to American author Paul Streitz, Seymour and the princess had an illegitimate son — raised as Edward de Vere, the seventeenth Earl of Oxford — who was the real Shakespeare. Streitz's additional claim that Kate's children could descend from an illegitimate son of Oxford and the queen is preposterous.

Kate's children have bloodlines from two namesake sons of Edward Seymour: Edward Seymour of Berry Pomeroy (son of Katherine Fillol), and Edward Seymour, the first Earl of Hertford (son of the duke's second wife Anne Stanhope and brother of Katherin Seymour). Hertford married Lady Catherine Grey, sister of Lady Jane who was queen for just nine days.

Elizabeth I was furious when Catherine Grey delivered two sons without permission and both were declared illegitimate (See Hypothetical Queen Catherines, Page 46).

Katherin Seymour and her siblings probably descended from Katherine of Flanders and Aoife through all of their grandparents.

Elizabeth I's governess and longtime companion Kat Ashley kept all of the monarch's most intimate secrets.

The PEDIGREE of
Katherin (Lady) SEYMOUR

Born: abt. 1541   Died: abt. 1591

HRH Charles's 12-Great Aunt.   Lady Diana's 12-Great Aunt.

Husband/Partner: **James FARWELL**
Child: **William FARWELL**

```
                              /-- John (III; of Wolf Hall) SEYMOUR  (1450? - 1491)
                         /           \-- Elizabeth COKER  +
                   /-- John (IV; Sir; of Wolf Hall) SEYMOUR
                   |        \          /-- George (Sir; of Littlecote) DARELL  +
                   |         \-- Elizabeth (of Littlecote) DARELL  (Wilts.)
                   /                     \-- Margaret STOURTON  +
            /-- Edward (K.G.) SEYMOUR
            |      \                      /-- Philip (Sir; of Nettlestead) WENTWORTH  +
            |       |            /-- Henry (Sir; of Nettlestead) WENTWORTH
            |       |           /           \-- Mary (de) CLIFFORD  +
            |       \-- Margery WENTWORTH  (? - 1550)
            |                   \           /-- John III (Sir; of Broxbourne) de SAY  +
            |                    \-- Anne (de) SAY
            /                                \-- Elizabeth CHEYNE (CHENEY)  +
```

-Katherin (Lady) SEYMOUR

```
            \                        /-- Richard (II; Sir; of RAMPTON) STANHOPE  +
            |                 /-- John (Knight; of Rampton) STANHOPE
            |                /           \-- Elizabeth MARKHAM  +
            |          /-- Thomas (Sir; of Rampton) STANHOPE  (? - 1474+)
            |          |     /          \-- Elizabeth (of Bashall) TALBOT  +
            |     /-- prob. Edward (of RAMPTON) STANHOPE  (1469? - 1511)
            |     |    |     \          /-- John (II; Sir; of Somerleyton) JERNEGAN  +
            |     |    \-- Mary JERNINGHAM
            |     /                      \-- Isobel CLIFTON  +
            \-- Anne STANHOPE  (? - 1587)
                  \                      /-- William BOURCHIER (1st Baron FitzWARIN)  +
                   |            /-- Fulk BOURCHIER (2nd/10th Baron FitzWARIN)
                   |           /           \-- Thomasine HANKFORD (Baroness FitzWARIN)  +
                   \-- Elizabeth BOURCHIER
```

KATHERINE FILLOL'S AFFAIR

HENRY VIII's brother-in-law Edward Seymour KG and his teenaged first wife Katherine Fillol (or Filliol) lived for about seven years at Wolf Hall, made famous by Hilary Mantel's novel.

In 1527, Katherine was excluded from her father Sir William Fillol's will and allegedly sent to a nunnery because she was 'apt to bestow her favours too liberally'. Years later, someone wrote a marginal note at the College of Arms that she was divorced after being 'known' by her father-in-law.

It is therefore possible that John Seymour IV (shown above) sired Katherin Seymour's half-brothers John and Edward. Descendants of Edward (of Berry Pomeroy) inherited the dukedom of Somerset after the male line from his namesake half-brother and Lady Catherine Grey failed in the 1700s.

ELIZABETHAN CATHERINES

ELIZABETH I had close connections with quite a few Catherines, including her stepmother Catherine Parr, her alleged half-sister Catherine Carey, and the latter's namesake niece.

It seems that Elizabeth's governess had the most influence because the princess once wrote: 'Anne Boleyn gave me life, but Kat Ashley gave me love.' Kat (nee Champernowne), not to be confused with Sir Walter Raleigh's mother Katherine Champernowne, died childless in 1565.

Henry VIII's last wife Catherine Parr was actively involved in Elizabeth's education, even while the princess was estranged from her father. 'I believe that you are destined by Heaven to be Queen of England,' Catherine wrote.

Elizabeth never acknowledged Catherine Carey as her half-sister (as well as her first cousin) but the bond between them was evident when the queen gave Catherine a lavish funeral and an epitaph in Westminster Abbey. Catherine had eight daughters, including Katherine Knollys and her sister Lettice, mother of Robert Devereux.

As shown opposite, Catherine Carey's brother Henry, who may also have been sired by Henry VIII, had a daughter named Catherine who married Charles Howard KG.

One of Elizabeth I's close friends was Lady

Prince William descends from Katherine Knyvett, the notoriously corrupt keeper of Elizabeth I's jewels. Another Catherine Knyvett (died 1622) had a daughter named Katherine Carey, not to be confused with Henry VIII's alleged illegitimate daughter and her niece.

The PEDIGREE of
Catherine (Hon.) CAREY
Born: abt. 1540   Died: 1603

Lady Diana's 10-Great Grandmother.

Husband/Partner: **Charles (K.G.) HOWARD**
Children: **Mary (Lady) HOWARD** ; **William (3rd Baron of EFFINGHAM) HOWARD**

```
                              /-- Edmund TUDOR  +
                       /-- Henry VII TUDOR (King) of ENGLAND
                      /       \-- Margaret BEAUFORT  +
               /-- Henry VIII TUDOR  (London 1491 - 1547 London)
               |      \ / OR: prob. not William (Esq.) CAREY  +
               |       |           /-- Edward IV `of Rouen' PLANTAGENET-YORK  +
               |       \-- Elizabeth (of YORK) PLANTAGENET
               /               \-- Elizabeth (Lady) WOODVILLE  +
       /-- Henry (Baron HUNSDON; K.G.) CAREY  (1526 - 1596)
       |       \                /-- William (K.B.; of Blickling) BOLEYN  +
       |       |        /-- Thomas (K.G.) BOLEYN  (1477 - 1539)
       |       |       /        \-- Margaret (Lady) BUTLER  +
       |       \-- Mary BOLEYN  (Norfolk 1504? - 1543 Staffords.)
       |               \           /-- Thomas HOWARD (Earl of SURREY)  +
       |                \-- Elizabeth (Lady) HOWARD
       /                        \-- Elizabeth (Heiress) TILNEY (TYLNEY)  +
```
Catherine (Hon.) CAREY
```
       |                   /-- William (Gwilym) ap DAFYDD (MORGAN) of ARKESTON
       |                  /        \-- Anne (Mary) DELAHAY  +
       |-- Thomas (Sir; of Arkston) MORGAN  (1495? - 1562)
       |       |        \           /-- Thomas (Sir; of Pencoed) MORGAN  +
       |       |         \-- Elizabeth (of Pencoed) MORGAN  (1478? - ?)
       \-- Anne MORGAN  (1529 - 1607)
```

Katherine Dudley who married Katherine Pole's son Henry Hastings KG in a 'triple wedding' with Katherine's brother Guildford Dudley and the ill-fated Lady Jane Grey, plus Jane's sister Catherine and Edward Seymour, the first Earl of Hertford.

Kate's children descend from Catherine Grey and both Catherine Careys, all of whom had numerous bloodlines from Katherine Swynford, Katherine of Flanders and Aoife.

THE ESSEX RING LEGEND

ELIZABETH I gave a ring to Catherine Carey's grandson Robert Devereux, Earl of Essex, saying if he was ever in trouble he could send it to her and be instantly forgiven.

In 1601, facing death after a failed rebellion, Essex mistakenly dispatched the ring to his aunt Catherine Carey (right), wife of Essex's enemy Charles Howard KG, the Earl of Nottingham (circled opposite). Years after Essex's execution, Elizabeth was furious when the countess made a deathbed confession.

The PEDIGREE of
Katherine CARY
Husband/Partner: Henry (Sir; of Wolverton) LONGUEVILLE
Child: Edward (1st Baronet; of Wolverton) LONGUEVILLE

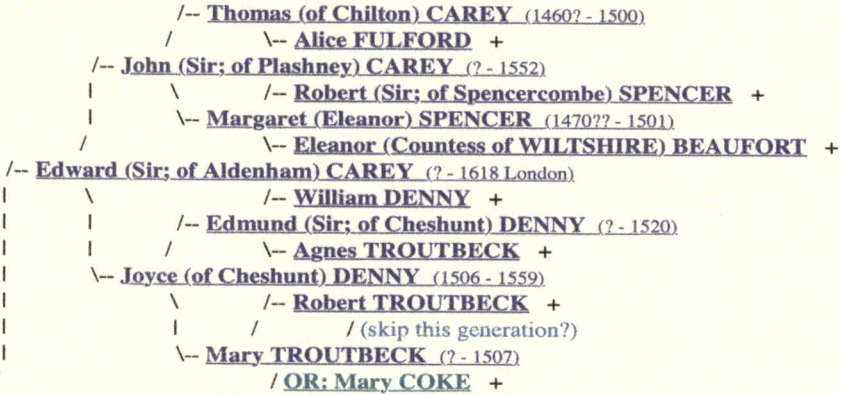

```
                              /-- Thomas (of Chilton) CAREY  (1460? - 1500)
                          /            \-- Alice FULFORD  +
                  /-- John (Sir; of Plashney) CAREY  (? - 1552)
                  |         \          /-- Robert (Sir; of Spencercombe) SPENCER  +
                  |          \-- Margaret (Eleanor) SPENCER  (1470?? - 1501)
                  /                    \-- Eleanor (Countess of WILTSHIRE) BEAUFORT  +
          /-- Edward (Sir; of Aldenham) CAREY  (? - 1618 London)
          |       \              /-- William DENNY  +
          |        |      /-- Edmund (Sir; of Cheshunt) DENNY  (? - 1520)
          |        |      /        \-- Agnes TROUTBECK  +
          |        \-- Joyce (of Cheshunt) DENNY  (1506 - 1559)
          |                \      /-- Robert TROUTBECK  +
          |                 |    /        / (skip this generation?)
          |                 \-- Mary TROUTBECK  (? - 1507)
          /                     / OR: Mary COKE  +
```
-Katherine CARY
```
          |              /-- Thomas (Knight of the Bath) KNYVET  (? - 1512)
          |          /          \-- Eleanor TYRRELL (TYRELL)  +
          |  /-- Henry (Knight; of Charlton) KNYVET (KNYVETT)
          |  |       \          /-- Thomas HOWARD (Earl of SURREY)  +
          |  |        \-- Muriel (Lady) HOWARD  (? - 1515 Lambeth)
          |  /                  \-- Elizabeth (Heiress) TILNEY (TYLNEY)  +
          \-- Catherine KNYVETT  (? - 1622 Aldenham)
```

KATHERINE CONNECTIONS

THESE TWO Katherines, who both had namesake daughters, were related to many other namesakes connected to Kate and her children.

Katherine Carey (Cary), the daughter of Catherine Knyvett and mother of Catherine Longueville, was distantly related to Henry VIII's alleged illegitimate daughter Catherine Carey and her namesake niece through Thomas Howard, the Earl of Surrey (See chart on previous page).

Margaret (Eleanor) Spencer was a sister of Kate's ancestor Katherine Spencer, and Sir Edmund Denny of Cheshunt was the great-grandfather of Prince William's ancestor Catherine Denny (See charts on Pages 199 and 229).

Kate's children descend from Katherine Carey's sister Elizabeth Carey, and also from Katherine de Vere's brother Edward de Vere, the seventeenth Earl of Oxford, who was an alleged illegitimate son of Elizabeth I and one of many Shakespeare contenders (See Seymour Sex Secrets, Page 232). Prince George and his siblings also descend from Katherine de Vere's second cousin twice removed, also named Katherine de Vere,

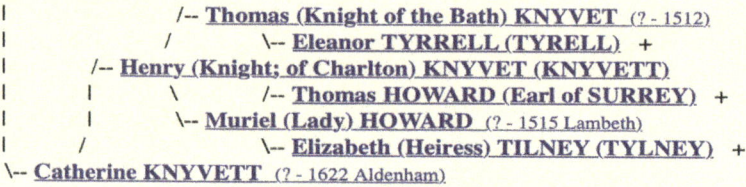

Catherine Knyvett (died 1622) was a first cousin once removed of Henry VIII's fifth wife Catherine Howard.

The PEDIGREE of

Katherine de VERE

Born: abt. 1540   Died: 1600

Husband/Partner: Edward (3rd Lord) WINDSOR
Children: Henry (5th Lord) WINDSOR ; Katherine (m. Robert Audley of Berechurch)

```
                        /-- Robert (Sir) de VERE  +
              /-- John (Esq.) de VERE  (1433 - by 1488)
             /              \-- Joan (Jean) COURTENAY  +
      /-- John (K.G.) de VERE  (1490? - 1540)
     |       \/ OR: prob. not John (K.G.) de VERE [alt ped]  +
     |        |        /-- Walter (Gent.) KILRINGTON  (Devon)
     |        \-- Alice KILRINGTON (COLBROKE)  (1468? - ?)
     /                 \-- Joan (Jane) TRESYTHENY  +
  /-- John de VERE (16th Earl) of OXFORD  (1516? - 1562)
  |      \              /-- William (of Kibblestone) TRUSSEL  +
  |      |       /-- Edward TRUSSEL (TRUSSELL)  (? - 1499)
  |      |      |       \-- Bridget KENE  +
  |      |      /              / or: Margaret KYME
  |      \-- Elizabeth (of KIBBLESTONE) TRUSSEL
```

-Katherine de VERE

```
  |          /-- Ralph (K.G.) NEVILL  (1497 - 1549)
  |         |      \           /-- William of Vyne (1st Lord?) of SANDYS  +
  |         |       \-- Edith SANDYS  (1470? - 1529 (or '37))
  |         |            \/ OR: poss. Edith SANDYS [alt ped]  +
  |         |             \-- Margaret CHENEY  +
  |         /                  / or: prob. not Margaret CURWEN (
  \-- Dorothy (Lady of WESTMORLAND) NEVILL  (? - 1546?)
         \              /-- Henry (K.G.) STAFFORD  +
         |       /-- Edward (K.G.) STAFFORD
         |      /       \-- Catherine WYDEVILLE (WYDVILLE)  +
         \-- Catherine (Lady) STAFFORD  (1499? - 1555)
                \       /-- Henry (K.G.) PERCY  +
                 \-- Eleanor (Lady) PERCY  (? - 1530 London)
                      \-- prob. Maud (Lady) HERBERT  +
```

who was probably illegitimate (See The Starbucks Mermaid, Page 42).

Catherine Woodville (shown above), grandmother of Katherine de Vere's grandmother Lady Catherine Stafford, was a first cousin once removed of Kate's ancestor Catherine Clifford.

Both Katherine Carey and Katherine de Vere (right) descended from Katherine of Flanders and Aoife through all of their grandparents. And both Katherines had bloodlines from Kate's ancestor Edmund Beaufort, including one through Lady Catherine Stafford (See Catherine of Valois' Lover, Page 184).

BEAUFORT BASTARD BLOODLINES

KATE'S children have bloodlines from the illegitimate offspring of two Henry Beauforts, one of whom descended from Henry I's illegitimate son Henry FitzHenry, a direct ancestor of two illegitimate Henry Fitzroys (See opposite).

Prince William's ancestor Catherine Denny descended from Henry FitzHenry through Sir Henry Beaufort's illegitimate son Charles Somerset KG (See chart on Page 229). And Katherine Stradling's assumed mother was Cardinal Henry Beaufort's illegitimate daughter Joan Beaufort (not to be confused with her namesake aunt).

Cardinal Beaufort (pictured above with Joan of Arc) allegedly slept with Alice FitzAlan. However, as explained on wikitree.com Joan Beaufort's mother must have been someone else.

The cardinal and his Beaufort siblings were born while John of Gaunt was married to Peter the Cruel's illegitimate daughter Constance of Castile, whose legitimate daughter Catherine of Lancaster was a direct ancestor of Catherine of Aragon and Catherine of Braganza.

(The oldest Beaufort was possibly sired by Katherine's first husband Hugh Swynford. If so, Kate's ancestor John 'Fairborn' Beaufort was not 'gotten in double adultery', as alleged by Richard III and his supporters.)

Even though they were legitimised by both parliament and the pope, the Beauforts were barred from the throne by their half-brother Henry IV, seemingly fulfilling an ancient prophecy: 'Thou shalt get kings though thou be none'.

Katherine Swynford (arms inset above) and daughter Joan Beaufort were buried in Lincoln Cathedral which once boasted one of St Catherine's fingers. The cathedral stood in for Westminster Abbey in The Da Vinci Code *film.*

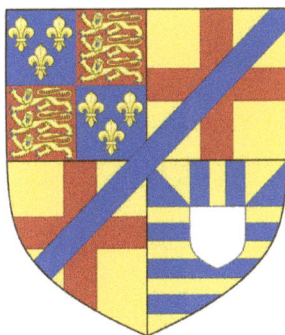

The PEDIGREE of

Katherine STRADLING

Born: Gloucests. abt. 1423

Lady Diana's 15-Great Grandmother.

Husband/Partner: Maurice (Esq.; of Olveston) DENNIS
Child: Walter (Knight) DENNIS

```
                    /-- Edward (Knight) STRADLING  (? - 1367+ (or '94))
                    |      \-- poss. Eleanor (STRONGBOW) STRADLING  +
                    /          | or: another Alienor
          /-- William (Knight) STRADLING  (Wales ? - 1412+)
          |      \      /-- Roger (Sir) BERKEROLLES  +
          |      \-- Gwenlian BERKEROLLES  (Wales by 1340 - ?)
          /          \-- Catherine (de) TURBERVILLE  +
   /-- Edward (Sir; of St. Donats) STRADLING
   |      \      /-- Richard ST. BARBE  +
   |      |   /-- John (Knight) ST. BARBE
   |      \-- Isabel (BARBE) ST. BARBE  (Wales)
   |          \      /-- Hugh (Esq.) LONGLAND  +
   |          \-- Margaret LONGLAND
   /              \-- Margaret de FURNEAUX  +
```

- Katherine STRADLING

```
   \              /-- Edward II (King) of ENGLAND  +
   |           /-- Edward III (WINDSOR; King) of ENGLAND
   |           |   \-- Isabella `the She-Wolf' of FRANCE  +
   |        /-- John (BEAUFORT) of GAUNT
   |        /      \-- Philipa d' AVESNES (Countess) of HAINAULT  +
   |     /-- Henry (Cardinal of England) BEAUFORT  (1376? - 1447)
   |     |      \      /-- Paon (Sir; of GUIENNE) de ROET  +
   |     |   \-- Katherine ROELT
   |     |      \-- poss. Catherine d' AVESNES  +
   |     /          | or: prob. another of AVESNES family
   \-- Joan (Jane) BEAUFORT  (Midx. 1402+ - ?)
```

Arthur Plantagenet   Henry Fitzroy I   Henry Fitzroy II

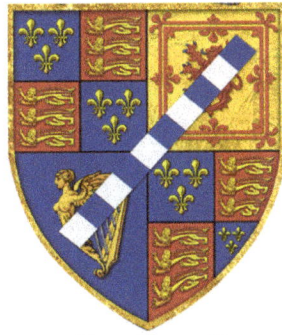

Four Beaufort descendants, all Knights of the Garter, displayed their own illegitimacies with bends sinister on their arms. Edward IV's bastard son Arthur Plantagenet was a half-brother of Kate's ancestor Margaret Plantagenet (See chart on Page 63).

Kate's children descend from Catherine Clinton, sister of Henry VIII's illegitimate son Henry Fitzroy, and also from his namesake who was an illegitimate son of Charles II and his long-term mistress Barbara Palmer.

Note: Catherine Turberville (shown above), whose relatives inspired Thomas Hardy's novel *Tess of the d'Urbervilles,* had an all-female bloodline from Aoife.

SCOTTISH BASTARD BLOODLINES

IF THE predominantly English Kate Middleton is well and truly descended from illegitimate offspring of William I of Scotland, nicknamed 'The Lion', a majority of people with British heritage probably have the same distinction.

As well, many millions of people must descend from James I of Scotland and Katherine Swynford's granddaughter Joan Beaufort (shown opposite), not to be confused with her namesake first cousin who was an illegitimate daughter of Cardinal Henry Beaufort (See previous page).

Kate descends from three illegitimate daughters of William the Lion (circled above): from Margaret FitzWilliam through William Fairfax and Katherine Ellis; from Aufrica of Scotland through Catherine Mortimer's husband Thomas Beauchamp; and from Isabel 'the bastard princess' through Jane Lambton.

Prince William descends from Joan Beaufort and her second husband through Catherine Stewart (died c1515) whose maternal grandfather William Sinclair

built Rosslyn Chapel (See Debunking the Da Vinci Code, Page 172).

According to fabpedigree.com Kate's children have a bloodline from William Sinclair's daughter Catherine Sinclair (shown opposite) but not through Margaret Catherine Stewart whose mother is unknown. Either way, Prince George and his siblings descend from an illegitimate daughter of Margaret Catherine's half-brother Alexander Stewart, the Bishop of Moray.

Kate's children also descend from James IV's illegitimate daughter Catherine Stewart (died c1554), and from Robert the Bruce's great-granddaughter Katherine Stewart.

Joan Beaufort, who had an all-female bloodline from Aoife, had nearly 40 grandchildren including Catherine Stewart (died c.1515).

— 240 —

Margaret (Catherine) STEWART

Born: ? Died: aft. 1542

Lady Diana's 15-Great Grandmother.

Husband/Partner: **Patrick (Sir; of KINCAVEL) HAMILTON**
Child: **James (of Kincavel) HAMILTON**

```
                          /-- James I STEWART (37th King) of SCOTS
                         /        \-- Annabella (of Stoball) DRUMMOND  +
              /-- James II `the Fiery Face' STEWART  (1430 - 1460)
             |        \          /-- John `Fairborn' (K.G.; de) BEAUFORT  +
             |         \-- Joan (Joanna) BEAUFORT  (1407? - 1445)
             /                    \-- Margaret (of Kent) HOLAND  +
     /-- Alexander STEWART (Duke) of ALBANY  (1454 - 1485)
    |        \              /-- Jan (II) van EGMOND  +
    |         |        /-- Arnold van EGMOND (Duke) of GUELDERS  +
    |         |       /    \-- Maria van ARKEL  +
    |         \-- Mary GUELDERS (von EGMOND)
    |                  \        /-- Adolf (I; IV) von KLEVE  +
    |                   \-- Katherina (Duchess) von KLEVE  (1417 - 1479)
    /                            \-- Marie VALOIS of BURGUNDY  +
```

-Margaret (Catherine) STEWART

```
    |                       /-- Henry (of Roslin) ST. CLAIR (SINCLAIR)
    |                      /       \-- Isabel of STRATHEARN  +
    |              /-- Henry II SINCLAIR (ST. CLAIR)  (? - 1422)
    |             /           \-- Jean (of Dirleton Castle) HALIBURTON  +
    |     /-- William SINCLAIR (ST. CLAIR)  (? - 1480?)
    |    |        \          /-- William (Knight; of Nithsdale) DOUGLAS  +
    |    |         \-- Egidia (Jill) DOUGLAS  (? - 1438?)
    |    /                    \-- Egidia (Princess) STEWART  +
    \-- Catherine SINCLAIR
         \/ or: Not! (NN), a mistress
         |                  /-- Archibald (3rd Earl of) DOUGLAS  +
         |          /-- Archibald Tyneman (4th Earl of) DOUGLAS
         |         |        \-- Joanna (Jean) MORAY  +
         |         /            / OR: prob. not Joanna MURRAY  +
         \-- Elizabeth (Margaret?) DOUGLAS  (? - 1451?)
```

'KATIE, BAR THE DOOR'

LEGEND has it that Kate Barlass suffered a broken arm while trying to prevent the assassination of James I in a sewer. Her real name may have been Catherine Douglas, presumably related to Catherine Sinclair's mother (shown above), but nobody knows for certain. Many believe the heroic Kate was Elizabeth Douglas who married Richard Lovell of Ballumbie.

Rossetti's poem 'The King's Tragedy' (1881) includes the line 'Catherine, keep the door!'

THE REAL LADY MACBETH

IN 2017, Kate must have been shocked to see herself portrayed as a modern-day Lady Macbeth in *King Charles III,* a 'neo-Shakespearean' TV film set after the death of Elizabeth II.

As Jasper Rees wrote in *The Telegraph:* 'It may never be possible to see the Duchess of Cambridge in quite the same light, with Charlotte Riley riveting as a dark-eyed schemer goading her husband to patricidal treachery.' Kate will be even more embarrassed if there is a sequel featuring William V and Queen Catherine.

While the fictional Kate plots to depose her father-in-law during a constitutional crisis involving freedom of the press, Shakespeare's Lady Macbeth (above) descends into madness after her husband murders King Duncan in his bed.

The real Duncan, nicknamed 'the Gracious', was murdered in 1040 by the real Macbeth, the second husband of Gruoch ingen Boîte who was a first cousin of Duncan's wife Bethoc MacDuff.

Kate is descended from King Duncan through three illegitimate daughters of William I. And on fabpedigree.com Kate has a bloodline from Gruoch through Jane Lambton, Muriel Hastings, Muriel Dinham, Muriel Courtenay, Muriel de Moels and Muriel de Soules.

Prince William has many possible descents from Gruoch, including one through Joan Beaufort's

Charlotte Riley, who played Kate with a 'touch of Lady Macbeth' in King Charles III, *played Catherine Earnshaw in a 2009 version of* Wuthering Heights.

The PEDIGREE of

Katherine (Lady) STEWART

HRH Charles's 19-Great Grandmother. Lady Diana's 17-Great Grandmother.
Husband/Partner: David (of Glenesk) LINDSAY
Children: Alexander (de) LINDSAY ; Alexander LINDSAY ; Elizabeth LINDSAY (of Crawford)

```
          /-- Walter (Sir) STEWART (STEWARD)  (1292? - 1327)
    |            \         /-- Walter de BURGH  +
    |             \-- Egidia de BURGH  (1255? - ?)
    |                    \ / or: prob. not Margaret de BONKYL, q.v.
    |                    I / OR: prob. not Cecilia of DUNBAR & MARCH  +
    |                     \-- Avelina (of Shere) FitzJOHN  +
    /                            / or: Maud de LACY, q.v.
 /-- Robert II `the Steward' STEWART  (1316 - 1390)
    |         \               /-- Robert VII BRUCE  +
    |          I     /-- Robert (I; `the Good'; the) BRUCE
    |          I    /      \-- Margaret (Countess) of CARRICK  +
    |          \-- Marjorie (Marjory Mary; de) BRUCE
    |                \      /-- Donald (6th Earl) de MAR  +
    |                 \-- Isobel (Isabel Matilda) de MAR
    /                      \-- Elen verch LLYWELYN  +
```

- Katherine (Lady) STEWART

```
    |                /-- William (III; 4th/5th Earl of) ROSS
    |               /       \-- Jean COMYN  +
    |        /-- Hugh MacTAGGART (5th? Earl of; de) ROSS
    |       |        \        /-- Hugh (Sir; of TOWIE) de BERKELEY  +
    |       |         \-- Euphemia de BARCLAY
    |       |               / OR: Euphemia GRAHAM  +
    |       /               / OR: prob. not Euphemia de BALLIOL  +
    \-- Euphemia (of ROSS) LESLIE  (1330? - 1387)
```

granddaughter Catherine Stewart (died c1515); another through James IV's illegitimate daughter Catherine Stewart (died c1554); and another through James I's aunt Katherine Stewart who, as shown above, was a great-granddaughter of Robert the Bruce. (According to wikitree.com and geneanet.org Katherine Stewart's first name may have been Elizabeth or Jean.)

Robert the Bruce and his namesake father, who had an all-female bloodline from Aoife, were descended from Henry I's illegitimate son Robert of Gloucester. And Elen verch Llywelyn (shown above) was an alleged daughter of King John's illegitimate daughter Joan of North Wales.

Macbeth was first performed early in James I's reign and Shakespeare was well aware of the monarch's alleged descent from the legendary Banquo who, like Katherine Swynford's illegitimate children, was supposedly told: 'Thou shalt get kings though thou be none.'

The inclusion of Princess Diana's ghost in *King Charles III* was obviously inspired by scenes in Shakespeare's play in which Macbeth is haunted by Banquo's ghost.

Note: Through Katherine Stewart, Robert the Bruce and Lulach 'the Fool', the dark-skinned Charles II had a bloodline from Gruoch's grandfather Kenneth 'the Brown' (See next page).

BLACK BOY'S MISTRESSES

CHARLES II was undoubtedly dark-skinned, hence his nickname 'Black Boy', and so was Charles Lennox (inset), the Merry Monarch's illegitimate son with Louise de Kerouaille (above).

One remote possibility is that Charles II inherited something from Lady Macbeth's grandfather Kenneth III who was nicknamed 'the Brown', presumably because of his swarthiness although that may have been his hair colour. It is much more likely that Charles II took after Caterina Sforza's Medici relatives, including Lorenzo the Magnificent (See chart on Page 73).

Through Princess Diana, Kate's children descend from Charles Lennox, who reportedly had a 'black complexion', and also from his half-brother Henry Fitzroy, a bastard son of Catherine of Braganza's arch-rival Barbara Palmer.

Prince George and his siblings may descend from Mary Crofts, an illegitimate daughter of Charles II and Lucy Walter, but there are no known bloodlines from his best known mistress, the legendary Nell Gwyn. Her illegitimate son Charles Beauclerk had a namesake son who allegedly had an illegitimate child with Charles Lennox's illegitimate daughter Renee Lennox.

Following Charles III, Prince William will become the first British monarch descended from Charles II, and Kate will become the sixth Queen Catherine.

Pub signs like this one were once common in Britain.

FABPEDIGREE.COM

The PEDIGREE of

Charles (Knight of the Garter) LENNOX

1st Duke of RICHMOND; (FitzROY)

Born: 1672   Died: 1723

Lady Diana's 7-Great Grandfather.

Wife/Partner: Anne BRUDENELL
Children: Anne (Countess) LENNOX ; Charles (K.G.) LENNOX ; Louisa (Lady) LENNOX

```
                              /-- Henry STUART (STEWART) (1545 - 1567)
                         /            \-- Margaret (Lady) DOUGLAS  +
                    /-- James I STUART (King) of GREAT BRITAIN
                 /            \-- Mary STUART (42nd Queen) of SCOTS  +
            /-- Charles I STUART (King) of ENGLAND  (1600 - 1649)
         |         \         /-- Frederick (Fredrik) II (King) of DENMARK  +
         |          \-- Anne (Princess) of DENMARK
         /                   \-- Sophia von MECKLENBURG-GUSTROW  +
    /-- Charles II STUART (King) of ENGLAND  (1630 - 1685)
   |         \            /-- Antoine (Anton) de BOURBON  +
   |          |        /-- Henry IV BOURBON (King) of FRANCE  (1553 - 1610)
   |          |       /        \-- Jeanne d' ALBRET (Queen) de NAVARRE  +
   |           \-- Henriette Marie (de) BOURBON
   |                   \            /-- Francesco (Francis) I de MEDICI of ITALY  +
   |                    \-- Maria de MEDICI (MEDICIS)
   /                           \-- Joanna HABSBURG (Archduchess) of AUSTRIA  +
```

- Charles (K.G.) LENNOX

```
   |              /-- Rene de PENANCOET
   |             /        \-- Guillemette BARBIER  +
   |        /-- Guilliame de PENANCOET  (? - 1690)
   |       /            \-- Julienne Emery (Heiress) du PONT-L'ABBE
   \-- Louise Renee (de PENANCOET) de KEROUAILLE  (1649 - 1734)
         \              /-- Vincent de PLOEUC  +
          |         /-- Sebastien de PLOEUC (Marquis) de TIMEUR
          |        /        \-- Suzanne de COATANEZRE  (? - 1593+ )
           \-- Marie Anne de PLOEUC de TIMEUR  (? - 1709)
```

CATHERINE CONNECTIONS

ONE OF Charles II's lesser known mistresses was Catherine Pegge (right), daughter of Catherine Kniveton and mother of the king's illegitimate daughter Catherine FitzCharles, who either died young or became a nun in a French abbey and died aged 101. James II matched his brother by having a mistress named Catherine who had a namesake illegitimate daughter (See next page).

Through Catherine of Foix, Charles II and James II had the same mitochondrial DNA as Catherine the Great.

JAMES THE 'BESHITTEN'...

PICTURED above with his father Charles I, who was beheaded in 1649, James II thoroughly deserved the insulting nickname bestowed by his Irish allies after the disastrous Battle of the Boyne, not least because his initials were branded on thousands of African slaves.

In 1688, just three years after succeeding his brother Charles II, James II was overthrown by their nephew William of Orange, husband of James' daughter Mary, in the Glorious Revolution. It was probably fortunate that first cousins William and Mary had no children.

William III and his royal uncles had the same mitochondrial DNA (haplogroup H) inherited from Catherine of Foix (See chart on Page 103). Surprisingly, so did James II's half-Polish grandson Bonnie Prince Charlie, and so did the prince's alleged illegitimate son Charles Godefroi whose fate is unknown. (Google 'Jacobite succession' for the alternative line of British monarchs.)

Unlike his beauty-loving brother, James II preferred unattractive mistresses, including Arabella Churchill and Catherine Sedley (See opposite). Kate's children descend from Arabella's illegitimate daughter Henrietta FitzJames who had a bloodline from Aoife through James II and Catherine of Aragon's sister Joanna the Mad.

Interestingly, Catherine Sedley's mother Lady Catherine Savage went mad soon after the birth of her namesake daughter and became fully convinced that she was Queen of England married to Charles II.

Catherine Darnley shares this monument in Westminster Abbey with second husband John Sheffield, Duke of Buckingham, a close friend of the poet Alexander Pope who features in The Da Vinci Code. *Nearby in Henry VII chapel is a statue of St Catherine of Alexandria trampling on Roman emperor Maxentius.*

The PEDIGREE of

Catherine (Lady) DARNLEY

Born: 1681   Died: 1743
Husbands/Partners: James ANNESLEY ; John (K.G.) SHEFFIELD
Child: Catherine (Lady) ANNESLEY

```
                        /-- James I STUART (King) of GREAT BRITAIN
                       /         \-- Mary STUART (42nd Queen) of SCOTS  +
              /-- Charles I STUART (King) of ENGLAND  (1600 - 1649)
             |          \          /-- Frederick (Fredrik) II (King) of DENMARK  +
             |           \-- Anne (Princess) of DENMARK
             /                     \-- Sophia von MECKLENBURG-GUSTROW  +
      /-- James II STUART (King) of ENGLAND
     |          \                  /-- Antoine (Anton) de BOURBON  +
     |           |      /-- Henry IV BOURBON (King) of FRANCE  (1553 - 1610)
     |           |     /          \-- Jeanne d' ALBRET (Queen) de NAVARRE  +
     |           \-- Henriette Marie (de) BOURBON
     |                  \          /-- Francesco (Francis) I de MEDICI of ITALY  +
     |                   \-- Maria de MEDICI (MEDICIS)
     /                              \-- Joanna HABSBURG (Archduchess) of AUSTRIA  +
```

Catherine (Lady) DARNLEY

```
     |                  /-- John (2nd Baronet; of Southfleet) SEDLEY
     |                 /          \-- Elizabeth DARRELL  +
     |          /-- Charles (5th Baronet; of Southfleet) SEDLEY
     |         |        \          /-- Henry SAVILE  +
     |         |         \-- Elizabeth SAVILE  (? - 1650?)
     |         /                   \-- Margaret DACRE  +
     \-- Catherine SEDLEY  (1657 - 1717 Somersets.)
                 \                  /-- Thomas (2nd Baronet) SAVAGE  +
                  |      /-- John (2nd Earl RIVERS) SAVAGE  (1606 - 1654)
                  |     |          \-- Elizabeth DARCY  +
                  |     /          / OR: Elizabeth d' ARCY [alt ped]  +
                  \-- Catherine (Lady) SAVAGE
                         \          /-- Wm. PARKER (Lord MORLEY & MONTEAGLE)  +
                          \-- Catherine PARKER  (1605? - ?)
```

...AND HIS WITTY WHORE

WHEN she met Charles II's mistress Louise de Kerouaille and William III's alleged mistress Elizabeth Hamilton at George I's court, James II's lover Catherine Sedley (right) famously said: 'God! Who would have thought that we three whores should meet here.'

Catherine Sedley descended from Katherine of Flanders and Aoife through all of her grandparents, including Catherine Parker who had the same first name as her daughter, granddaughter, great-grand-daughter and great-great-granddaughter. Catherine Sedley also descended from the Stockeld Middletons.

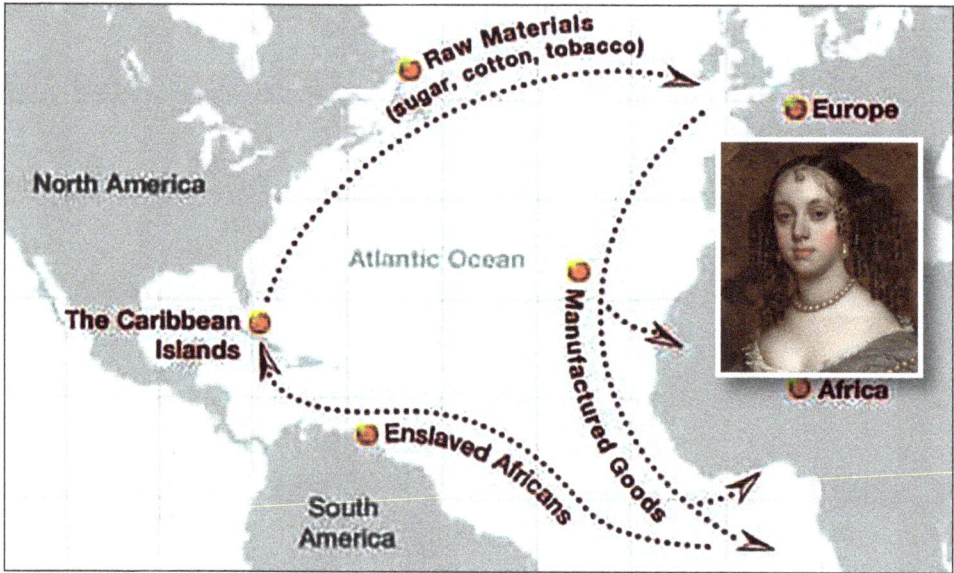

FROM BRAGANZA TO *BRIDGERTON*

WHEN the Portuguese princess Catherine of Braganza (inset above) married Charles II in 1662, nobody could have foreseen that her fondness for tea would result in a triangular trade route supplying African slaves to the Caribbean sugar plantations. And when Charlotte of Mecklenburg-Strelitz married George III a century later, it was unimaginable that 'Britain's first black queen' would inspire an acclaimed TV series.

Coincidentally, both queens descended from Madragana, the Moorish mistress of Affonso III of Portugal (See Katalin of the Cumans, Page 38).

Queen Charlotte opposed slavery and joined an estimated 400,000 Britons who boycotted West Indian sugar in the early 1790s. Many switched to 'East India sugar not made by slaves' and others drank unsweetened tea.

Bridgerton, with its references to slavery and George III's madness, is much more than a colourblind fantasy featuring Guyanese-British actress Golda Rosheuvel as Queen Charlotte. And the casting of Simone Ashley, who has Indian Tamil heritage, as Kate Sharma is notable because Prince William has a rare form of Indian DNA inherited from Katherine Scott Forbes (See chart on Page 8).

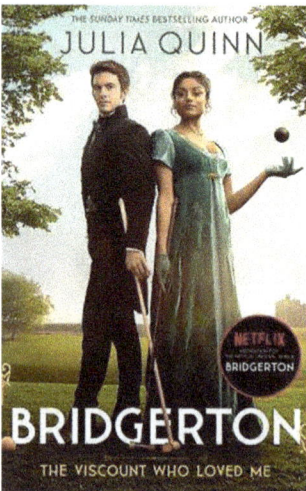

In May 2022, glamour.com gleefully claimed that Kate had channelled her 'inner Bridgerton sister' by wearing a mint green high-neck dress at a Buckingham Palace garden party.

The TV series based on novels by Julia Quinn features Simone Ashley as Kate Sharma and Jonathan Bailey as the viscount who loves her.

— 248 —

THE PEDIGREE OF

Katherine de BRAGANCA (Princess) of PORTUGAL

Born: 1638   Died: 1705

Husband/Partner: Charles II STUART (King) of ENGLAND

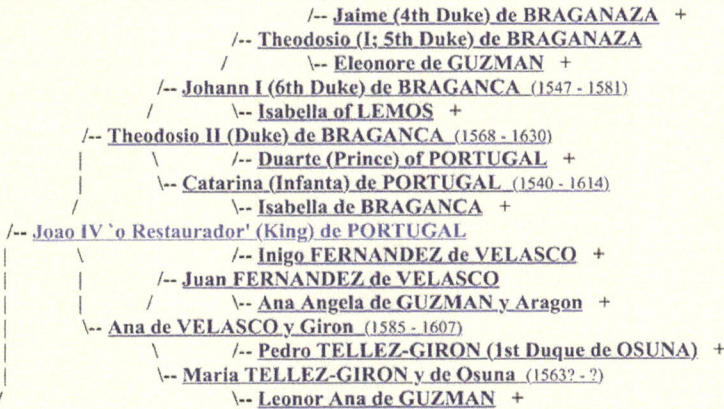

```
                                    /-- Jaime (4th Duke) de BRAGANAZA  +
                          /-- Theodosio (I; 5th Duke) de BRAGANAZA
                         /          \-- Eleonore de GUZMAN  +
                  /-- Johann I (6th Duke) de BRAGANCA  (1547 - 1581)
                 /          \-- Isabella of LEMOS  +
          /-- Theodosio II (Duke) de BRAGANCA  (1568 - 1630)
         |         \          /-- Duarte (Prince) of PORTUGAL  +
         |          \-- Catarina (Infanta) de PORTUGAL  (1540 - 1614)
         |         /          \-- Isabella de BRAGANCA  +
      /-- Joao IV 'o Restaurador' (King) de PORTUGAL
     |         \                   /-- Inigo FERNANDEZ de VELASCO  +
     |          |          /-- Juan FERNANDEZ de VELASCO
     |          |         /          \-- Ana Angela de GUZMAN y Aragon  +
     |          \-- Ana de VELASCO y Giron  (1585 - 1607)
     |                    /-- Pedro TELLEZ-GIRON (1st Duque de OSUNA)  +
     |          \-- Maria TELLEZ-GIRON y de Osuna  (1563? - ?)
     /                    \-- Leonor Ana de GUZMAN  +
```

-Katherine de BRAGANCA (Princess) of PORTUGAL

```
     \                   /-- Juan Alfonso de GUZMAN  +
     |          /-- Juan Carlos de GUZMAN  (? - 1556)
     |         /          \-- Ana de ARAGON  +
     |    /-- Afonso Perez de GUZMAN  (1550? - 1615)
     |   /          \-- Leonor Manrique (de ZUNIGA) SOTOMAYOR  +
     /-- Juan Manuel Domingo Alonso Perez de GUZMAN (& de Silva)
     |         \          /-- Rui Gomes da SILVA (Principe de EBOLI)  +
     |          \-- Ana de SYLVA & Mendoza  (1561 - 1610)
     |         /          \-- Ana de MENDOZA & LACERDA  +
     \-- Luisa Maria de GUZMAN  (1613 - 1666)
```

Kate's children descend from Queen Charlotte through Elizabeth II who acknowledged her African heritage soon after her coronation. Prince George and his siblings also descend from British Prime Minister Charles Grey (after whom Earl Grey tea was named) whose government abolished slavery throughout the British Empire in 1833.

Catherine of Braganza descended from Madragana through Catarina de Lacerda, and from Aoife through Catarina de Portugal (shown above).

KATE'S CROOKED ANCESTOR

TEA imported by the East India Company was too expensive for the working classes and for many years the demand was met by smugglers, probably including Kate's maternal ancestor Thomas Hay Webster.

According to *The Daily Express* (23rd May, 2020), Webster was a 'swashbuckling pirate' but it seems that he was nothing more than a 'rogue and a vagabond'. He was lucky to escape death or transportation after a violent clash with government agents near Margate in 1821 but later spent time in jail for other offences.

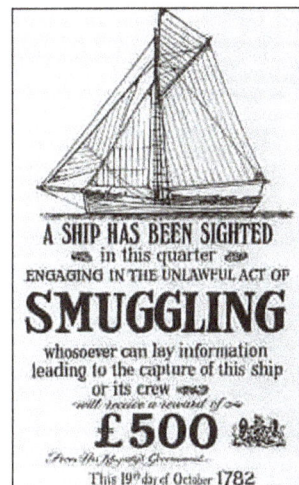

A SHIP HAS BEEN SIGHTED
in this quarter
ENGAGING IN THE UNLAWFUL ACT OF

SMUGGLING

whosoever can lay information
leading to the capture of this ship
or its crew
will receive a reward of

£500

From His Majesty's Government.

This 19th day of October 1782

CATHERINES OF WINDSOR

EXACTLY 600 years after the first Queen Catherine supposedly caused the early death of Henry V by giving birth to the future Henry VI at Windsor, the future Queen Catherine was preparing to move her family to a cottage not far from the castle which dates from the 11th century.

Henry V died in France in August 1422, seven years after his famous victory at Agincourt and less than nine months after Catherine of Valois (inset above) seemingly defied an ancient prophecy: 'Henry born at Monmouth shall small time reign and much get, but Henry born at Windsor shall long reign and lose all' (See Page 112).

The tomb of the mentally unstable Henry VI, who lost everything during the Wars of the Roses, is in St George's Chapel at Windsor, not far from Catherine of Aragon's closet. In 1547, Henry III's last wife Catherine Parr watched his funeral

from the closet, and in 1863 Queen Victoria sat in the same spot when the future Edward VII married Alexandra of Denmark (See Mitochondrial Marriages, Page 96).

Catherine of Aragon's pomegranate emblem can be seen high above the castle's Henry VIII gateway, and a long hidden image of her namesake saint can be seen in the Catherine Room named after Charles II's wife Catherine of Braganza.

This depiction of St Catherine of Alexandria by Guido Reni was first recorded in the King's Closet at Windsor in 1792.

Antonio Verrio's ceiling painting in the Queen's Presence Chamber, The Apotheosis of Catherine of Braganza (above), shows the queen under a canopy surrounded by mythical and allegorical figures.

When she becomes queen, Kate will have effective control over all of the artworks at Windsor, including The Negro Page by Aelbert Cuyp which caused a minor sensation in 2016 when photographed at Kensington Palace during a visit by US President Barack Obama.

Kate will eventually join the Order of the Garter founded along similar lines to the ancient Order of St Catherine (See Page 30). St George's Chapel is the order's spiritual home and Kate was there in 2008 when Prince William became the thousandth knight.

Barring unforeseen circumstances, Kate and William will be buried in a vault in front of the altar, not far from the tomb of her most recent royal ancestor Edward IV.

KATE'S NEW HOME

ADELAIDE Cottage is less than a kilometre from the castle and a reasonable distance from Royal Lodge, home of Kate's disgraced uncle-in-law Prince Andrew.

Commissioned by William IV for his wife Adelaide of Saxe-Meiningen, the cottage probably needs refurbishment but, after an expensive upgrade of their Kensington Palace quarters, Kate and the future William V will reportedly leave the cottage the way it is.

KATE AND THE KOHINOOR CURSE

HANGING over Kate and her stepmother-in-law Camilla is a 700-year-old curse involving one of the world's most famous gems and an even older curse threatening their husbands.

The Kohinoor diamond, gifted to Queen Victoria by the East India Company in 1850, had previously been owned by numerous rulers who died violently, supposedly because of a curse first recorded in 1306: 'He who owns this diamond will own the world, but will also know all its misfortunes. Only God, or a woman, can wear it with impunity.'

Camilla and Kate must have been hugely relieved in early 2023 when it was announced that the Kohinoor would be removed from the Queen Mother's crown due to be worn at Charles III's coronation. However, the Kohinoor curse will linger for as long as it remains in Britain and the queen consort's crown will remain controversial because the replacement Cullinan diamonds are an unpleasant reminder of South African colonialism.

Regardless of the Kohinoor curse, it seems that Queen Victoria was the victim of an historical hoodoo outlined by British author David Maislish in *Assassination: The Royal Family's 1000-Year Curse* (2012). After years of painstaking research, he detailed the murder or attempted murder of every

The Queen Mother's crown

WIKIPEDIA

British monarch from the legendary King Canute, who failed to stop the incoming tide, to Elizabeth II.

Queen Victoria, who wore the Kohinoor as a brooch, survived eight assassination attempts, starting with Edward Oxford's attack in 1840 (pictured above). The sixth attack was in June 1850, shortly before the queen was presented with the Kohinoor at Buckingham Palace. One year later, the diamond attracted large crowds at the Great Exhibition in London but most people were unimpressed. Soon after, the gem was recut and polished.

Edward VII was nearly killed by a teenage gunman in Belgium in 1900, and Edward VIII was targeted by MI5 informant George McMahon in London in 1936. An attempt on Elizabeth II in Australia in 1970 made headlines but, incredibly, an attempted assassination in New Zealand by Christopher John Lewis in 1981 was kept secret for more than 30 years.

The Kohinoor is currently with other crown jewels in the Tower of London and will probably remain there for quite some time because of competing ownership claims by India, Pakistan, Iran and Afghanistan.

Note: In 2019, ISIS extremists were urged to kill Kate by poisoning food bought from supermarkets identified on an encrypted website.

WIKIPEDIA

An alleged victim of the Kohinoor curse was Catherine Singh, daughter of the last maharaja to own the diamond. Catherine died childless and so did her seven siblings.

FROM KATE TO CATHERINE I?

CATHERINE I could be crowned on Westminster Abbey's famous Cosmati Pavement (above) before the end of this century because the two main requirements are easily imaginable: that Prince George's first child is a girl, and that she is named after her grandmother who was married on the pavement in 2011. And if Prince George marries a matrilineal descendant of Catherine of Foix, which is unlikely but not impossible, Britain's Catherine I could have the same mitochondrial DNA as Russia's Catherine the Great.

The Cosmati Pavement was commissioned in 1268 by the father of Britain's first Princess Katherine whose brother Edward I stole from Scotland the legendary Stone of Scone which sits under the Coronation Chair (inset). The chair was named after Edward the Confessor who gave the abbey some of St Catherine of Alexandria's holy oil from her Mt Sinai monastery.

A mysterious inscription on the Cosmati Pavement predicts that the world will end 19,683 years from when it was laid down.

Afterword

READERS can make up their own minds about the implied question in this book: Was Kate Middleton, a commoner with many working class ancestors, destined to be Britain's sixth Queen Catherine? Like all of them, and most of her 200 namesakes listed in the index, Kate descends from William the Conqueror who introduced to Britain the cult of St Catherine of Alexandria. And was Kate fated to get married in Westminster Abbey (where the conqueror was crowned in 1066) on the feast day of St Catherine of Siena?

Belief in predestination is no less ridiculous than Dan Brown's plagiarised notion about Jesus and Mary Magdalene having just a few living descendants protected by the non-existent Priory of Sion. That said, I thoroughly enjoyed Brown's bestselling novel and the film starring Tom Hanks, especially the connections to Leonardo da Vinci, the Knights Templar and Rosslyn Chapel.

While I admit that identification of mitochondrial bloodlines through some of Kate's namesakes (including Catherine of Foix and Katharina von Pfannberg) is arbitrary, DNA from two living descendants of Katherine Swynford enabled scientists to identify the remains of Richard III, father of the illegitimate Katherine Plantagenet and uncle of Kate's illegitimate ancestor Margaret Plantagenet. And, fortuitously, a sample from Kate's grandfather-in-law Prince Philip (who had the same mitochondrial DNA as Catherine the Great's illegitimate son) matched the remains of Alexey Romanov.

I encourage everyone to delve into British history bearing in mind that, like Kate, they probably descend from several royal bastards. One of my bloodlines is through an illegitimate daughter of George Pitt, the second Baron Rivers, who descended from an illegitimate great-grandson of Katherine Swynford's illegitimate son John 'Fairborn' Beaufort.

Finally, an eBook version of *The Catherine Code* should be available from my planned website later this year and feedback will be most welcome.

Bob Casey
Hobart, Tasmania
June 2023

INDEX OF CATHERINES

www.ingramcontent.com/pod-product-compliance
Lightning Source LLC
Chambersburg PA
CBHW040254100426
42811CB00011B/1258